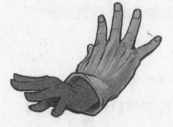

Volume 20! Thanks for picking it up! My little
sister's friend's son is a fan of Jiro, and I hear
he was influenced enough to start taking guitar
lessons! Jiro is one rocking girl who can play
both guitar and bass! Rock on, Kyoka Jiro!!

KOHEI HORIKOSHI

MY HERO ACADEMIA

20

SHONEN JUMP Manga Edition

STORY & ART KOHEI HORIKOSHI

TRANSLATION & ENGLISH ADAPTATION **Caleb Cook**
TOUCH-UP ART & LETTERING **John Hunt**
DESIGNER **Julian [JR] Robinson**
SHONEN JUMP SERIES EDITOR **John Bae**
GRAPHIC NOVEL EDITOR **Mike Montesa**

BOKU NO HERO ACADEMIA © 2014 by Kohei Horikoshi
All rights reserved.
First published in Japan in 2014 by SHUEISHA Inc., Tokyo.
English translation rights arranged by SHUEISHA Inc.

The stories, characters and incidents mentioned in this publication are entirely fictional.

Printed in the U.S.A.

Published by VIZ Media, LLC
P.O. Box 77010
San Francisco, CA 94107

10 9 8 7 6 5 4 3 2
First printing, August 2019
Second printing, April 2020

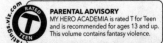

PARENTAL ADVISORY
MY HERO ACADEMIA is rated T for Teen
and is recommended for ages 13 and up.
This volume contains fantasy violence.

shonenjump.com

MY HERO ACADEMIA vol. 20

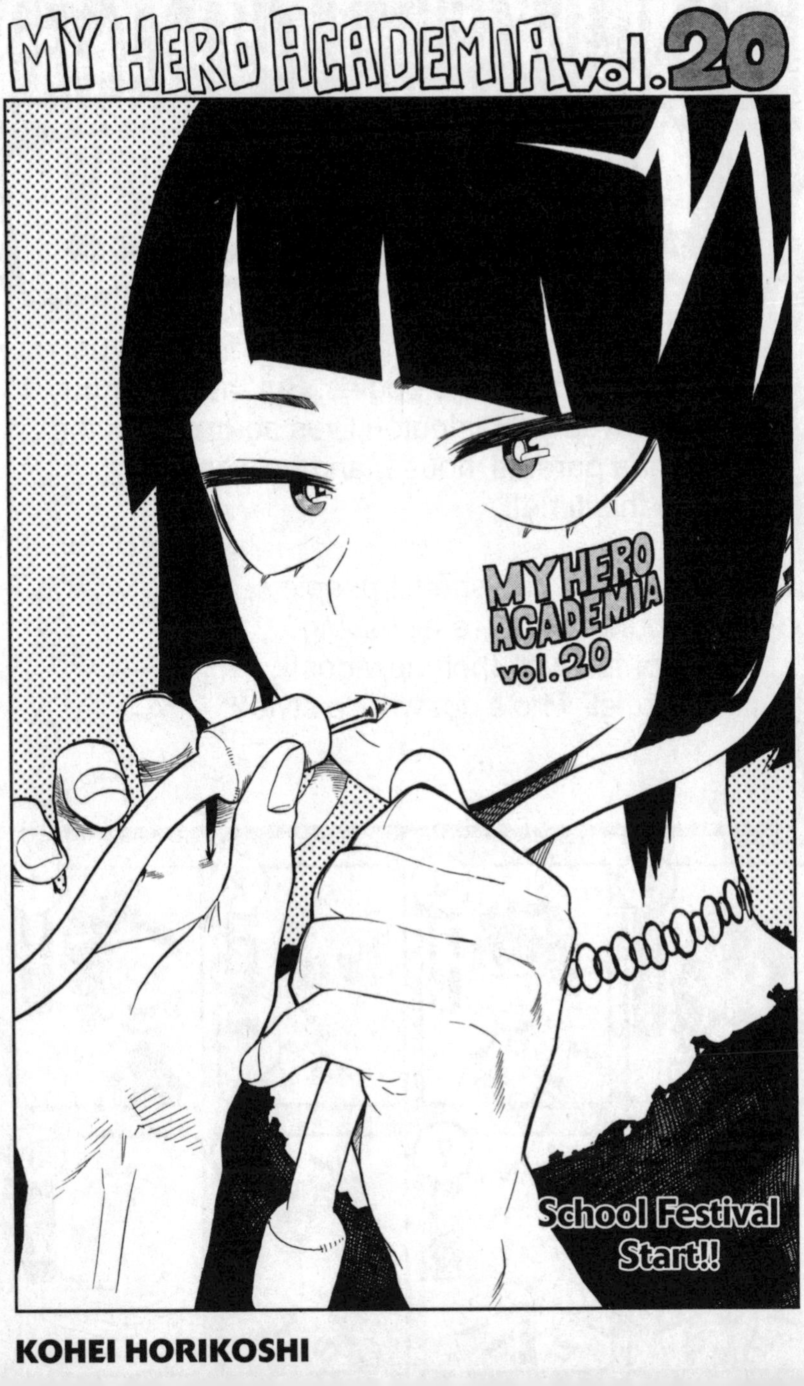
MY HERO
ACADEMIA
vol. 20
School Festival
Start!!

KOHEI HORIKOSHI

HEAD-HAIR SHUFFLE CHARACTER LINEUP!!

It's terrible!! Last time, the Meddler jumbled up class 1-A's brains and bodies. But this other guy named Swop T. Hairington lives across from the Meddler's parents' house, and he's causing trouble this time!!

His Quirk lets him shuffle people's hair around!! They're all having plenty of fun with their new dos!! Can you tell who's got whose style?!

Hmph.
EVIL

1
IZUKU MIDORIYA
2
ALL MIGHT
3
KATSUKI BAKUGO
4
OCHACO URARAKA
5
SHOTA AIZAWA
6
SHOTO TODOROKI
7
TENYA IDA
8
MOMO YAOYOROZU

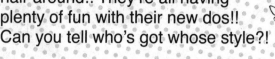

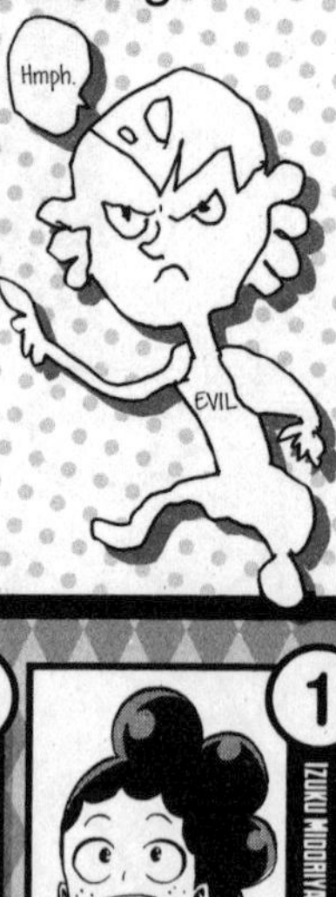

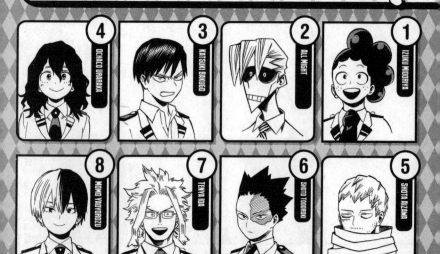

One day, people began manifesting special abilities that came to be known as "Quirks," and before long, the world was full of superpowered humans. But with the advent of these exceptional individuals came an increase in crime, and governments alone were unable to deal with the situation. At the same time, others emerged to oppose the spread of evil! As if straight from the comic books, these heroes keep the peace and are even officially authorized to fight crime. Our story begins when a certain Quirkless boy and lifelong hero fan meets the world's number one hero, starting him on his path to becoming the greatest hero ever!

STORY

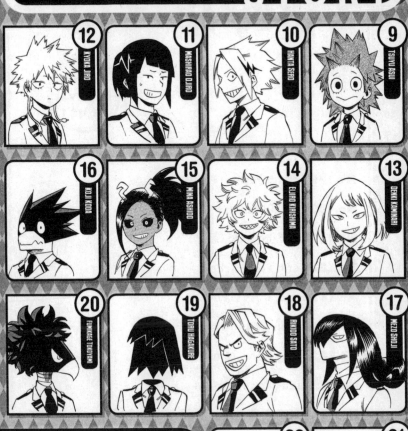

9
TSUYU ASUI
10
HANTA SERO
11
MASHIRAO OJIRO
12
KYOKA JIRO
13
DENKI KAMINARI
14
EIJIRO KIRISHIMA
15
MINA ASHIDO
16
KOJI KODA
17
MEZO SHOJI
18
RIKIDO SATO
19
TORU HAGAKURE
20
FUMIKAGE TOKOYAMI

21
YUGA AOYAMA
22
MINORU MINETA

ANSWERS: (1) MINETA, (2) SHOJI, (3) IIDA, (4) AIZAWA, (5) OJIRO, (6) SATO, (7) ALL MIGHT, (8) TODOROKI, (9) KIRISHIMA, (10) KAMINARI, (11) JIRO, (12) BAKUGO, (13) URARAKA, (14) ASHIDO, (15) YAOYOROZU, (16) TOKOYAMI, (17) ASUI, (18) AOYAMA, (19) SERO, (20) MIDORIYA, (21) HAGAKURE, (22) KODA

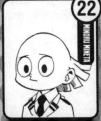

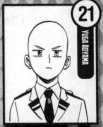

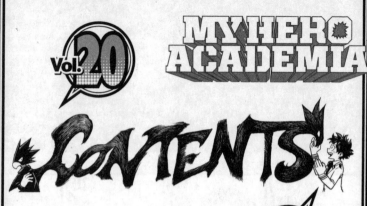

MY HERO ACADEMIA

Vol. 20

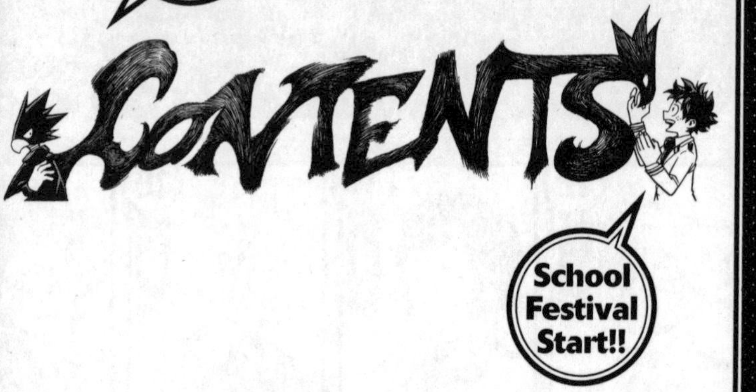
CONTENTS
School Festival Start!!

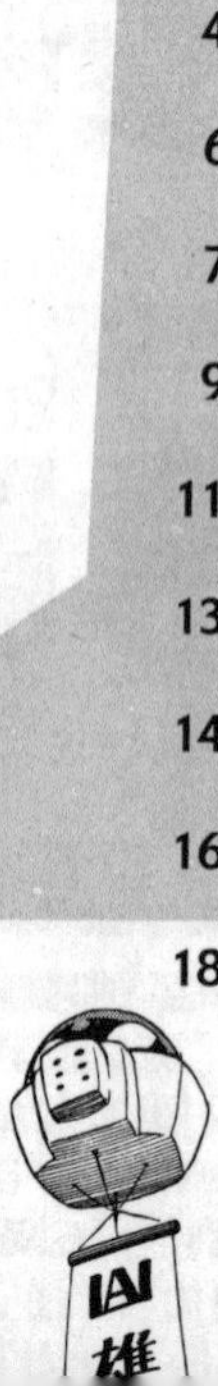
雄

No. 178 - The Woman Called La Brava

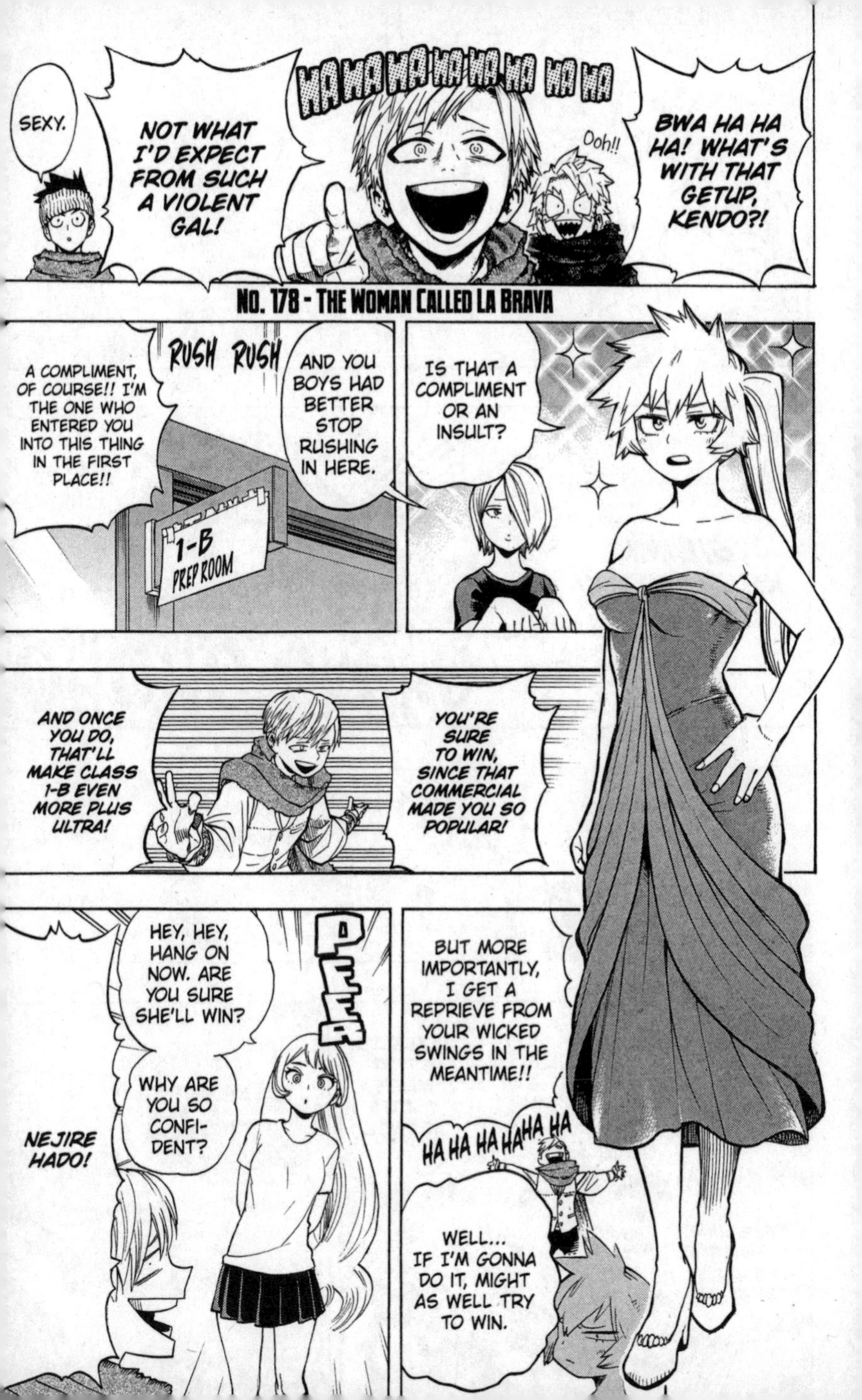
BWA HA HA HA! WHAT'S WITH THAT GETUP, KENDO?!
Ooh!!
HA HA HA HA HA HA HA HA
NOT WHAT I'D EXPECT FROM SUCH A VIOLENT GAL!
SEXY.
IS THAT A COMPLIMENT OR AN INSULT?
AND YOU BOYS HAD BETTER STOP RUSHING IN HERE.
RUSH RUSH
A COMPLIMENT, OF COURSE!! I'M THE ONE WHO ENTERED YOU INTO THIS THING IN THE FIRST PLACE!!
1-B PREP ROOM
YOU'RE SURE TO WIN, SINCE THAT COMMERCIAL MADE YOU SO POPULAR!
AND ONCE YOU DO, THAT'LL MAKE CLASS 1-B EVEN MORE PLUS ULTRA!
BUT MORE IMPORTANTLY, I GET A REPRIEVE FROM YOUR WICKED SWINGS IN THE MEANTIME!!
HA HA HA HAHA HA
WELL... IF I'M GONNA DO IT, MIGHT AS WELL TRY TO WIN.
PEER
HEY, HEY, HANG ON NOW. ARE YOU SURE SHE'LL WIN?
WHY ARE YOU SO CONFI-DENT?
NEJIRE HADO!

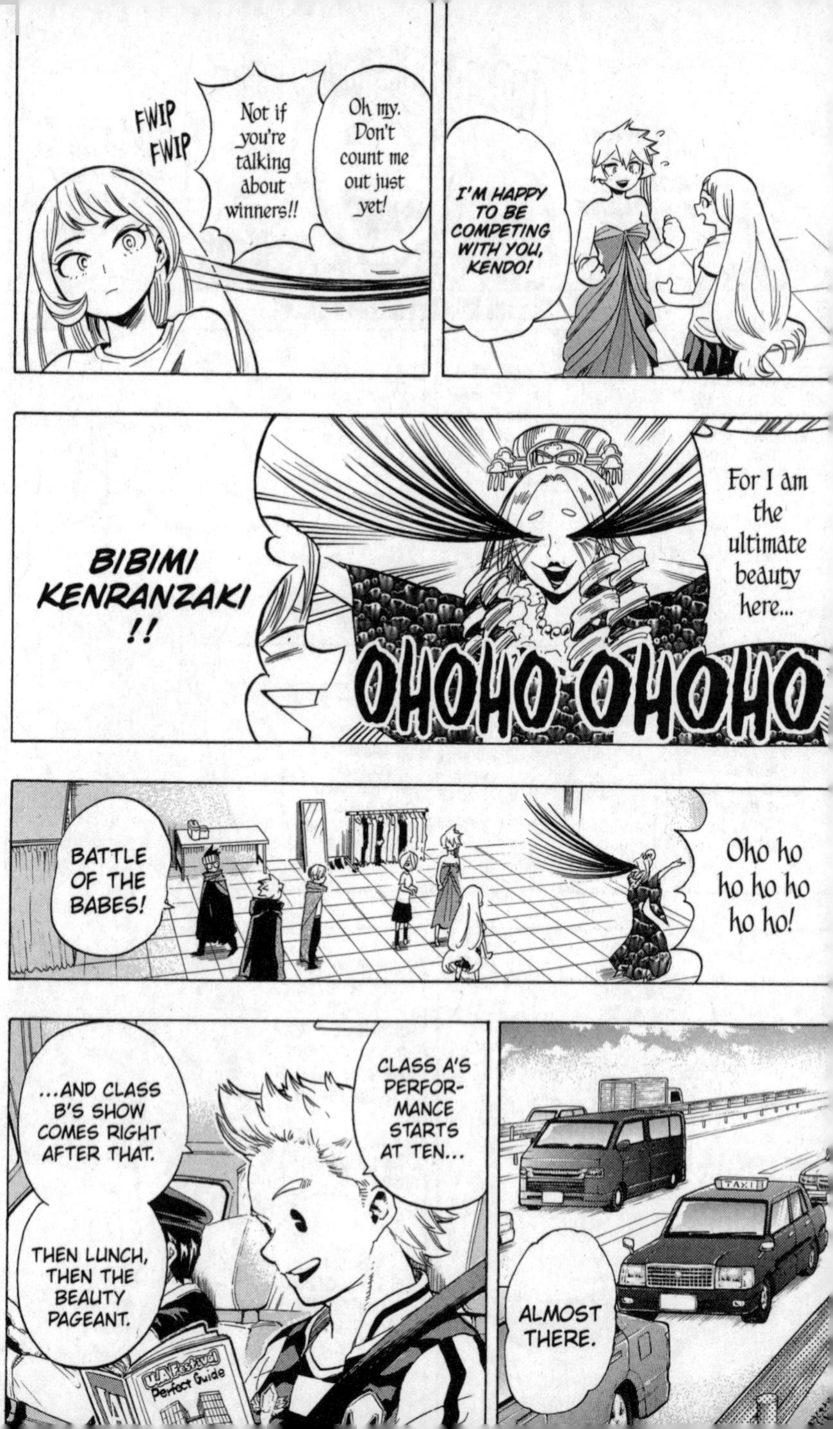
I'M HAPPY TO BE COMPETING WITH YOU, KENDO!
Oh my. Don't count me out just yet!
Not if you're talking about winners!!
FWIP FWIP
For I am the ultimate beauty here...
OHOHO OHOHO
BIBIMI KENRANZAKI !!
Oho ho ho ho ho ho ho!
BATTLE OF THE BABES!
ALMOST THERE.
TAXI
CLASS A'S PERFORMANCE STARTS AT TEN...
...AND CLASS B'S SHOW COMES RIGHT AFTER THAT.
THEN LUNCH, THEN THE BEAUTY PAGEANT.
U.A. Festival Perfect Guide

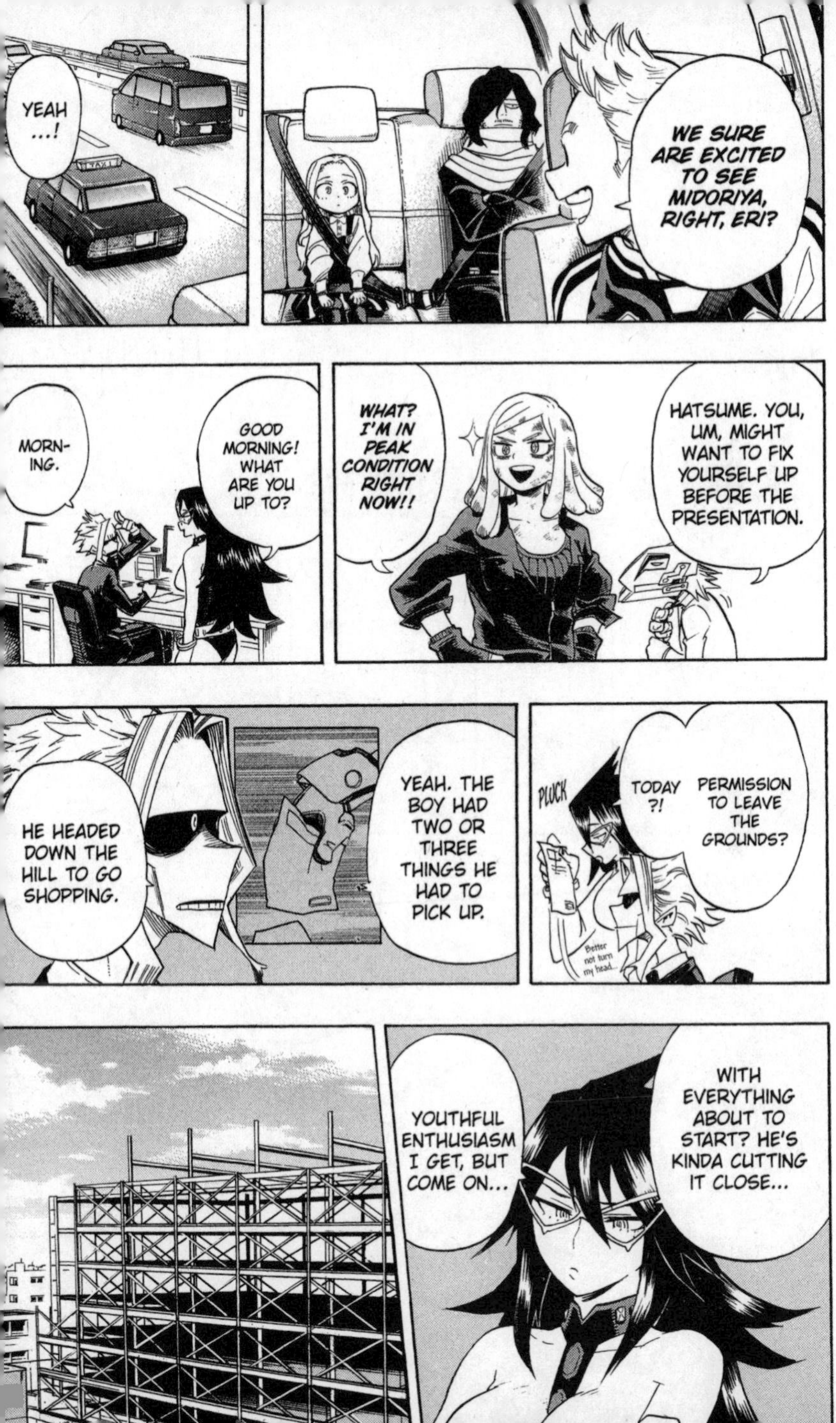
WE SURE ARE EXCITED TO SEE MIDORIYA, RIGHT, ERI?
YEAH ...!
HATSUME. YOU, UM, MIGHT WANT TO FIX YOURSELF UP BEFORE THE PRESENTATION.
WHAT? I'M IN PEAK CONDITION RIGHT NOW!!
GOOD MORNING! WHAT ARE YOU UP TO?
MORN-ING.
PERMISSION TO LEAVE THE GROUNDS?
TODAY?!
PLUCK
Better not turn my head...
YEAH. THE BOY HAD TWO OR THREE THINGS HE HAD TO PICK UP.
HE HEADED DOWN THE HILL TO GO SHOPPING.
WITH EVERYTHING ABOUT TO START? HE'S KINDA CUTTING IT CLOSE...
YOUTHFUL ENTHUSIASM I GET, BUT COME ON...

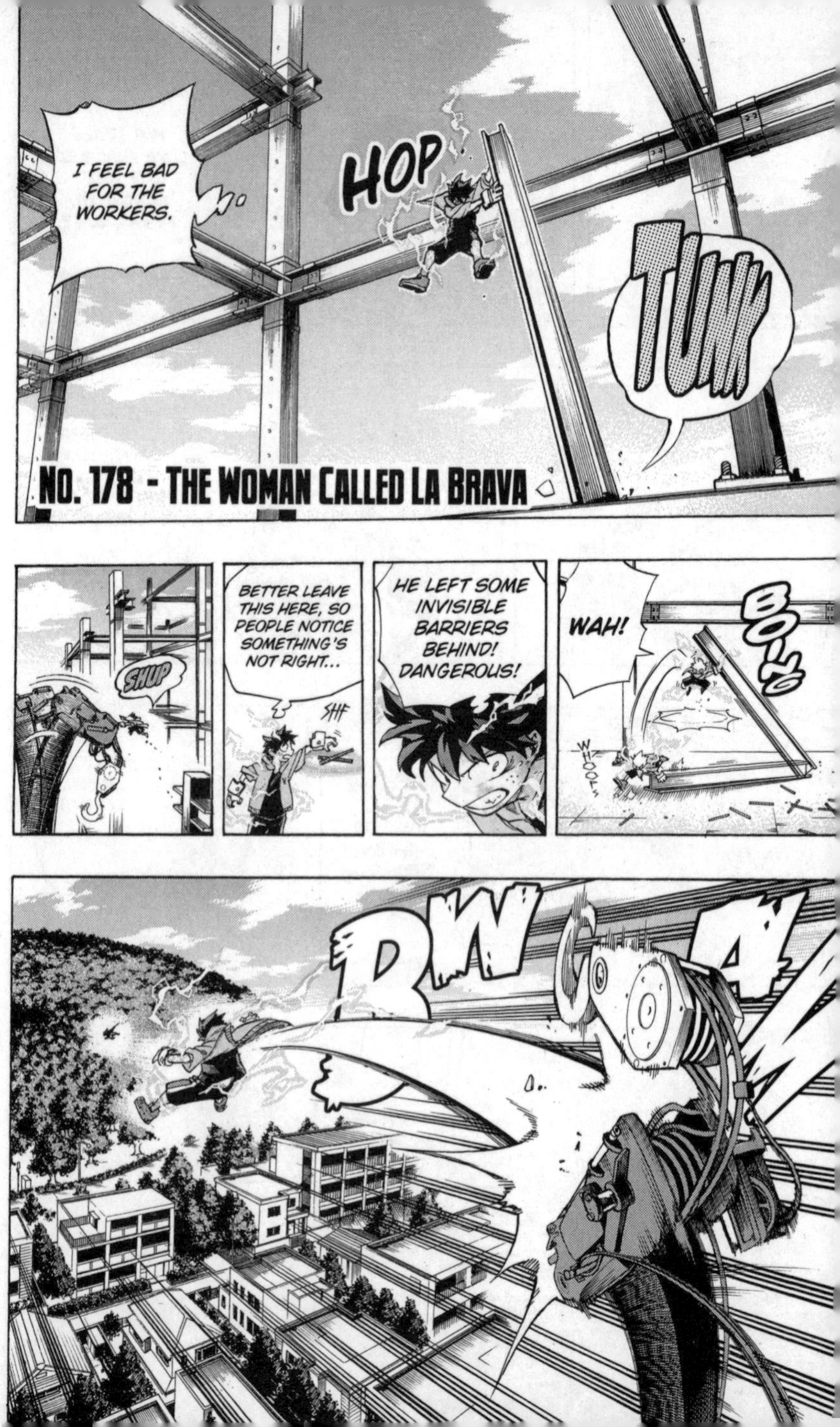
TUNK
HOP
I FEEL BAD FOR THE WORKERS.
No. 178 - The Woman Called La Brava
BOING
WAH!
HE LEFT SOME INVISIBLE BARRIERS BEHIND! DANGEROUS!
BETTER LEAVE THIS HERE, SO PEOPLE NOTICE SOMETHING'S NOT RIGHT...
SHF
SHUP

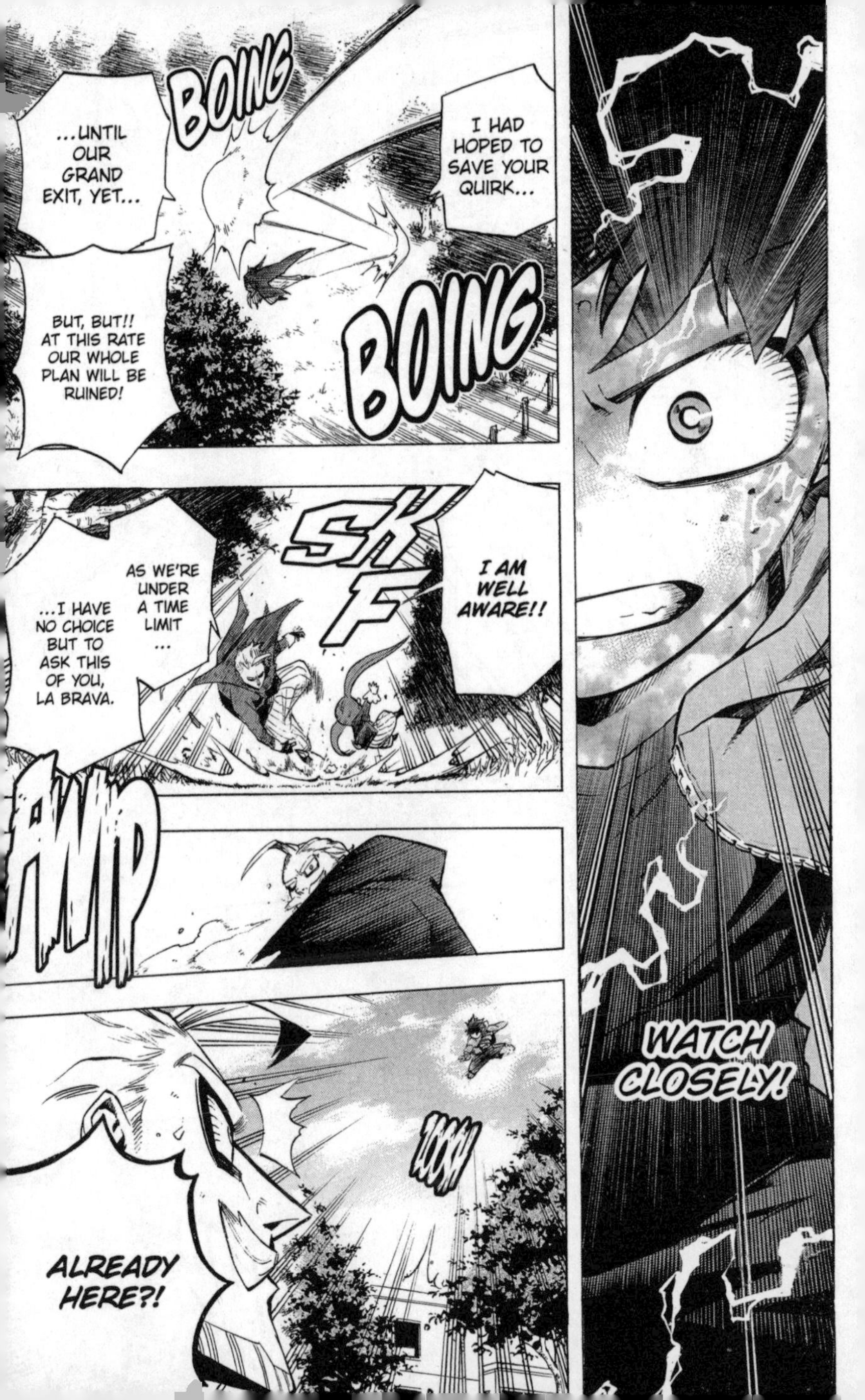
WATCH CLOSELY!
I HAD HOPED TO SAVE YOUR QUIRK...
BOING
...UNTIL OUR GRAND EXIT, YET...
BOING
BUT, BUT!! AT THIS RATE OUR WHOLE PLAN WILL BE RUINED!
SKF
I AM WELL AWARE!!
AS WE'RE UNDER A TIME LIMIT...
...I HAVE NO CHOICE BUT TO ASK THIS OF YOU, LA BRAVA.
PAMP
ALREADY HERE?!

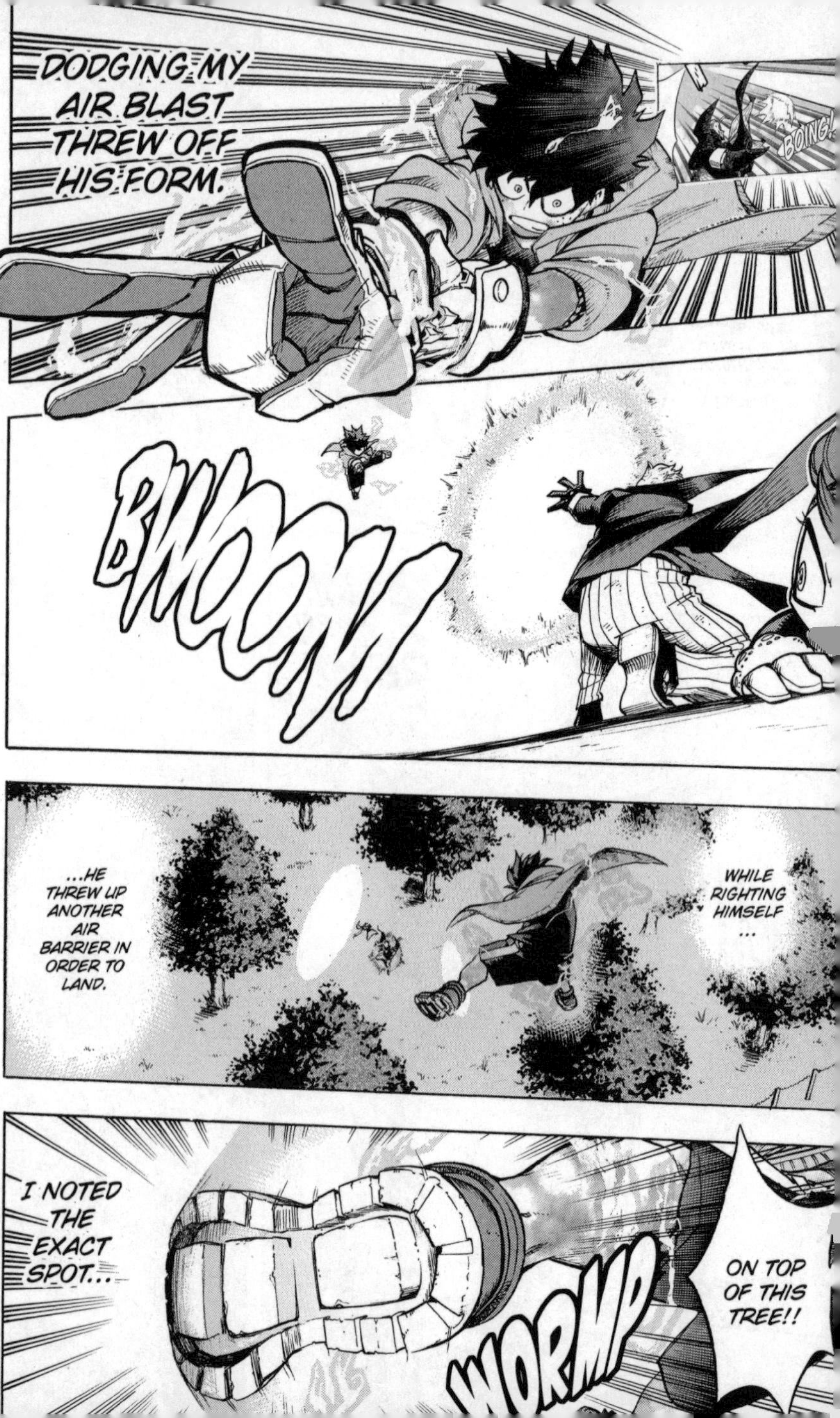
BOING!
DODGING MY AIR BLAST THREW OFF HIS FORM.
BWOOOM
WHILE RIGHTING HIMSELF...
...HE THREW UP ANOTHER AIR BARRIER IN ORDER TO LAND.
I NOTED THE EXACT SPOT...
ON TOP OF THIS TREE!!
WORMP

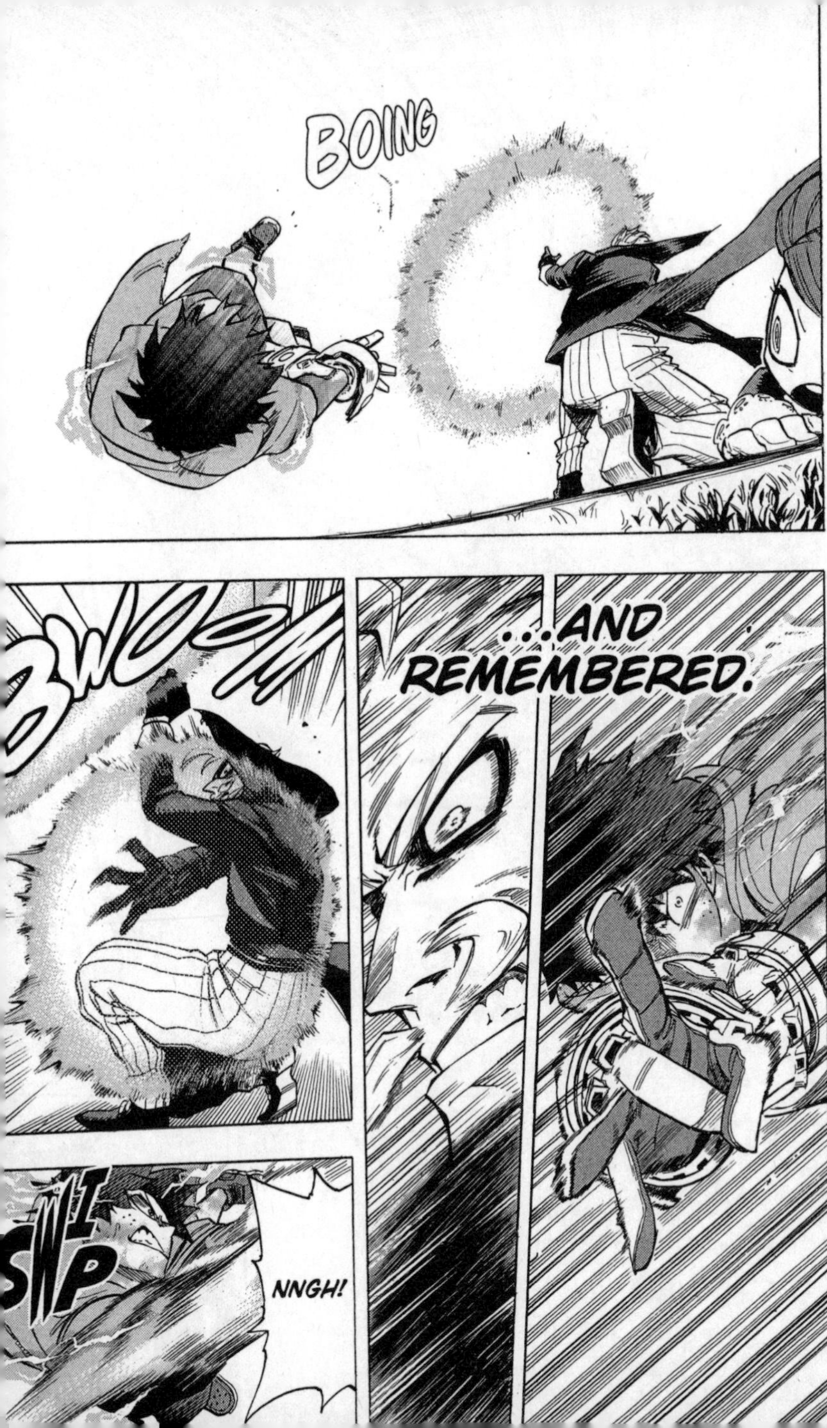
BOING
...AND
REMEMBERED.
BWOOOM
NNGH!

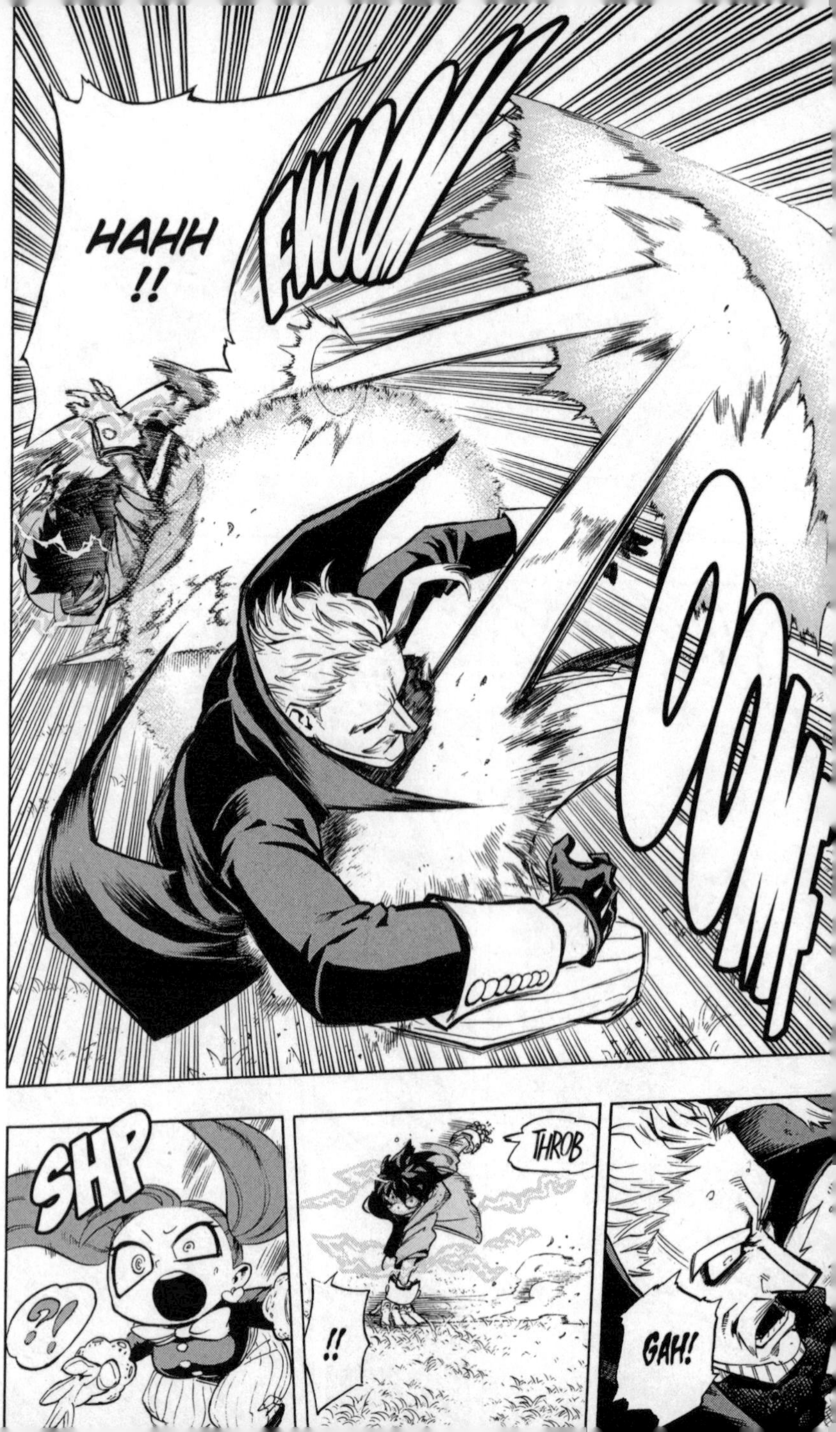
FWOO
OOMF
HAHH !!
GAH!
THROB
!!
SHP
?!

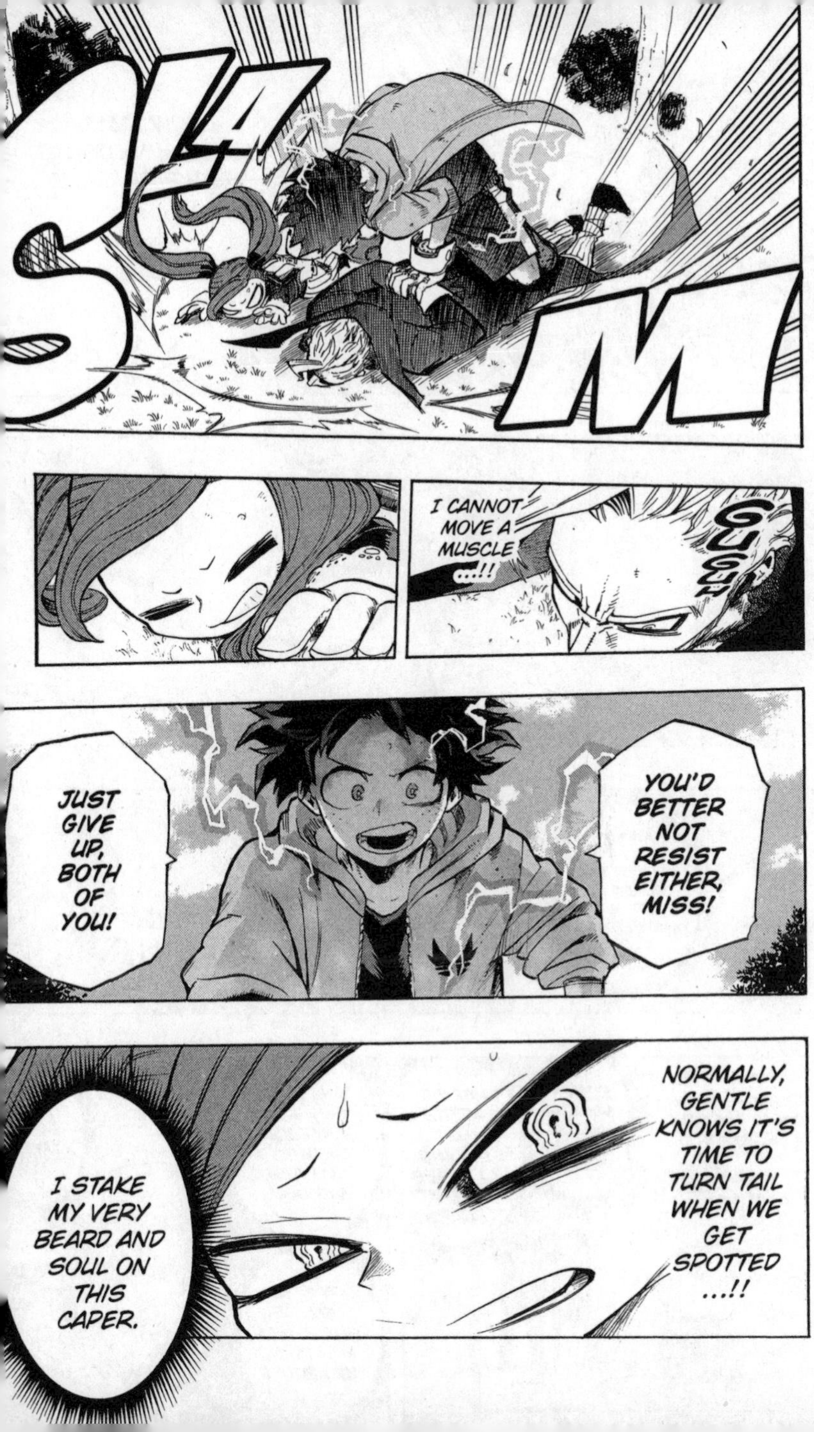
SLAM
I CANNOT MOVE A MUSCLE ...!!
GUGUH
YOU'D BETTER NOT RESIST EITHER, MISS!
JUST GIVE UP, BOTH OF YOU!
NORMALLY, GENTLE KNOWS IT'S TIME TO TURN TAIL WHEN WE GET SPOTTED ...!!
I STAKE MY VERY BEARD AND SOUL ON THIS CAPER.

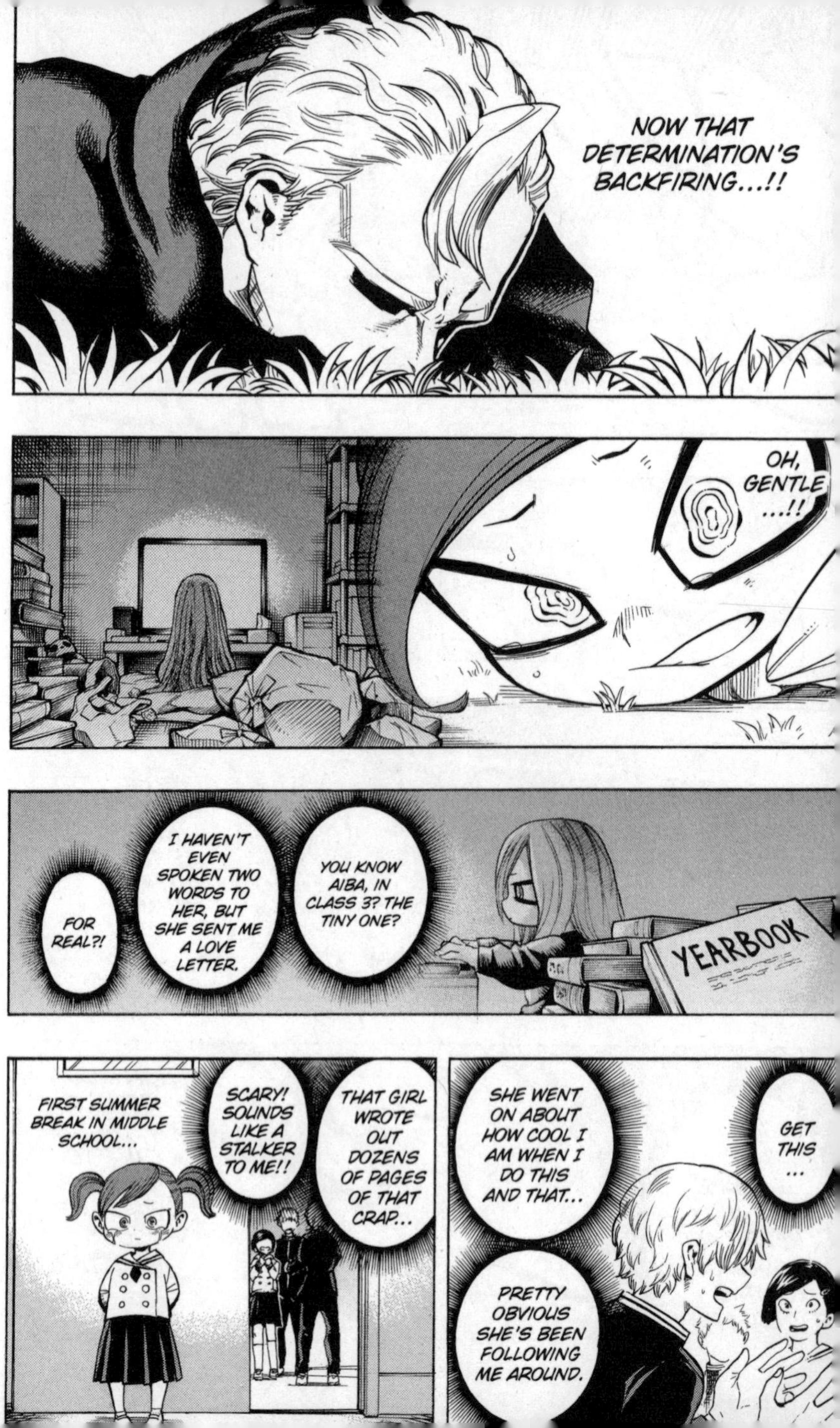
NOW THAT DETERMINATION'S BACKFIRING...!!
OH, GENTLE ...!!
YOU KNOW AIBA, IN CLASS 3? THE TINY ONE?
I HAVEN'T EVEN SPOKEN TWO WORDS TO HER, BUT SHE SENT ME A LOVE LETTER.
FOR REAL?!
YEARBOOK
GET THIS ...
SHE WENT ON ABOUT HOW COOL I AM WHEN I DO THIS AND THAT...
PRETTY OBVIOUS SHE'S BEEN FOLLOWING ME AROUND.
THAT GIRL WROTE OUT DOZENS OF PAGES OF THAT CRAP...
SCARY! SOUNDS LIKE A STALKER TO ME!!
FIRST SUMMER BREAK IN MIDDLE SCHOOL...

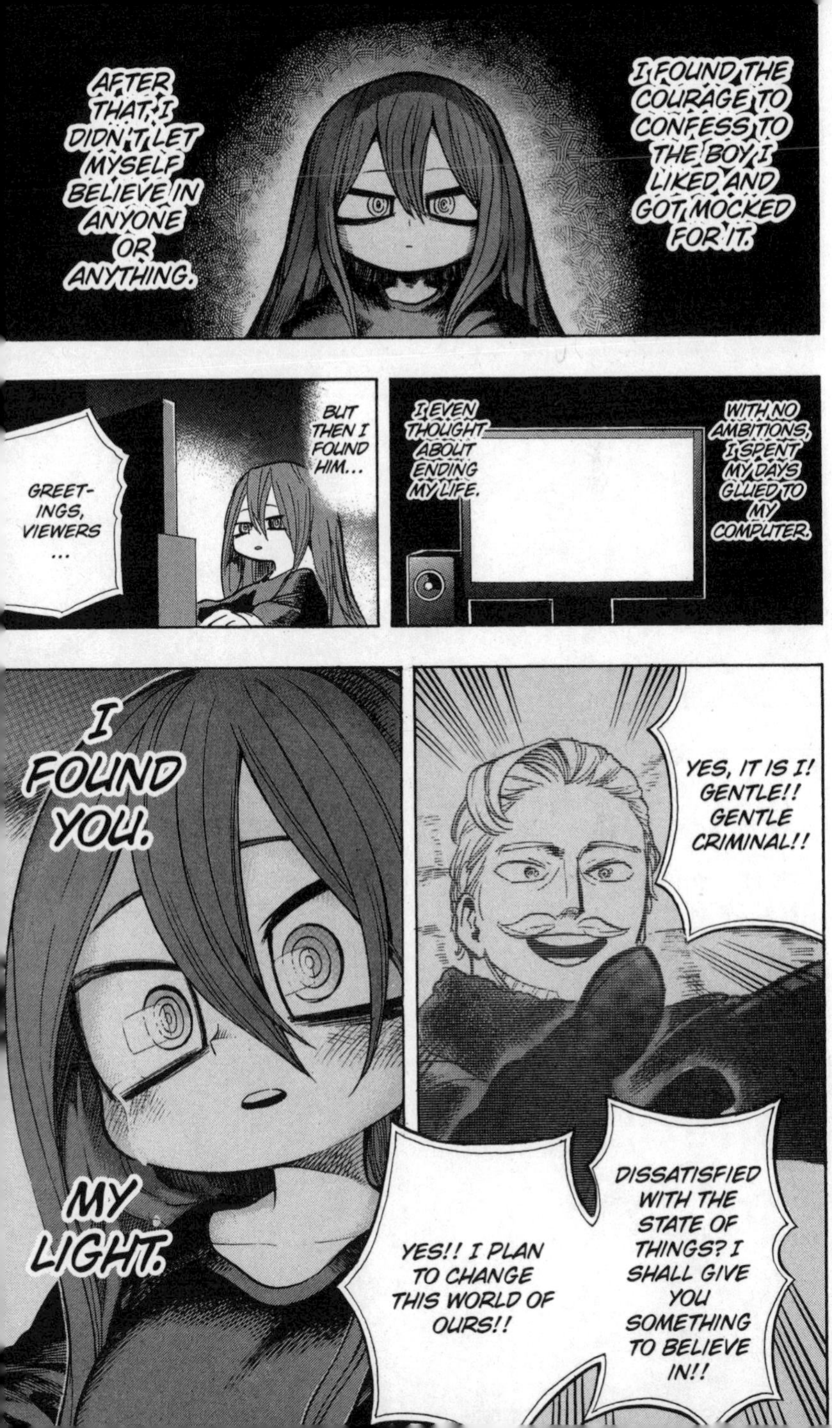
I FOUND THE COURAGE TO CONFESS TO THE BOY I LIKED AND GOT MOCKED FOR IT.
AFTER THAT, I DIDN'T LET MYSELF BELIEVE IN ANYONE OR ANYTHING.
WITH NO AMBITIONS, I SPENT MY DAYS GLUED TO MY COMPUTER.
I EVEN THOUGHT ABOUT ENDING MY LIFE.
BUT THEN I FOUND HIM...
GREETINGS, VIEWERS ...
YES, IT IS I! GENTLE!! GENTLE CRIMINAL!!
DISSATISFIED WITH THE STATE OF THINGS? I SHALL GIVE YOU SOMETHING TO BELIEVE IN!!
YES!! I PLAN TO CHANGE THIS WORLD OF OURS!!
I FOUND YOU.
MY LIGHT.

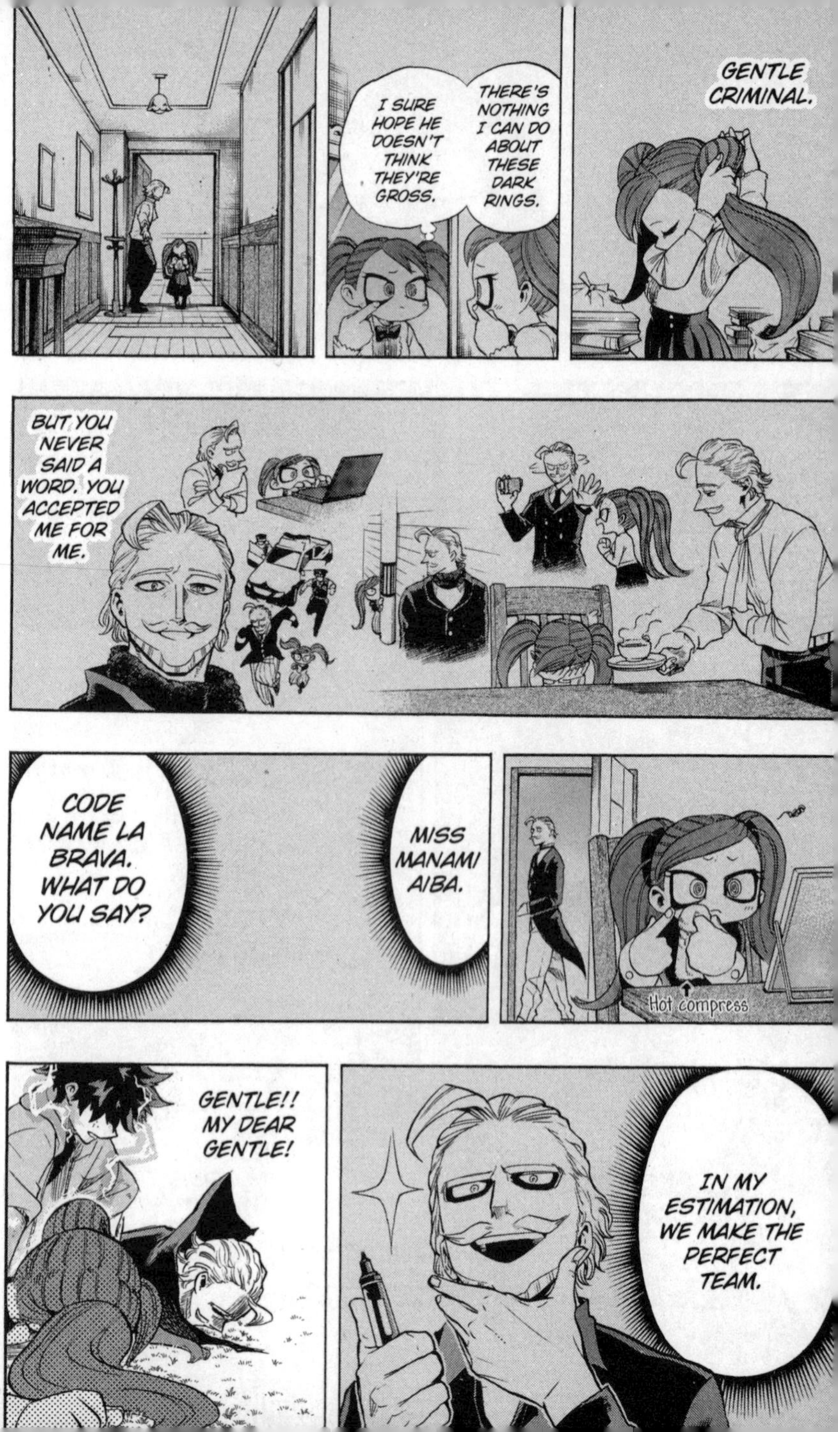
GENTLE CRIMINAL.
THERE'S NOTHING I CAN DO ABOUT THESE DARK RINGS.
I SURE HOPE HE DOESN'T THINK THEY'RE GROSS.
BUT YOU NEVER SAID A WORD. YOU ACCEPTED ME FOR ME.
Hot compress
MISS MANAMI AIBA.
CODE NAME LA BRAVA. WHAT DO YOU SAY?
IN MY ESTIMATION, WE MAKE THE PERFECT TEAM.
GENTLE!! MY DEAR GENTLE!

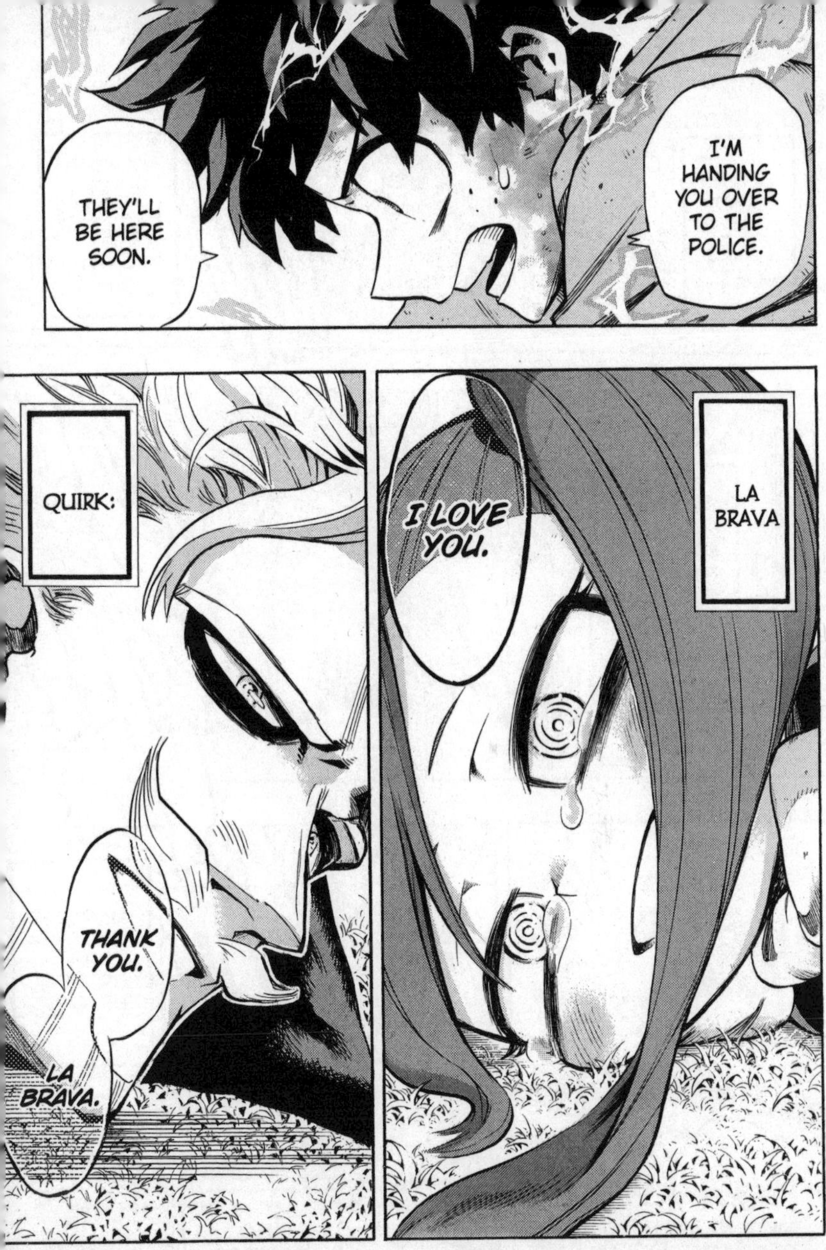
I'M HANDING YOU OVER TO THE POLICE.
THEY'LL BE HERE SOON.
LA BRAVA
I LOVE YOU.
QUIRK:
THANK YOU.
LA BRAVA.

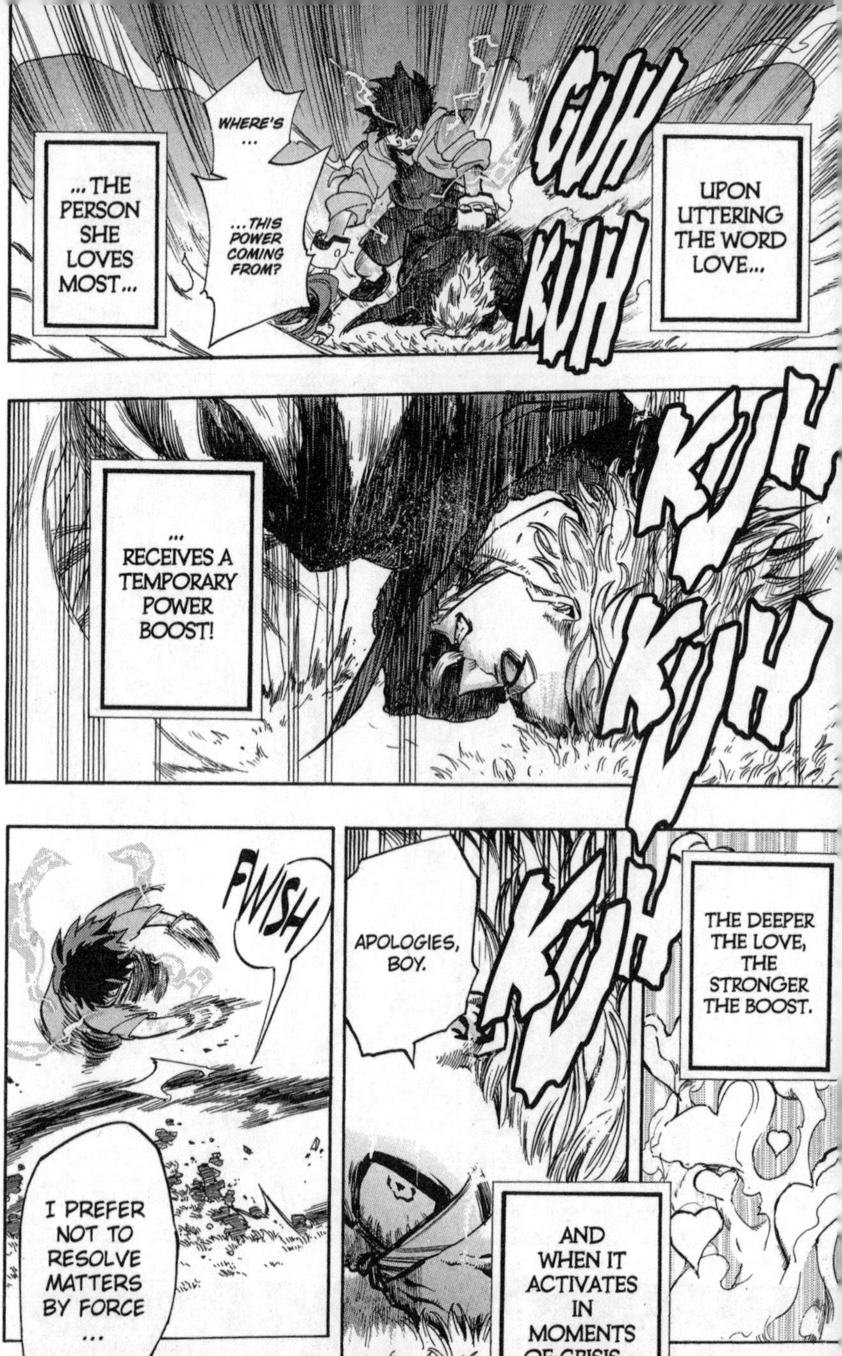
UPON UTTERING THE WORD LOVE...
GUH
KUH
WHERE'S ...
...THIS POWER COMING FROM?
...THE PERSON SHE LOVES MOST...
KUH
KUH
... RECEIVES A TEMPORARY POWER BOOST!
THE DEEPER THE LOVE, THE STRONGER THE BOOST.
KUH
APOLOGIES, BOY.
AND WHEN IT ACTIVATES IN MOMENTS OF CRISIS...
FWISH
I PREFER NOT TO RESOLVE MATTERS BY FORCE ...

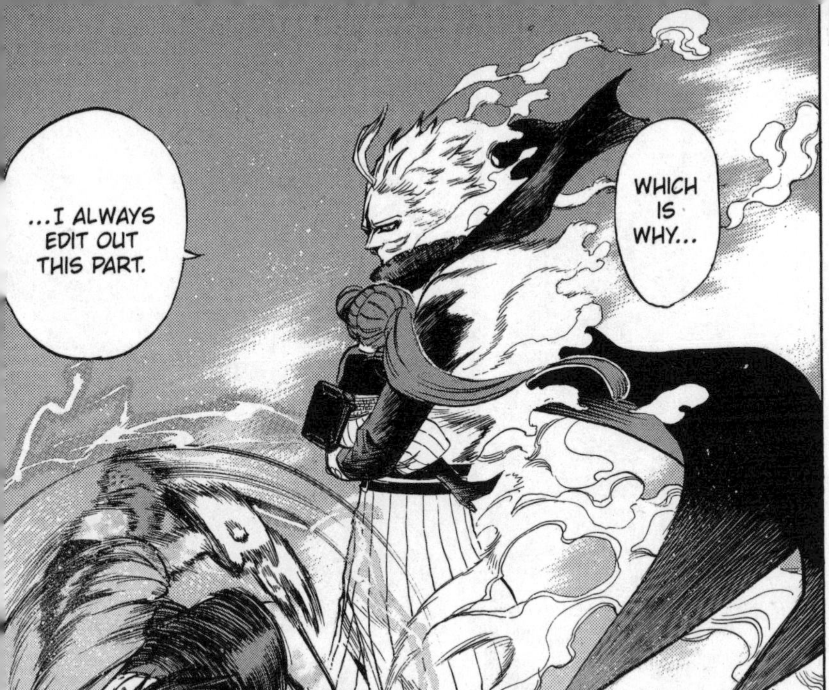
WHICH IS WHY...
...I ALWAYS EDIT OUT THIS PART.

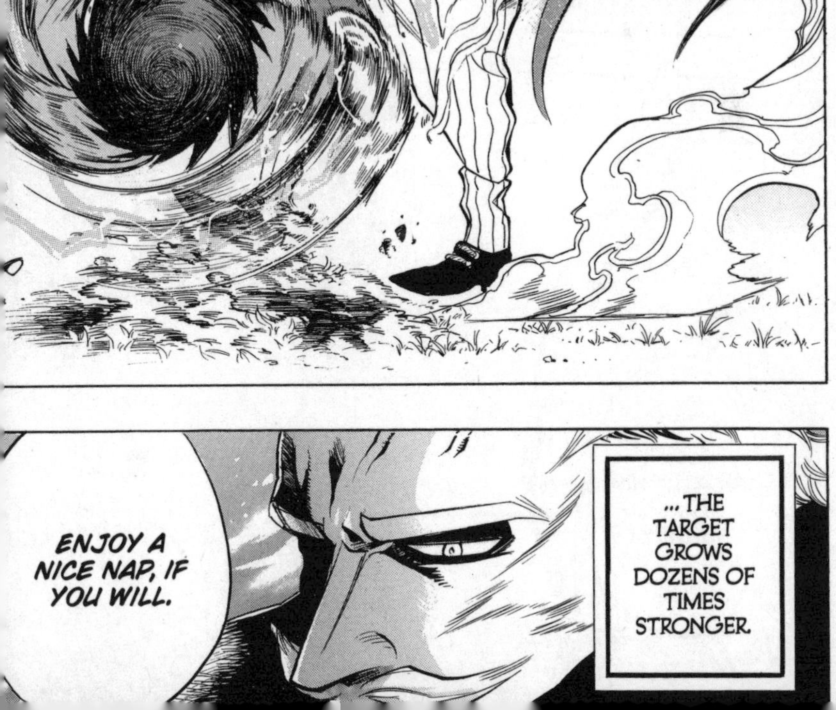
...THE TARGET GROWS DOZENS OF TIMES STRONGER.
ENJOY A NICE NAP, IF YOU WILL.

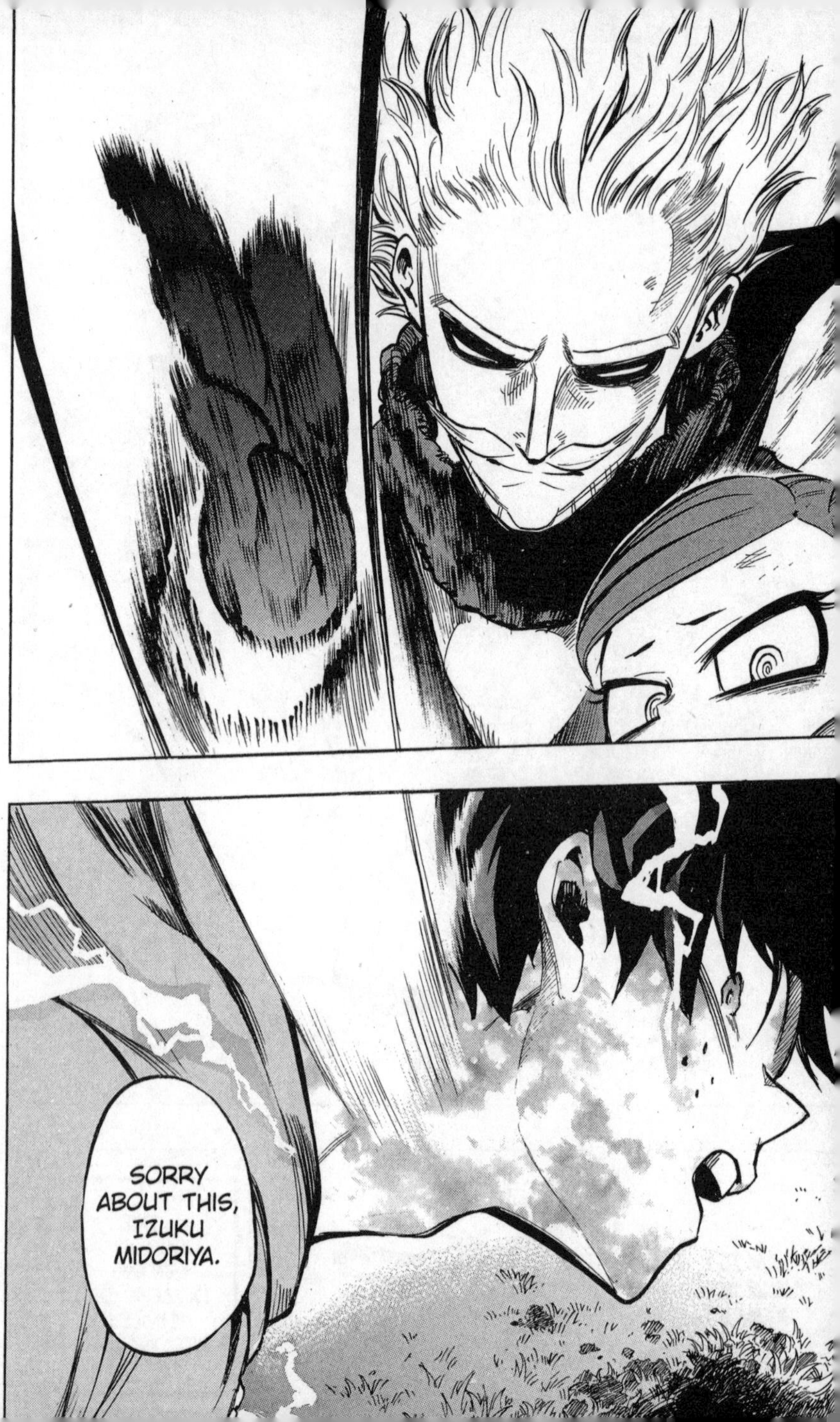
SORRY ABOUT THIS, IZUKU MIDORIYA.

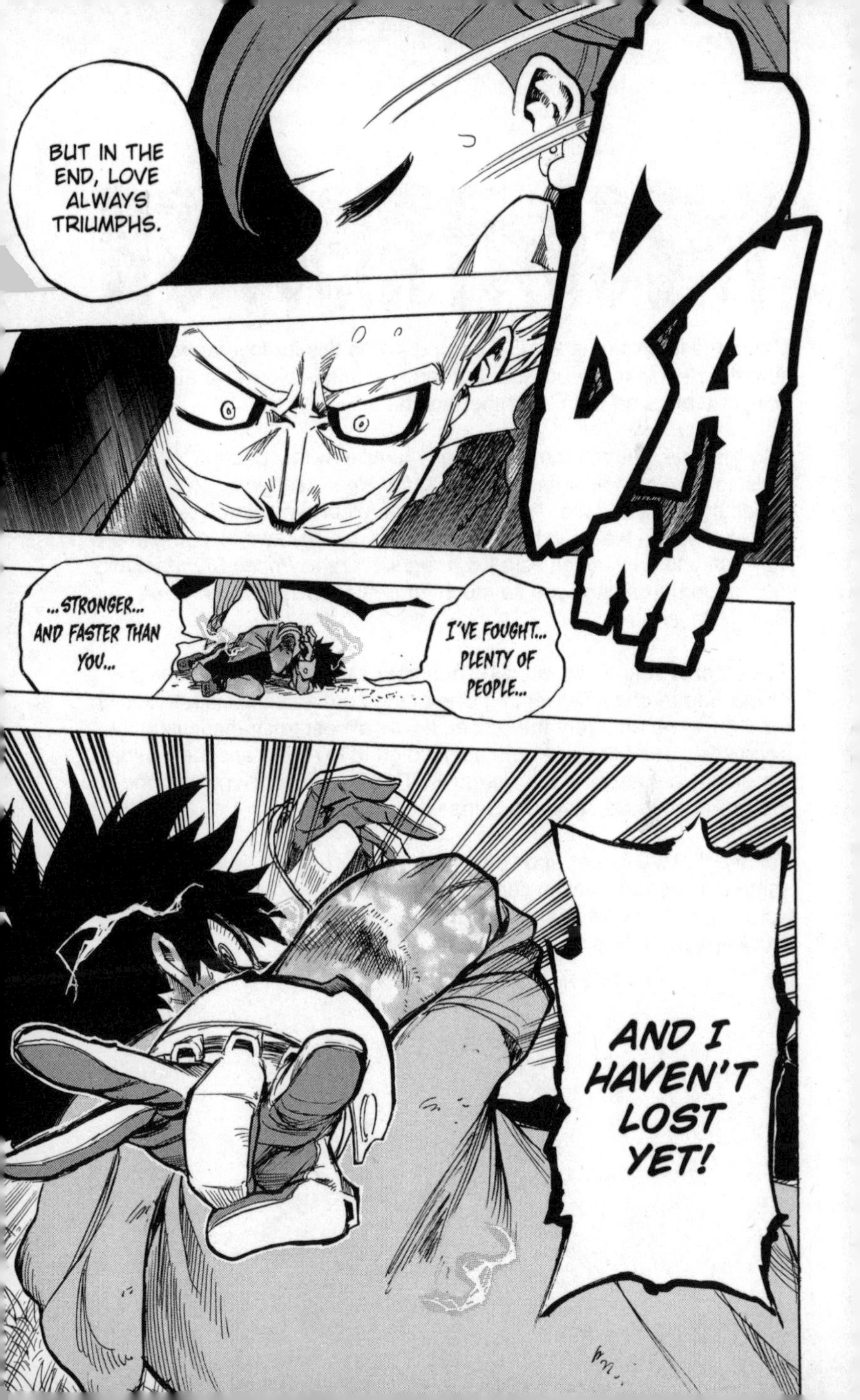
BUT IN THE END, LOVE ALWAYS TRIUMPHS.
DAM
I'VE FOUGHT... PLENTY OF PEOPLE...
...STRONGER... AND FASTER THAN YOU...
AND I HAVEN'T LOST YET!

THE CONTRIBUTION

We made it to volume 20! I've been drawing this for four years straight! And it's all thanks to you—the readers!! In this book, we've even got congratulatory art from two other artists!!

The first one, you're probably already familiar with—Betten Court is the artist for the spin-off series in *Jump+*, *My Hero Academia: Vigilantes*!! When they first told me, "You're getting a full-blown spin-off drawn by Betten Court," I was dumbstruck. It was especially awe-inspiring and a little scary to hear, since as a kid, I regularly read *Prince Standard* and *Ashita Dorobo*. Thank you so much for getting involved with *MHA*, Betten Sensei!

The other is Yoko Akiyama, who has her own serialization in *Jump+* called *Saguri-chan Tankentai*!! She started out as an assistant helping me with *MHA*, and from the outset, it was almost frustrating just how good she was at drawing cute girls. I'd grind my teeth and stew over the quality of her drawings, seriously. Thank you for all you've done and continue to do, Akiyama Sensei!!

Volume 5 of *Vigilantes* and volume 3 of *Saguri-chan* released at the same time as this book in Japan. They both have some illustrations from me, so if you're interested, go ahead and check those out! Doing art swaps like this is so exciting! I love it!

Akiyama Sensei's art is on page 60!!

Betten Sensei's art is on page 42!

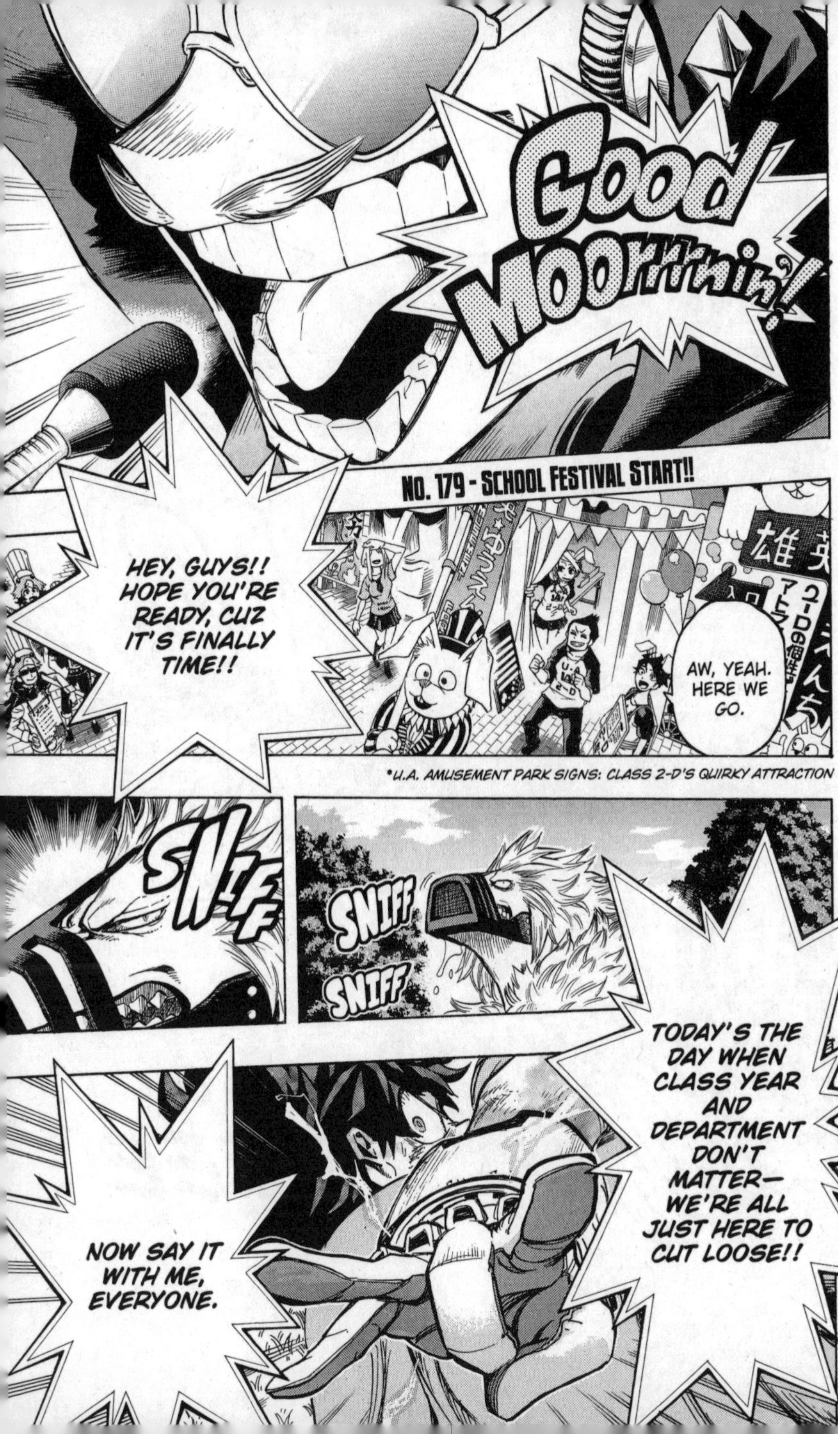
Good MOORrrnin'!
NO. 179 - SCHOOL FESTIVAL START!!
AW, YEAH. HERE WE GO.
HEY, GUYS!! HOPE YOU'RE READY, CUZ IT'S FINALLY TIME!!
*U.A. AMUSEMENT PARK SIGNS: CLASS 2-D'S QUIRKY ATTRACTION
SNIFF
SNIFF
SNIFF
TODAY'S THE DAY WHEN CLASS YEAR AND DEPARTMENT DON'T MATTER— WE'RE ALL JUST HERE TO CUT LOOSE!!
NOW SAY IT WITH ME, EVERYONE.

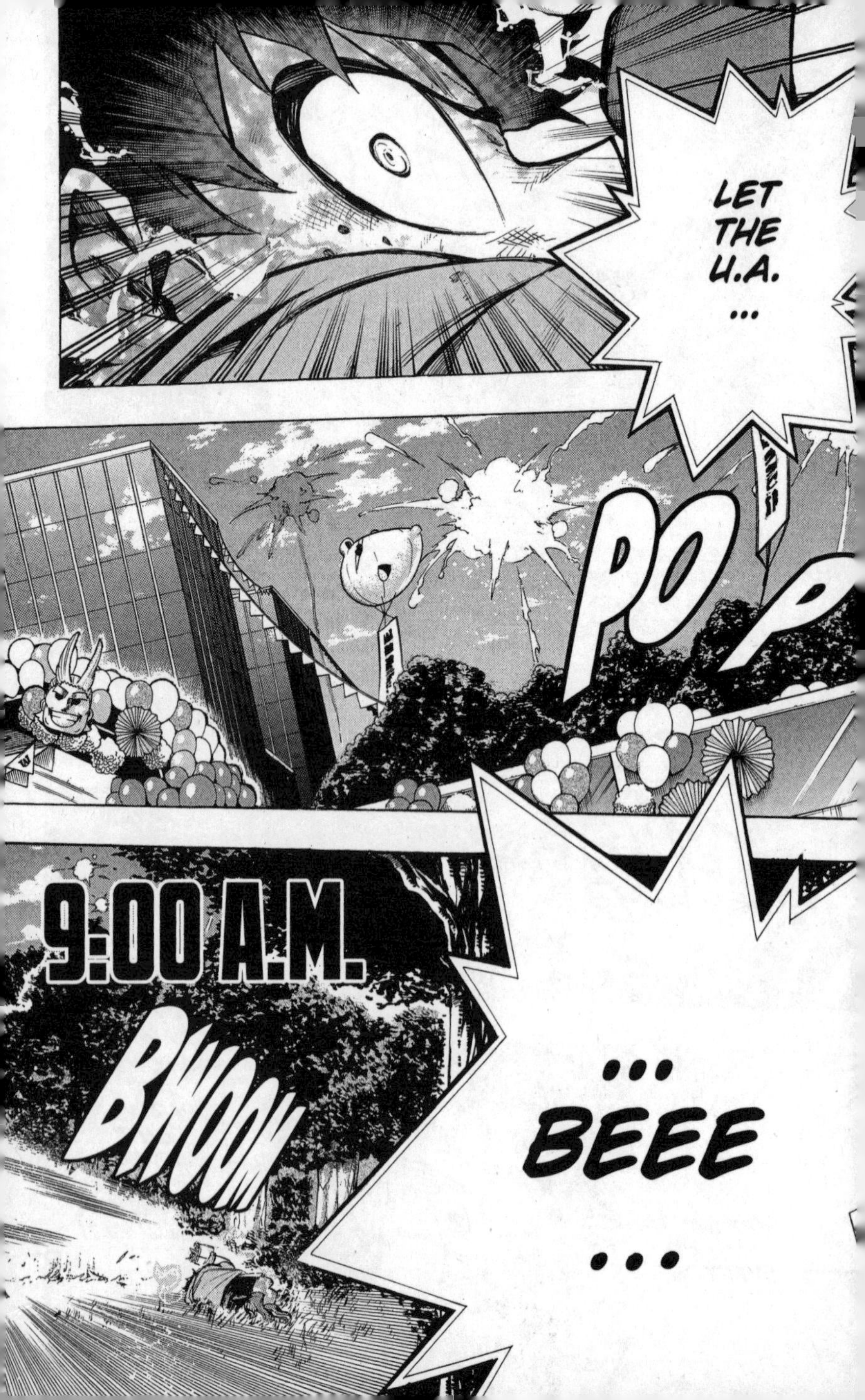
LET THE U.A. ...
POP
9:00 A.M.
... BEEE ...
BWOOM

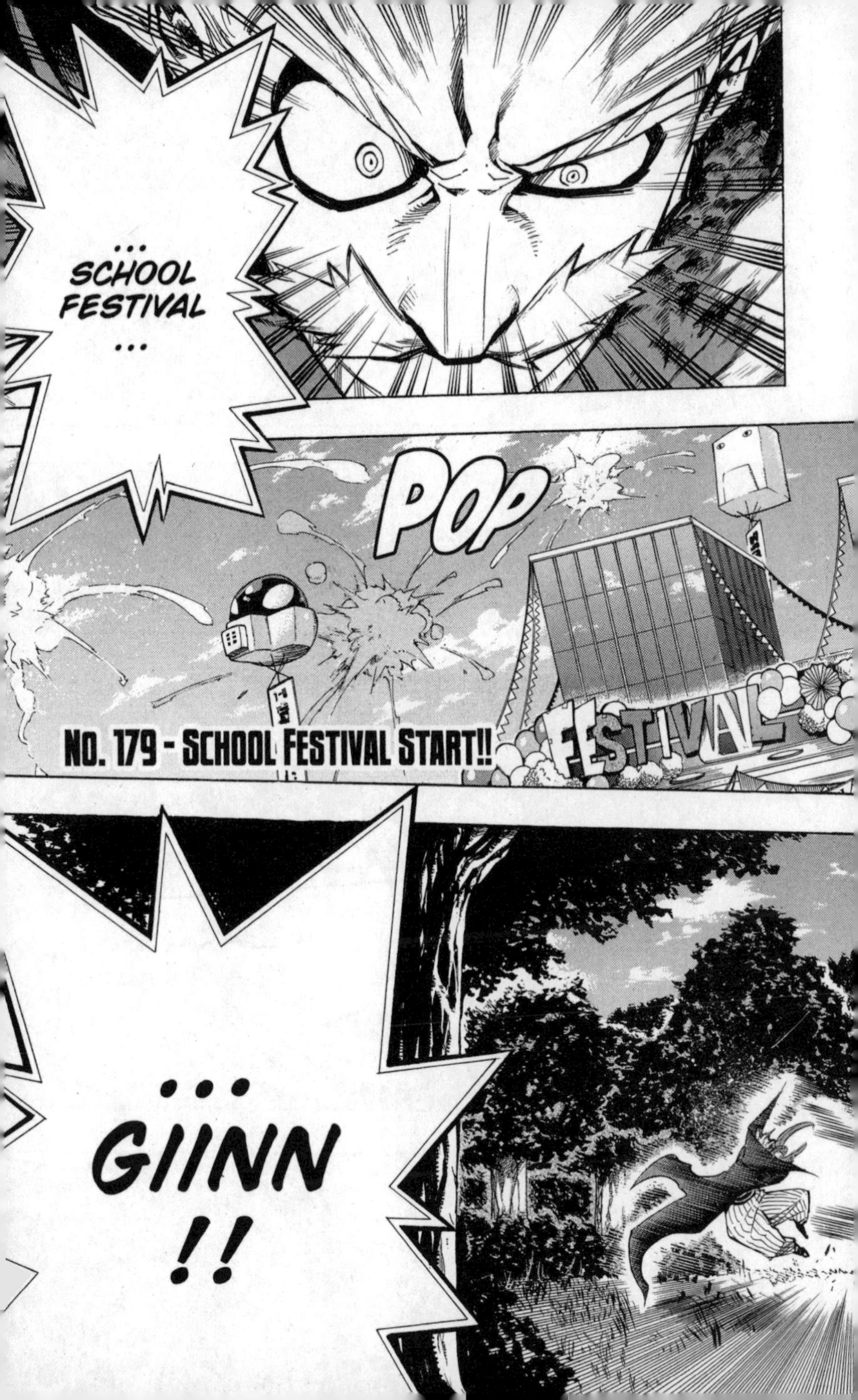

... SCHOOL FESTIVAL ...
POP
NO. 179 - SCHOOL FESTIVAL START!!
FESTIVAL
... GIINN !!

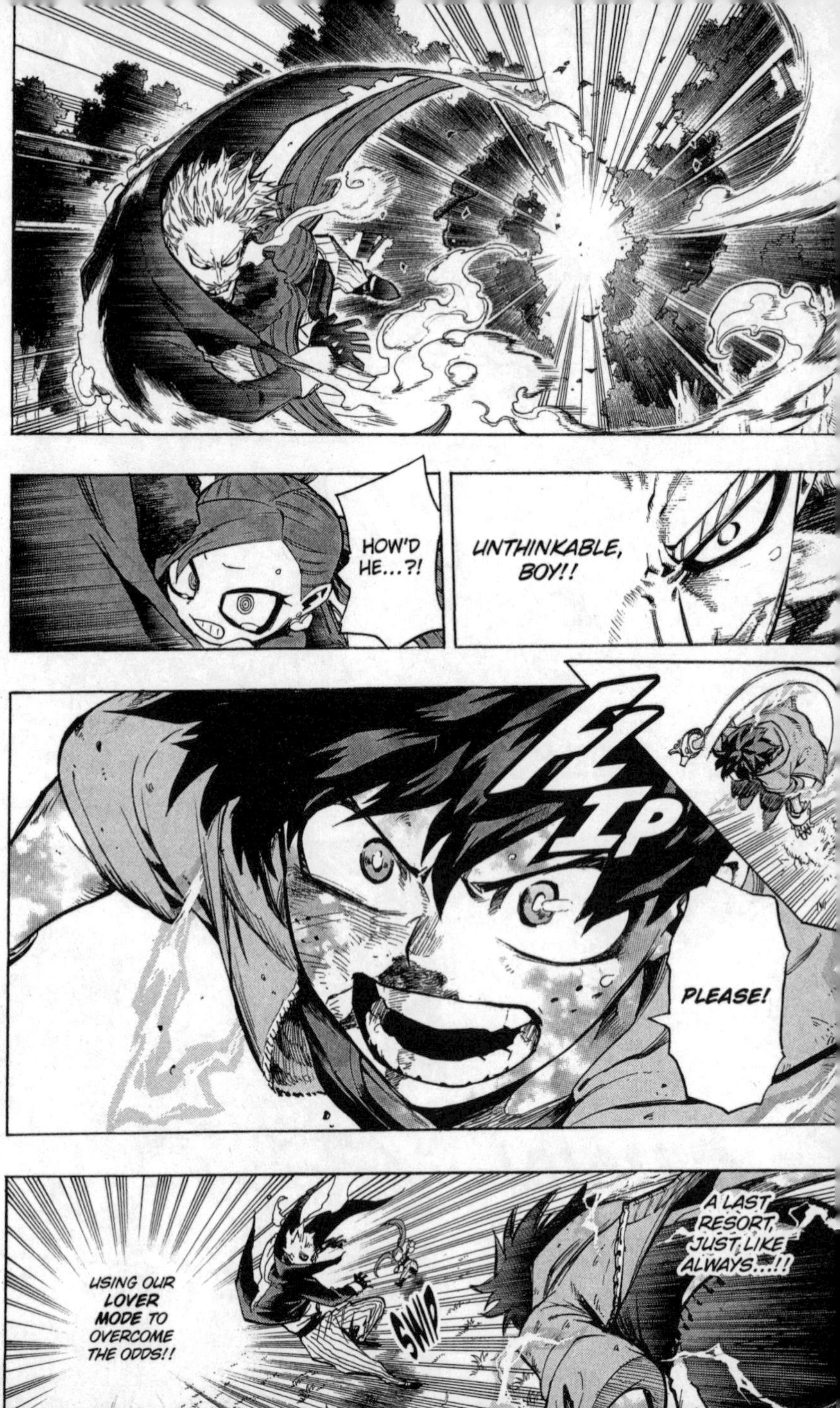
UNTHINKABLE, BOY!!
HOW'D HE...?!
FLIP
PLEASE!
A LAST RESORT, JUST LIKE ALWAYS...!!
SWIP
USING OUR LOVER MODE TO OVERCOME THE ODDS!!

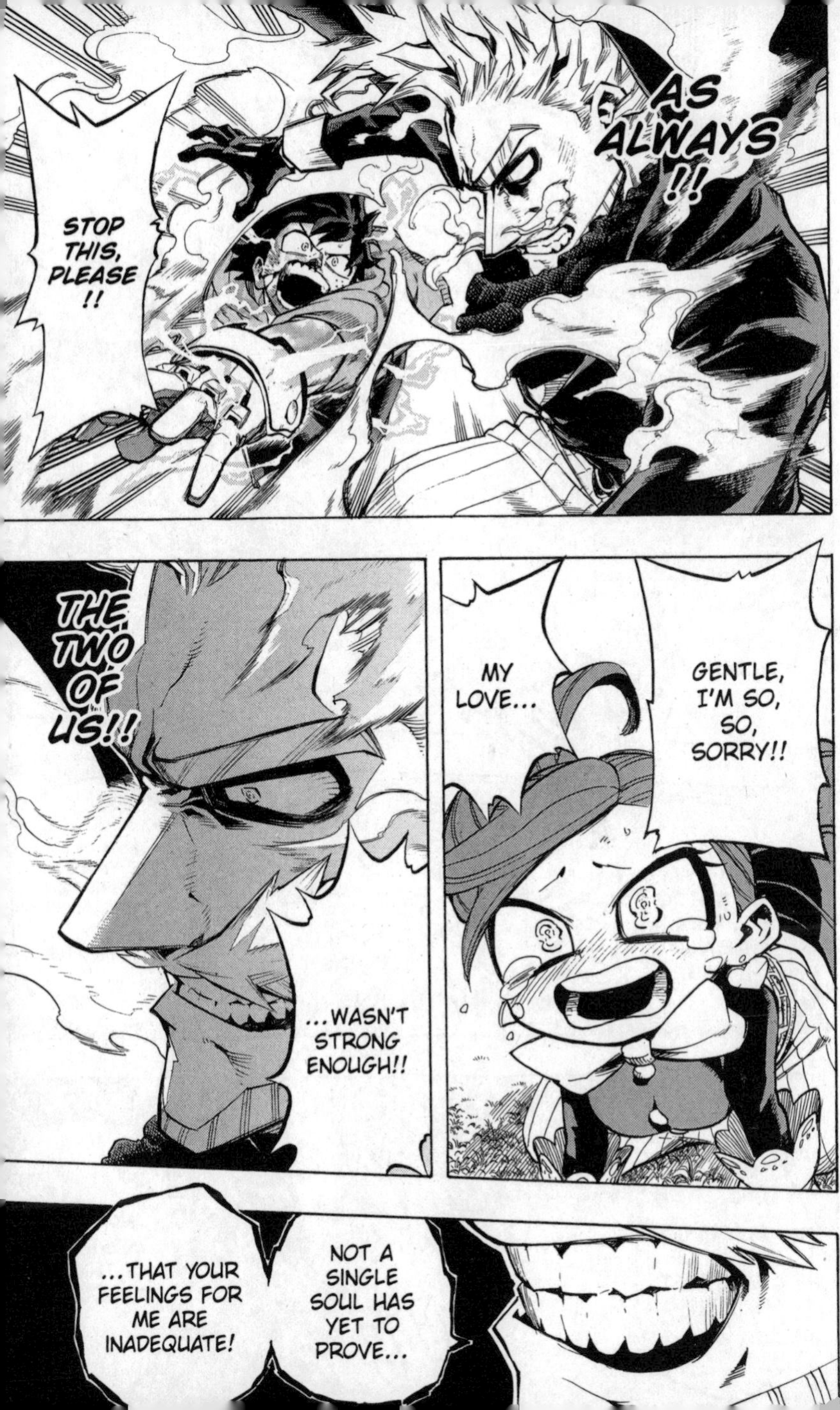
AS ALWAYS!!
STOP THIS, PLEASE!!
GENTLE, I'M SO, SO, SORRY!!
MY LOVE...
THE TWO OF US!!
...WASN'T STRONG ENOUGH!!
NOT A SINGLE SOUL HAS YET TO PROVE...
...THAT YOUR FEELINGS FOR ME ARE INADEQUATE!

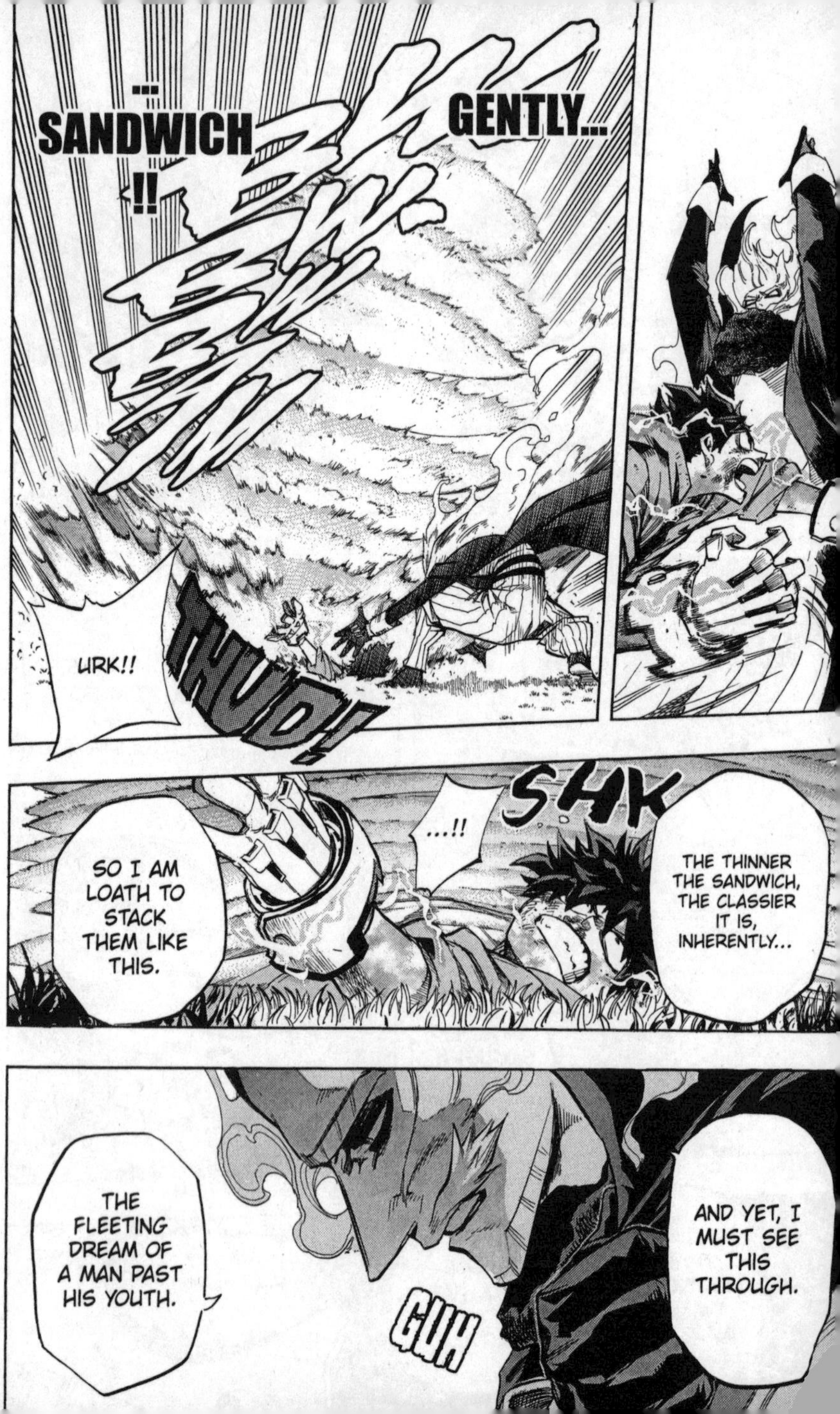
GENTLY...
...SANDWICH !!
THUD!
URK!!
SHK
THE THINNER THE SANDWICH, THE CLASSIER IT IS, INHERENTLY...
...!!
SO I AM LOATH TO STACK THEM LIKE THIS.
AND YET, I MUST SEE THIS THROUGH.
GUH
THE FLEETING DREAM OF A MAN PAST HIS YOUTH.

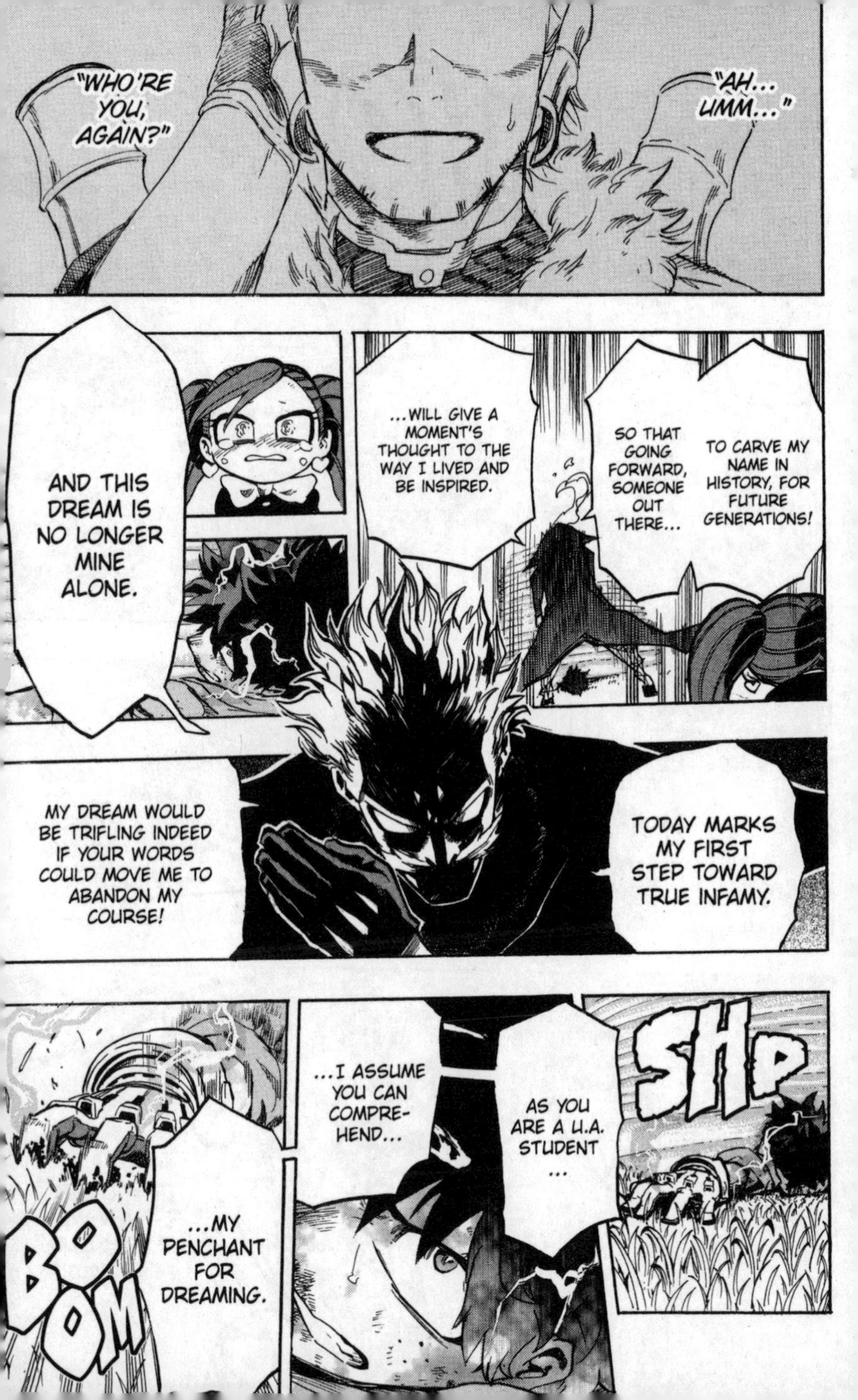
"AH... UMM..."
"WHO'RE YOU, AGAIN?"
TO CARVE MY NAME IN HISTORY, FOR FUTURE GENERATIONS!
SO THAT GOING FORWARD, SOMEONE OUT THERE...
...WILL GIVE A MOMENT'S THOUGHT TO THE WAY I LIVED AND BE INSPIRED.
AND THIS DREAM IS NO LONGER MINE ALONE.
TODAY MARKS MY FIRST STEP TOWARD TRUE INFAMY.
MY DREAM WOULD BE TRIFLING INDEED IF YOUR WORDS COULD MOVE ME TO ABANDON MY COURSE!
SHP
AS YOU ARE A U.A. STUDENT ...
...I ASSUME YOU CAN COMPRE-HEND...
...MY PENCHANT FOR DREAMING.
BOOM

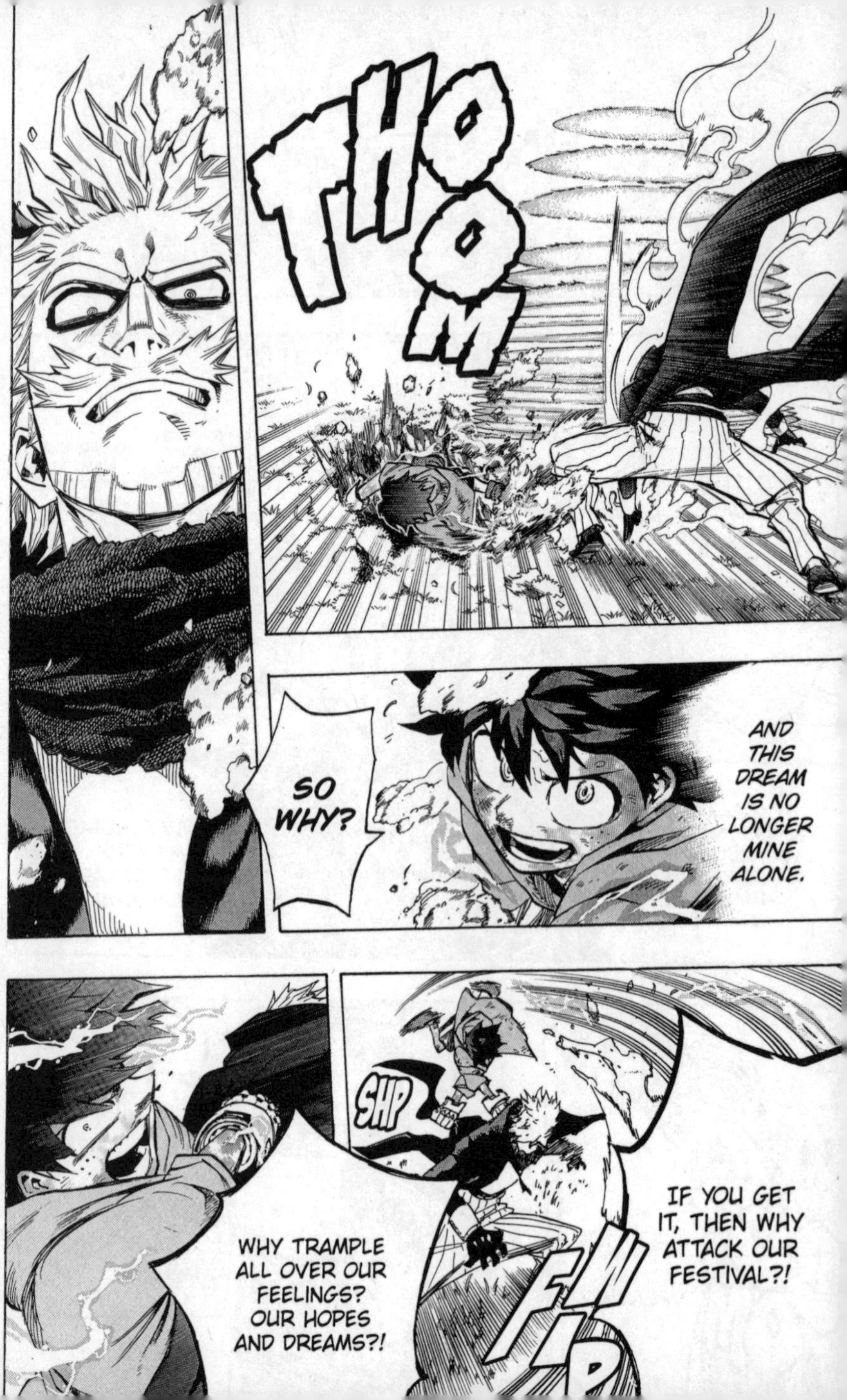
THOOM
AND THIS DREAM IS NO LONGER MINE ALONE.
SO WHY?
SHP
IF YOU GET IT, THEN WHY ATTACK OUR FESTIVAL?!
FWIP
WHY TRAMPLE ALL OVER OUR FEELINGS? OUR HOPES AND DREAMS?!

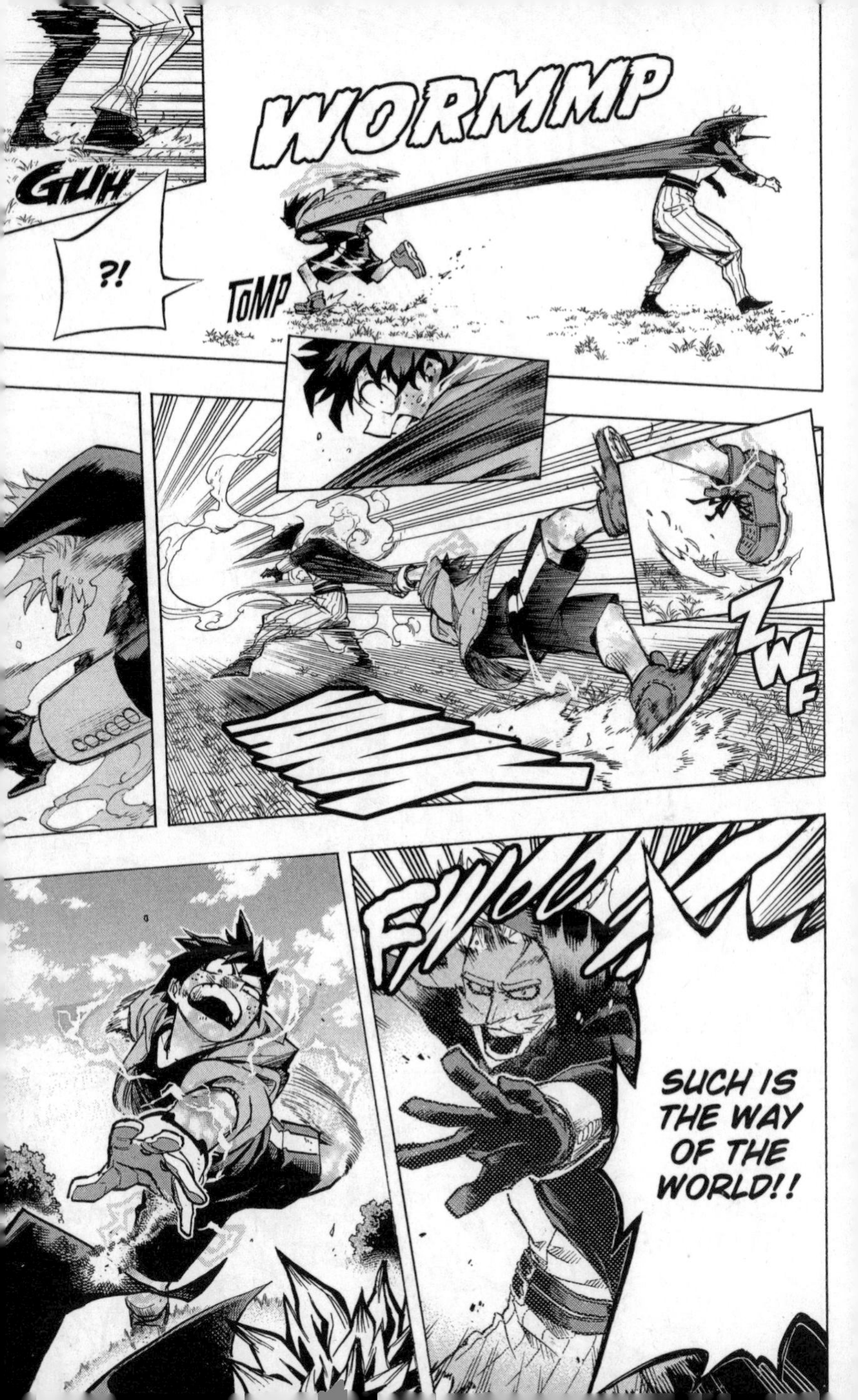
WORMMP
TOMP
?!
GUH
ZWF
SUCH IS THE WAY OF THE WORLD!!

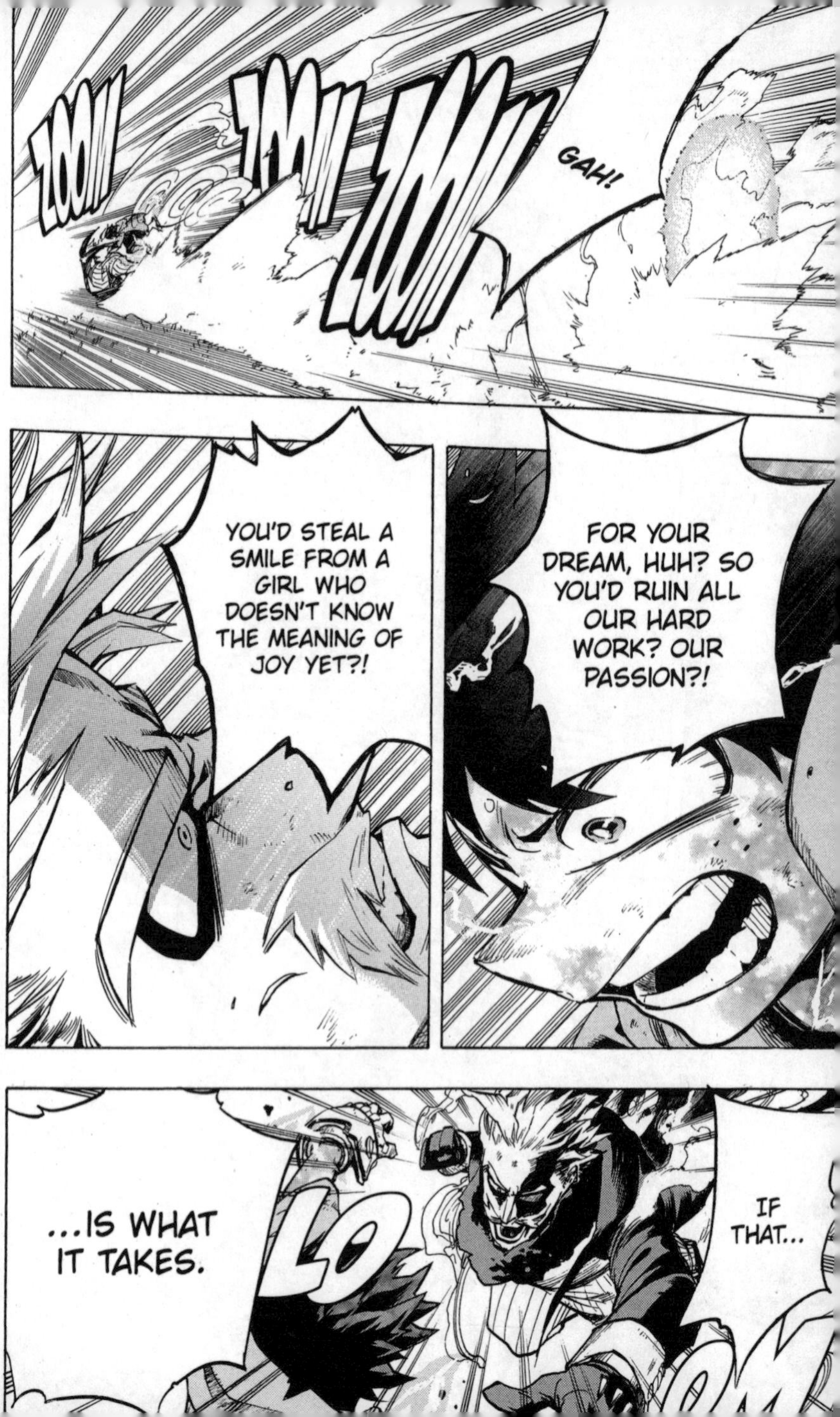
GAH!
ZOOM
ZOOM
FOR YOUR DREAM, HUH? SO YOU'D RUIN ALL OUR HARD WORK? OUR PASSION?!
YOU'D STEAL A SMILE FROM A GIRL WHO DOESN'T KNOW THE MEANING OF JOY YET?!
IF THAT...
...IS WHAT IT TAKES.

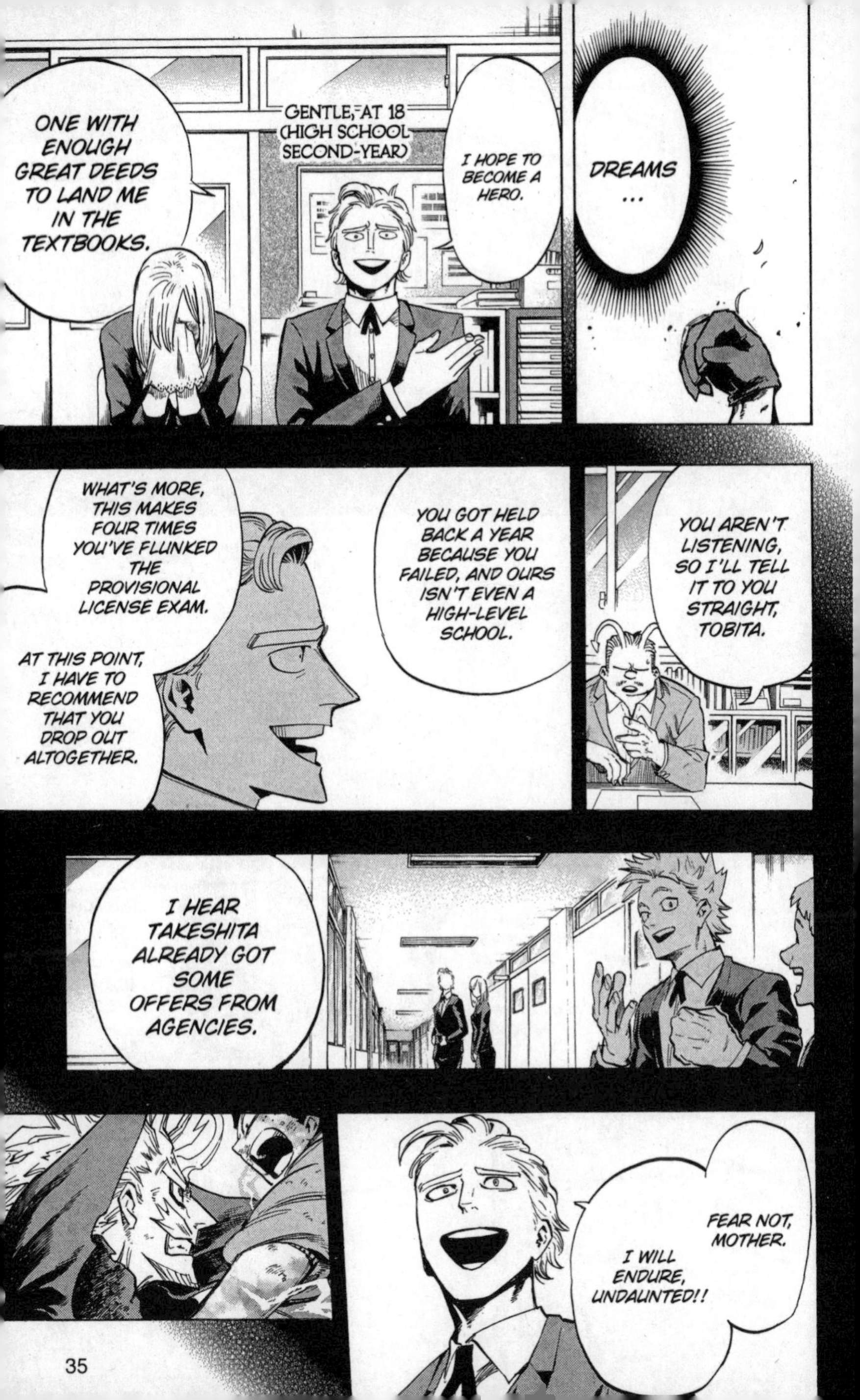
DREAMS ...
I HOPE TO BECOME A HERO.
GENTLE, AT 18 (HIGH SCHOOL SECOND-YEAR)
ONE WITH ENOUGH GREAT DEEDS TO LAND ME IN THE TEXTBOOKS.
YOU AREN'T LISTENING, SO I'LL TELL IT TO YOU STRAIGHT, TOBITA.
YOU GOT HELD BACK A YEAR BECAUSE YOU FAILED, AND OURS ISN'T EVEN A HIGH-LEVEL SCHOOL.
WHAT'S MORE, THIS MAKES FOUR TIMES YOU'VE FLUNKED THE PROVISIONAL LICENSE EXAM.
AT THIS POINT, I HAVE TO RECOMMEND THAT YOU DROP OUT ALTOGETHER.
I HEAR TAKESHITA ALREADY GOT SOME OFFERS FROM AGENCIES.
FEAR NOT, MOTHER.
I WILL ENDURE, UNDAUNTED!!

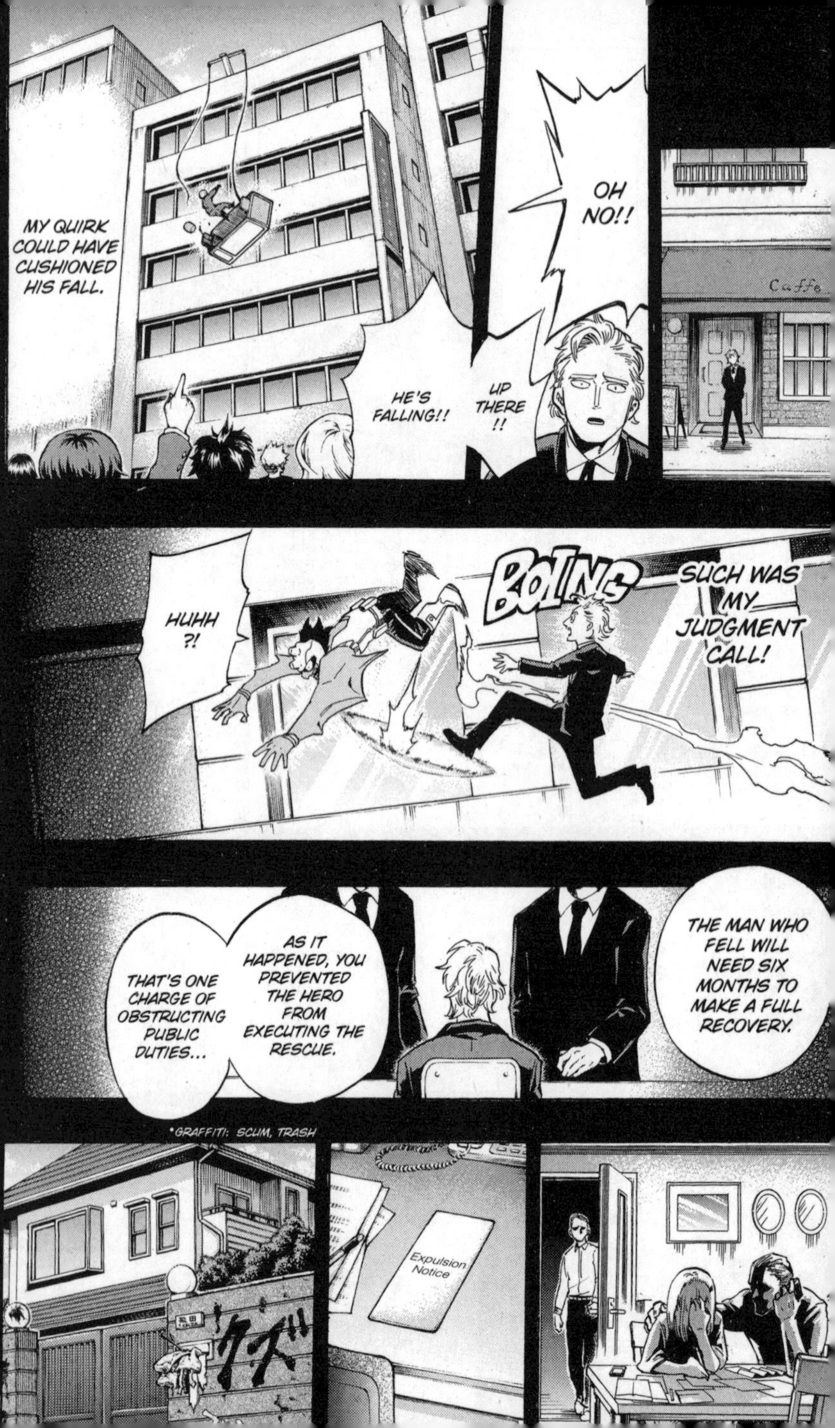
Caffe
OH NO!!
UP THERE !!
HE'S FALLING!!
MY QUIRK COULD HAVE CUSHIONED HIS FALL.
SUCH WAS MY JUDGMENT CALL!
BOING
HUHH ?!
THE MAN WHO FELL WILL NEED SIX MONTHS TO MAKE A FULL RECOVERY.
AS IT HAPPENED, YOU PREVENTED THE HERO FROM EXECUTING THE RESCUE.
THAT'S ONE CHARGE OF OBSTRUCTING PUBLIC DUTIES...
Expulsion Notice
クズ!!
*GRAFFITI: SCUM, TRASH

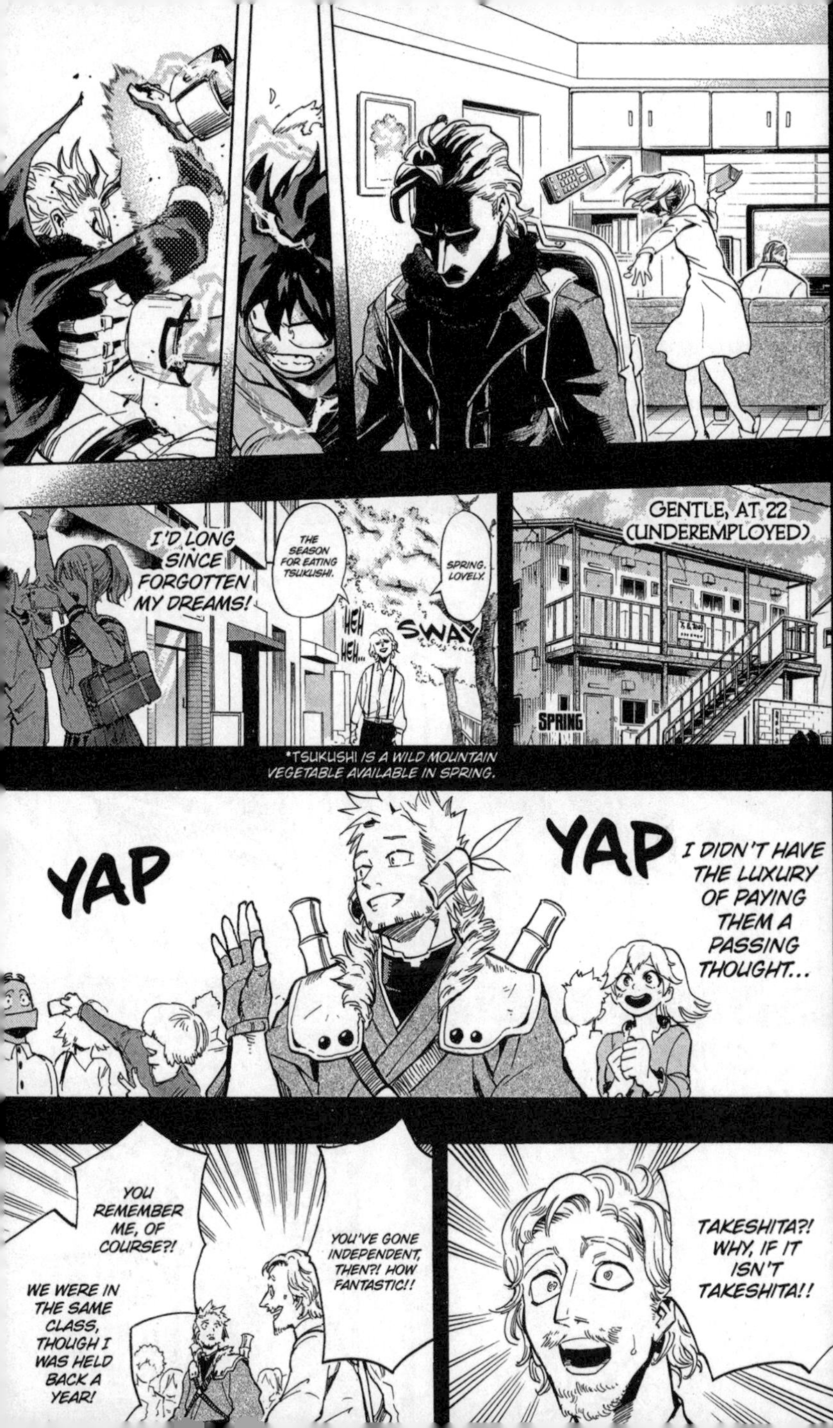
GENTLE, AT 22 (UNDEREMPLOYED)
SPRING
SPRING. LOVELY.
SWAY
THE SEASON FOR EATING TSUKUSHI.
HEH HEH...
I'D LONG SINCE FORGOTTEN MY DREAMS!
*TSUKUSHI IS A WILD MOUNTAIN VEGETABLE AVAILABLE IN SPRING.
I DIDN'T HAVE THE LUXURY OF PAYING THEM A PASSING THOUGHT...
YAP
YAP
TAKESHITA?! WHY, IF IT ISN'T TAKESHITA!!
YOU'VE GONE INDEPENDENT, THEN?! HOW FANTASTIC!!
YOU REMEMBER ME, OF COURSE?!
WE WERE IN THE SAME CLASS, THOUGH I WAS HELD BACK A YEAR!

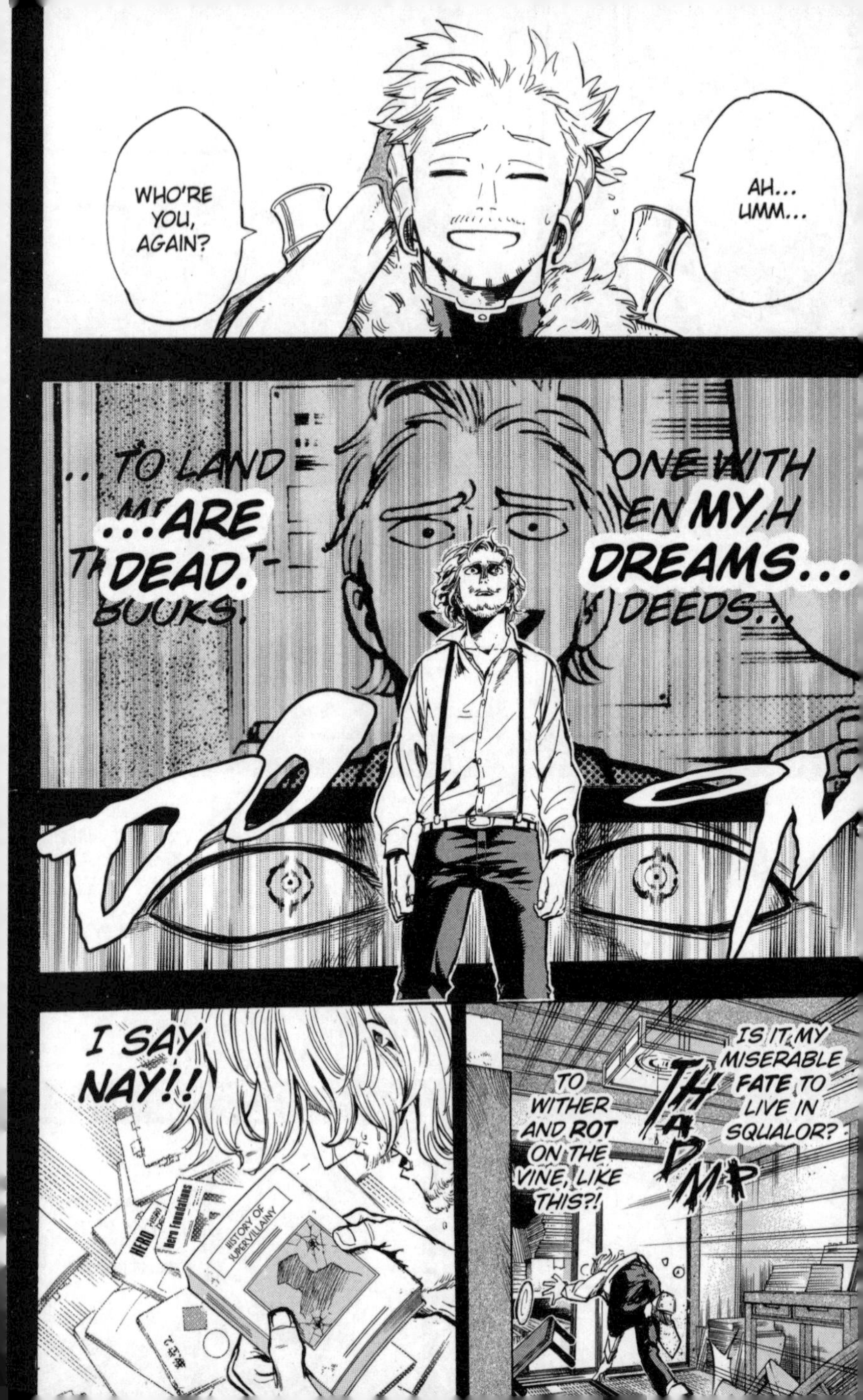
AH... UMM...
WHO'RE YOU, AGAIN?
ONE WITH
DEEDS...
...TO LAND
BOOKS.
MY DREAMS...
...ARE DEAD.
DOON
IS IT MY MISERABLE FATE TO LIVE IN SQUALOR?
TO WITHER AND ROT ON THE VINE, LIKE THIS?!
THADMP
I SAY NAY!!
HISTORY OF SUPERVILLAINY
Hero Foundations
HERO

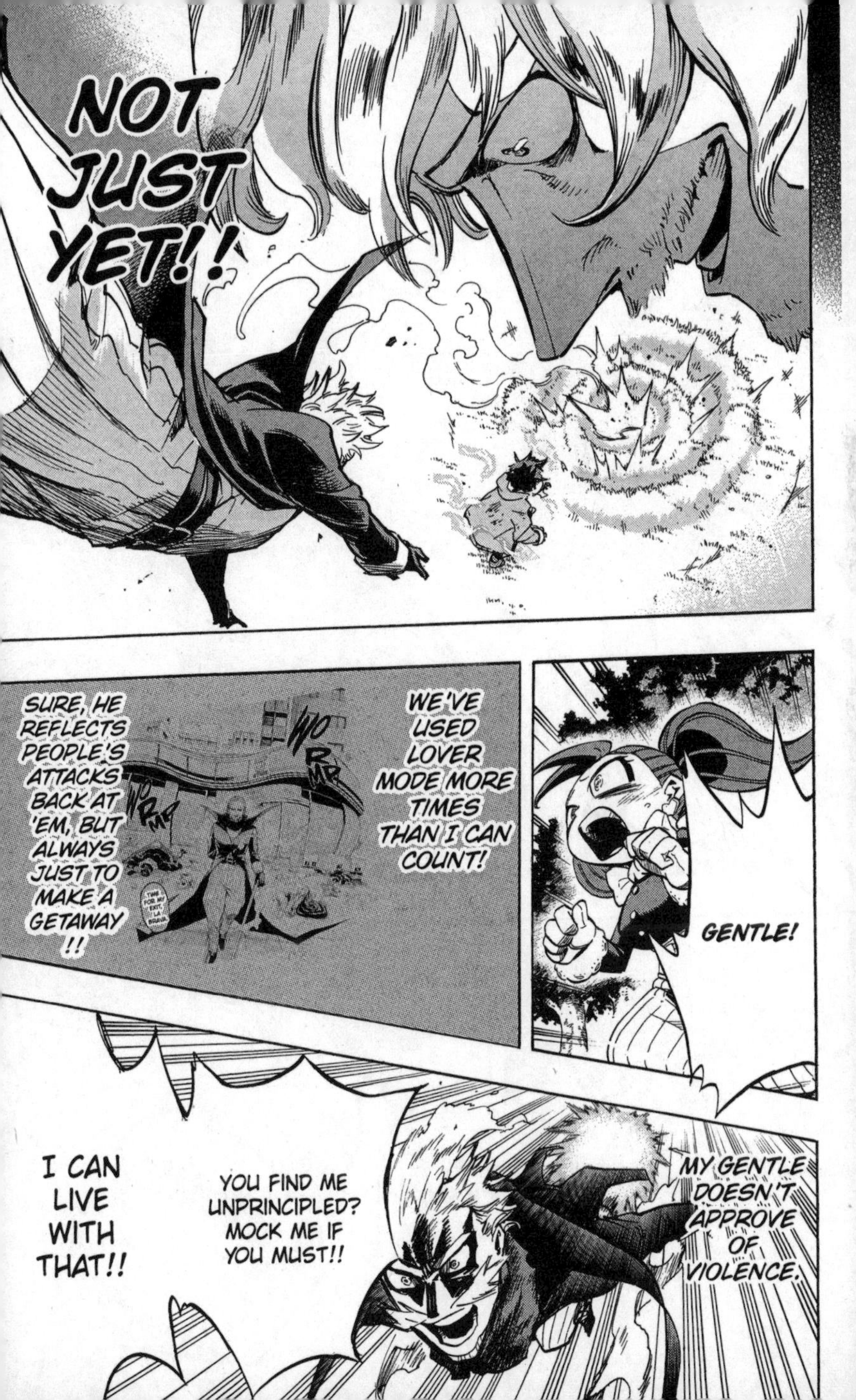
NOT JUST YET!!
GENTLE!
WE'VE USED LOVER MODE MORE TIMES THAN I CAN COUNT!
SURE, HE REFLECTS PEOPLE'S ATTACKS BACK AT 'EM, BUT ALWAYS JUST TO MAKE A GETAWAY!!
MY GENTLE DOESN'T APPROVE OF VIOLENCE.
YOU FIND ME UNPRINCIPLED? MOCK ME IF YOU MUST!!
I CAN LIVE WITH THAT!!

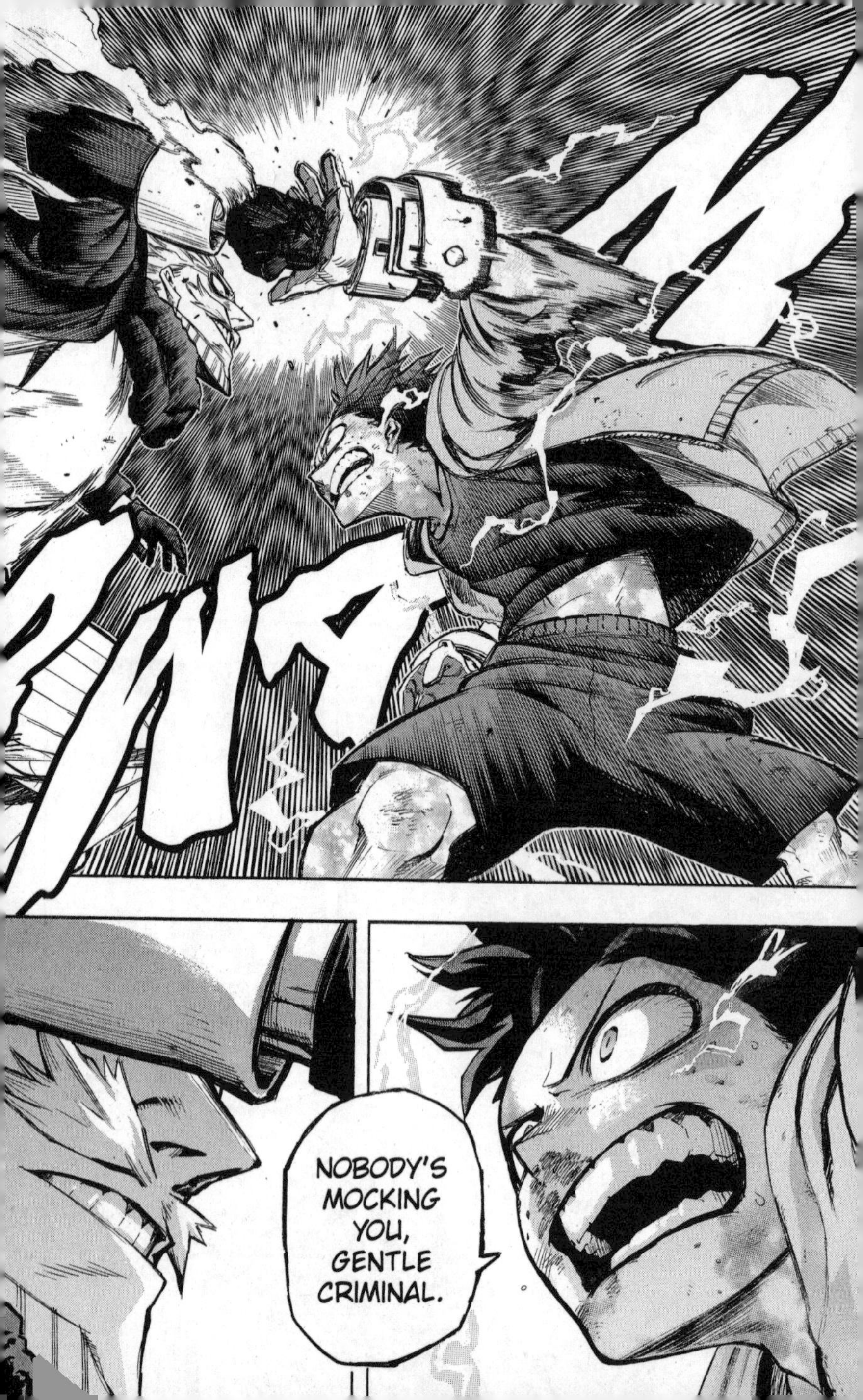
NOBODY'S MOCKING YOU, GENTLE CRIMINAL.

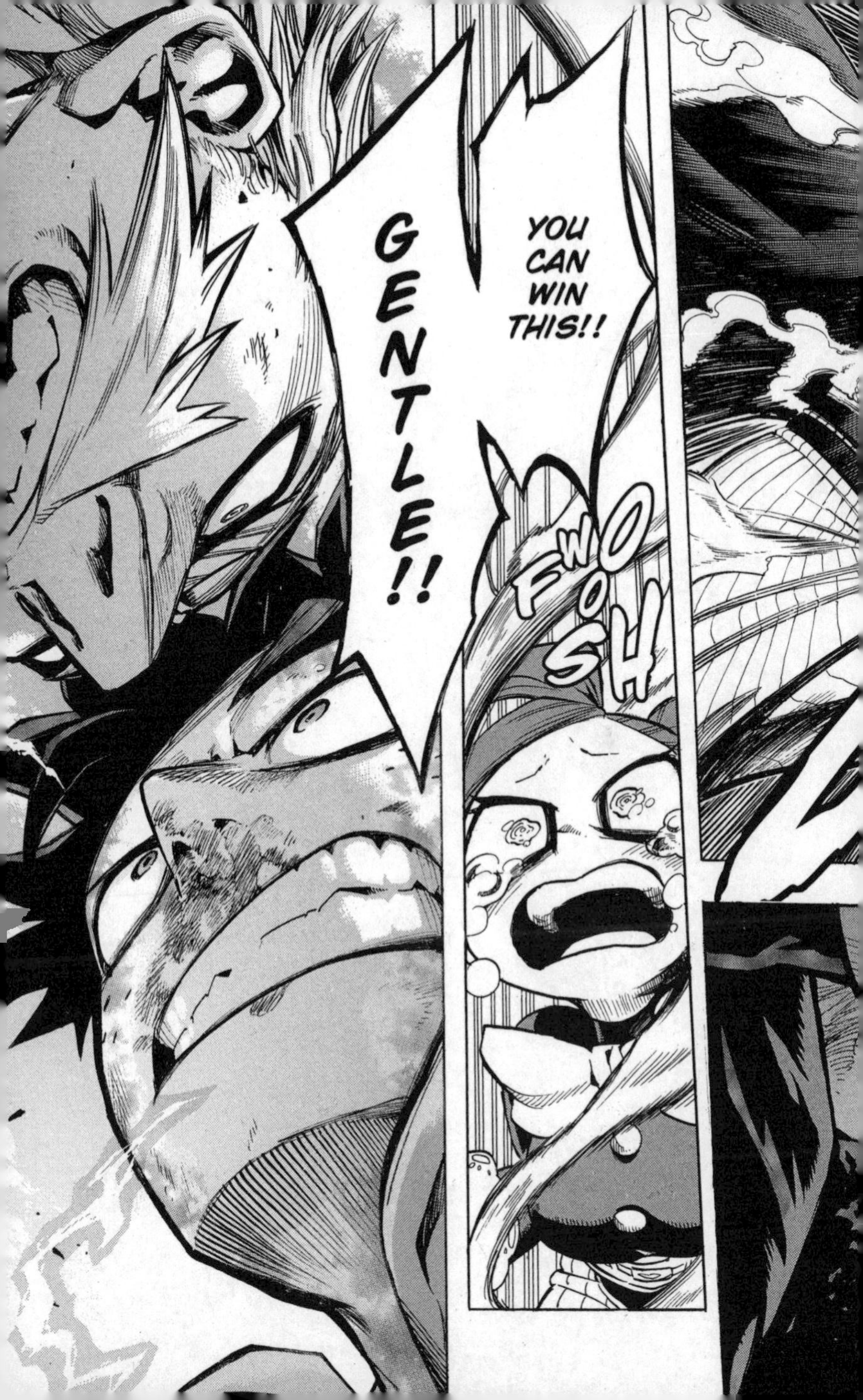
GENTLE!!
YOU CAN WIN THIS!!
FWOOSH

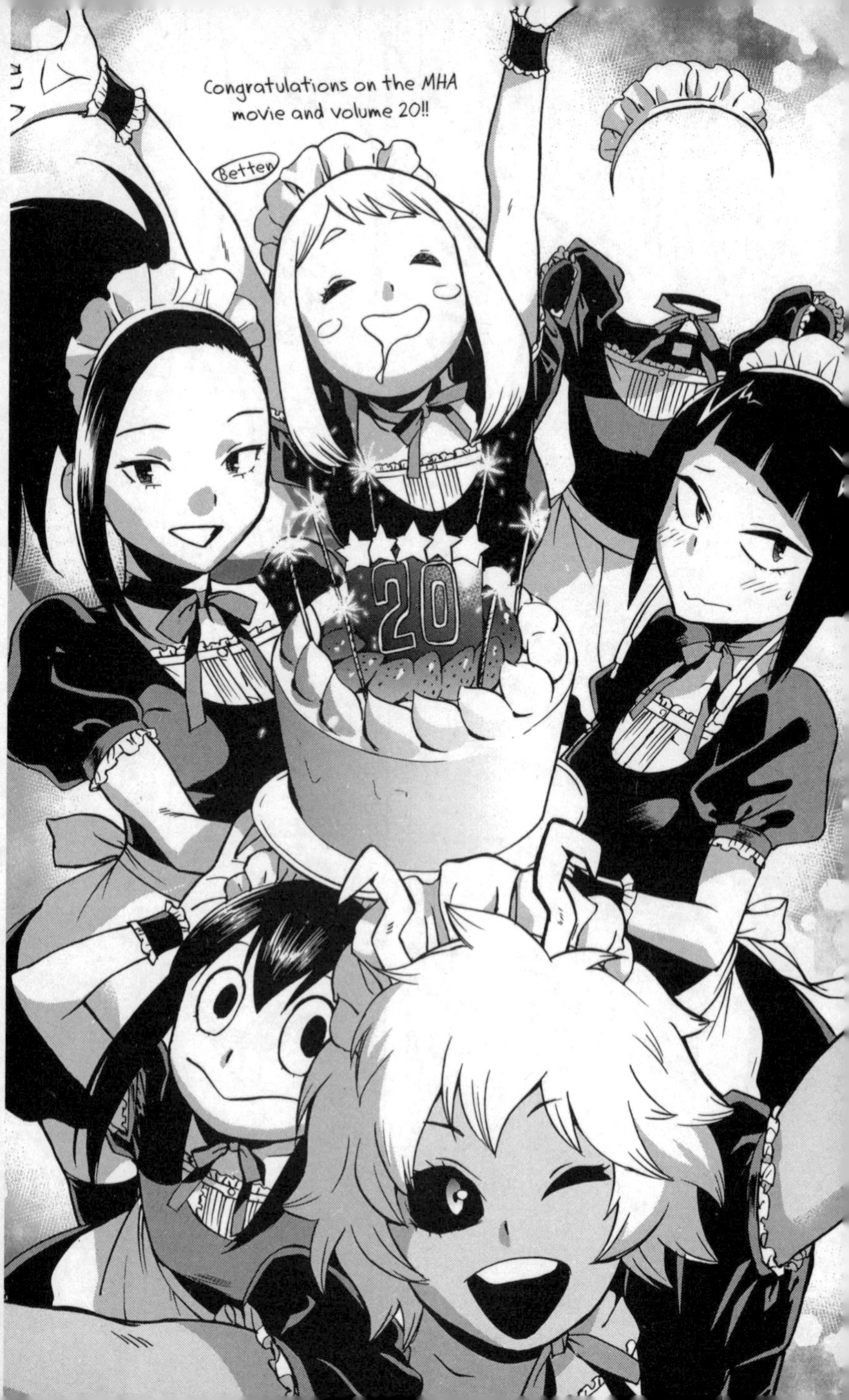
Congratulations on the MHA movie and volume 20!!
Betten
20

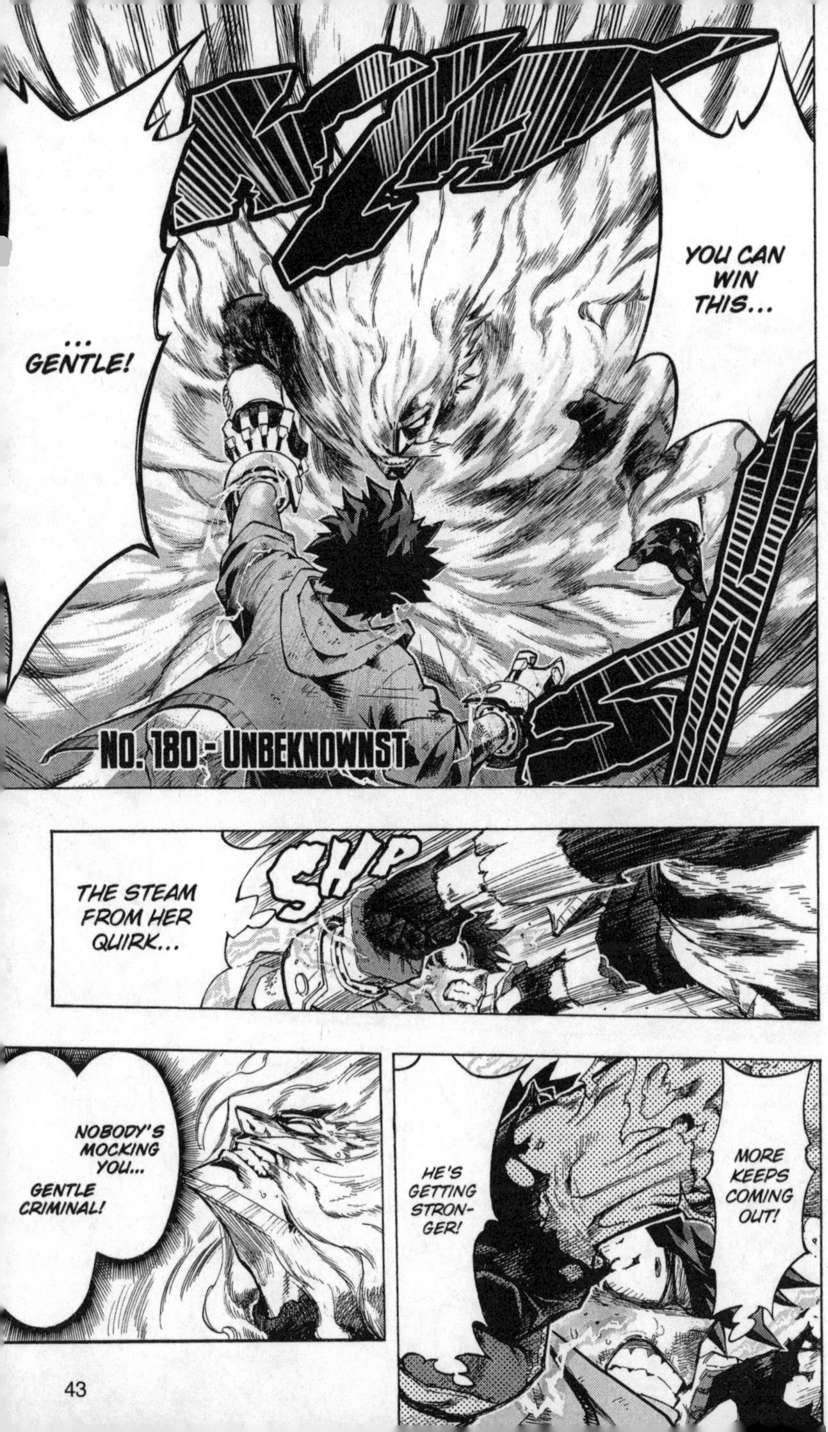
YOU CAN WIN THIS...
...GENTLE!
No. 180 - UNBEKNOWNST
SHP
THE STEAM FROM HER QUIRK...
MORE KEEPS COMING OUT!
HE'S GETTING STRONGER!
NOBODY'S MOCKING YOU...
GENTLE CRIMINAL!

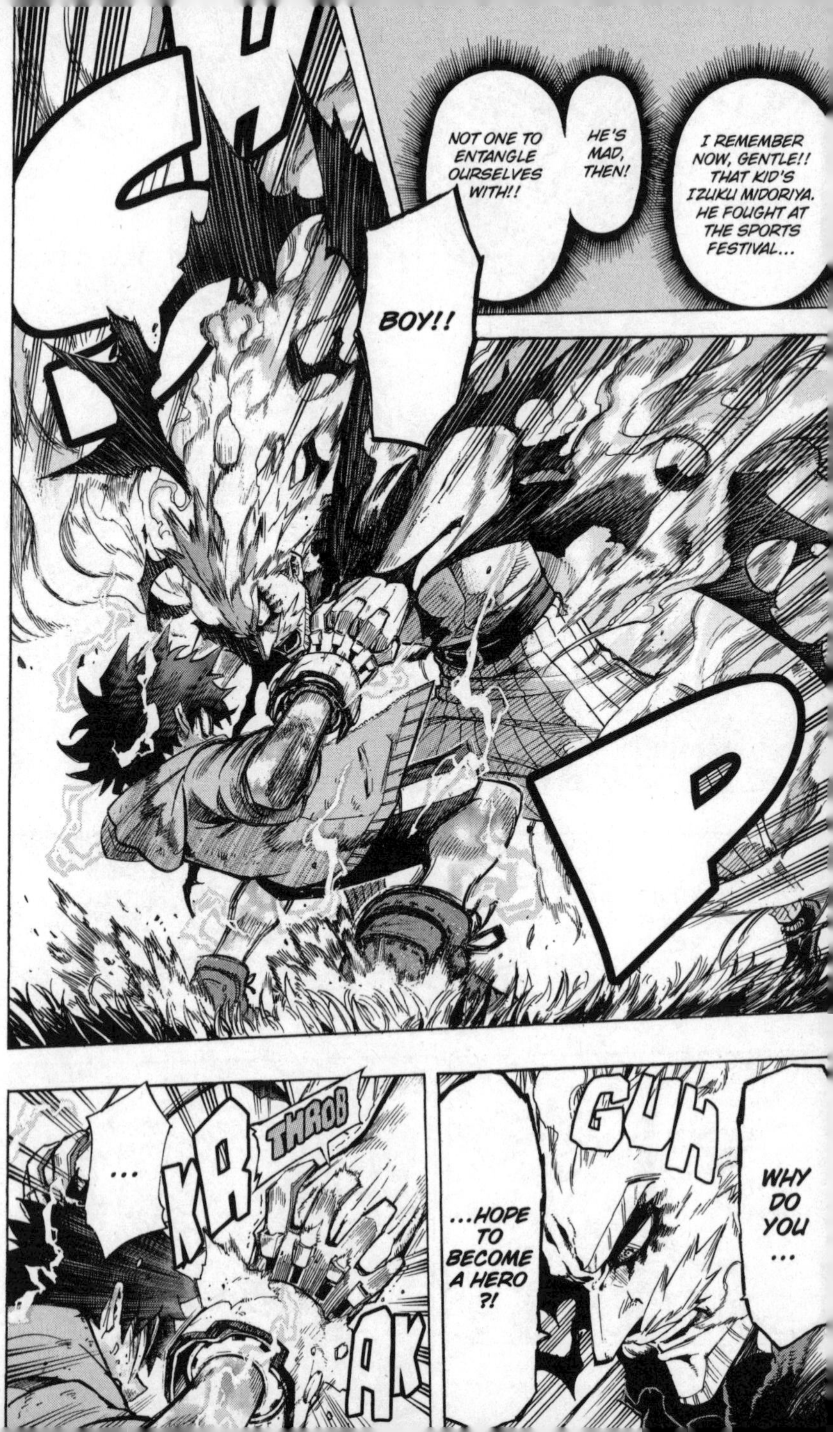
I REMEMBER NOW, GENTLE!! THAT KID'S IZUKU MIDORIYA. HE FOUGHT AT THE SPORTS FESTIVAL...
HE'S MAD, THEN!
NOT ONE TO ENTANGLE OURSELVES WITH!!
BOY!!
WHY DO YOU ...
GUH
...HOPE TO BECOME A HERO ?!
THROB
...

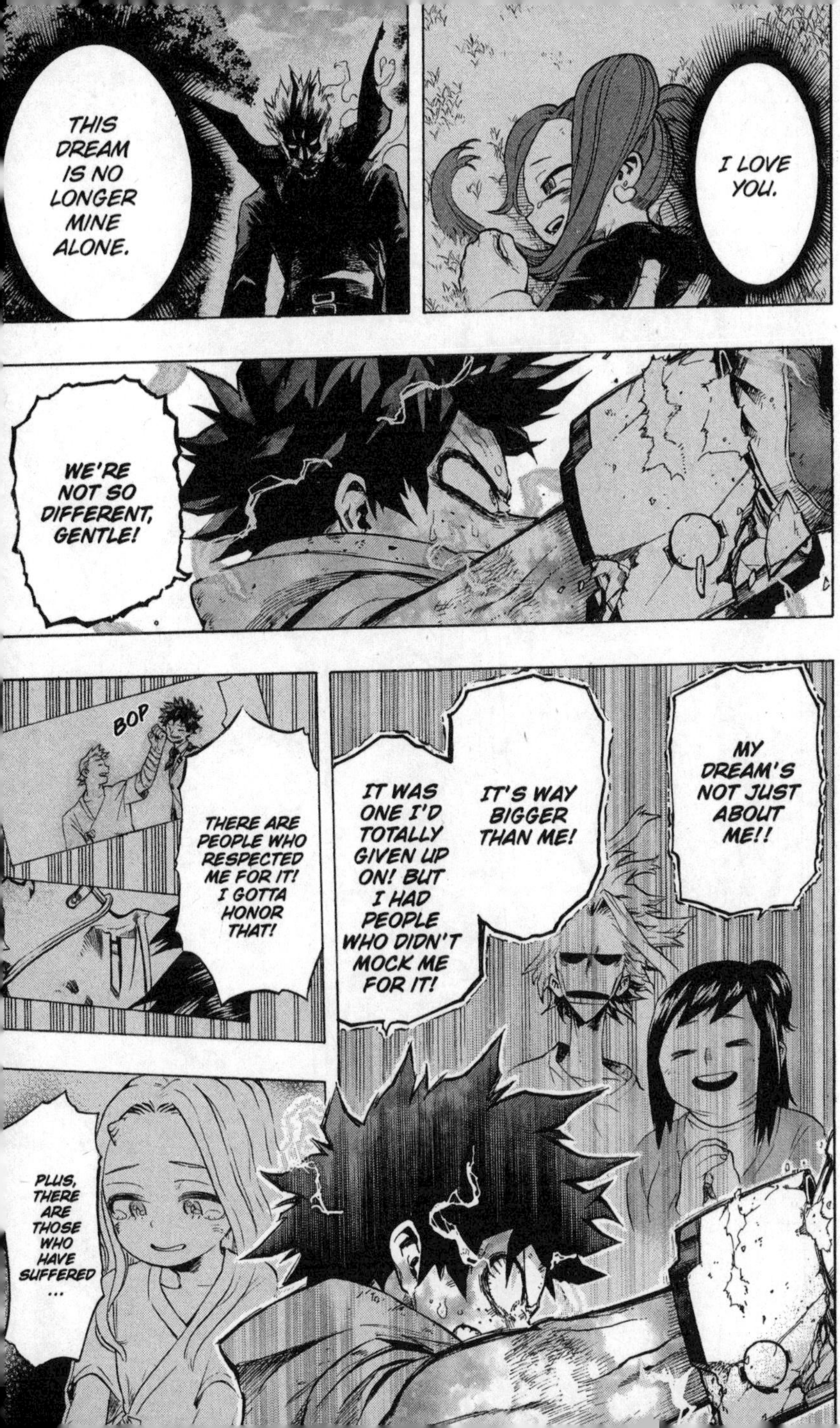
I LOVE YOU.
THIS DREAM IS NO LONGER MINE ALONE.
WE'RE NOT SO DIFFERENT, GENTLE!
MY DREAM'S NOT JUST ABOUT ME!!
IT'S WAY BIGGER THAN ME!
IT WAS ONE I'D TOTALLY GIVEN UP ON! BUT I HAD PEOPLE WHO DIDN'T MOCK ME FOR IT!
BOP
THERE ARE PEOPLE WHO RESPECTED ME FOR IT! I GOTTA HONOR THAT!
PLUS, THERE ARE THOSE WHO HAVE SUFFERED ...

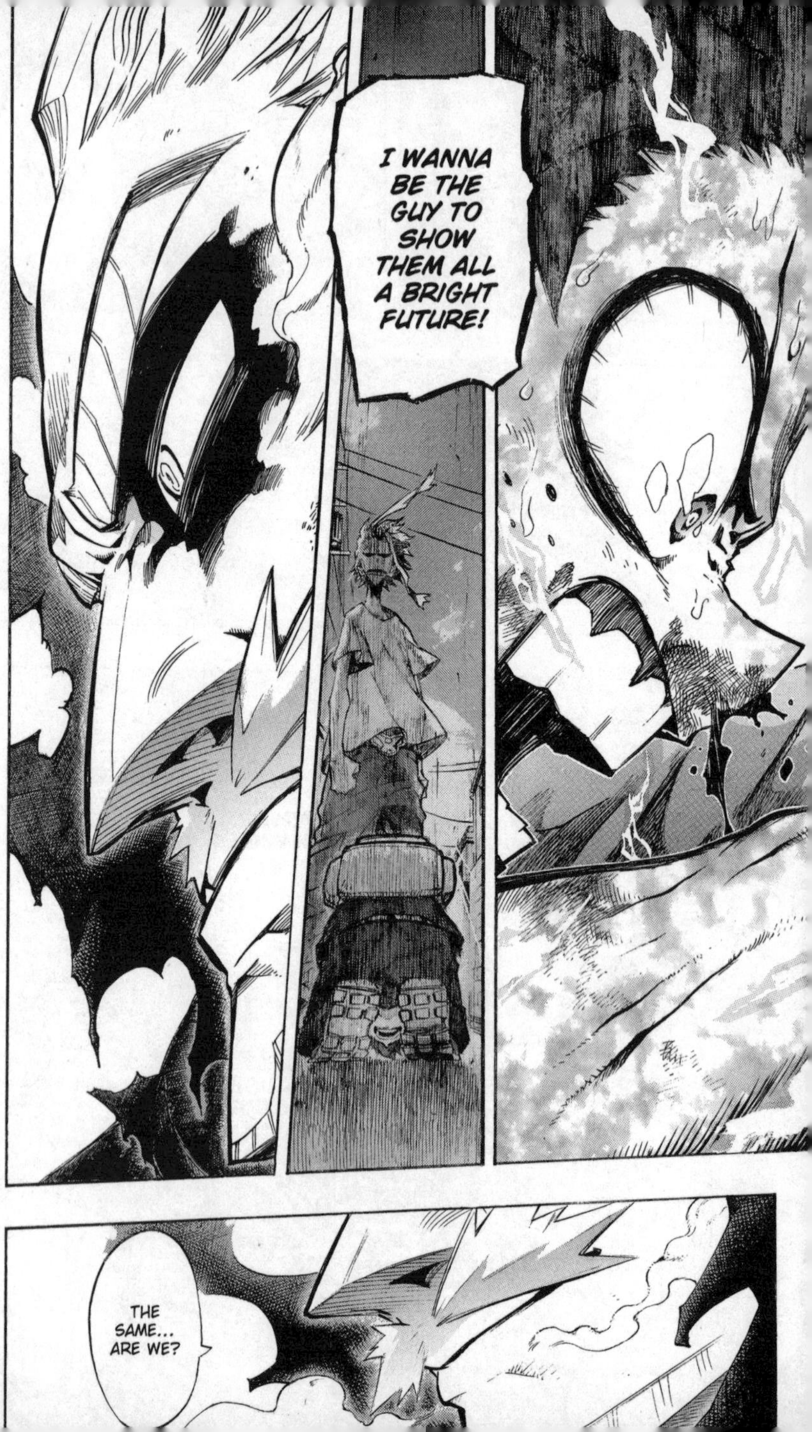
I WANNA BE THE GUY TO SHOW THEM ALL A BRIGHT FUTURE!
THE SAME... ARE WE?

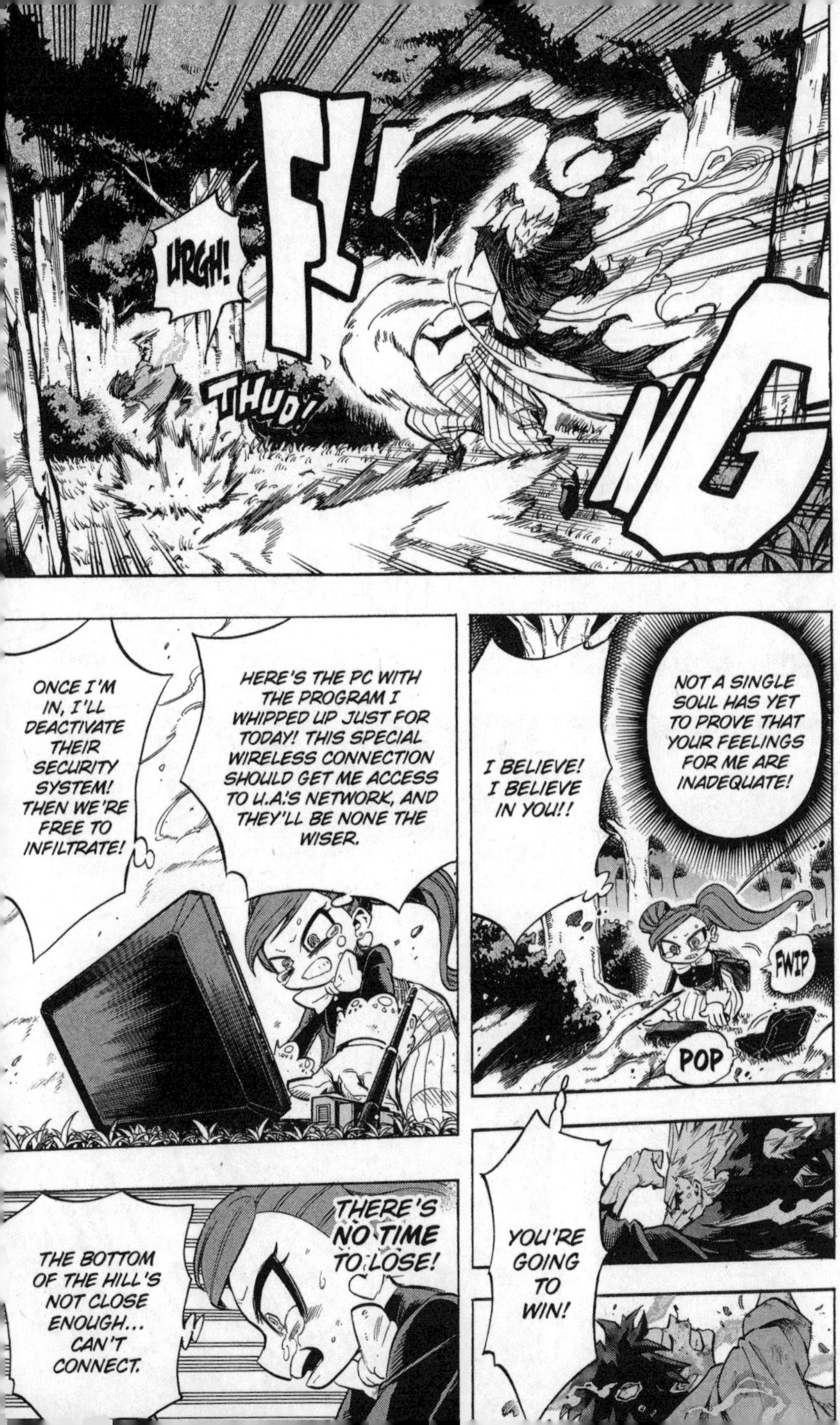
URGH!
THUD!
NOT A SINGLE SOUL HAS YET TO PROVE THAT YOUR FEELINGS FOR ME ARE INADEQUATE!
I BELIEVE! I BELIEVE IN YOU!!
FWIP
POP
YOU'RE GOING TO WIN!
HERE'S THE PC WITH THE PROGRAM I WHIPPED UP JUST FOR TODAY! THIS SPECIAL WIRELESS CONNECTION SHOULD GET ME ACCESS TO U.A.'S NETWORK, AND THEY'LL BE NONE THE WISER.
ONCE I'M IN, I'LL DEACTIVATE THEIR SECURITY SYSTEM! THEN WE'RE FREE TO INFILTRATE!
THERE'S NO TIME TO LOSE!
THE BOTTOM OF THE HILL'S NOT CLOSE ENOUGH... CAN'T CONNECT.

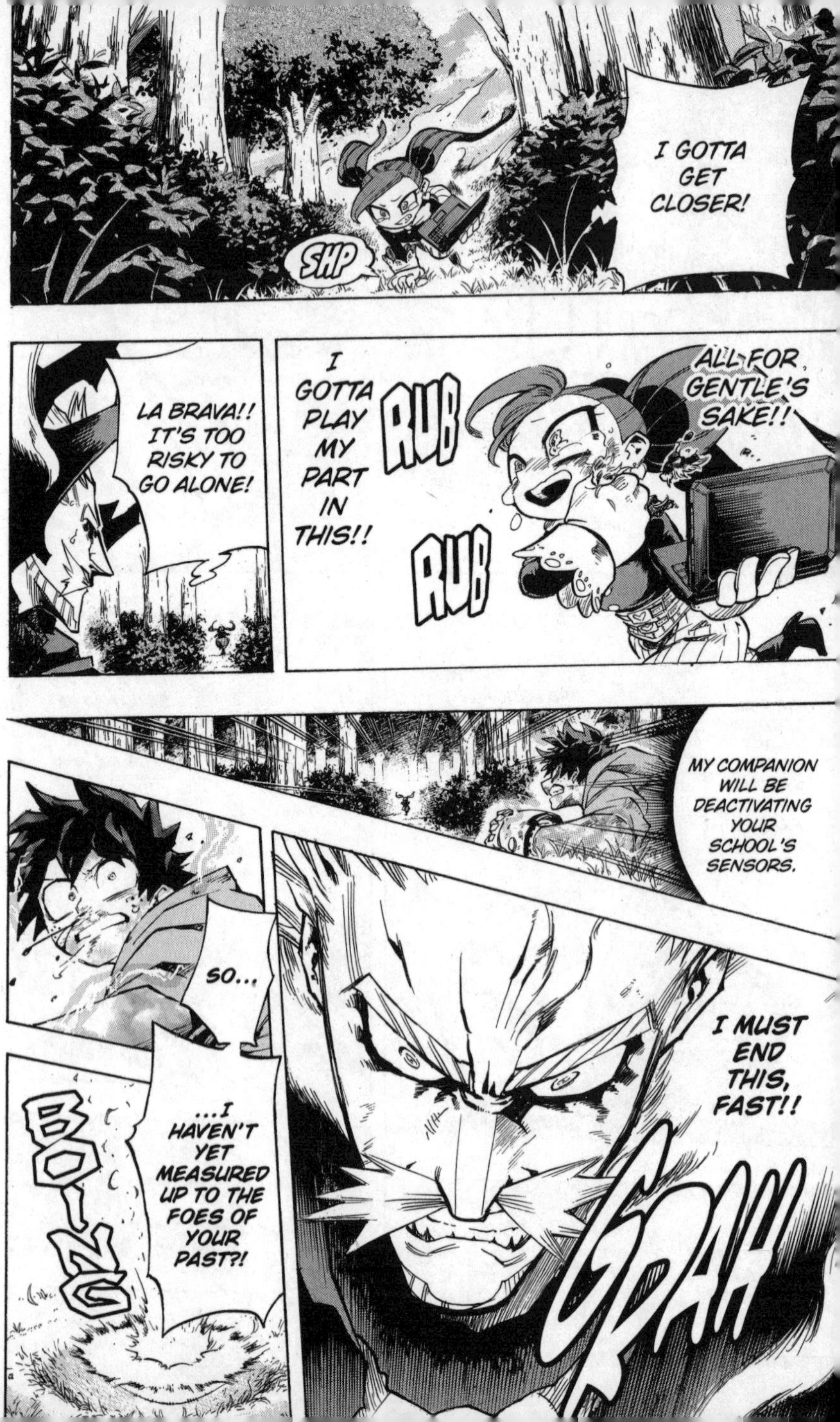
I GOTTA GET CLOSER!
SHP
ALL FOR GENTLE'S SAKE!!
RUB
RUB
I GOTTA PLAY MY PART IN THIS!!
LA BRAVA!! IT'S TOO RISKY TO GO ALONE!
MY COMPANION WILL BE DEACTIVATING YOUR SCHOOL'S SENSORS.
I MUST END THIS, FAST!!
GRAH
SO...
...I HAVEN'T YET MEASURED UP TO THE FOES OF YOUR PAST?!
BOING

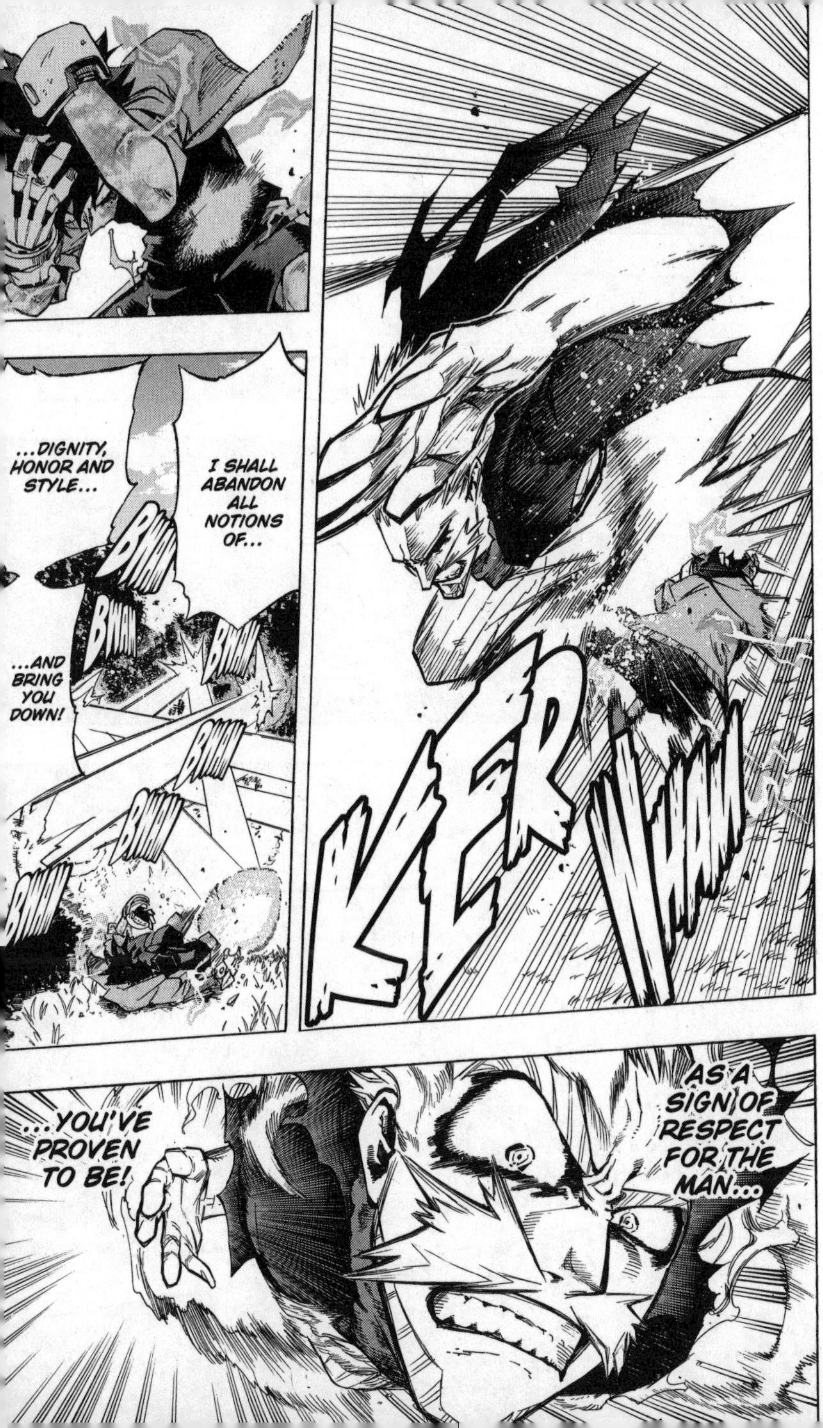
KERWHAM
I SHALL ABANDON ALL NOTIONS OF...
...DIGNITY, HONOR AND STYLE...
BWAM
BWAM
...AND BRING YOU DOWN!
AS A SIGN OF RESPECT FOR THE MAN...
...YOU'VE PROVEN TO BE!

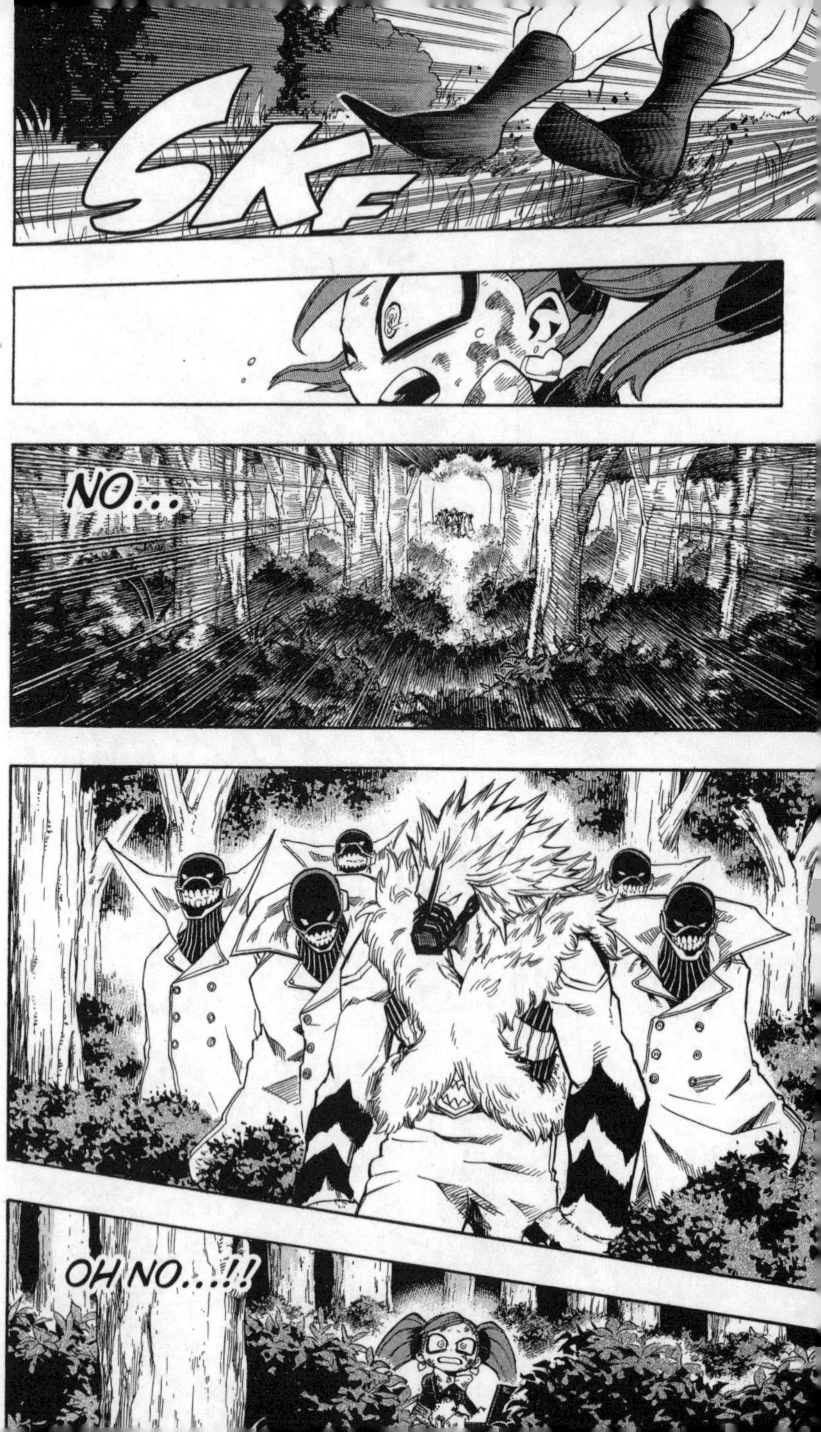
SKF
NO...
OH NO...!!

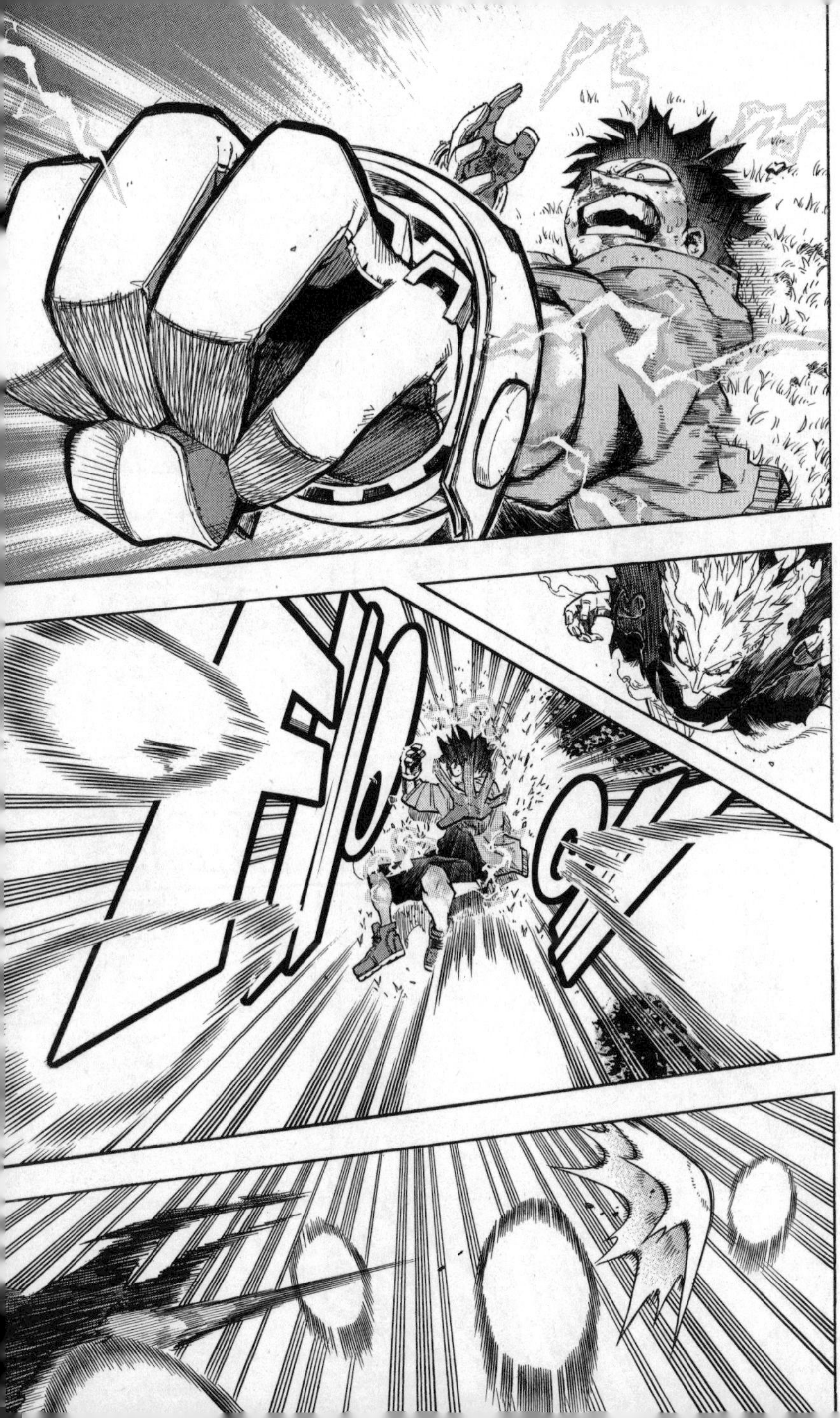

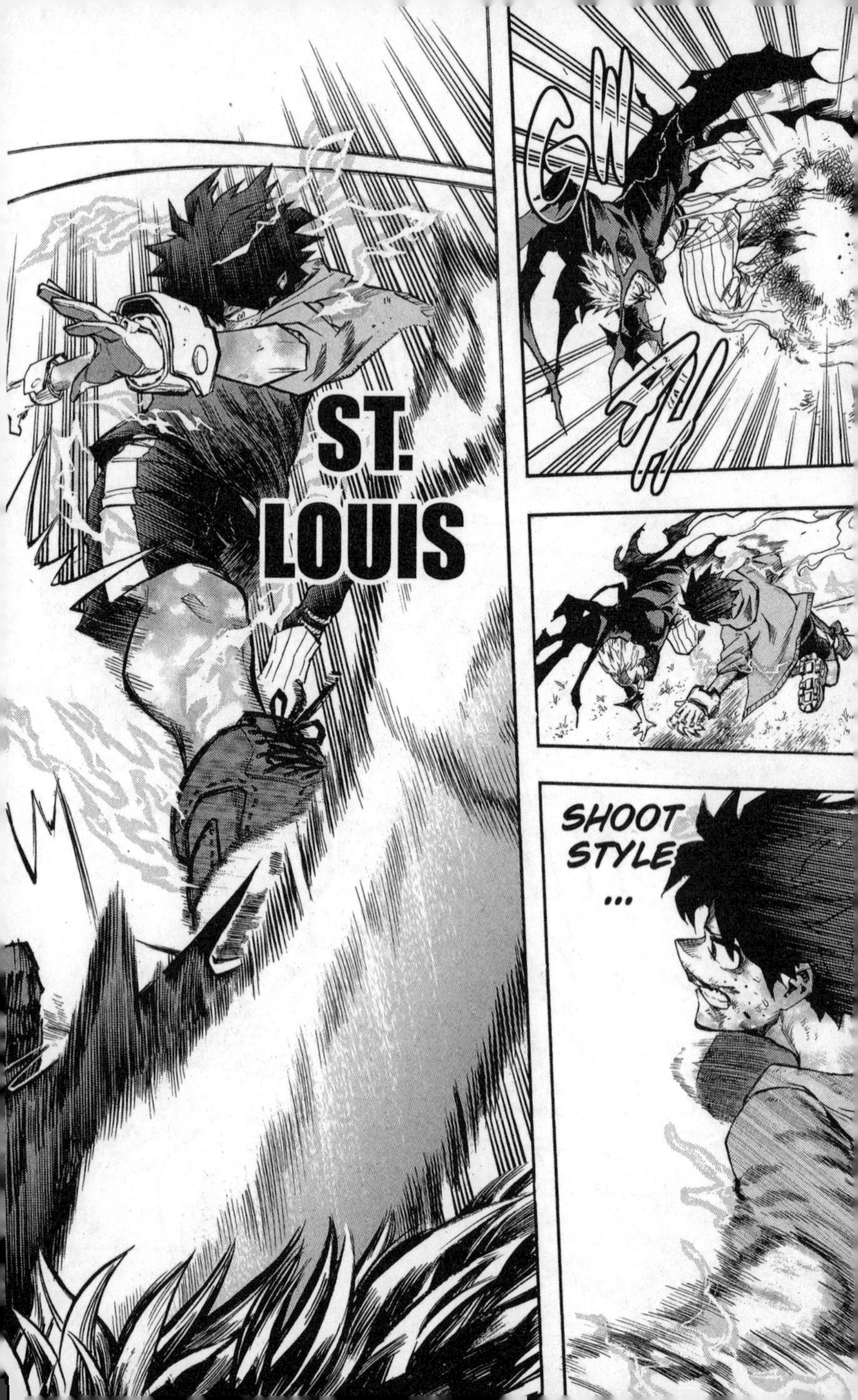
SHOOT STYLE ...
ST. LOUIS

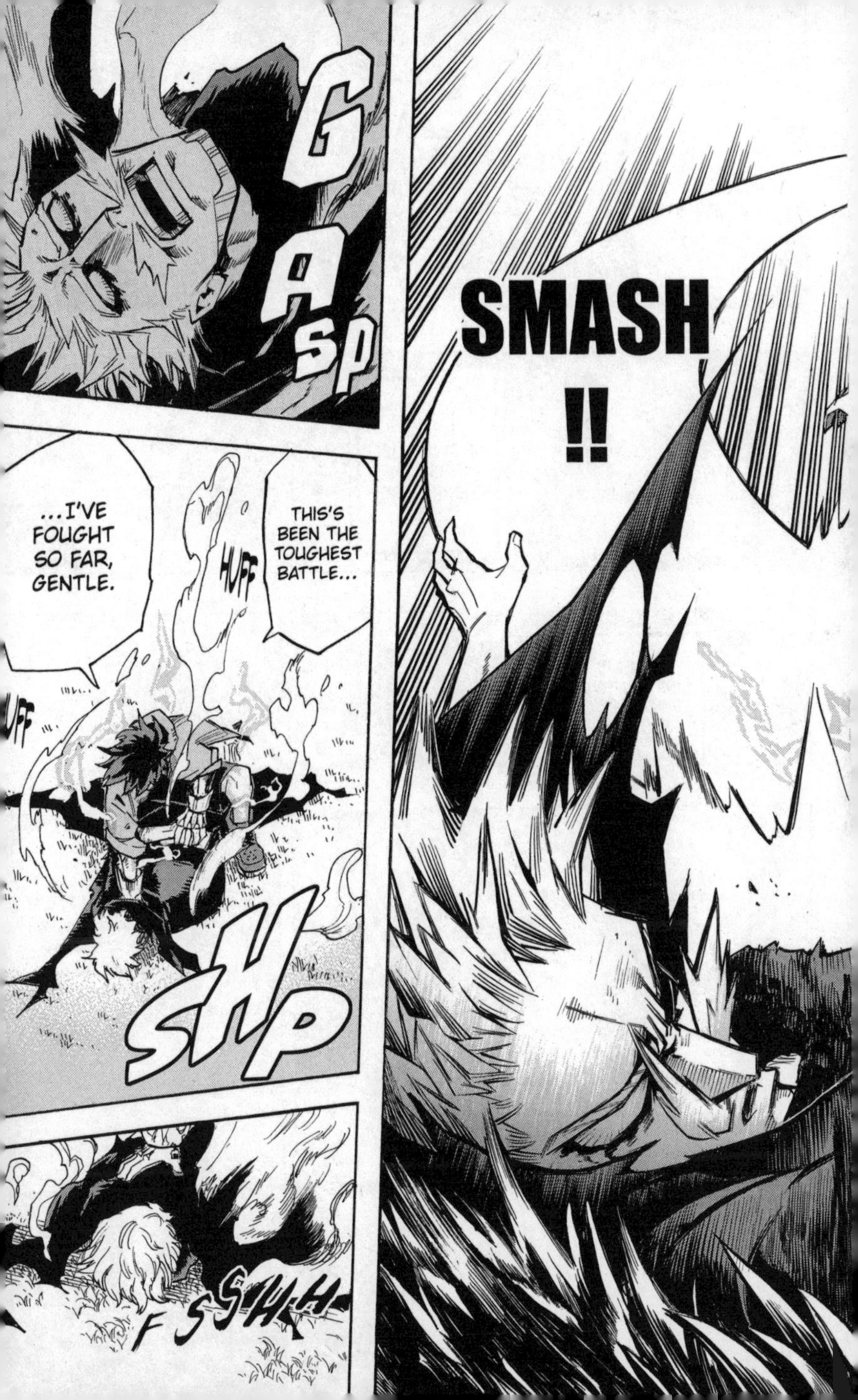
SMASH
!!
GASP
THIS'S BEEN THE TOUGHEST BATTLE...
...I'VE FOUGHT SO FAR, GENTLE.
HUFF
HUFF
SHHP
FSSHH

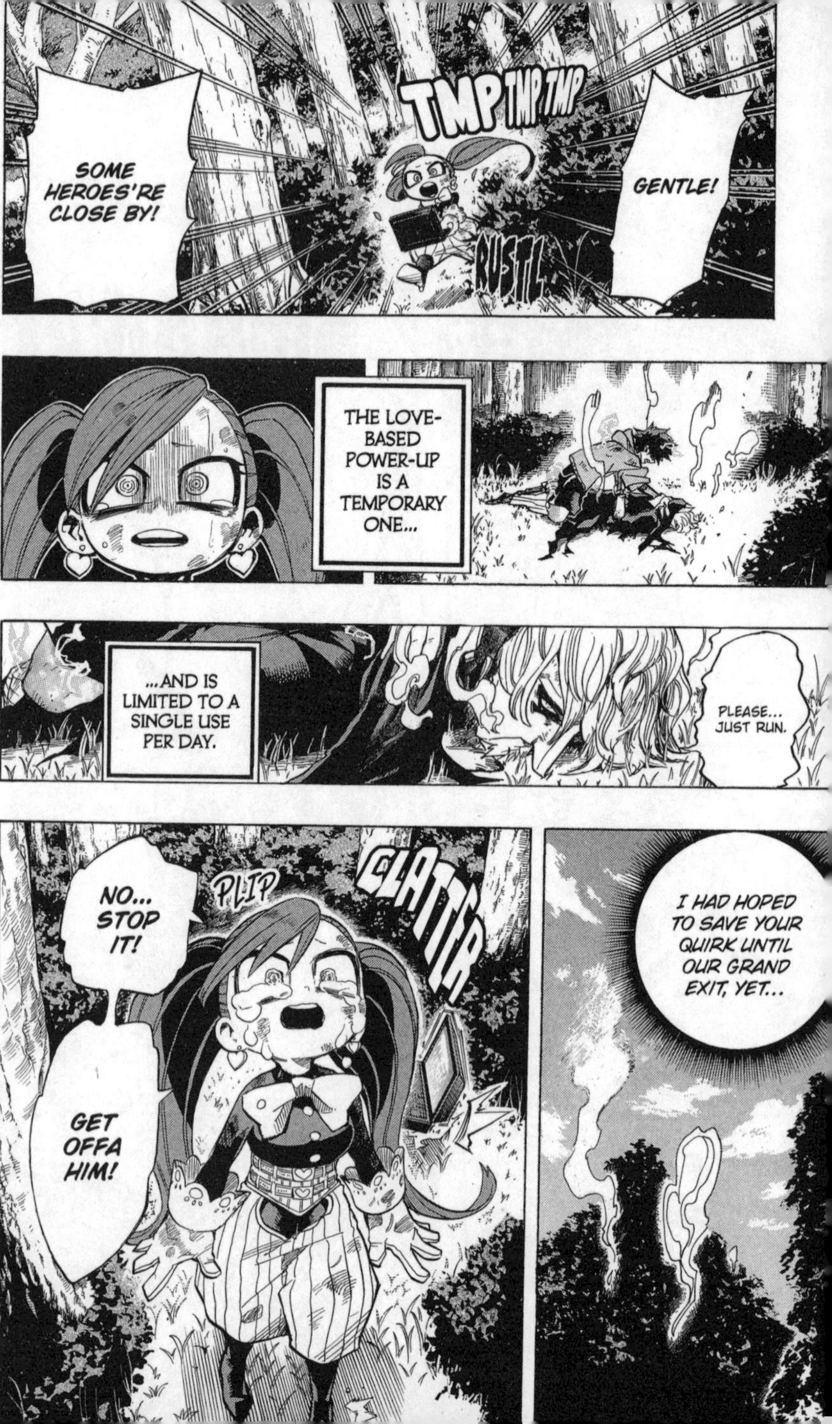
GENTLE!
TMP TMP TMP
SOME HEROES'RE CLOSE BY!
RUSTL
THE LOVE-BASED POWER-UP IS A TEMPORARY ONE...
PLEASE... JUST RUN.
...AND IS LIMITED TO A SINGLE USE PER DAY.
I HAD HOPED TO SAVE YOUR QUIRK UNTIL OUR GRAND EXIT, YET...
CLATTER
PLIP
NO... STOP IT!
GET OFFA HIM!

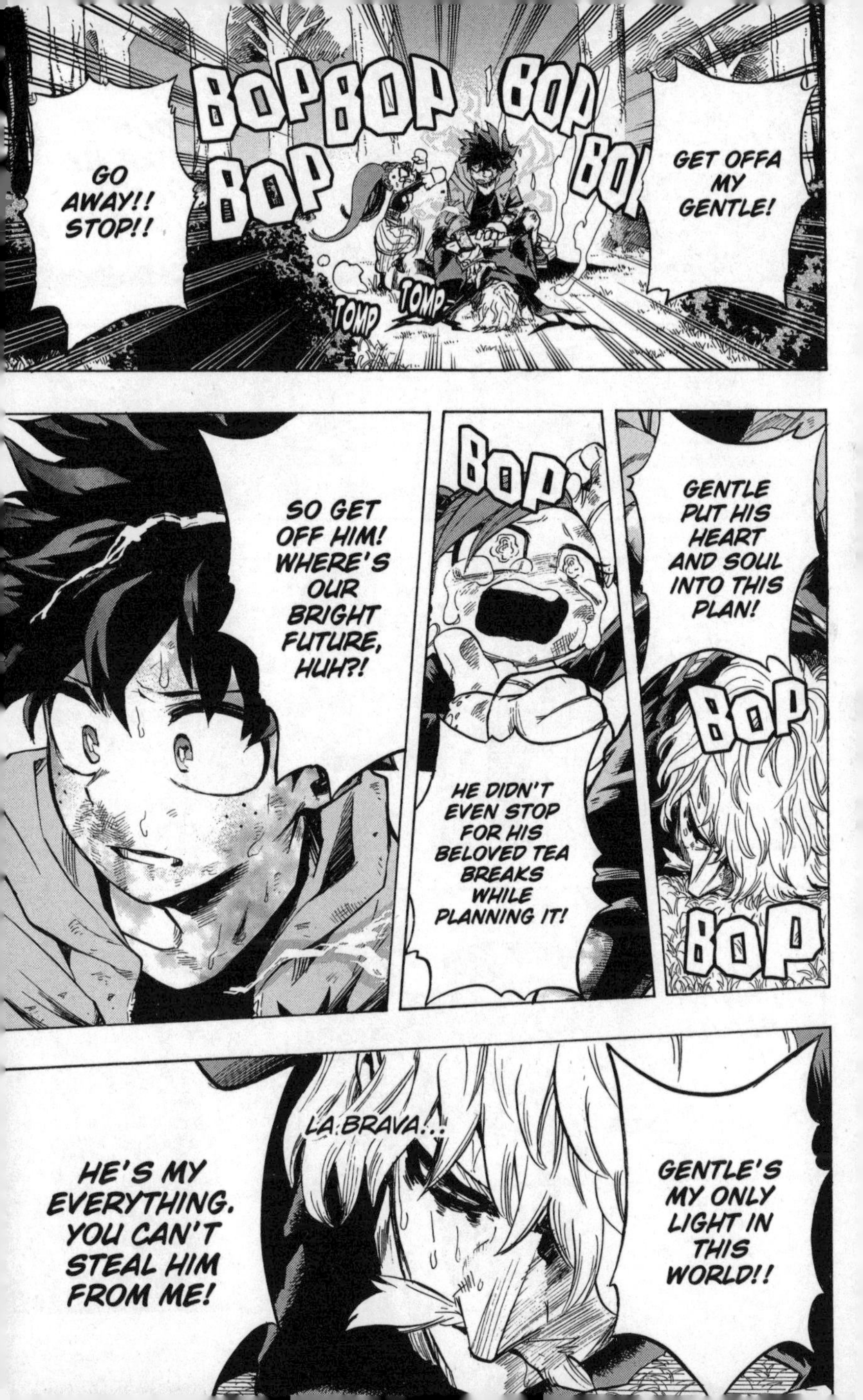
GET OFFA MY GENTLE!
BOP BOP BOP BOP
BOP
BOP
GO AWAY!! STOP!!
TOMP
TOMP
GENTLE PUT HIS HEART AND SOUL INTO THIS PLAN!
BOP
BOP
BOP
HE DIDN'T EVEN STOP FOR HIS BELOVED TEA BREAKS WHILE PLANNING IT!
SO GET OFF HIM! WHERE'S OUR BRIGHT FUTURE, HUH?!
GENTLE'S MY ONLY LIGHT IN THIS WORLD!!
LA BRAVA...
HE'S MY EVERYTHING. YOU CAN'T STEAL HIM FROM ME!

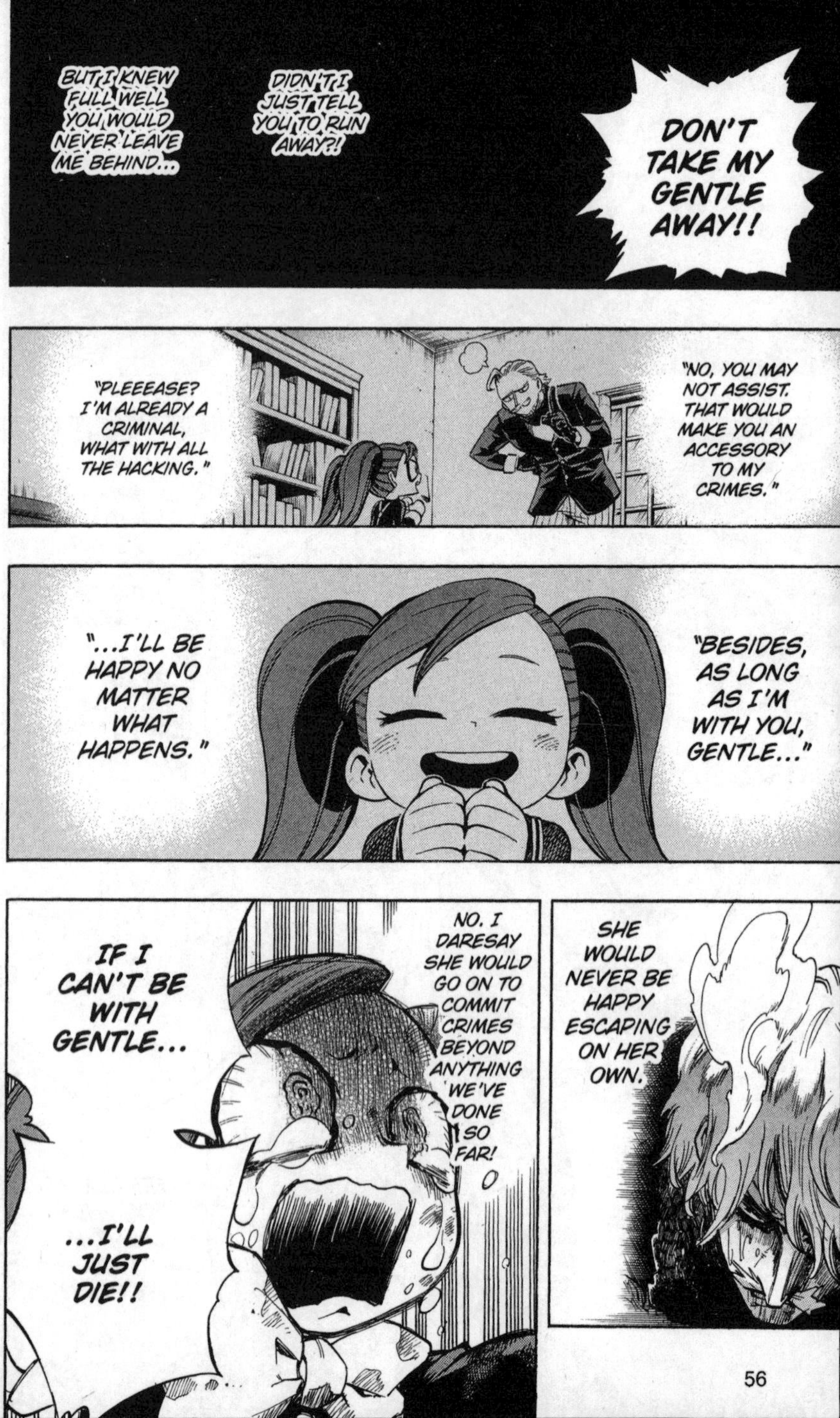
DON'T TAKE MY GENTLE AWAY!!
DIDN'T I JUST TELL YOU TO RUN AWAY?!
BUT I KNEW FULL WELL YOU WOULD NEVER LEAVE ME BEHIND...
"NO, YOU MAY NOT ASSIST. THAT WOULD MAKE YOU AN ACCESSORY TO MY CRIMES."
"PLEEEASE? I'M ALREADY A CRIMINAL, WHAT WITH ALL THE HACKING."
"BESIDES, AS LONG AS I'M WITH YOU, GENTLE..."
"...I'LL BE HAPPY NO MATTER WHAT HAPPENS."
SHE WOULD NEVER BE HAPPY ESCAPING ON HER OWN.
NO. I DARESAY SHE WOULD GO ON TO COMMIT CRIMES BEYOND ANYTHING WE'VE DONE SO FAR!
IF I CAN'T BE WITH GENTLE...
...I'LL JUST DIE!!

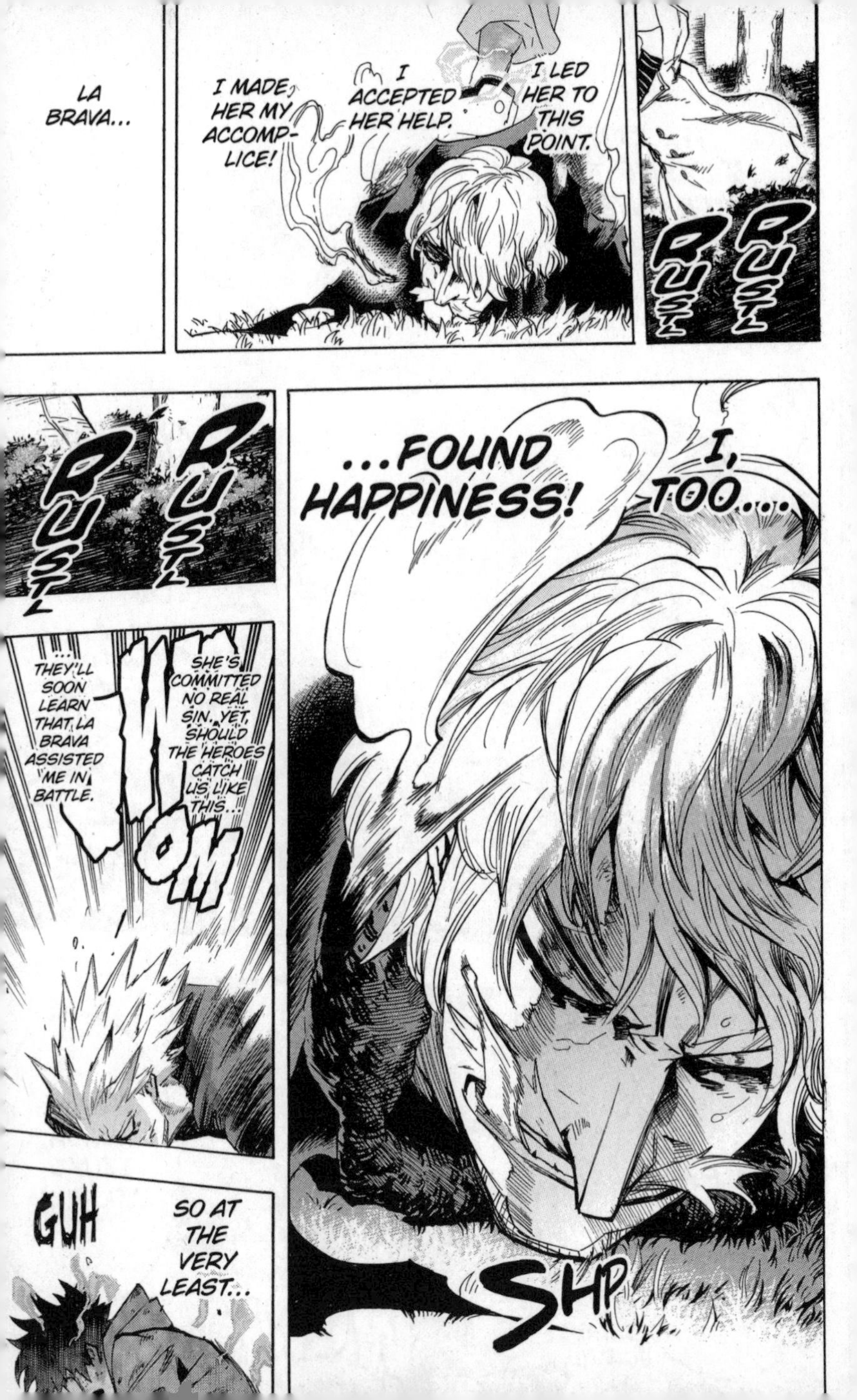
RUSTL
RUSTL
I LED HER TO THIS POINT.
I ACCEPTED HER HELP.
I MADE HER MY ACCOMPLICE!
LA BRAVA...
I, TOO...
...FOUND HAPPINESS!
SHP
RUSTL
RUSTL
SHE'S COMMITTED NO REAL SIN, YET, SHOULD THE HEROES CATCH US LIKE THIS...
...THEY'LL SOON LEARN THAT LA BRAVA ASSISTED ME IN BATTLE.
SO AT THE VERY LEAST...
GUH

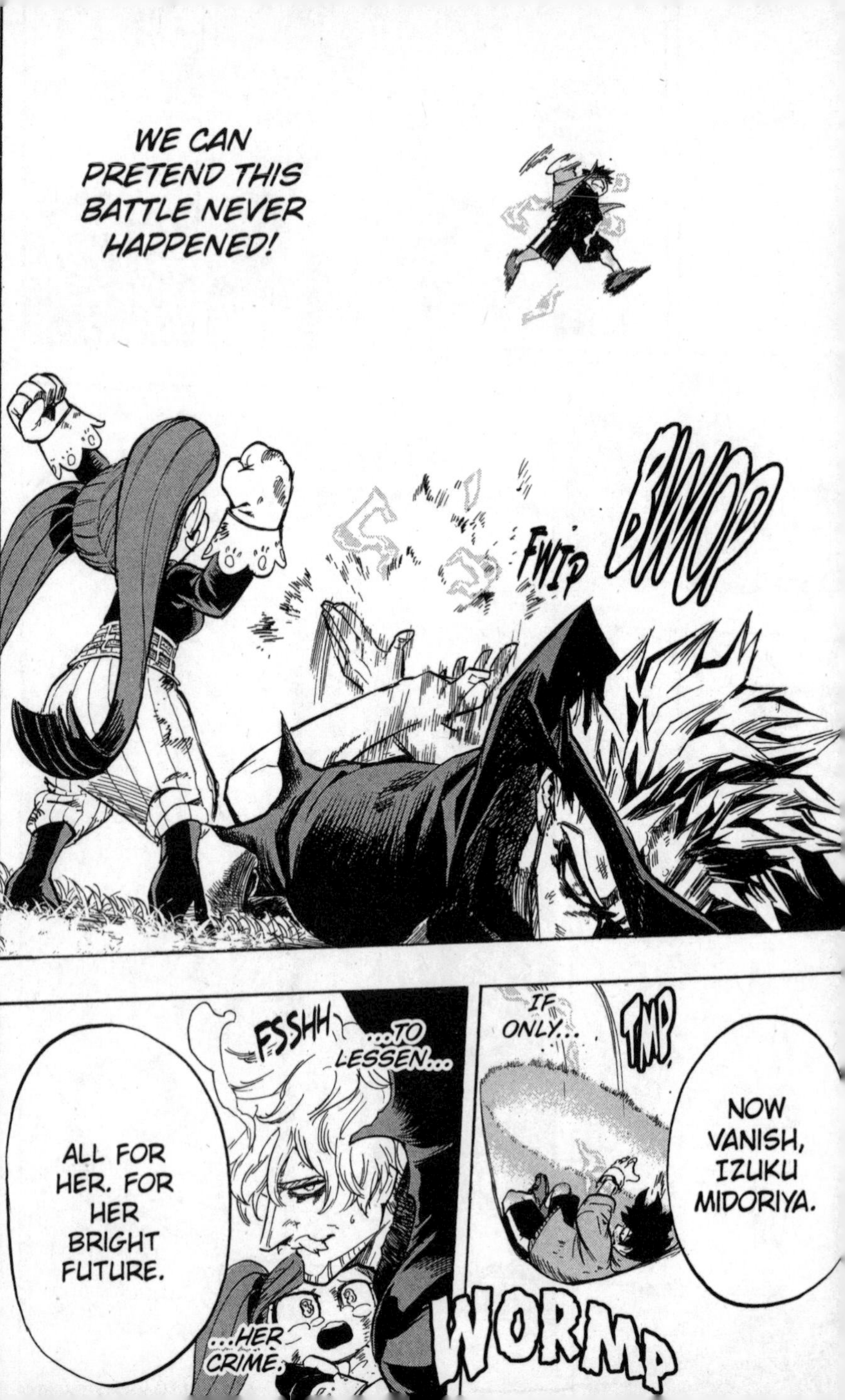
WE CAN PRETEND THIS BATTLE NEVER HAPPENED!
FWIP
TMP
IF ONLY...
NOW VANISH, IZUKU MIDORIYA.
WORMP
...TO LESSEN...
FSSHH
ALL FOR HER. FOR HER BRIGHT FUTURE.
...HER CRIME.

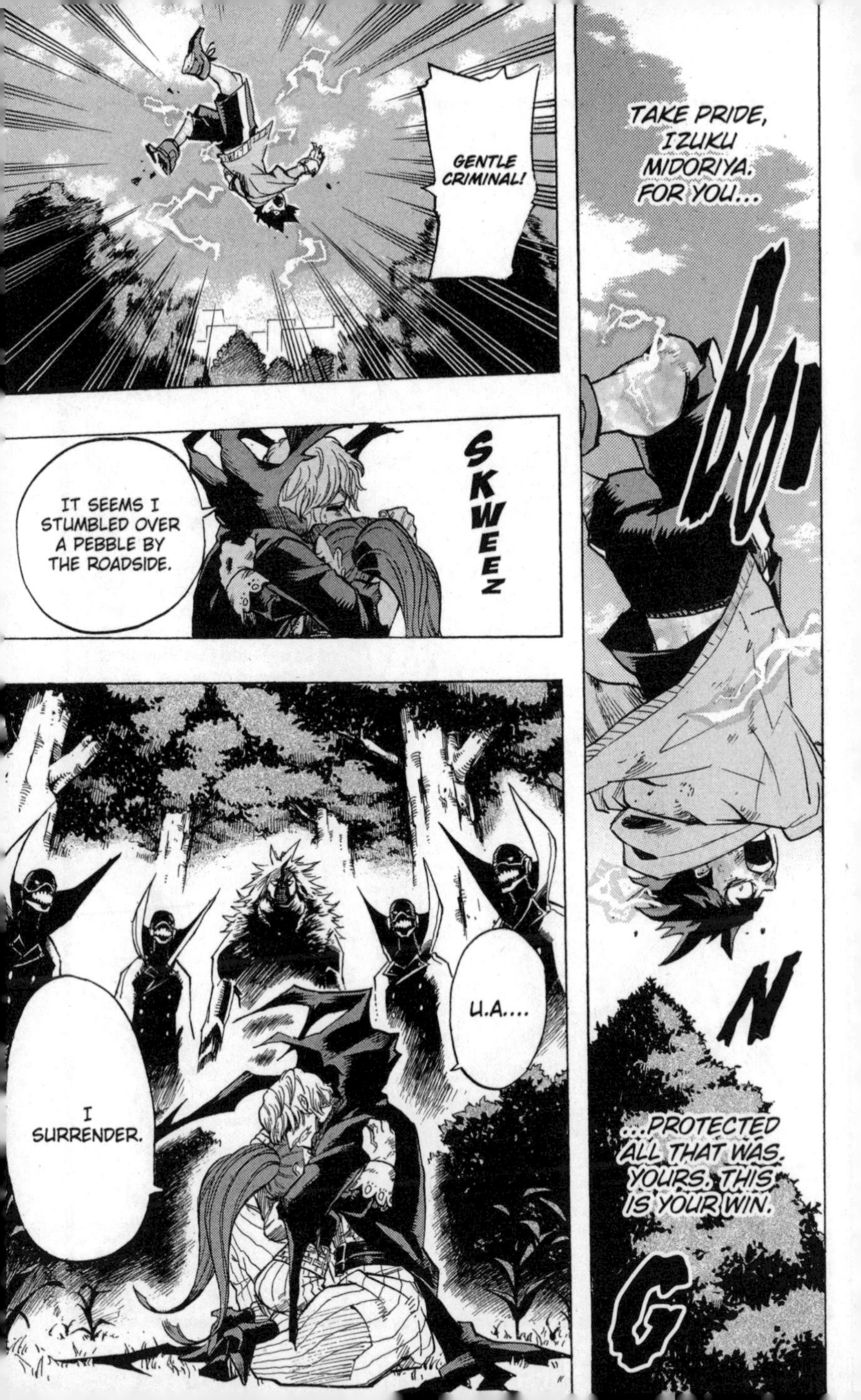
TAKE PRIDE, IZUKU MIDORIYA. FOR YOU...
...PROTECTED ALL THAT WAS YOURS. THIS IS YOUR WIN.
GENTLE CRIMINAL!
SKWEEZ
IT SEEMS I STUMBLED OVER A PEBBLE BY THE ROADSIDE.
U.A....
I SURRENDER.

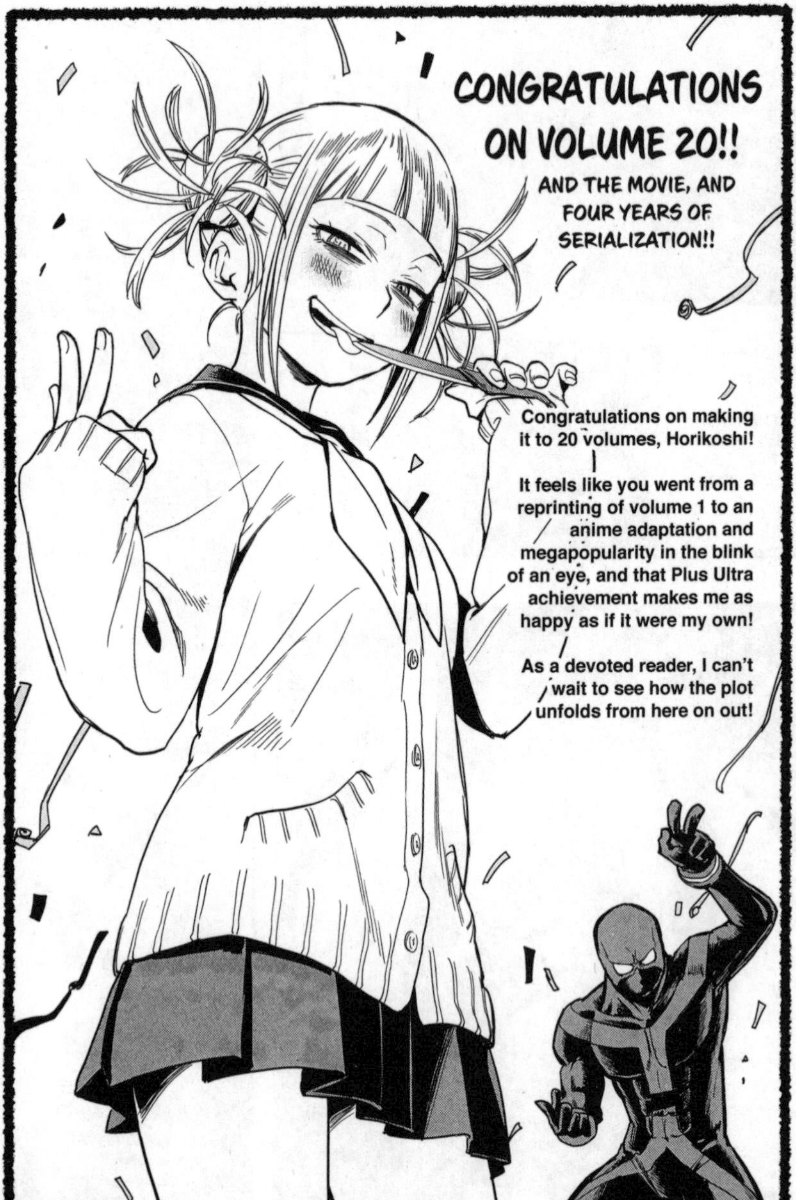
CONGRATULATIONS ON VOLUME 20!!
AND THE MOVIE, AND FOUR YEARS OF SERIALIZATION!!
Congratulations on making it to 20 volumes, Horikoshi!
It feels like you went from a reprinting of volume 1 to an anime adaptation and megapopularity in the blink of an eye, and that Plus Ultra achievement makes me as happy as if it were my own!
As a devoted reader, I can't wait to see how the plot unfolds from here on out!
YOKO AKIYAMA
あきやま陽光

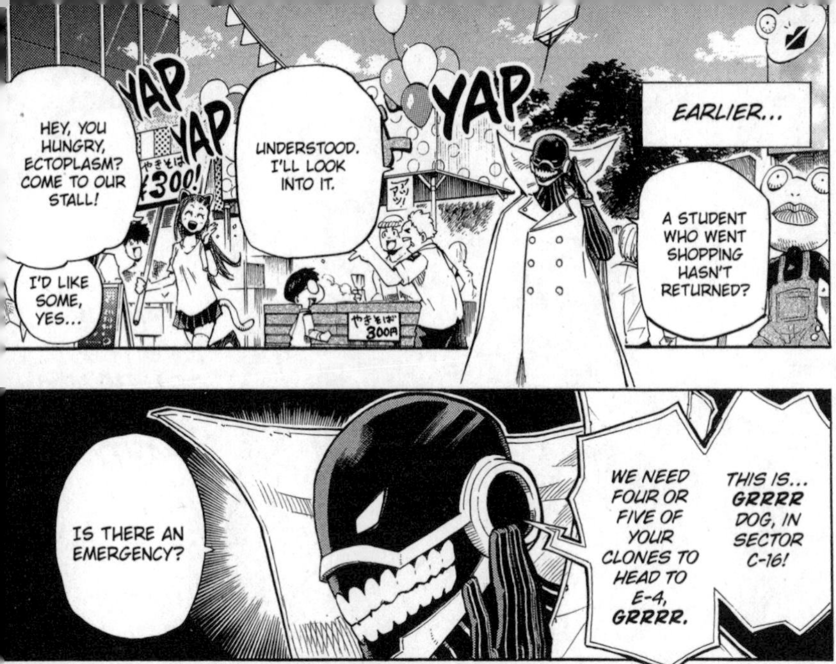
EARLIER...
A STUDENT WHO WENT SHOPPING HASN'T RETURNED?
YAP
YAP
UNDERSTOOD. I'LL LOOK INTO IT.
YAP
HEY, YOU HUNGRY, ECTOPLASM? COME TO OUR STALL!
I'D LIKE SOME, YES...
THIS IS... GRRRR DOG, IN SECTOR C-16!
WE NEED FOUR OR FIVE OF YOUR CLONES TO HEAD TO E-4, GRRRR.
IS THERE AN EMERGENCY?

No. 181 - For Someone Else

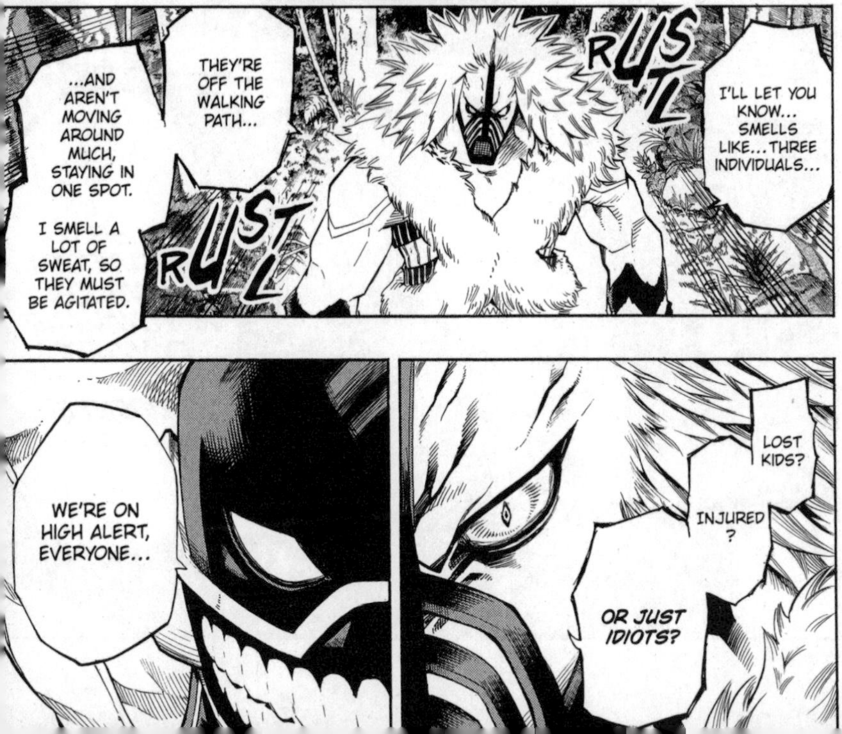
I'LL LET YOU KNOW... SMELLS LIKE... THREE INDIVIDUALS...
RUSTL
THEY'RE OFF THE WALKING PATH...
...AND AREN'T MOVING AROUND MUCH, STAYING IN ONE SPOT.
I SMELL A LOT OF SWEAT, SO THEY MUST BE AGITATED.
RUSTL
LOST KIDS?
INJURED?
OR JUST IDIOTS?
WE'RE ON HIGH ALERT, EVERYONE...

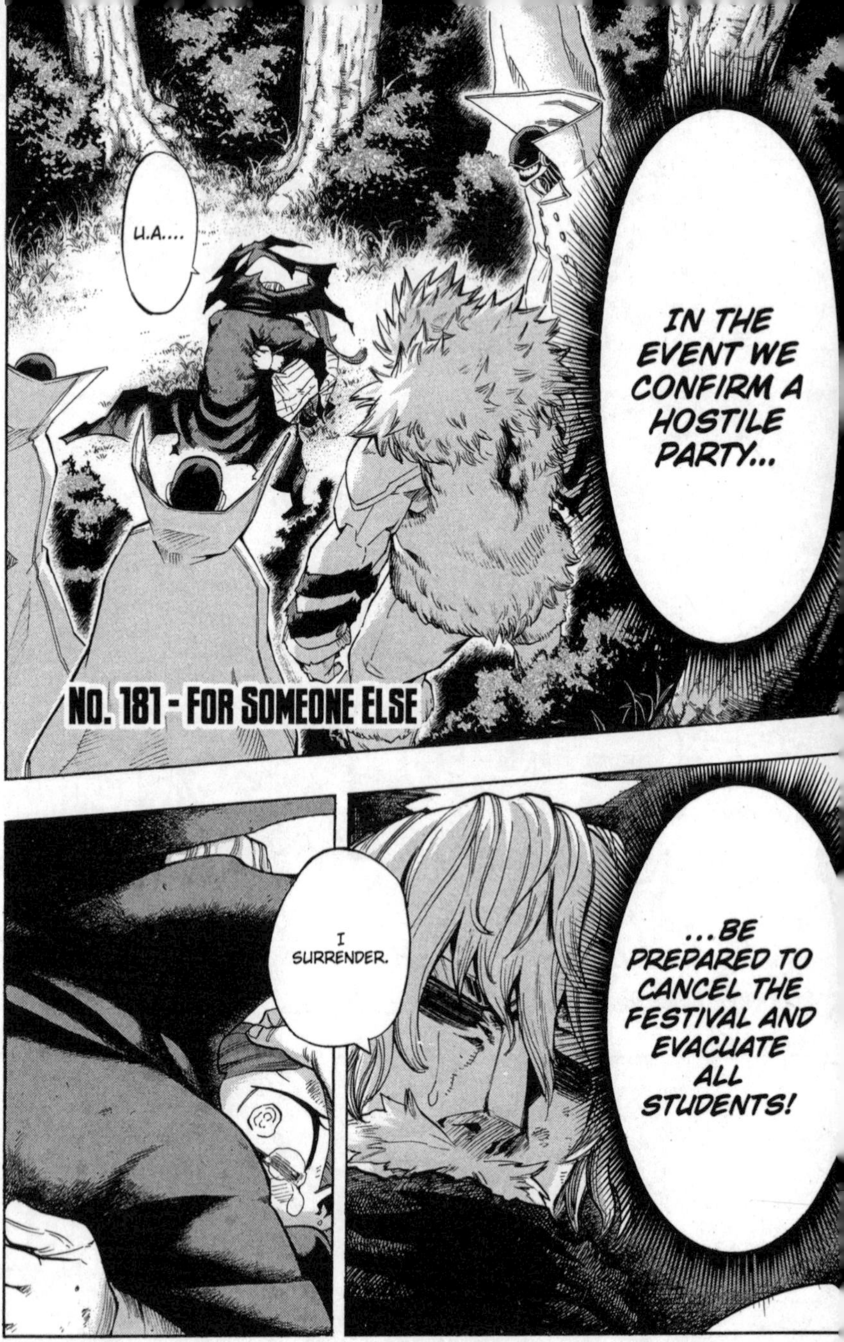
IN THE EVENT WE CONFIRM A HOSTILE PARTY...
U.A....
No. 181 - For Someone Else
...BE PREPARED TO CANCEL THE FESTIVAL AND EVACUATE ALL STUDENTS!
I SURRENDER.

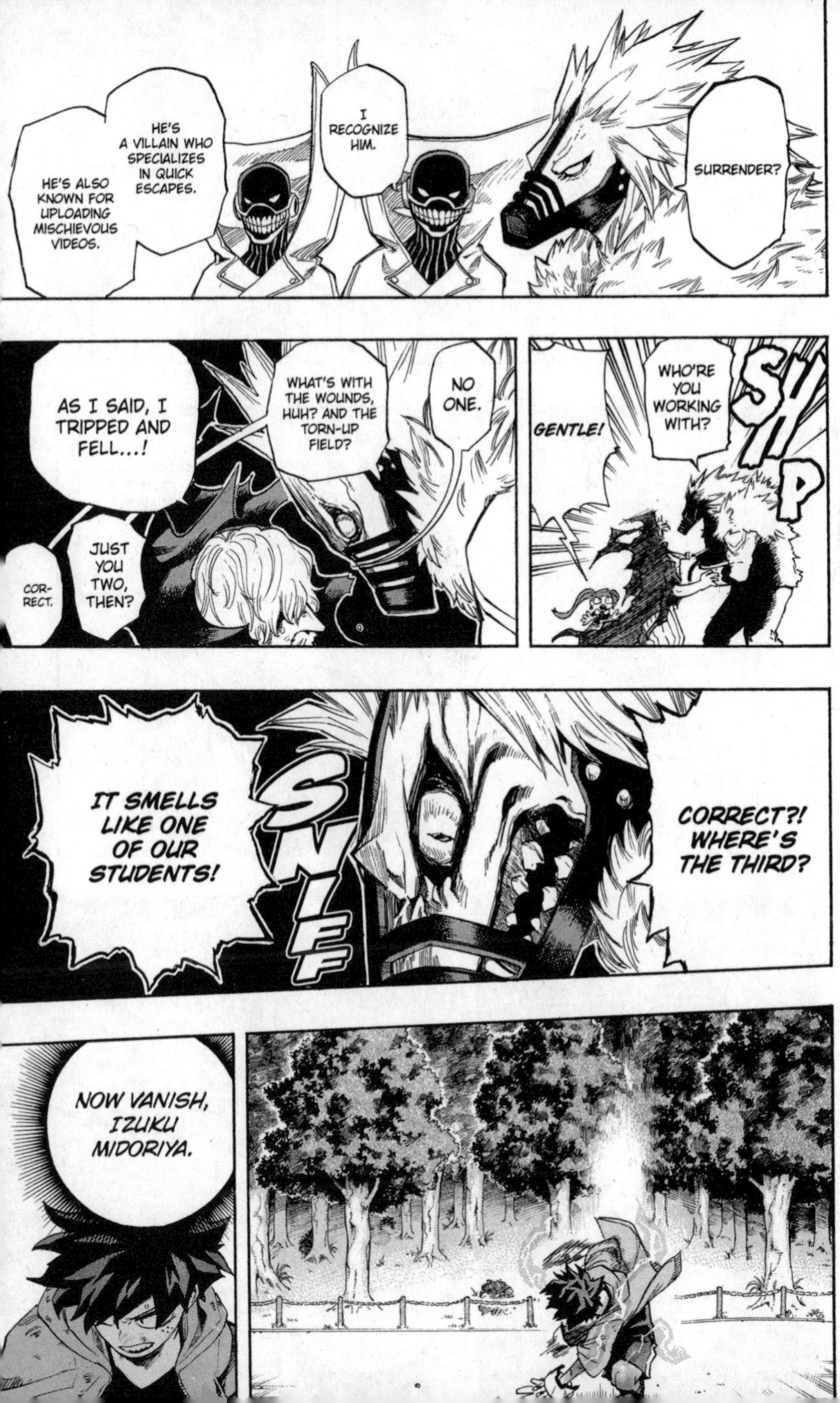
SURRENDER?
I RECOGNIZE HIM.
HE'S A VILLAIN WHO SPECIALIZES IN QUICK ESCAPES.
HE'S ALSO KNOWN FOR UPLOADING MISCHIEVOUS VIDEOS.
SHP
WHO'RE YOU WORKING WITH?
GENTLE!
NO ONE.
WHAT'S WITH THE WOUNDS, HUH? AND THE TORN-UP FIELD?
AS I SAID, I TRIPPED AND FELL...!
JUST YOU TWO, THEN?
CORRECT.
CORRECT?! WHERE'S THE THIRD?
SNIFF
IT SMELLS LIKE ONE OF OUR STUDENTS!
NOW VANISH, IZUKU MIDORIYA.

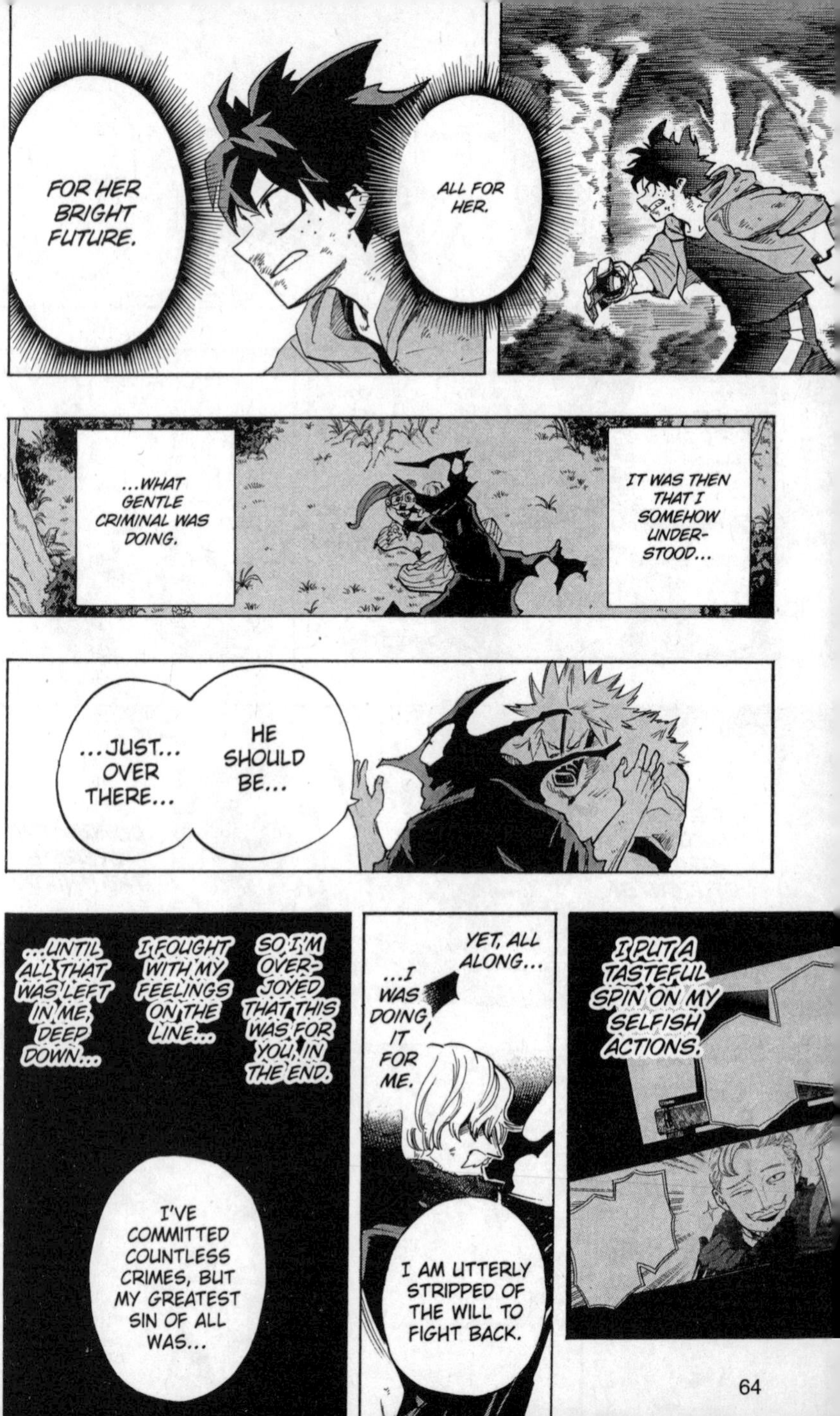
ALL FOR HER.
FOR HER BRIGHT FUTURE.
IT WAS THEN THAT I SOMEHOW UNDER-STOOD...
...WHAT GENTLE CRIMINAL WAS DOING.
HE SHOULD BE...
...JUST... OVER THERE...
I PUT A TASTEFUL SPIN ON MY SELFISH ACTIONS.
YET, ALL ALONG...
...I WAS DOING IT FOR ME.
I AM UTTERLY STRIPPED OF THE WILL TO FIGHT BACK.
SO I'M OVER-JOYED THAT THIS WAS FOR YOU, IN THE END.
I FOUGHT WITH MY FEELINGS ON THE LINE...
...UNTIL ALL THAT WAS LEFT IN ME, DEEP DOWN...
I'VE COMMITTED COUNTLESS CRIMES, BUT MY GREATEST SIN OF ALL WAS...

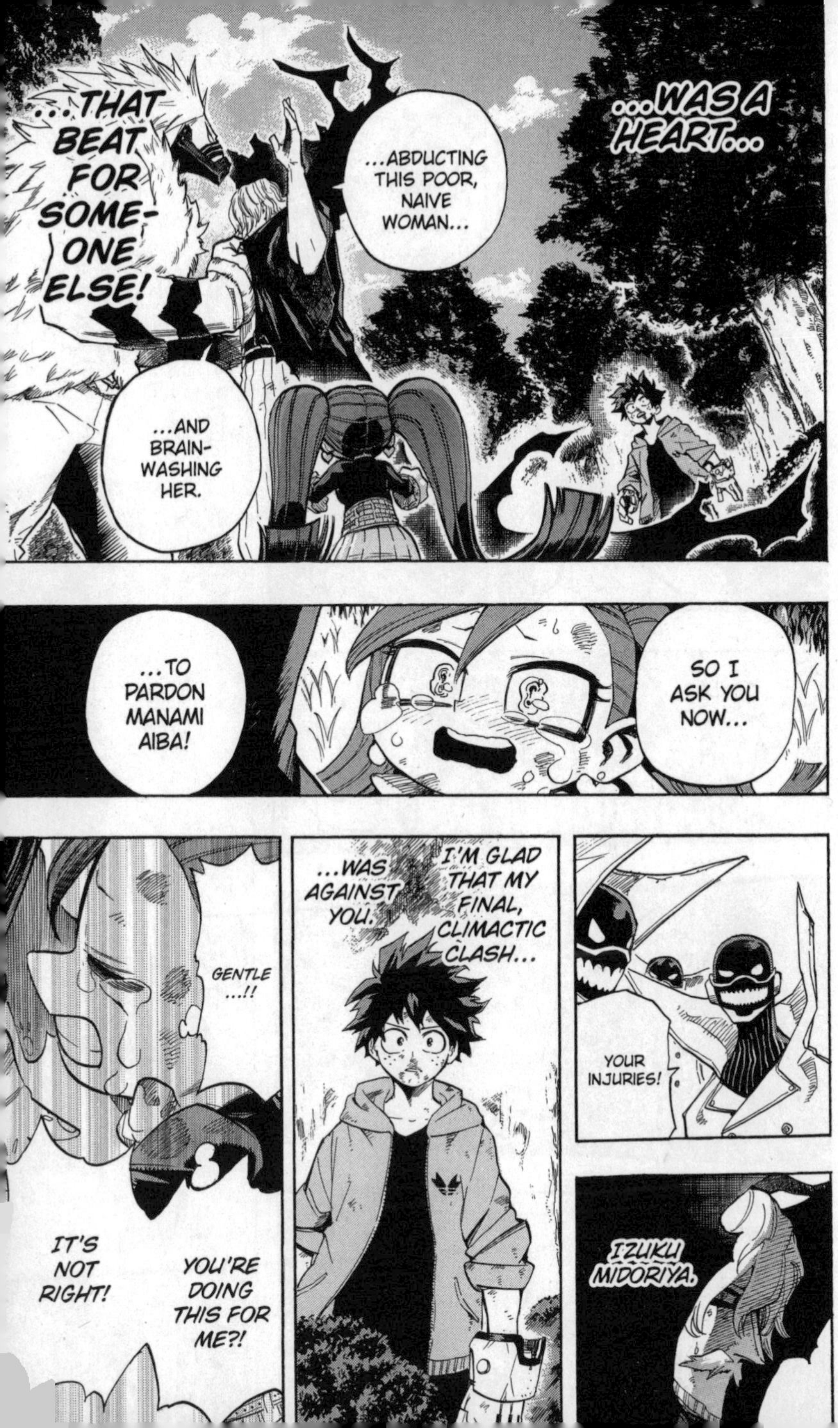
...WAS A HEART...
...THAT BEAT FOR SOMEONE ELSE!
...ABDUCTING THIS POOR, NAIVE WOMAN...
...AND BRAINWASHING HER.
SO I ASK YOU NOW...
...TO PARDON MANAMI AIBA!
YOUR INJURIES!
IZUKU MIDORIYA.
I'M GLAD THAT MY FINAL, CLIMACTIC CLASH...
...WAS AGAINST YOU.
GENTLE...!!
YOU'RE DOING THIS FOR ME?!
IT'S NOT RIGHT!

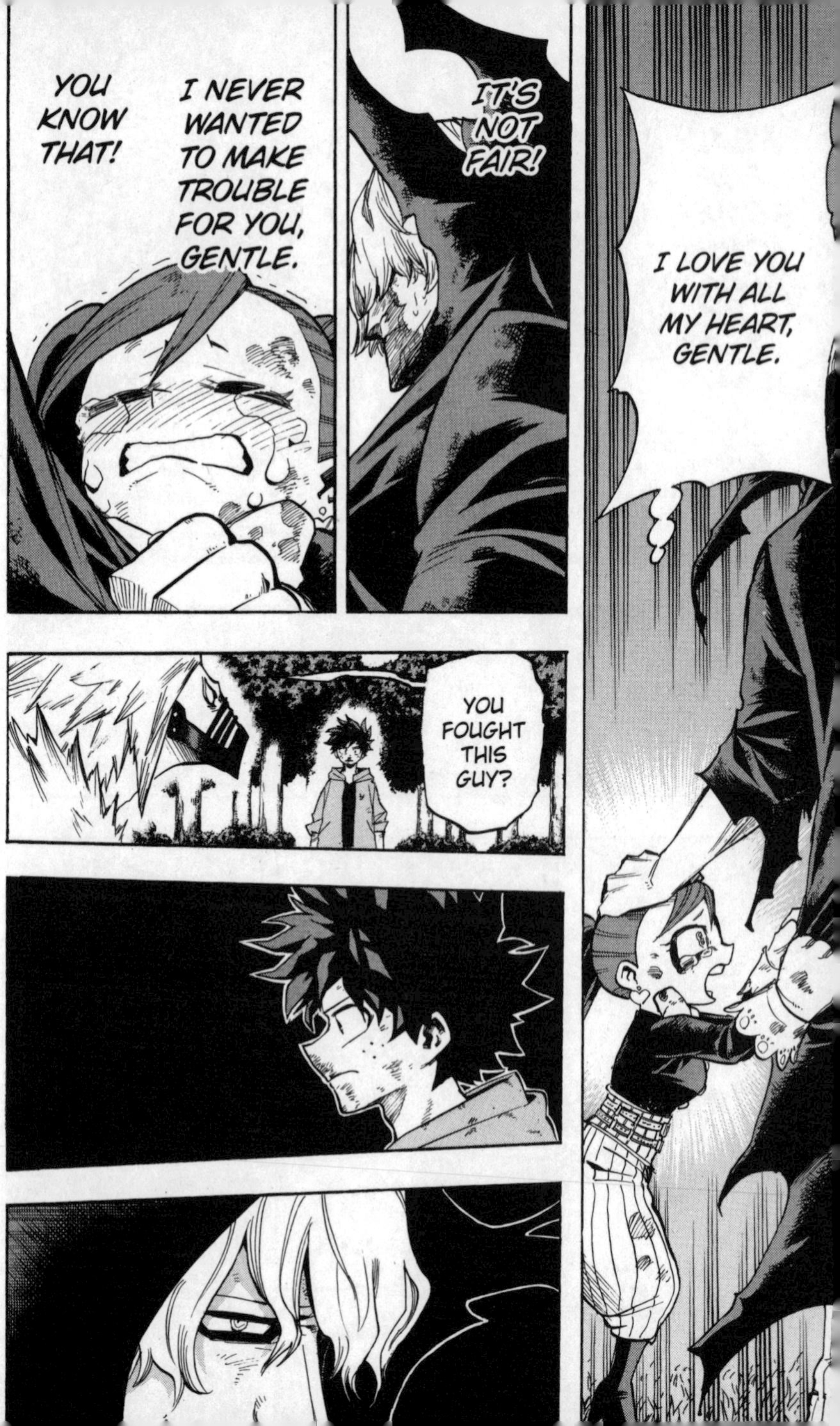
I LOVE YOU WITH ALL MY HEART, GENTLE.
IT'S NOT FAIR!
I NEVER WANTED TO MAKE TROUBLE FOR YOU, GENTLE.
YOU KNOW THAT!
YOU FOUGHT THIS GUY?

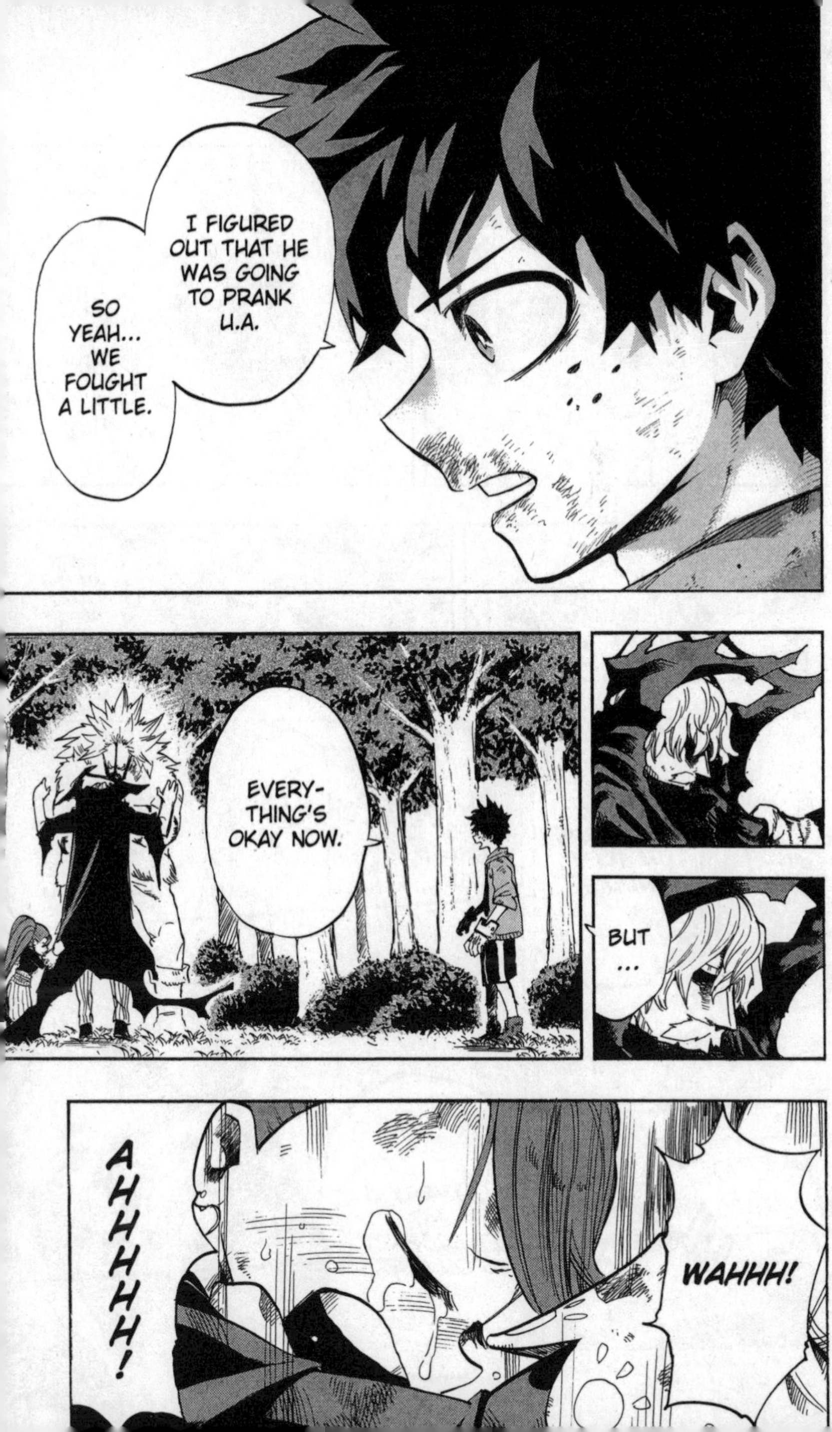
I FIGURED OUT THAT HE WAS GOING TO PRANK U.A.
SO YEAH... WE FOUGHT A LITTLE.
BUT...
EVERY-THING'S OKAY NOW.
WAHHH!
AHHHHH!

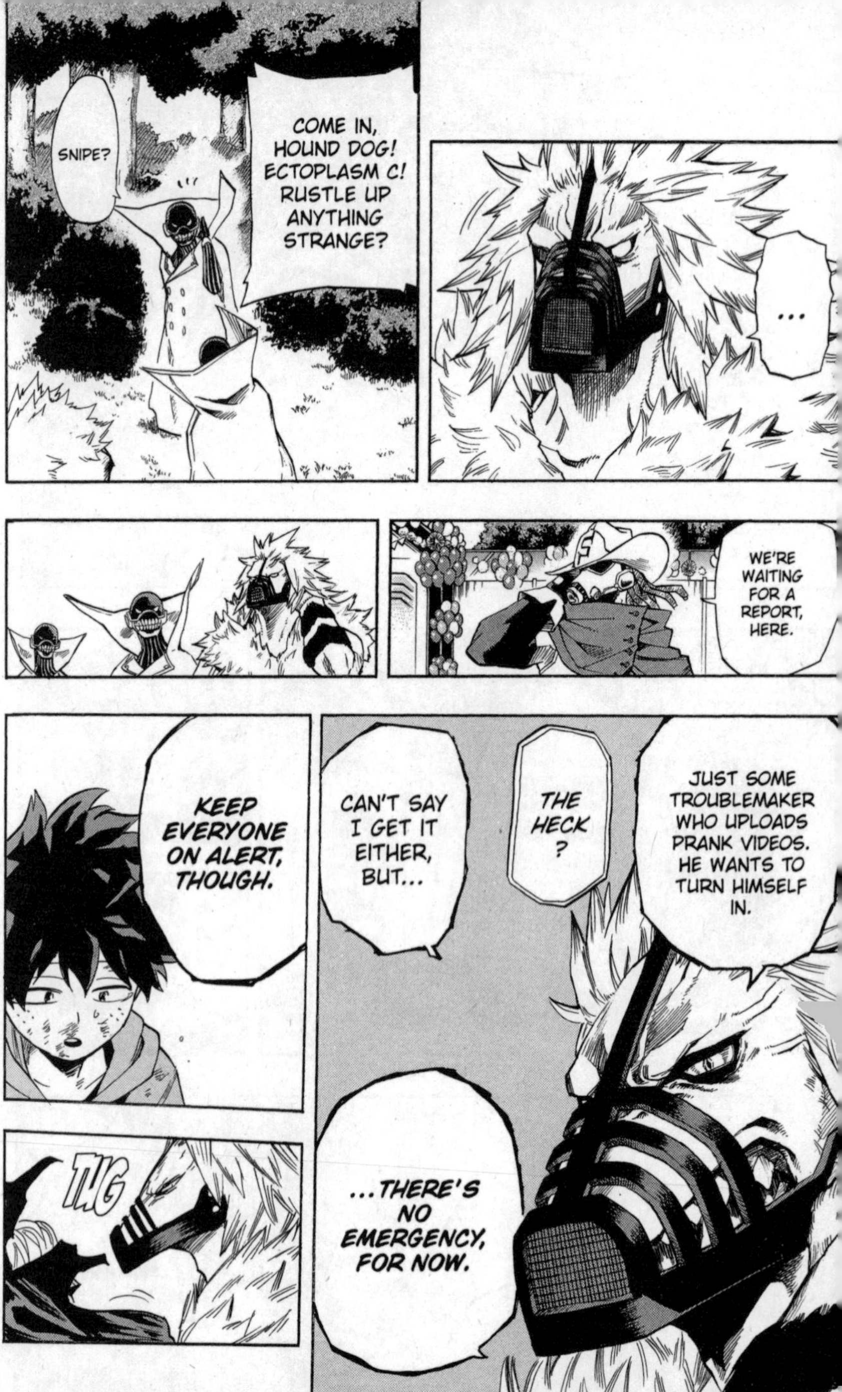
...
COME IN, HOUND DOG! ECTOPLASM C! RUSTLE UP ANYTHING STRANGE?
SNIPE?
WE'RE WAITING FOR A REPORT, HERE.
JUST SOME TROUBLEMAKER WHO UPLOADS PRANK VIDEOS. HE WANTS TO TURN HIMSELF IN.
THE HECK?
CAN'T SAY I GET IT EITHER, BUT...
...THERE'S NO EMERGENCY, FOR NOW.
KEEP EVERYONE ON ALERT, THOUGH.
THG

IZUKU MIDORIYA...

YOU'LL EXPLAIN YOURSELF IN DETAIL OVER AT THE POLICE STATION.

GENTLE CRIMINAL IS A MERE SHADOW OF A FAILED WOULD-BE HERO.

I, TOO, WAS ONCE ENROLLED IN A HERO COURSE.

YOU'D STEAL A SMILE FROM A GIRL WHO DOESN'T KNOW THE MEANING OF JOY YET?!

THOUGH I AM IN NO POSITION TO GIVE ADVICE...

THOSE FEELINGS OF YOURS—MAKE SURE TO SEE THEM THROUGH.

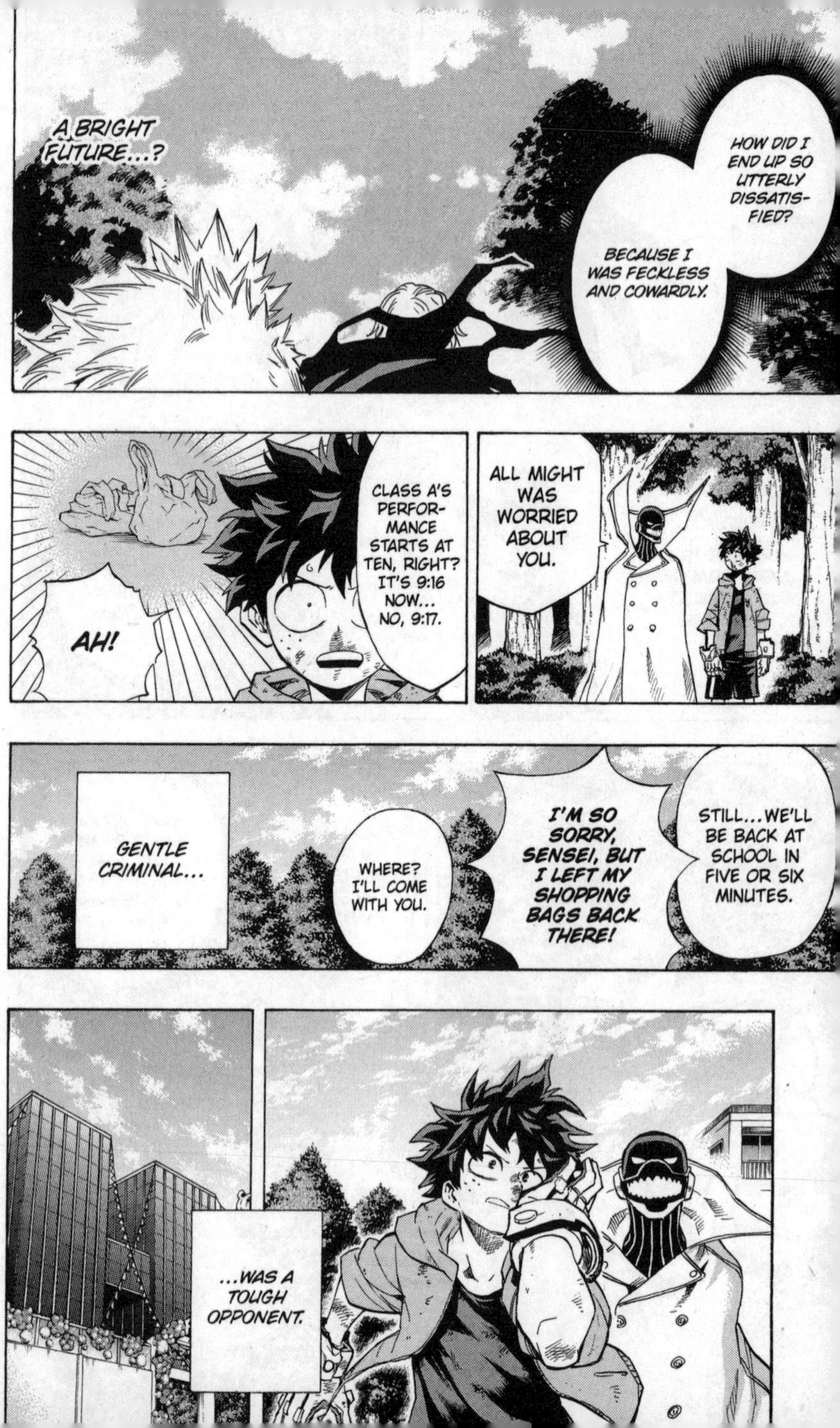
HOW DID I END UP SO UTTERLY DISSATIS-FIED?
BECAUSE I WAS FECKLESS AND COWARDLY.
A BRIGHT FUTURE...?
ALL MIGHT WAS WORRIED ABOUT YOU.
CLASS A'S PERFOR-MANCE STARTS AT TEN, RIGHT? IT'S 9:16 NOW... NO, 9:17.
AH!
STILL...WE'LL BE BACK AT SCHOOL IN FIVE OR SIX MINUTES.
I'M SO SORRY, SENSEI, BUT I LEFT MY SHOPPING BAGS BACK THERE!
WHERE? I'LL COME WITH YOU.
GENTLE CRIMINAL...
...WAS A TOUGH OPPONENT.

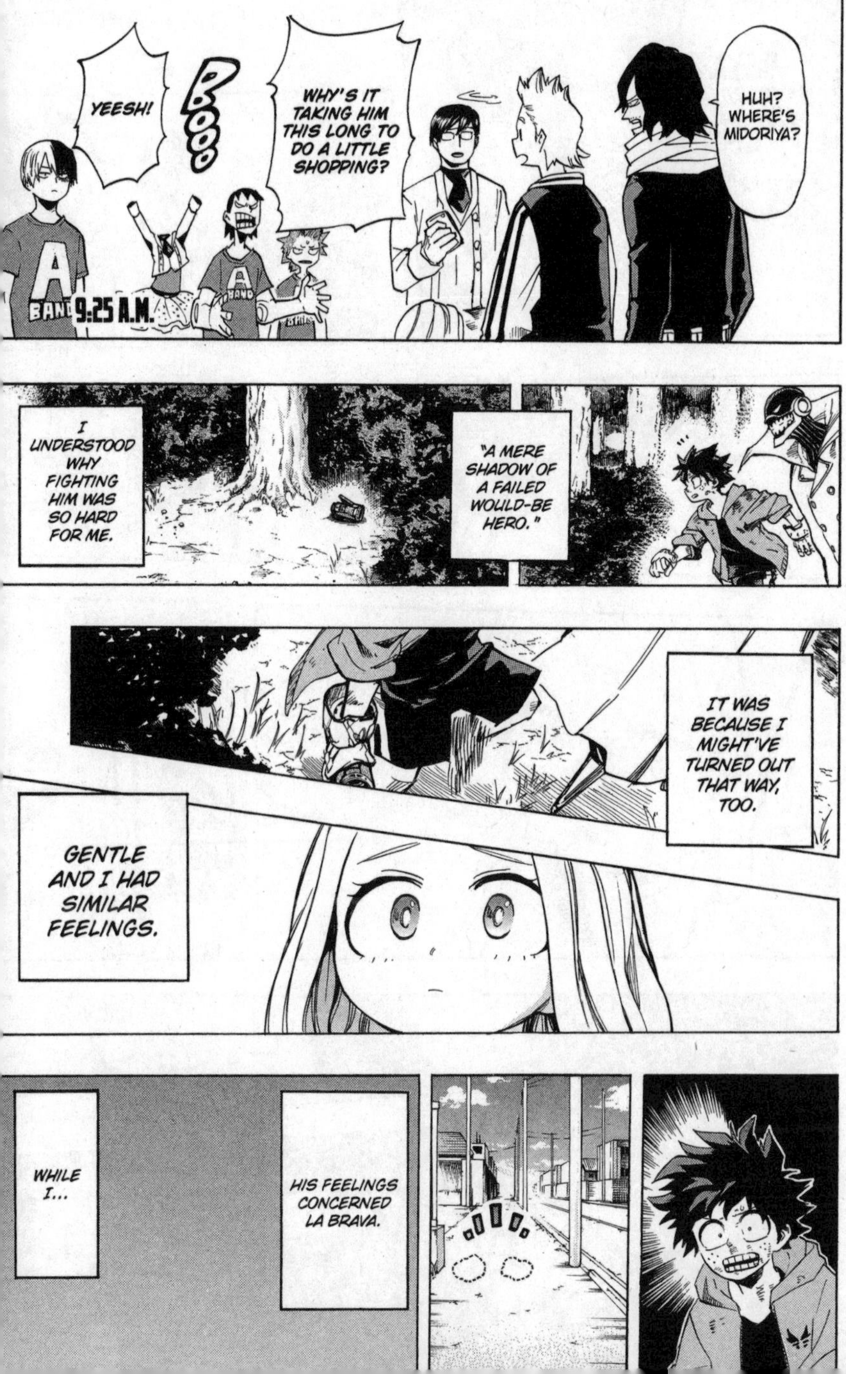
HUH? WHERE'S MIDORIYA?
WHY'S IT TAKING HIM THIS LONG TO DO A LITTLE SHOPPING?
BOOO
YEESH!
9:25 A.M.
"A MERE SHADOW OF A FAILED WOULD-BE HERO."
I UNDERSTOOD WHY FIGHTING HIM WAS SO HARD FOR ME.
IT WAS BECAUSE I MIGHT'VE TURNED OUT THAT WAY, TOO.
GENTLE AND I HAD SIMILAR FEELINGS.
HIS FEELINGS CONCERNED LA BRAVA.
WHILE I...

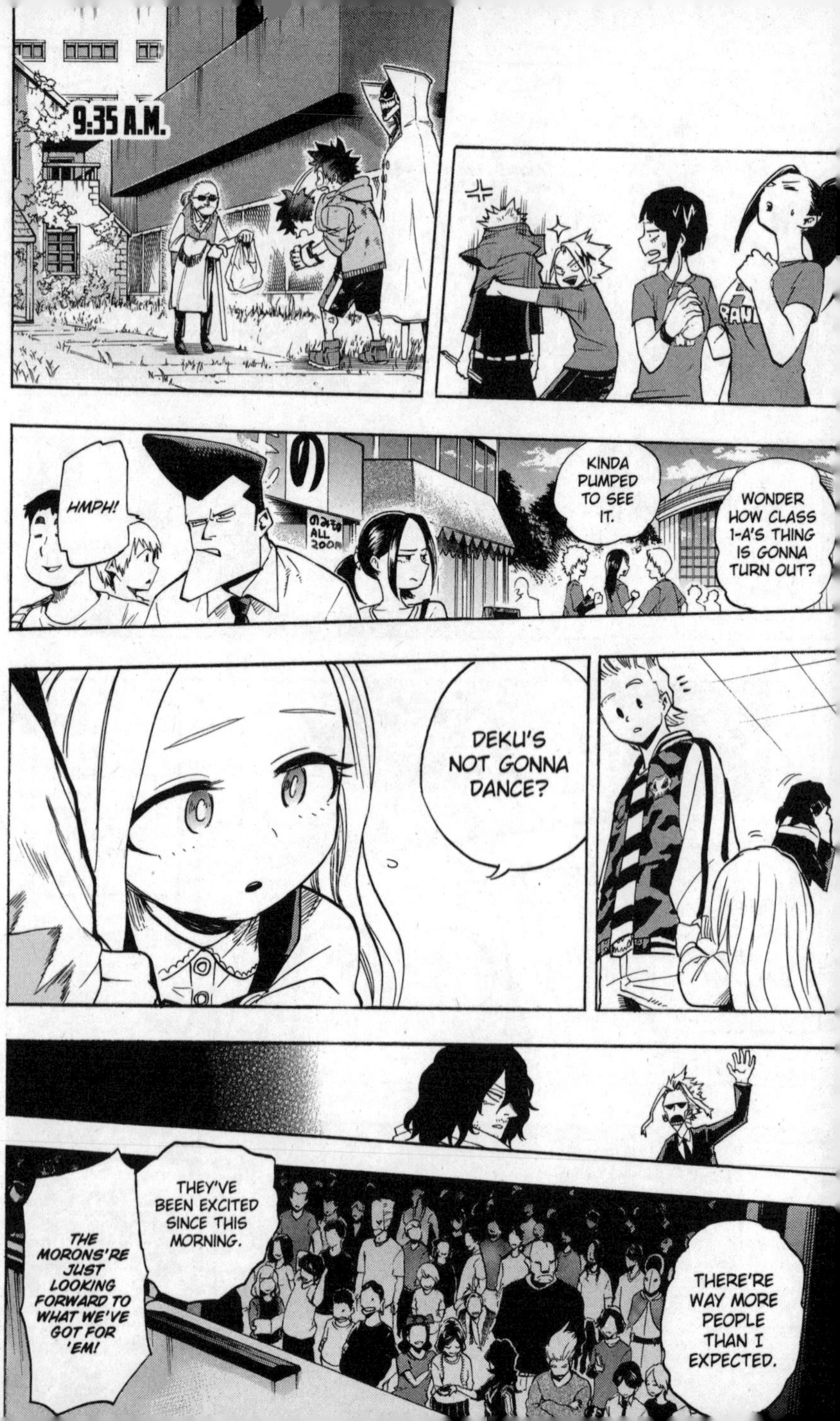
9:35 A.M.
WONDER HOW CLASS 1-A'S THING IS GONNA TURN OUT?
KINDA PUMPED TO SEE IT.
HMPH!
DEKU'S NOT GONNA DANCE?
THERE'RE WAY MORE PEOPLE THAN I EXPECTED.
THEY'VE BEEN EXCITED SINCE THIS MORNING.
THE MORONS'RE JUST LOOKING FORWARD TO WHAT WE'VE GOT FOR 'EM!

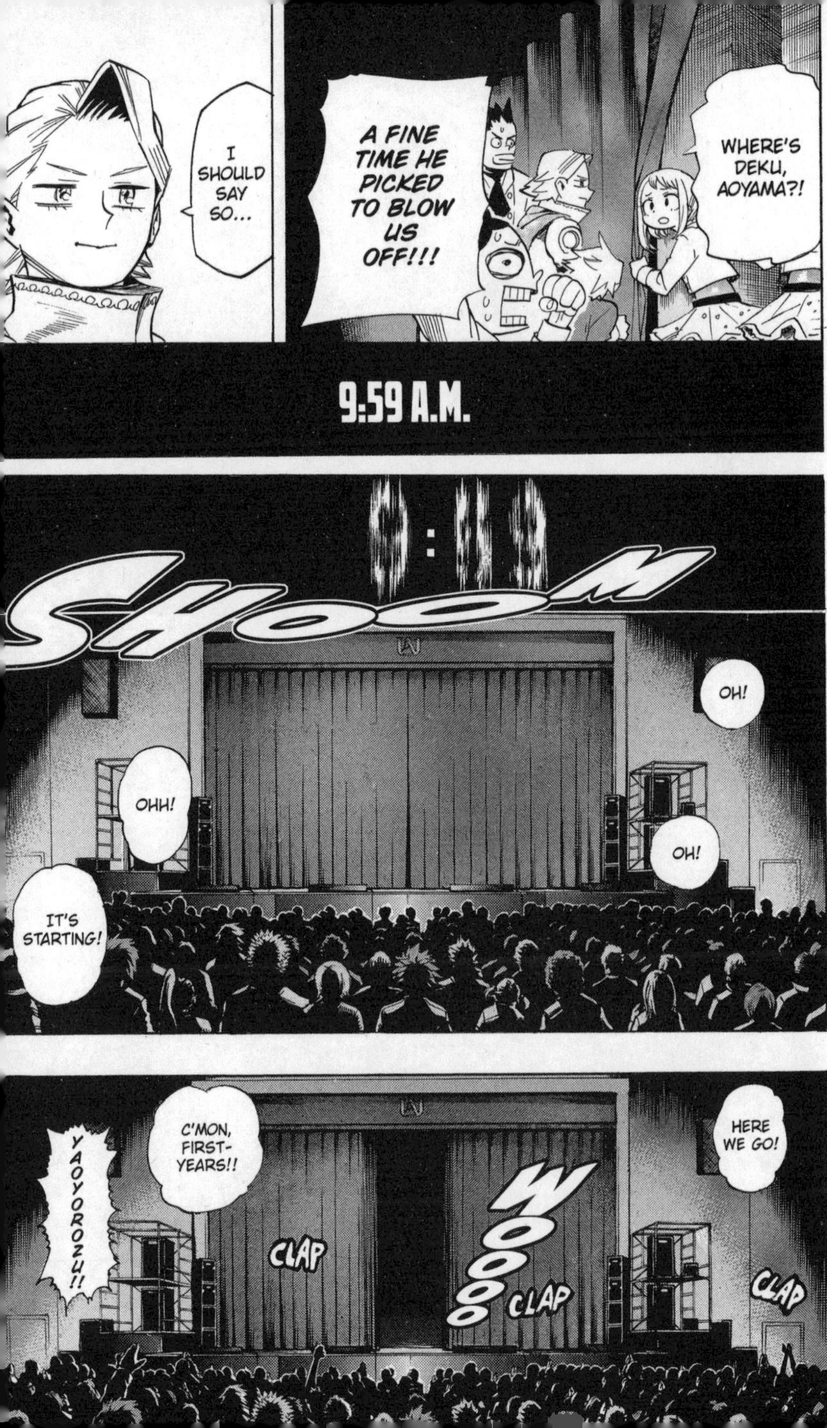
WHERE'S DEKU, AOYAMA?!
A FINE TIME HE PICKED TO BLOW US OFF!!!
I SHOULD SAY SO...
9:59 A.M.
SHOOM
OH!
OHH!
OH!
IT'S STARTING!
HERE WE GO!
C'MON, FIRST-YEARS!!
YAOYOROZU!!
WOOOOO
CLAP
CLAP
CLAP

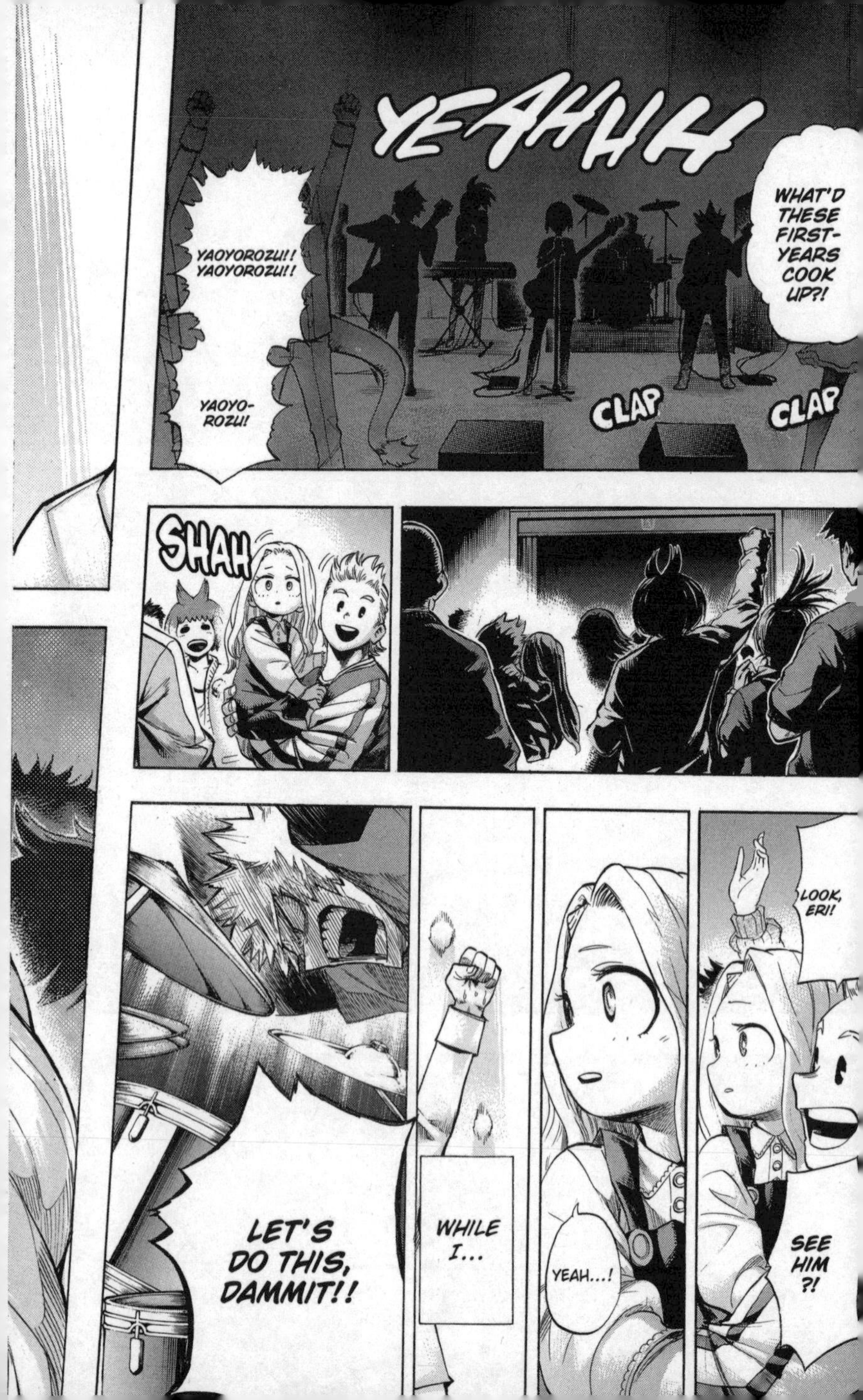
YEAHHH
WHAT'D THESE FIRST-YEARS COOK UP?!
YAOYOROZU!! YAOYOROZU!!
YAOYO-ROZU!
CLAP
CLAP
SHAH
LOOK, ERI!
SEE HIM?!
YEAH...!
WHILE I...
LET'S DO THIS, DAMMIT!!

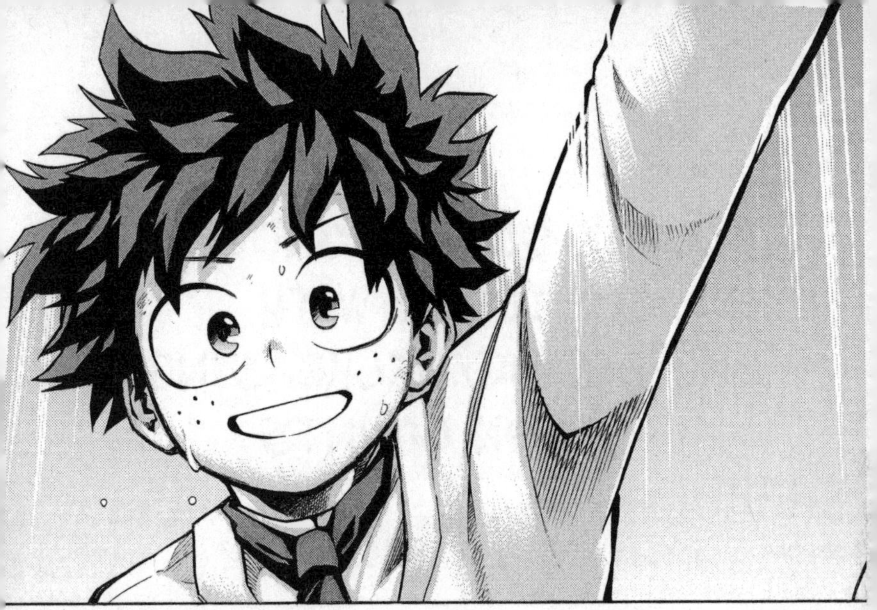

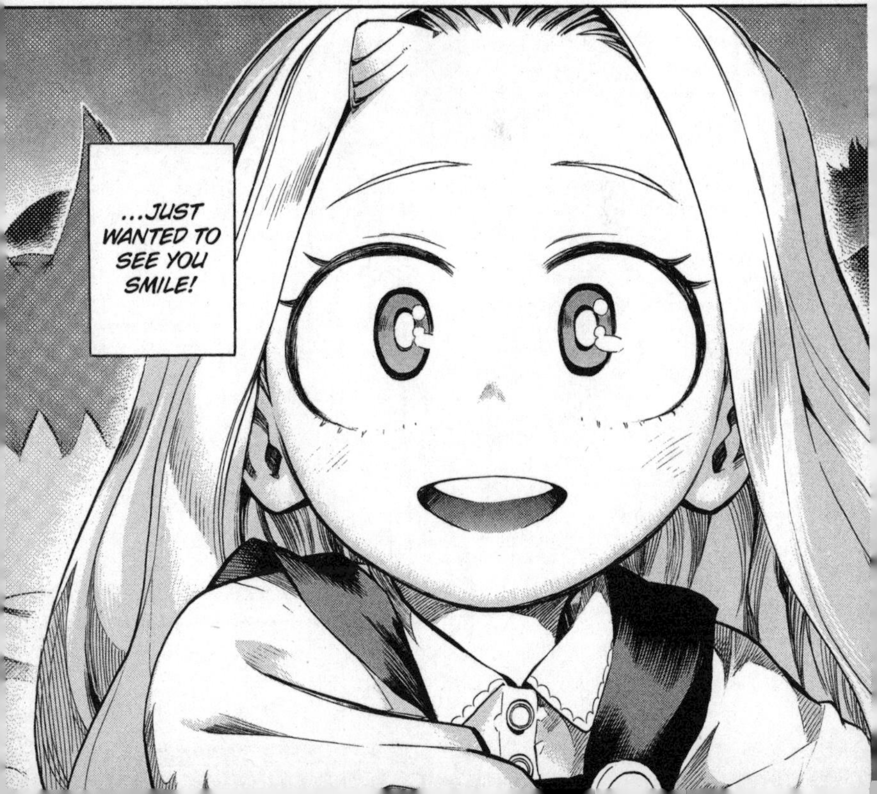
...JUST WANTED TO SEE YOU SMILE!

SUPER-DUPER WONDER COSTUMES WITH INCREASING/DECREASING BUTTON COUNTS

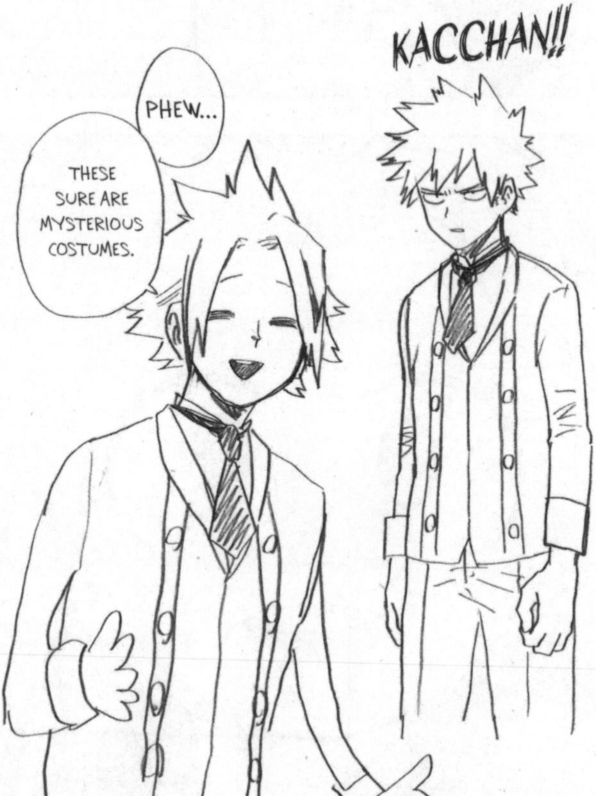

KACCHAN!!
PHEW...
THESE SURE ARE MYSTERIOUS COSTUMES.

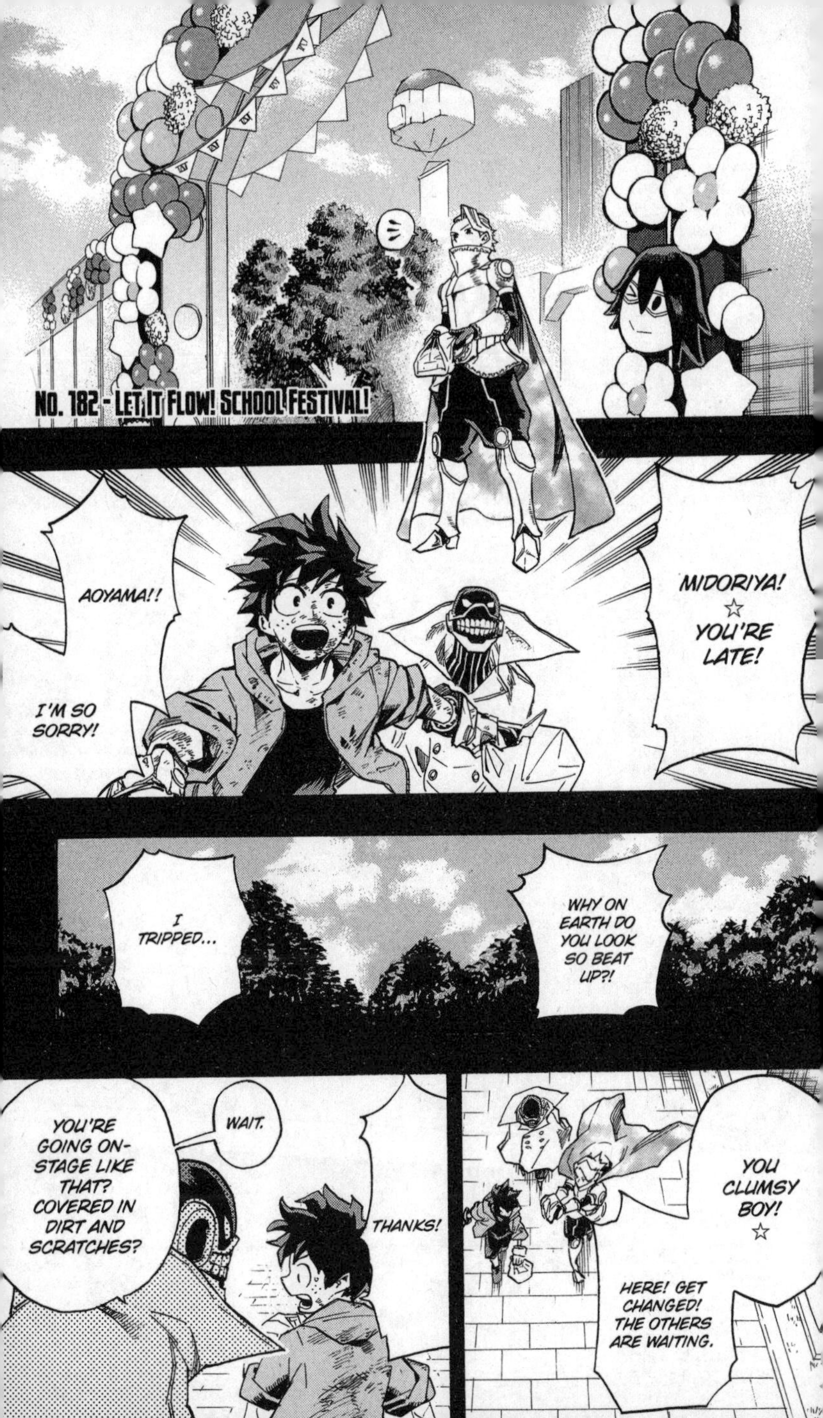
No. 182 - Let It Flow! School Festival!
MIDORIYA! ☆ YOU'RE LATE!
AOYAMA!!
I'M SO SORRY!
WHY ON EARTH DO YOU LOOK SO BEAT UP?!
I TRIPPED...
YOU CLUMSY BOY! ☆
HERE! GET CHANGED! THE OTHERS ARE WAITING.
WAIT.
YOU'RE GOING ON-STAGE LIKE THAT? COVERED IN DIRT AND SCRATCHES?
THANKS!

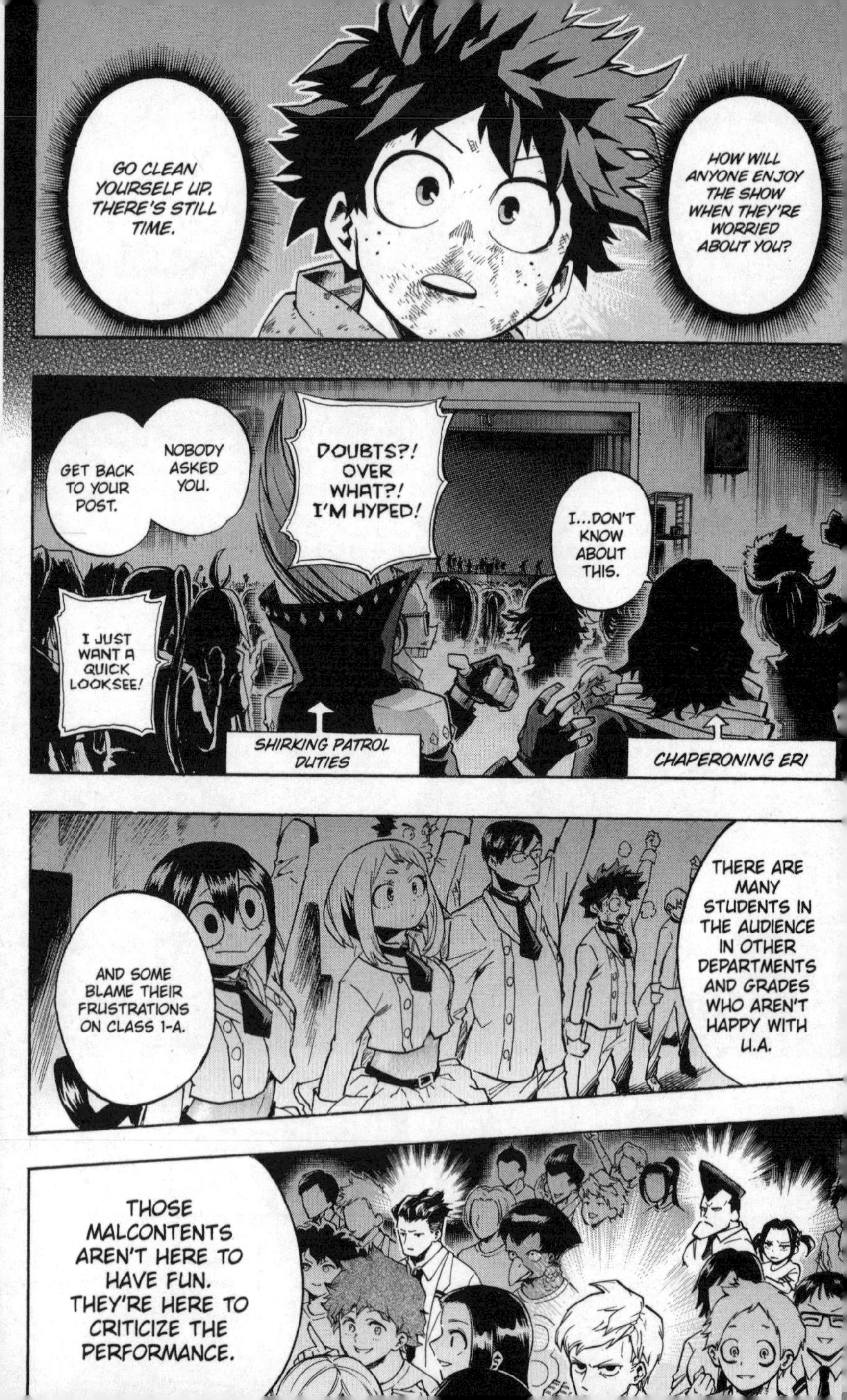
HOW WILL ANYONE ENJOY THE SHOW WHEN THEY'RE WORRIED ABOUT YOU?
GO CLEAN YOURSELF UP. THERE'S STILL TIME.
I...DON'T KNOW ABOUT THIS.
DOUBTS?! OVER WHAT?! I'M HYPED!
NOBODY ASKED YOU.
GET BACK TO YOUR POST.
CHAPERONING ERI
SHIRKING PATROL DUTIES
I JUST WANT A QUICK LOOKSEE!
THERE ARE MANY STUDENTS IN THE AUDIENCE IN OTHER DEPARTMENTS AND GRADES WHO AREN'T HAPPY WITH U.A.
AND SOME BLAME THEIR FRUSTRATIONS ON CLASS 1-A.
THOSE MALCONTENTS AREN'T HERE TO HAVE FUN. THEY'RE HERE TO CRITICIZE THE PERFORMANCE.

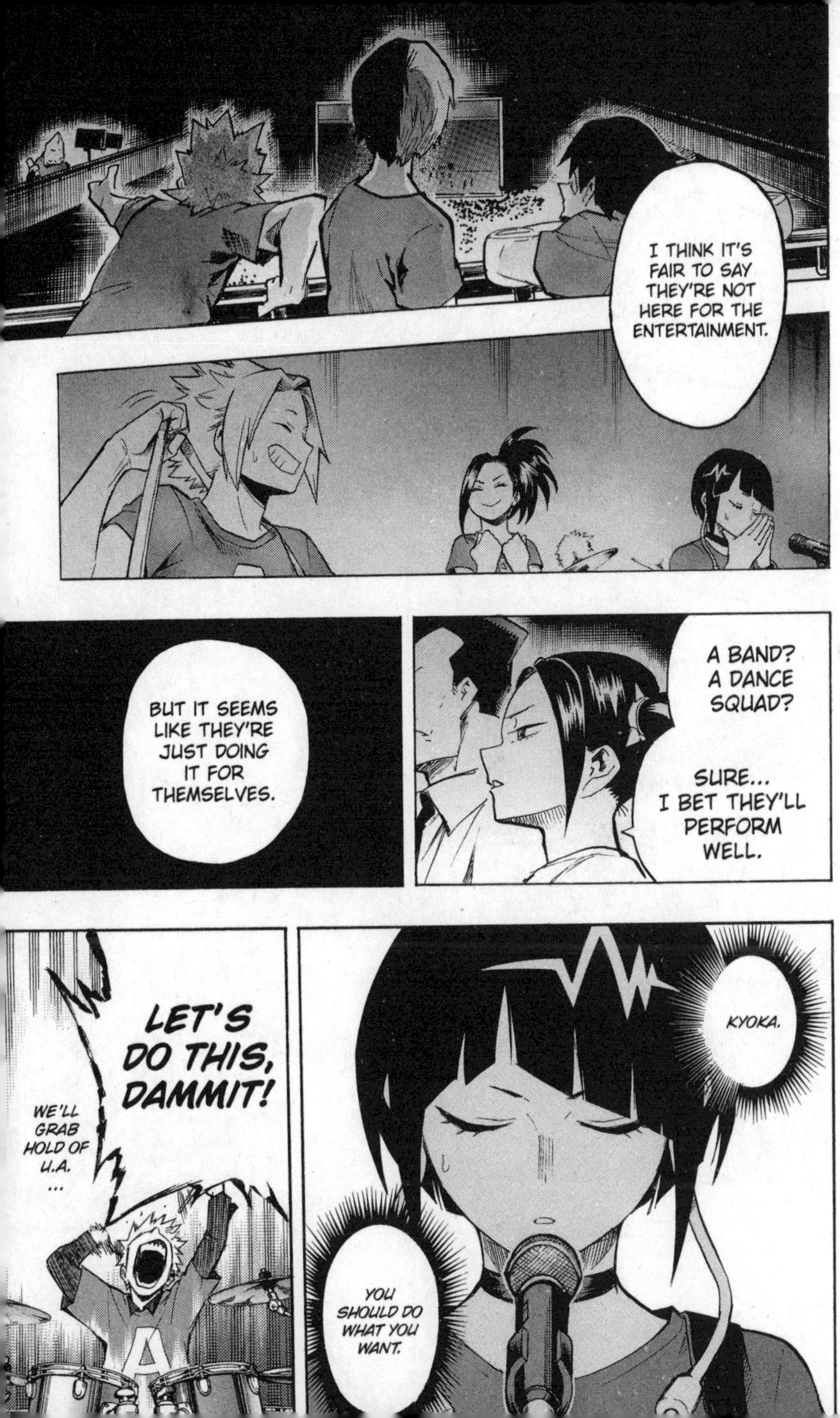
I THINK IT'S FAIR TO SAY THEY'RE NOT HERE FOR THE ENTERTAINMENT.
A BAND? A DANCE SQUAD?
SURE... I BET THEY'LL PERFORM WELL.
BUT IT SEEMS LIKE THEY'RE JUST DOING IT FOR THEMSELVES.
KYOKA.
YOU SHOULD DO WHAT YOU WANT.
LET'S DO THIS, DAMMIT!
WE'LL GRAB HOLD OF U.A. ...

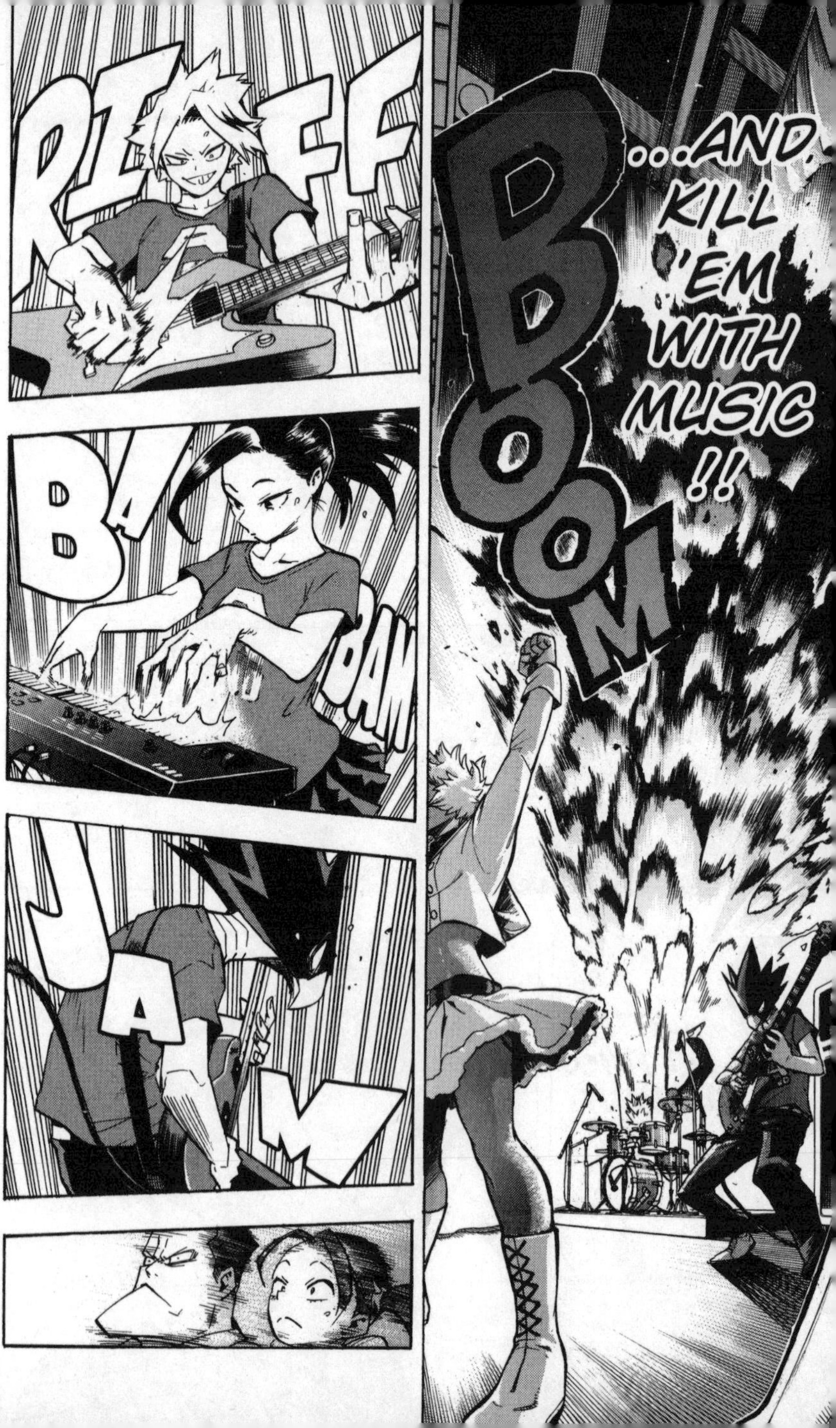
...AND KILL 'EM WITH MUSIC!!
BOOM
RIFF
BA
BAM
JAM

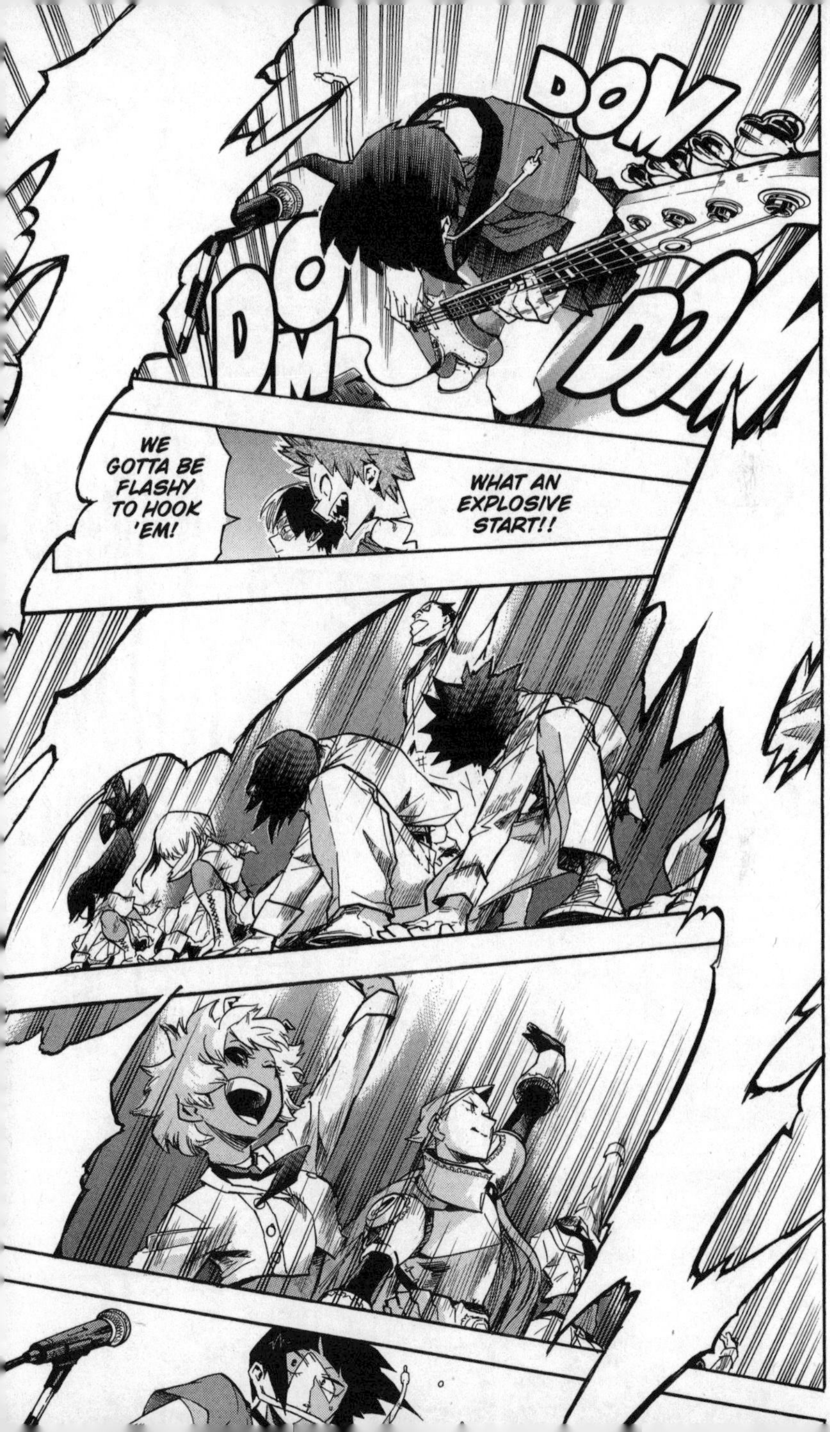
DOM
DOOM
DOM
WHAT AN EXPLOSIVE START!!
WE GOTTA BE FLASHY TO HOOK 'EM!

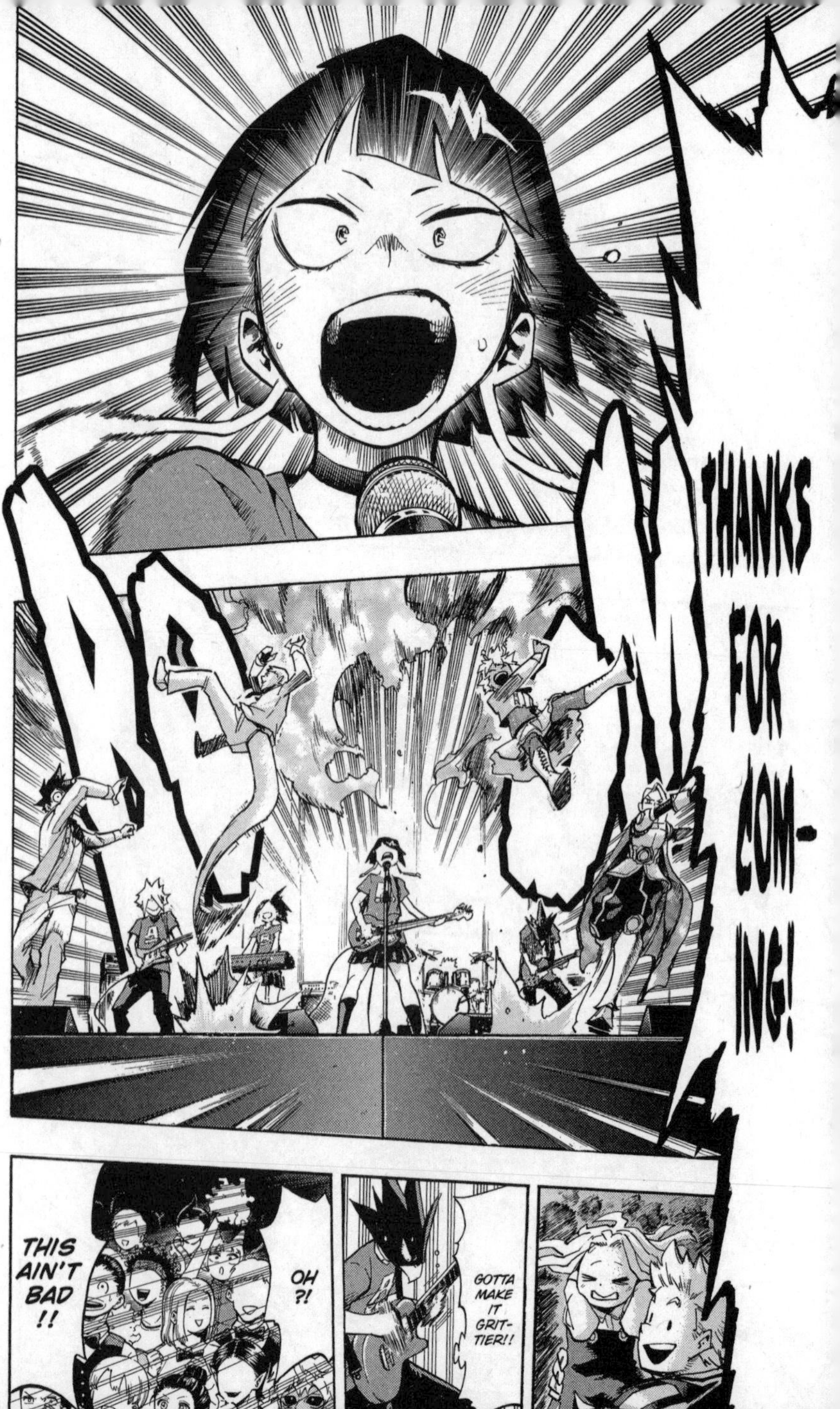
THANKS FOR COM-ING!
GOTTA MAKE IT GRIT-TIER!!
OH ?!
THIS AIN'T BAD !!

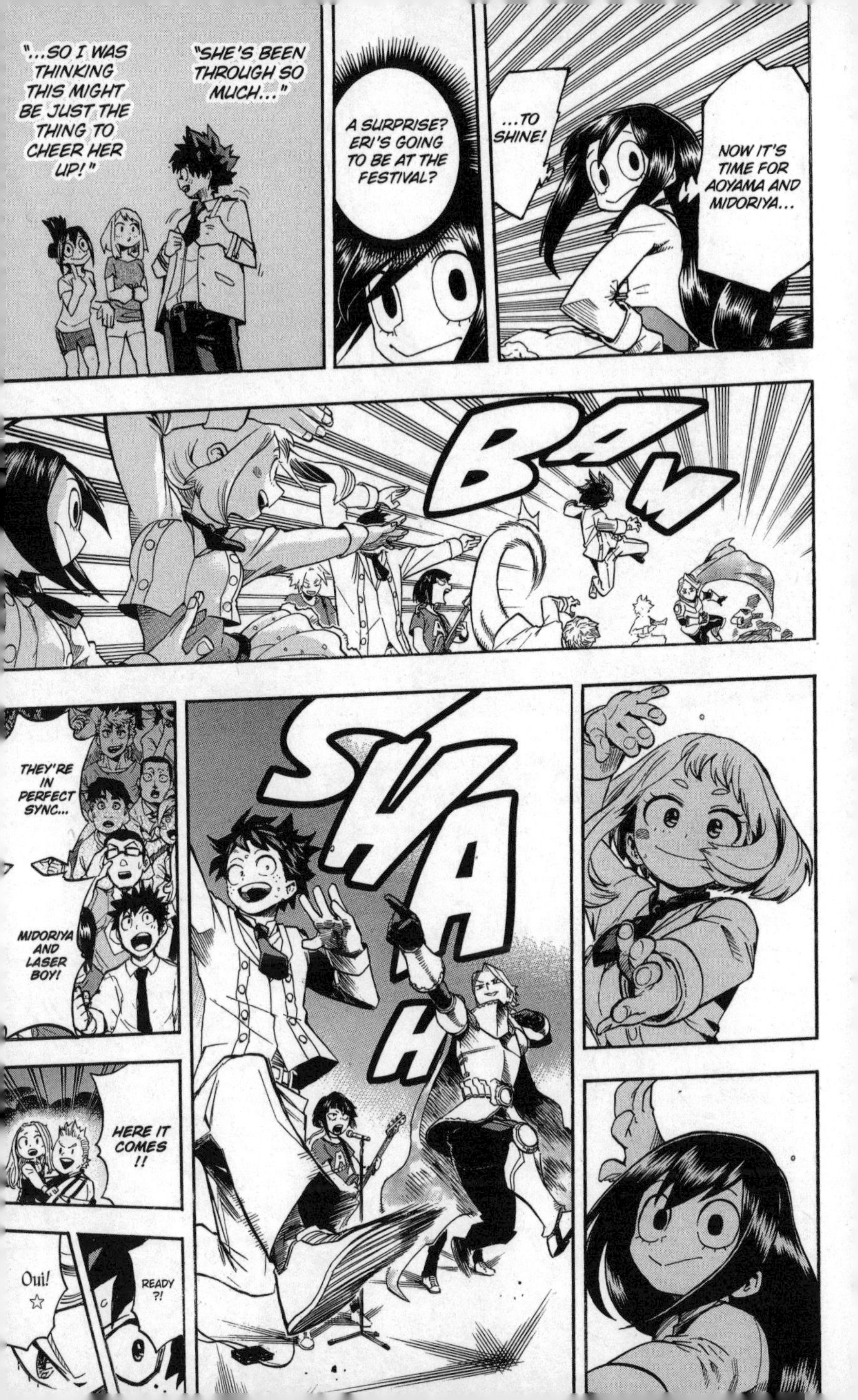
NOW IT'S TIME FOR AOYAMA AND MIDORIYA...
...TO SHINE!
A SURPRISE? ERI'S GOING TO BE AT THE FESTIVAL?
"SHE'S BEEN THROUGH SO MUCH..."
"...SO I WAS THINKING THIS MIGHT BE JUST THE THING TO CHEER HER UP!"
BAM
SHAAH
THEY'RE IN PERFECT SYNC...
MIDORIYA AND LASER BOY!
HERE IT COMES!!
READY?!
Oui! ☆

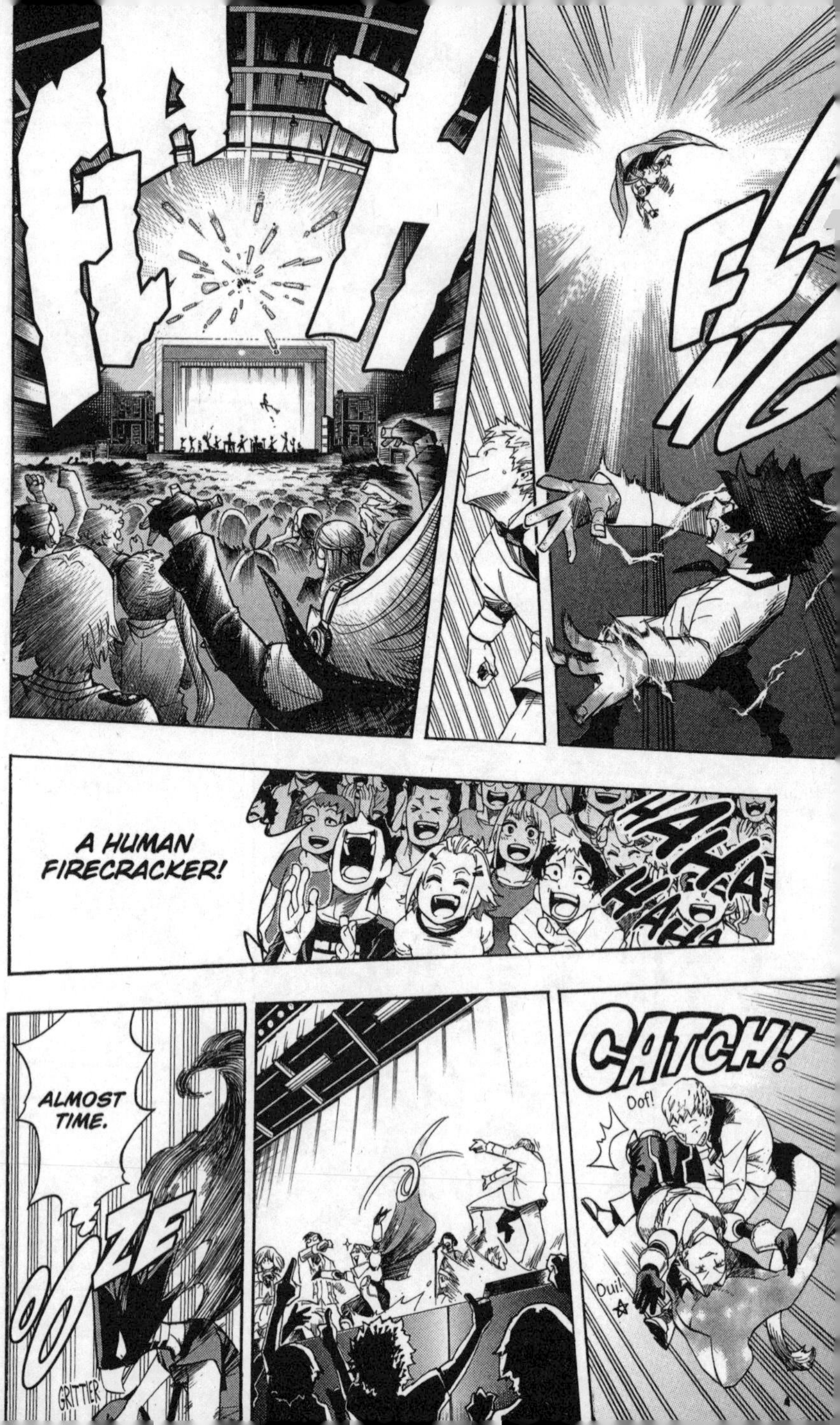
A HUMAN FIRECRACKER!
HAHA HAHA
CATCH!
Oof!
Oui! ☆
ALMOST TIME.
OOZE
GRITTIER

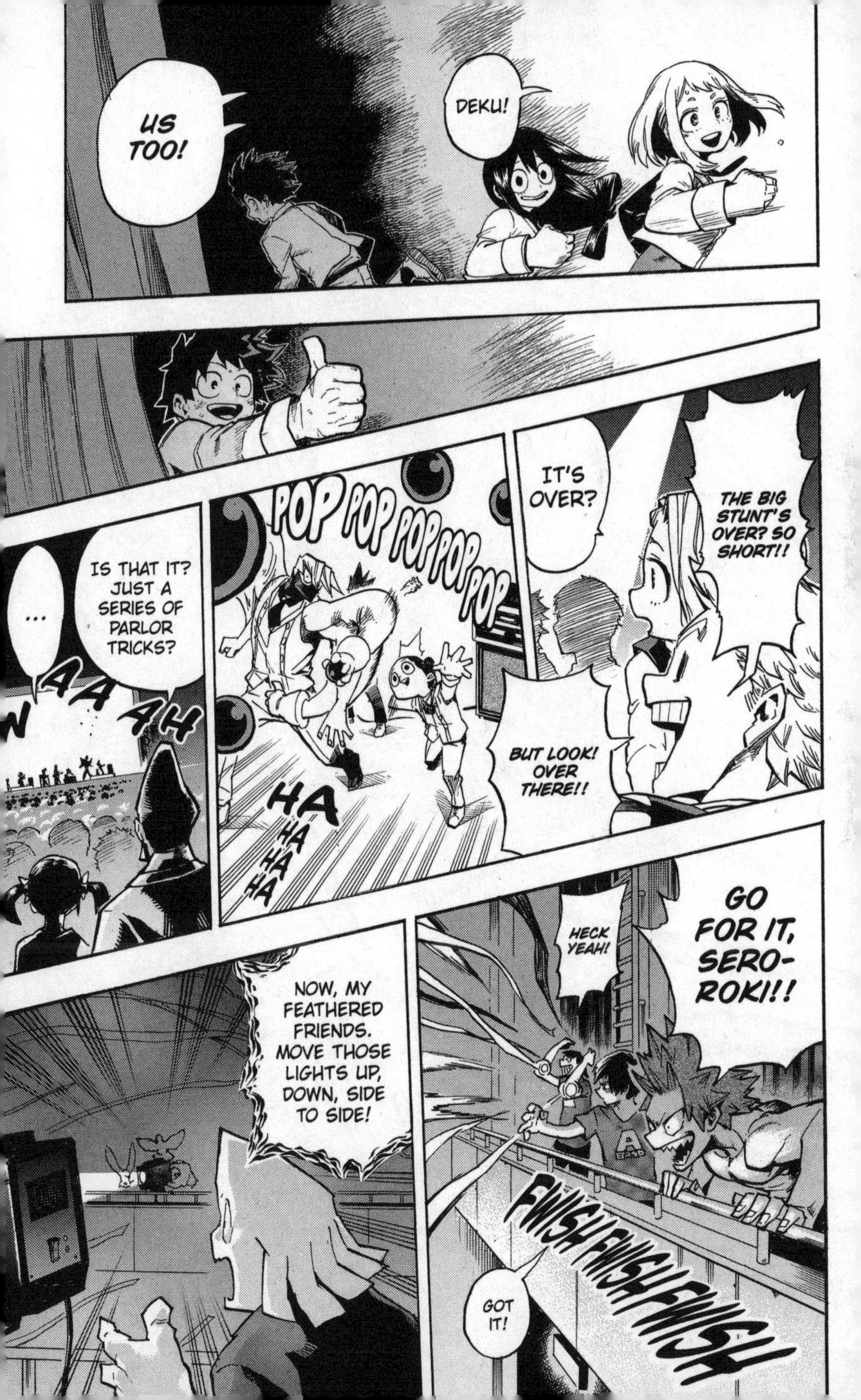
DEKU!
US TOO!
THE BIG STUNT'S OVER? SO SHORT!!
IT'S OVER?
BUT LOOK! OVER THERE!!
POP POP POP POP POP
HA HA HA HA HA
IS THAT IT? JUST A SERIES OF PARLOR TRICKS?
...
WAAAAAH
GO FOR IT, SERO-ROKI!!
HECK YEAH!
FWISH FWISH FWISH
GOT IT!
NOW, MY FEATHERED FRIENDS. MOVE THOSE LIGHTS UP, DOWN, SIDE TO SIDE!

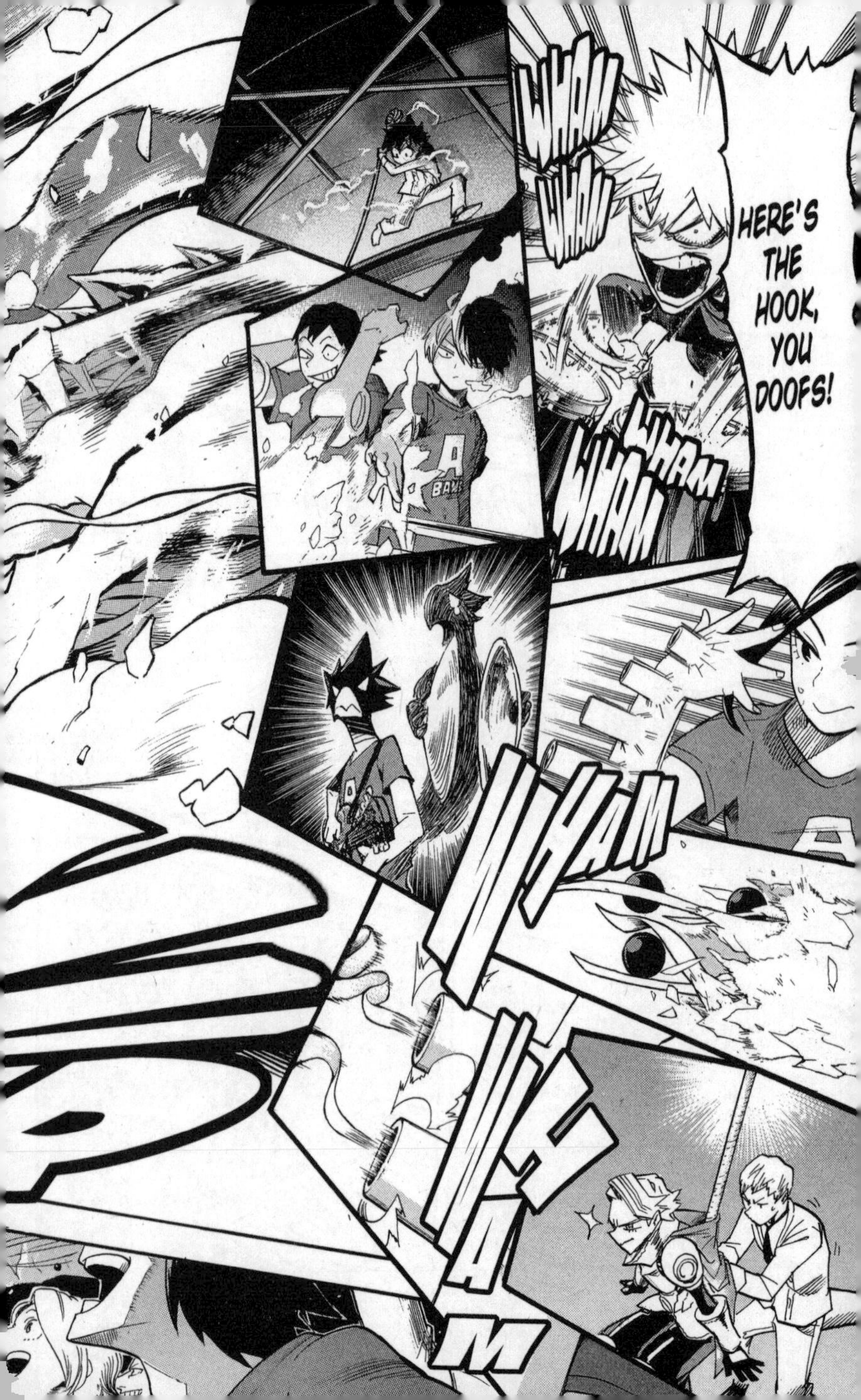
WHAM
WHAM
HERE'S THE HOOK, YOU DOOFS!
WHAM
WHAM
WHAM
WHAM

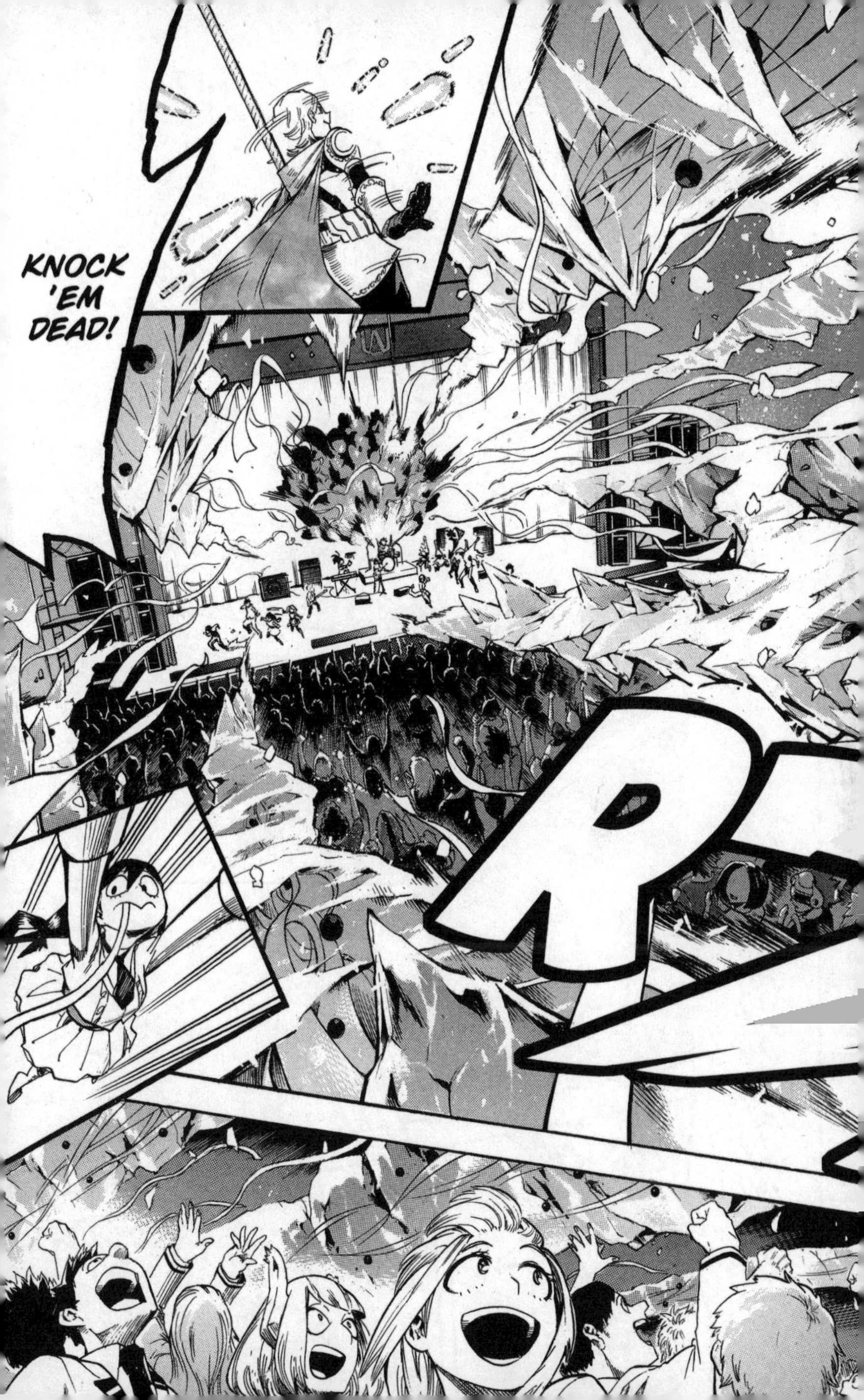
KNOCK 'EM DEAD!

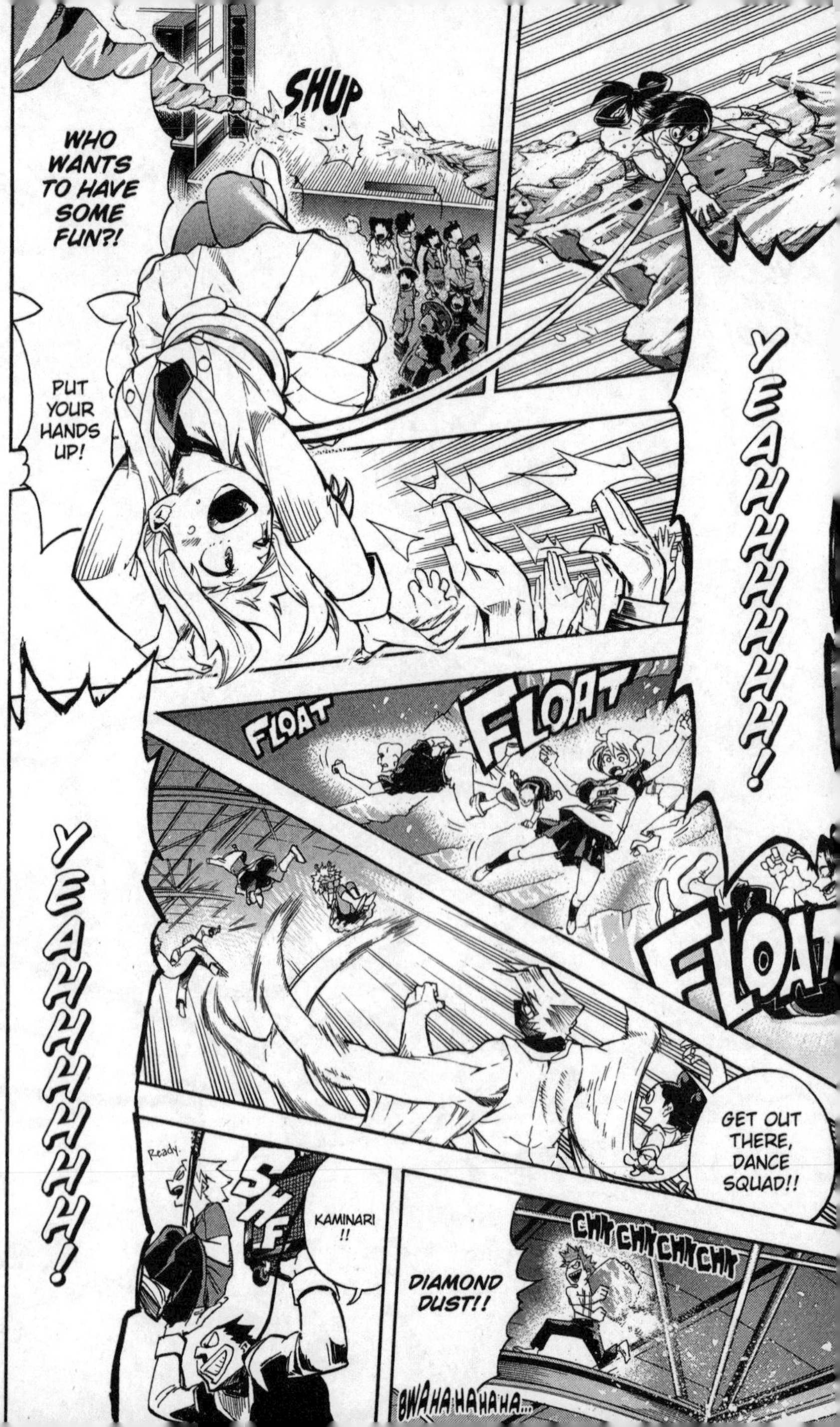
SHUP
WHO WANTS TO HAVE SOME FUN?!
PUT YOUR HANDS UP!
YEAHHHHHHHH!
FLOAT
FLOAT
FLOAT
YEAHHHHHHHH!
GET OUT THERE, DANCE SQUAD!!
CHK CHKCHKCHK
DIAMOND DUST!!
BWAHAHAHAHA...
KAMINARI!!
SHF
Ready.

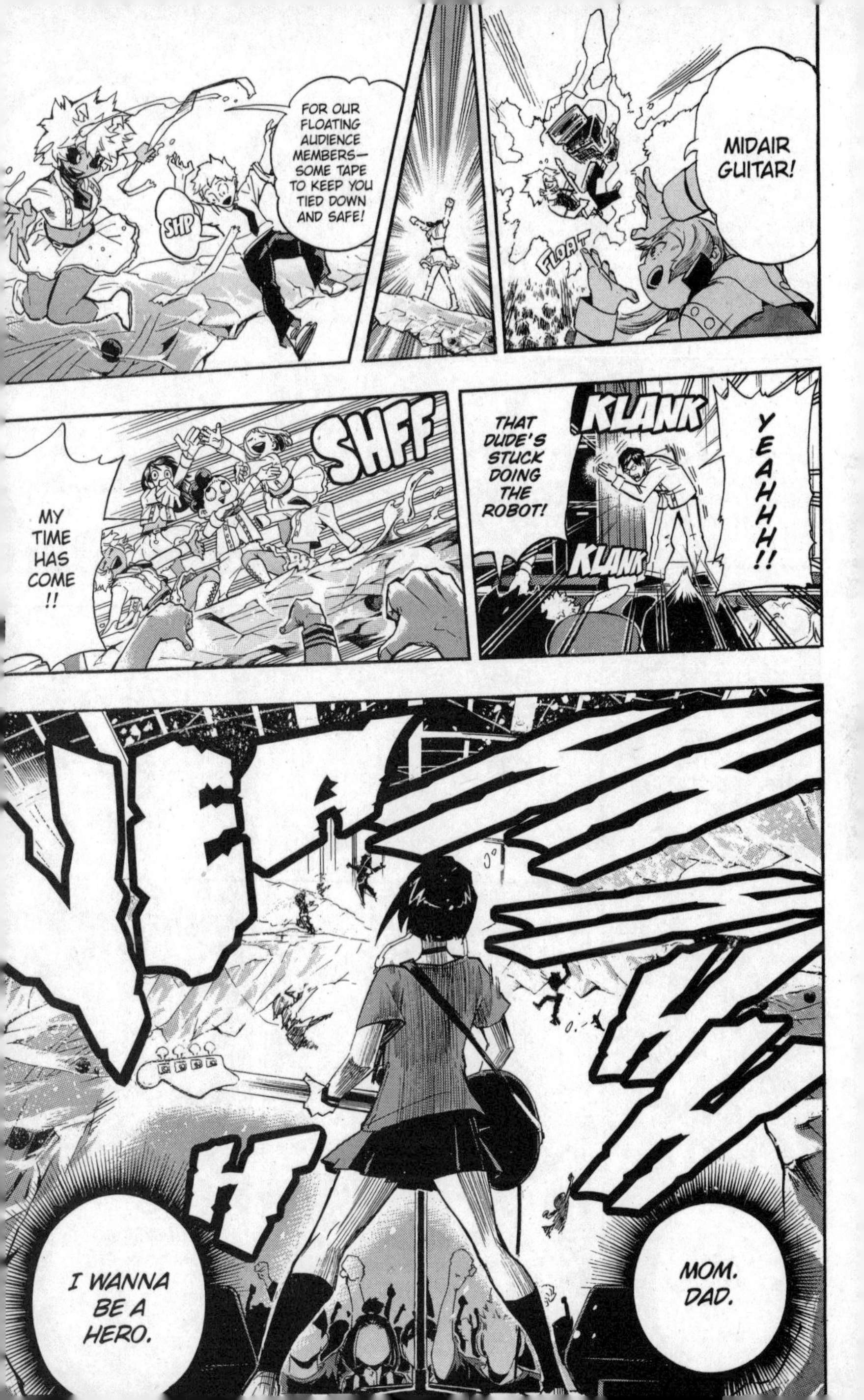
MIDAIR GUITAR!
FLOAT
FOR OUR FLOATING AUDIENCE MEMBERS— SOME TAPE TO KEEP YOU TIED DOWN AND SAFE!
SHP
YEAHHH!!
KLANK
THAT DUDE'S STUCK DOING THE ROBOT!
KLANK
SHFF
MY TIME HAS COME!!
MOM. DAD.
I WANNA BE A HERO.

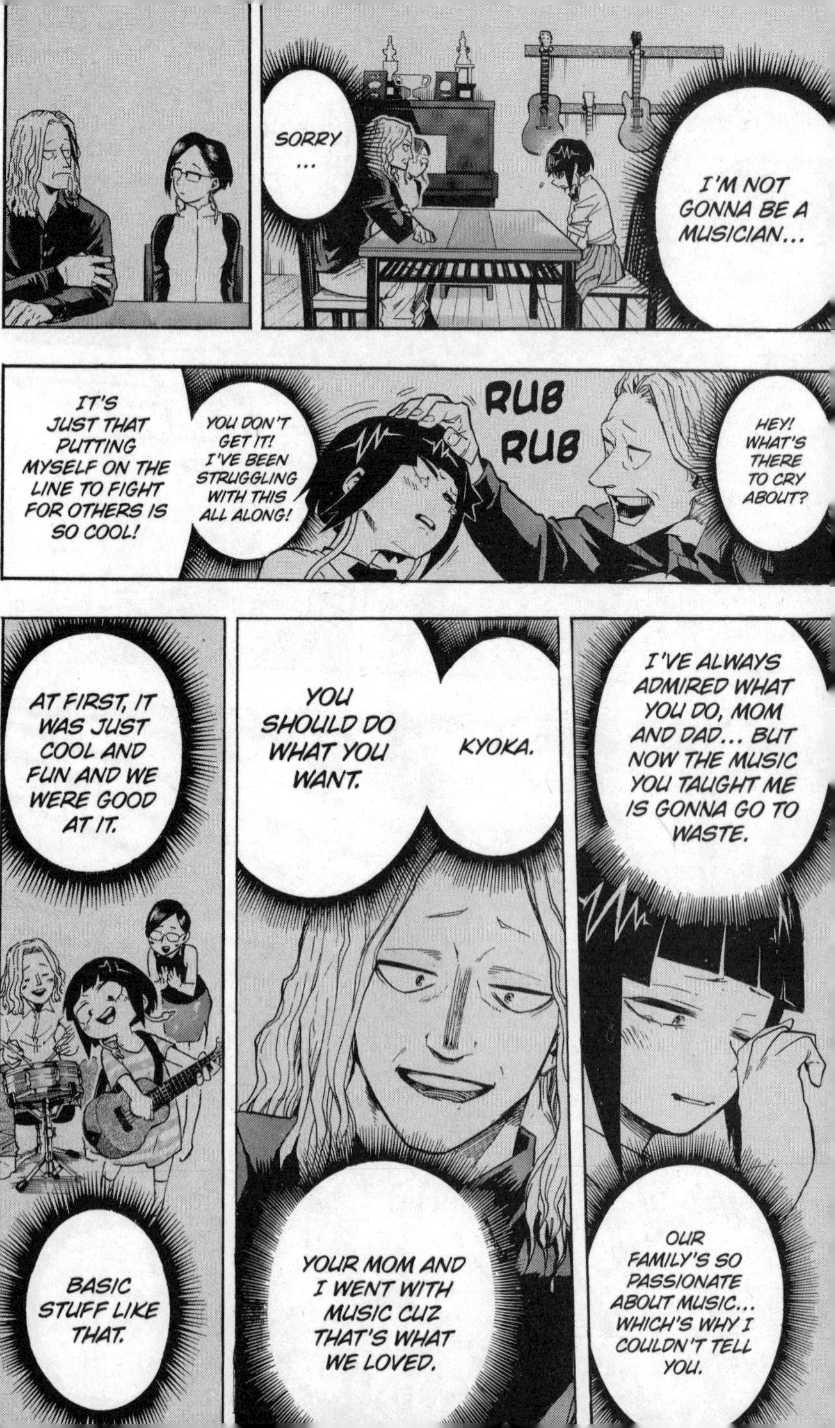
I'M NOT GONNA BE A MUSICIAN...
SORRY ...
HEY! WHAT'S THERE TO CRY ABOUT?
RUB RUB
YOU DON'T GET IT! I'VE BEEN STRUGGLING WITH THIS ALL ALONG!
IT'S JUST THAT PUTTING MYSELF ON THE LINE TO FIGHT FOR OTHERS IS SO COOL!
I'VE ALWAYS ADMIRED WHAT YOU DO, MOM AND DAD... BUT NOW THE MUSIC YOU TAUGHT ME IS GONNA GO TO WASTE.
OUR FAMILY'S SO PASSIONATE ABOUT MUSIC... WHICH'S WHY I COULDN'T TELL YOU.
KYOKA.
YOU SHOULD DO WHAT YOU WANT.
YOUR MOM AND I WENT WITH MUSIC CUZ THAT'S WHAT WE LOVED.
AT FIRST, IT WAS JUST COOL AND FUN AND WE WERE GOOD AT IT.
BASIC STUFF LIKE THAT.

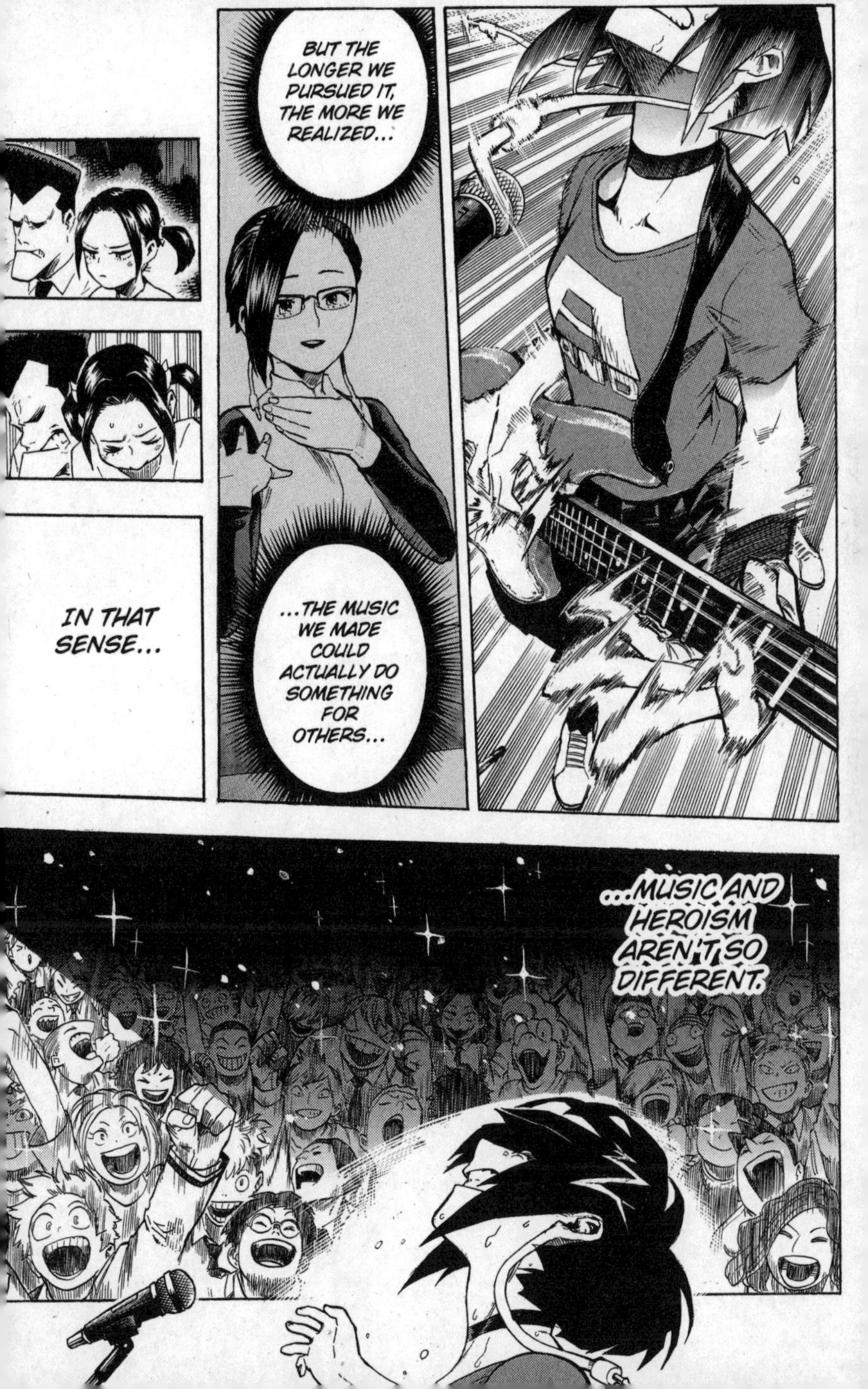
BUT THE LONGER WE PURSUED IT, THE MORE WE REALIZED...
...THE MUSIC WE MADE COULD ACTUALLY DO SOMETHING FOR OTHERS...
IN THAT SENSE...
...MUSIC AND HEROISM AREN'T SO DIFFERENT.

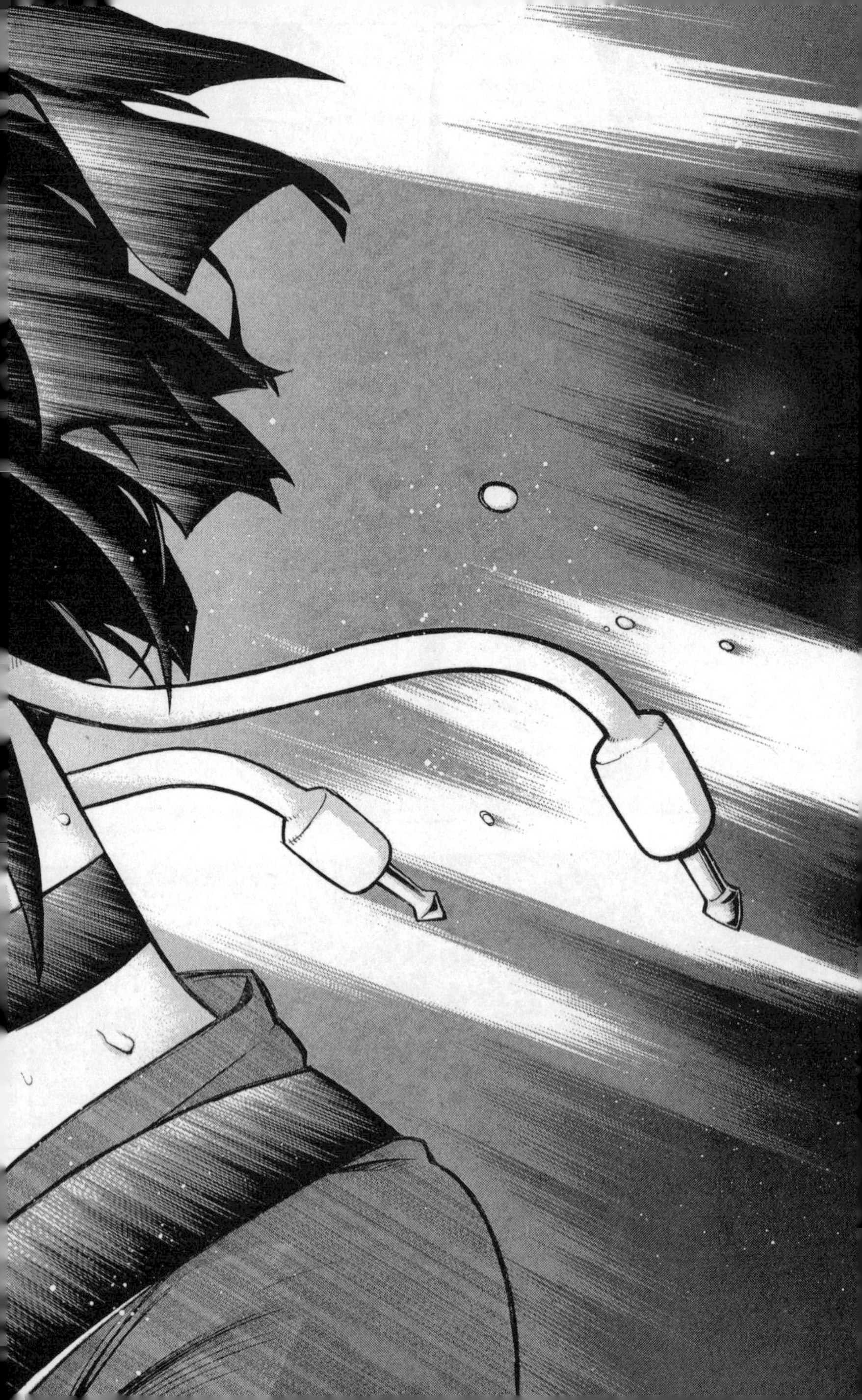

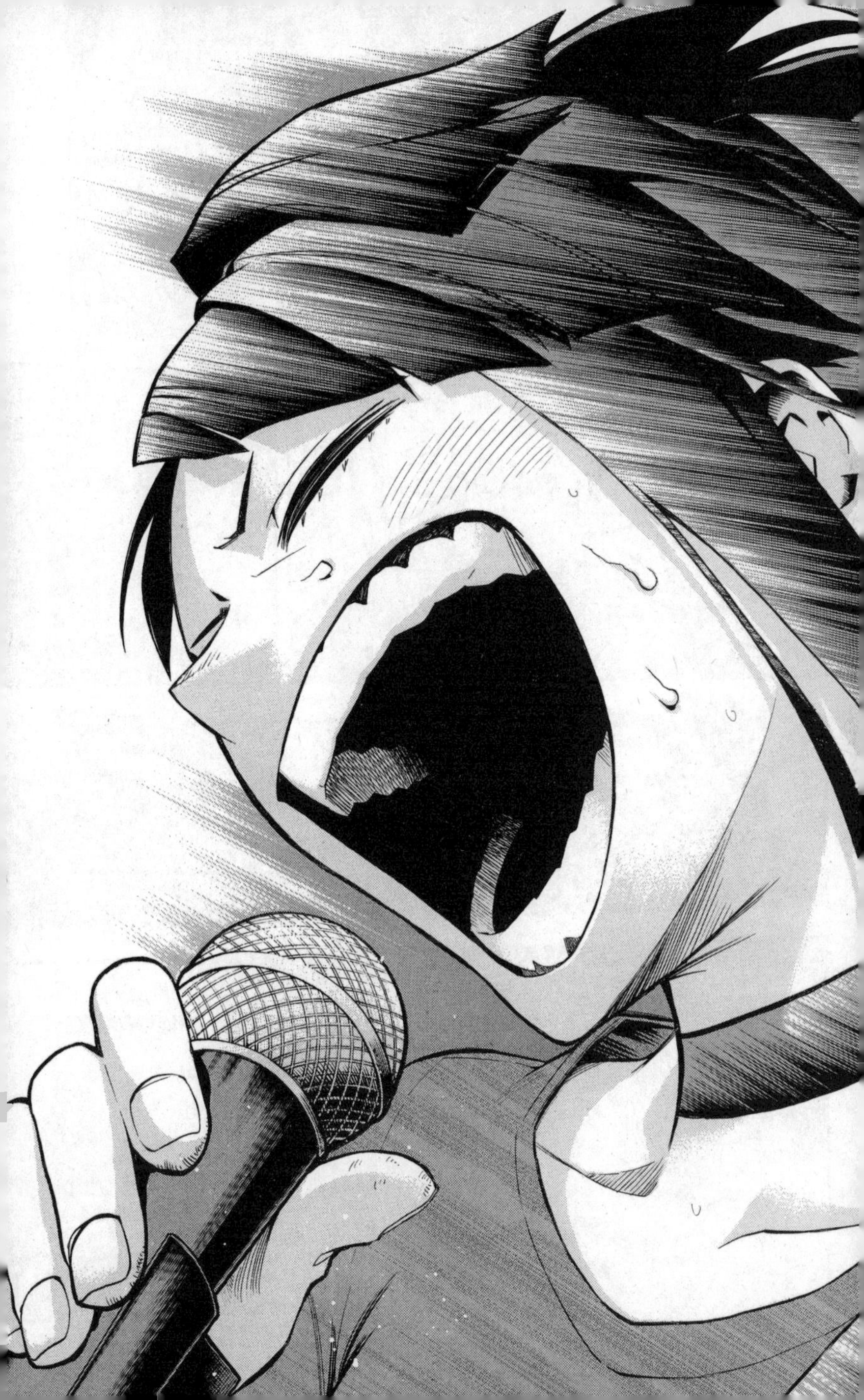

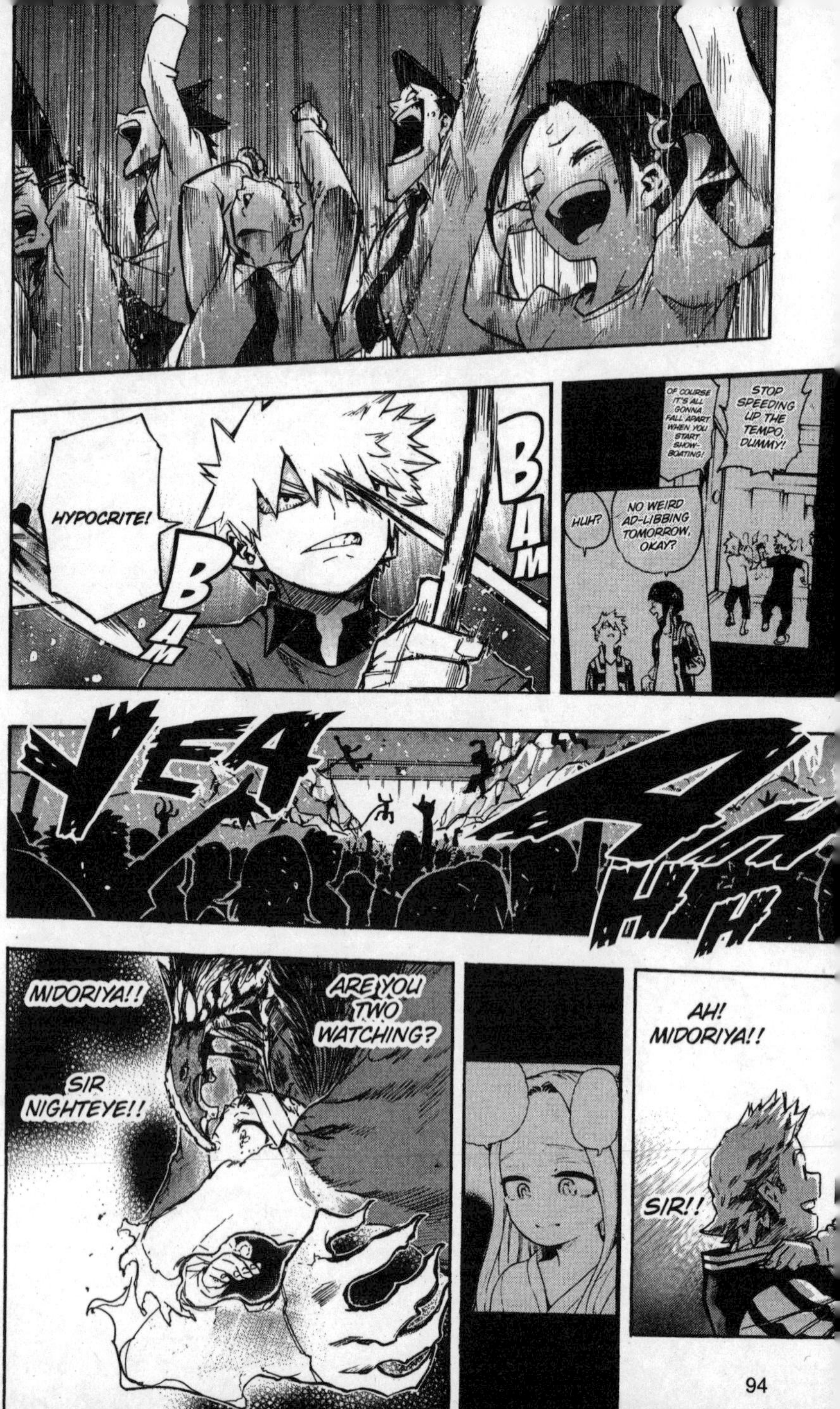
STOP SPEEDING UP THE TEMPO, DUMMY!
OF COURSE IT'S ALL GONNA FALL APART WHEN YOU START SHOW-BOATING!
NO WEIRD AD-LIBBING TOMORROW, OKAY?
HUH?
BAM
BAM
HYPOCRITE!
YEAAHH
AH! MIDORIYA!!
SIR!!
ARE YOU TWO WATCHING?
MIDORIYA!!
SIR NIGHTEYE!!

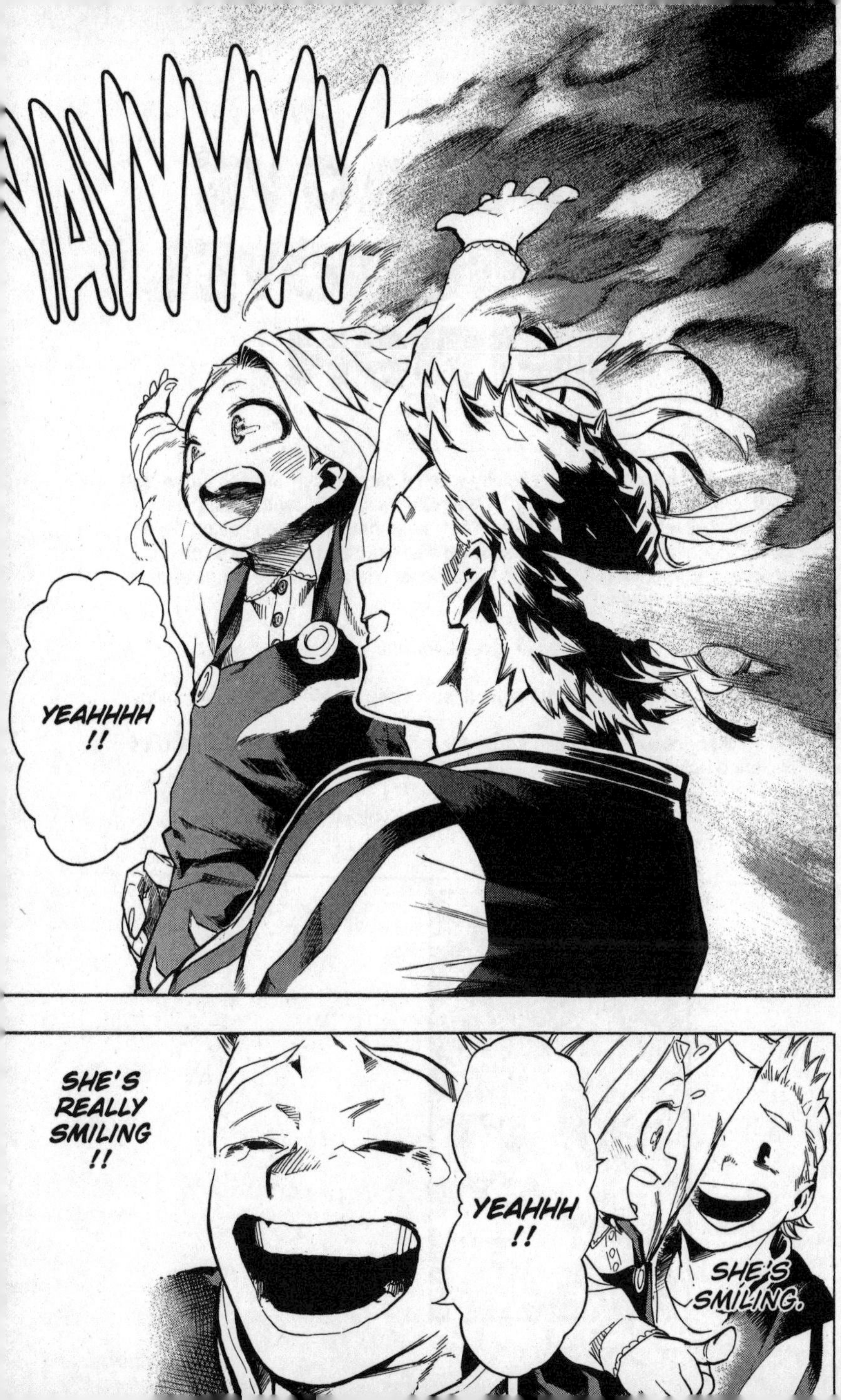
YAYYYYY
YEAHHHH !!
YEAHHH !!
SHE'S SMILING.
SHE'S REALLY SMILING !!

JUMP MAG VS. GRAPHIC NOVEL EDITION

Chapter 182.

This chapter was rough and sketchy when it came out in *Shonen Jump*, and I felt terrible about it. Especially for the readers who follow the story via the weekly chapters. Of all the chapters for this to happen… You couldn't even tell what was going on in some spots. It's all fixed up for this book, of course, and I've even added some additional bits and shifted things around to better fit my original vision.

Jiro's close-up gets a two-page spread, for one.

That's how I originally wanted to do it, so please think of this as an apology.

Still, I liked the version of Jiro I drew for the chapter in the magazine, so it's included below.

"You should do what you want." Thank you, Kyotoku (Jiro's dad).

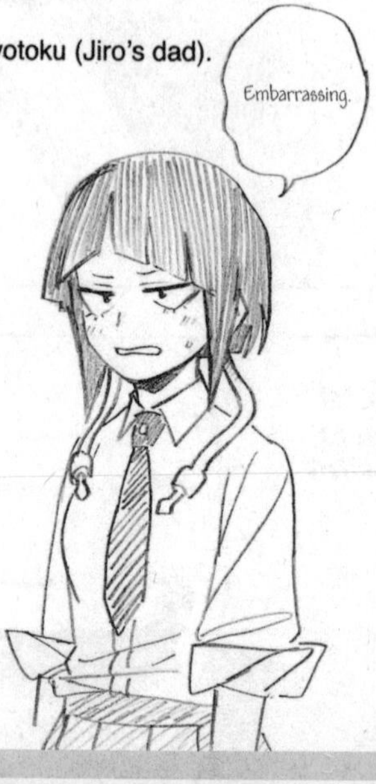
Embarrassing.

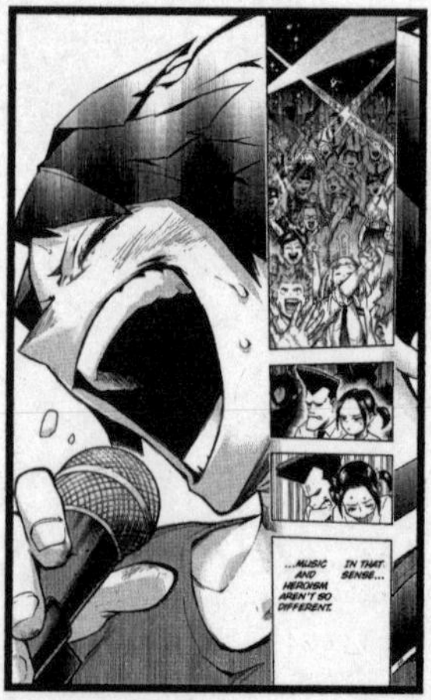
IN THAT SENSE...
...MUSIC AND HEROISM AREN'T SO DIFFERENT.

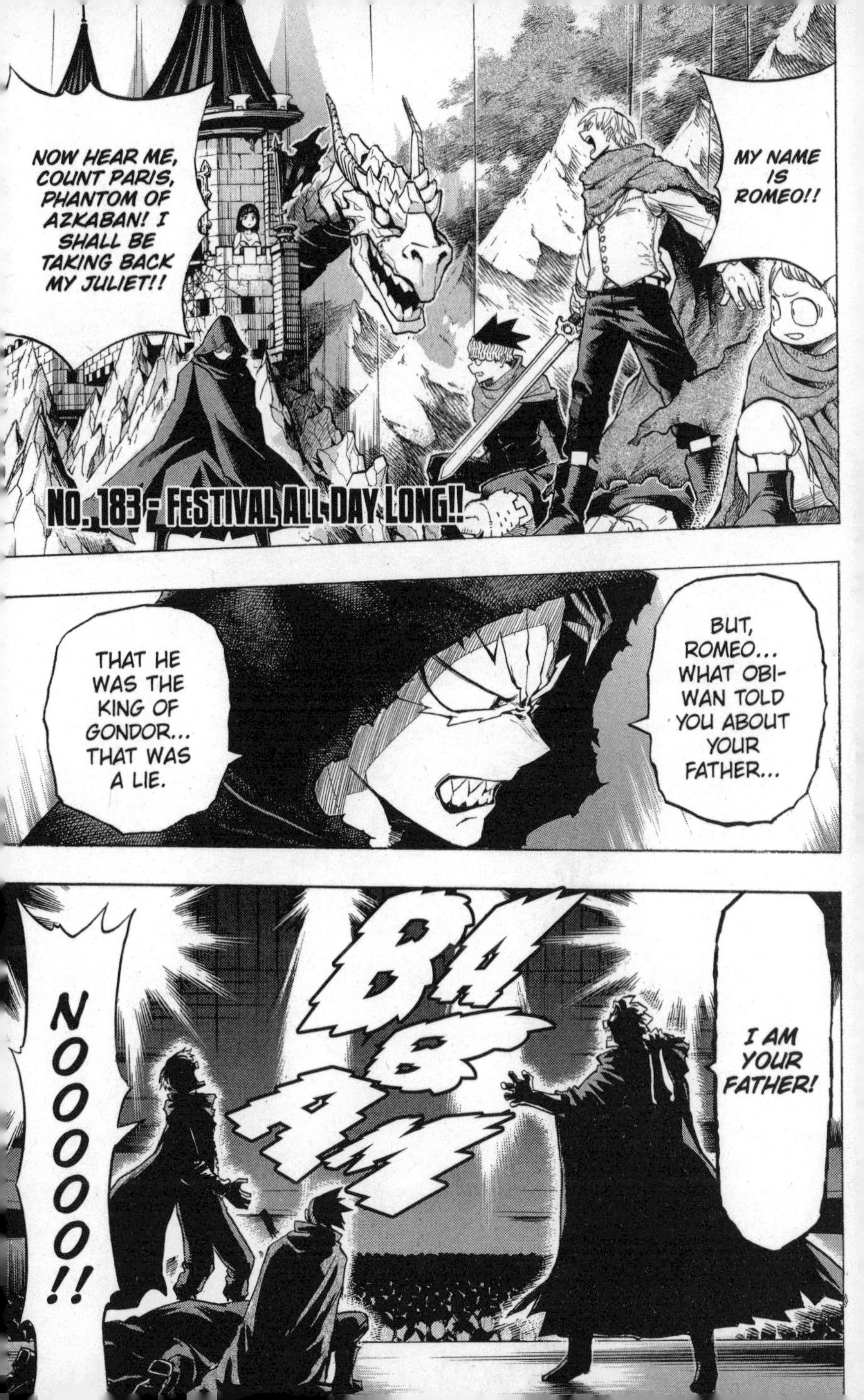
MY NAME IS ROMEO!!
NOW HEAR ME, COUNT PARIS, PHANTOM OF AZKABAN! I SHALL BE TAKING BACK MY JULIET!!
NO. 183 - FESTIVAL ALL DAY LONG!!
BUT, ROMEO... WHAT OBI-WAN TOLD YOU ABOUT YOUR FATHER...
THAT HE WAS THE KING OF GONDOR... THAT WAS A LIE.
I AM YOUR FATHER!
BAAAM
NOOOOOO!!

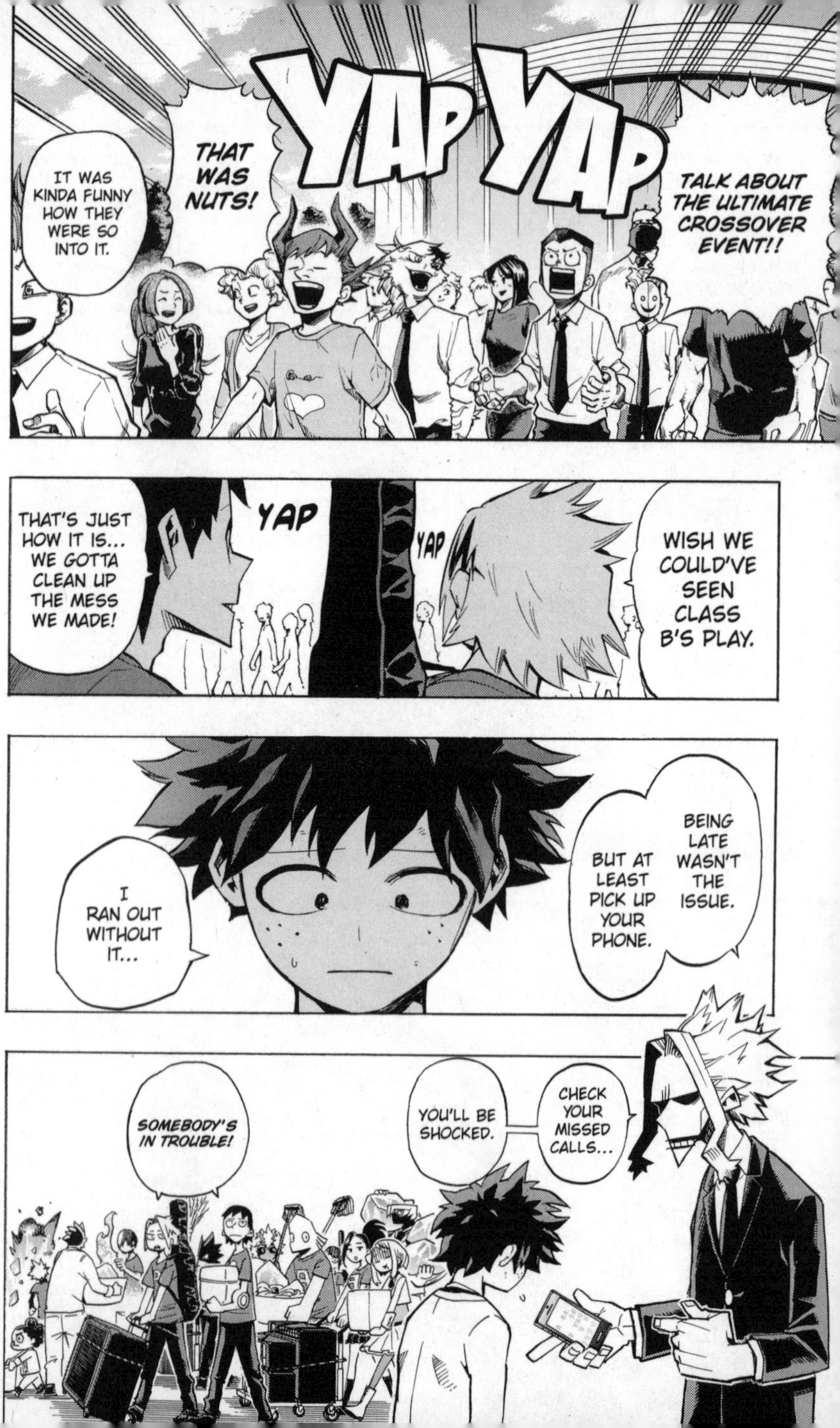
TALK ABOUT THE ULTIMATE CROSSOVER EVENT!!
YAP YAP
THAT WAS NUTS!
IT WAS KINDA FUNNY HOW THEY WERE SO INTO IT.
WISH WE COULD'VE SEEN CLASS B'S PLAY.
YAP
YAP
THAT'S JUST HOW IT IS... WE GOTTA CLEAN UP THE MESS WE MADE!
BEING LATE WASN'T THE ISSUE.
BUT AT LEAST PICK UP YOUR PHONE.
I RAN OUT WITHOUT IT...
CHECK YOUR MISSED CALLS...
YOU'LL BE SHOCKED.
SOMEBODY'S IN TROUBLE!

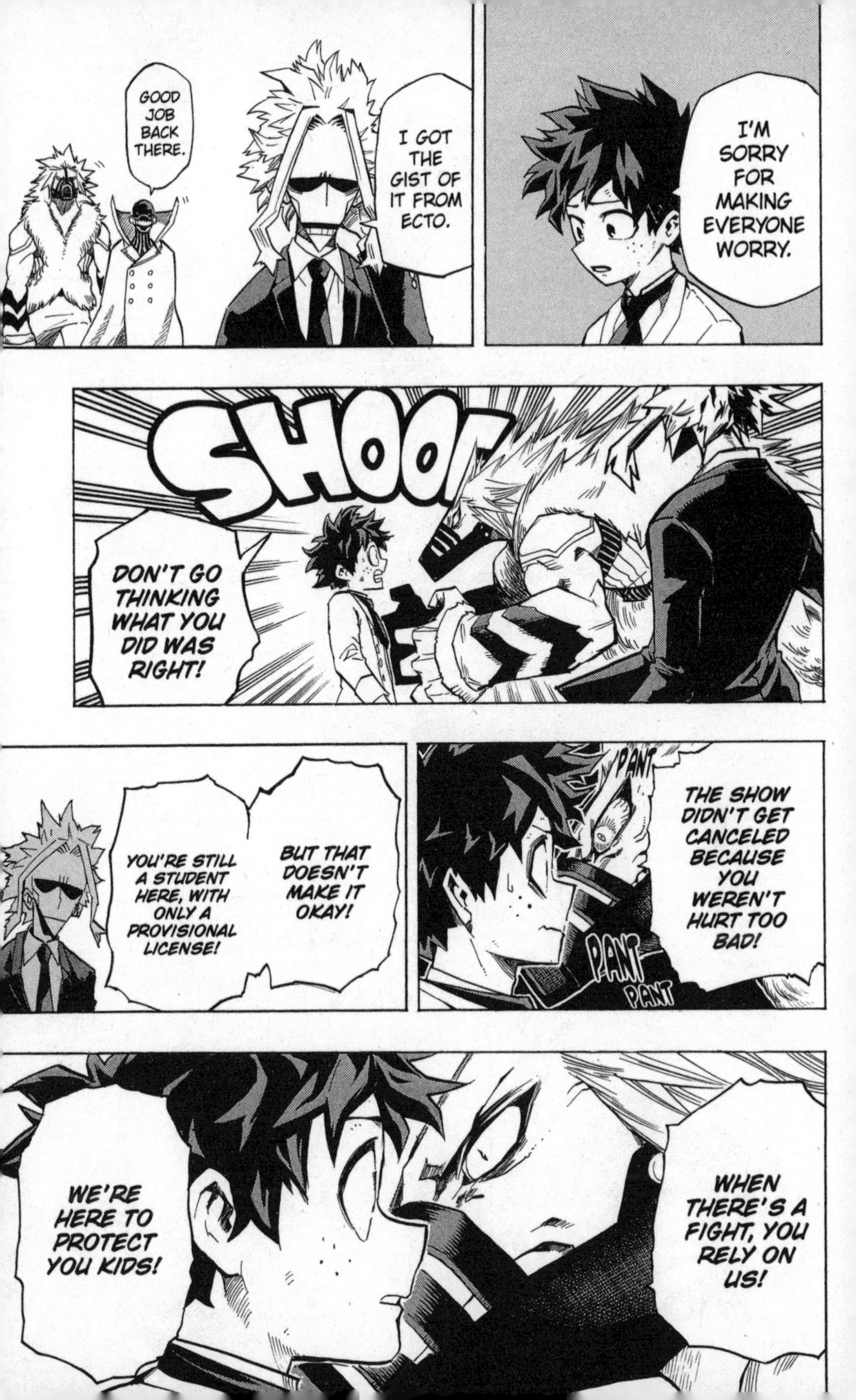
I'M SORRY FOR MAKING EVERYONE WORRY.
I GOT THE GIST OF IT FROM ECTO.
GOOD JOB BACK THERE.
SHOO
DON'T GO THINKING WHAT YOU DID WAS RIGHT!
PANT
THE SHOW DIDN'T GET CANCELED BECAUSE YOU WEREN'T HURT TOO BAD!
PANT
PANT
BUT THAT DOESN'T MAKE IT OKAY!
YOU'RE STILL A STUDENT HERE, WITH ONLY A PROVISIONAL LICENSE!
WHEN THERE'S A FIGHT, YOU RELY ON US!
WE'RE HERE TO PROTECT YOU KIDS!

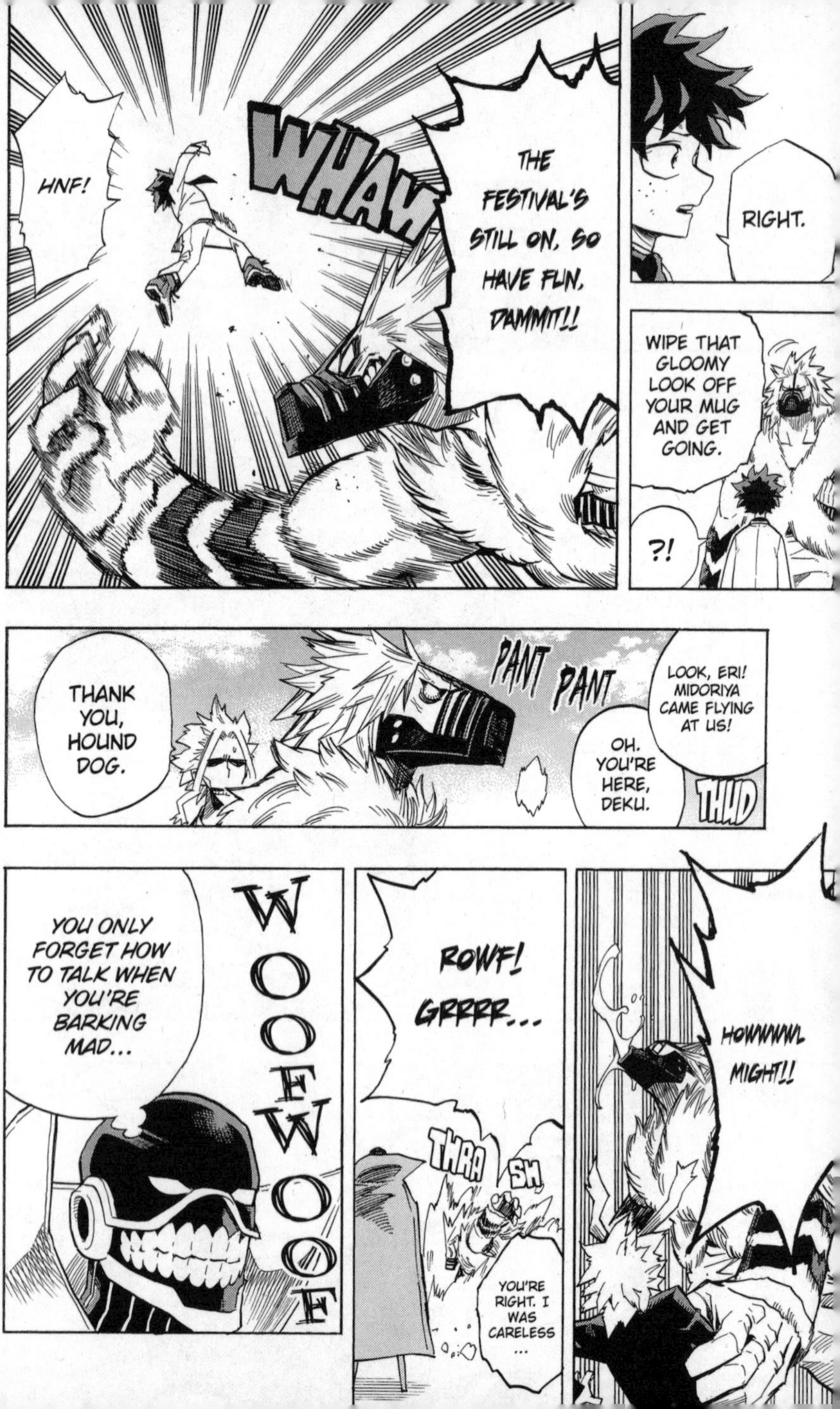
RIGHT.
WIPE THAT GLOOMY LOOK OFF YOUR MUG AND GET GOING.
?!
THE FESTIVAL'S STILL ON, SO HAVE FUN, DAMMIT!!
WHAM
HNF!
THUD
LOOK, ERI! MIDORIYA CAME FLYING AT US!
OH. YOU'RE HERE, DEKU.
PANT PANT
THANK YOU, HOUND DOG.
HOWWWL MIGHT!!
ROWF! GRRRR...
THRASH
YOU'RE RIGHT. I WAS CARELESS ...
WOOF WOOF
YOU ONLY FORGET HOW TO TALK WHEN YOU'RE BARKING MAD...

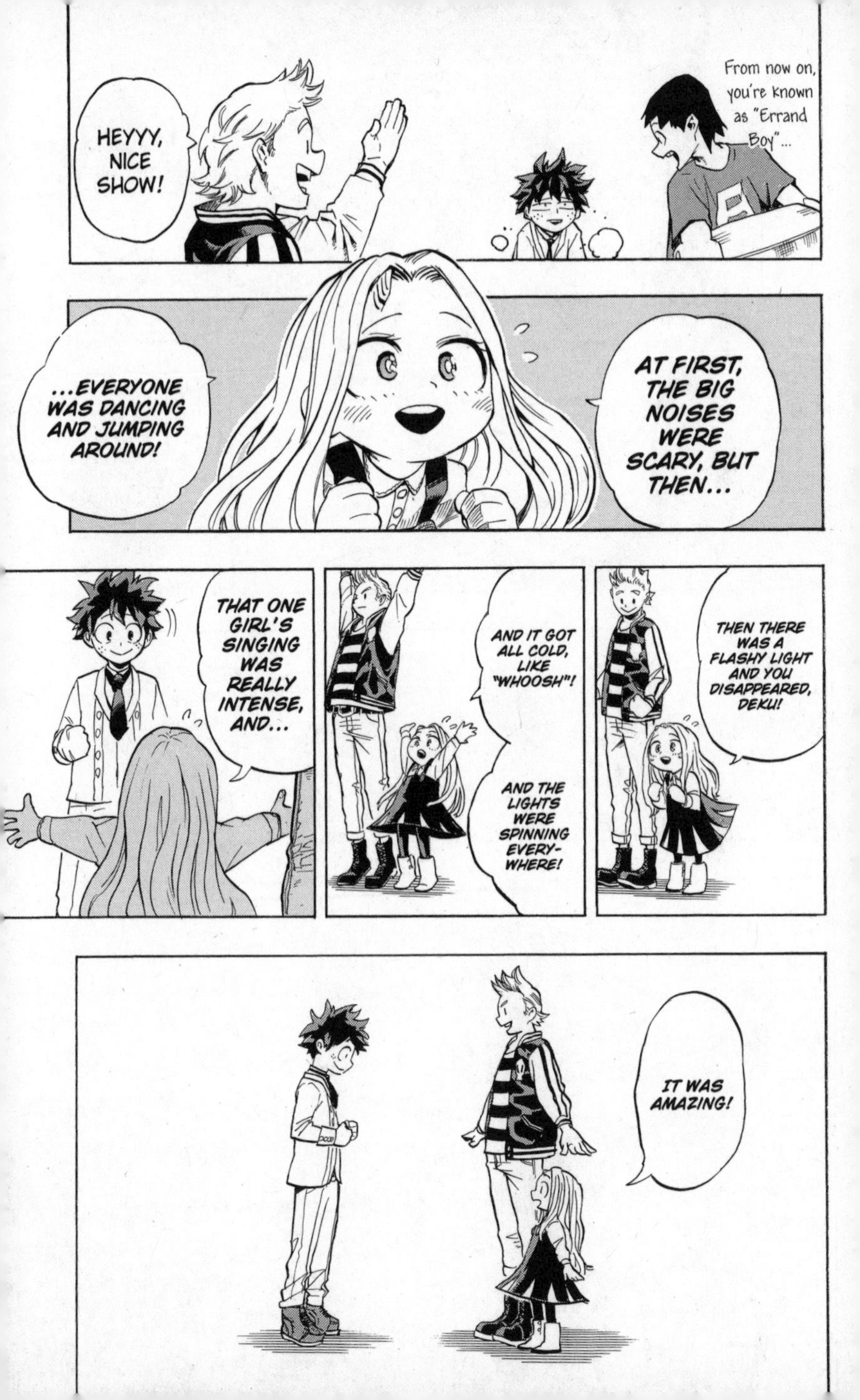
From now on, you're known as "Errand Boy"...
HEYYY, NICE SHOW!
AT FIRST, THE BIG NOISES WERE SCARY, BUT THEN...
...EVERYONE WAS DANCING AND JUMPING AROUND!
THEN THERE WAS A FLASHY LIGHT AND YOU DISAPPEARED, DEKU!
AND IT GOT ALL COLD, LIKE "WHOOSH"!
AND THE LIGHTS WERE SPINNING EVERY-WHERE!
THAT ONE GIRL'S SINGING WAS REALLY INTENSE, AND...
IT WAS AMAZING!

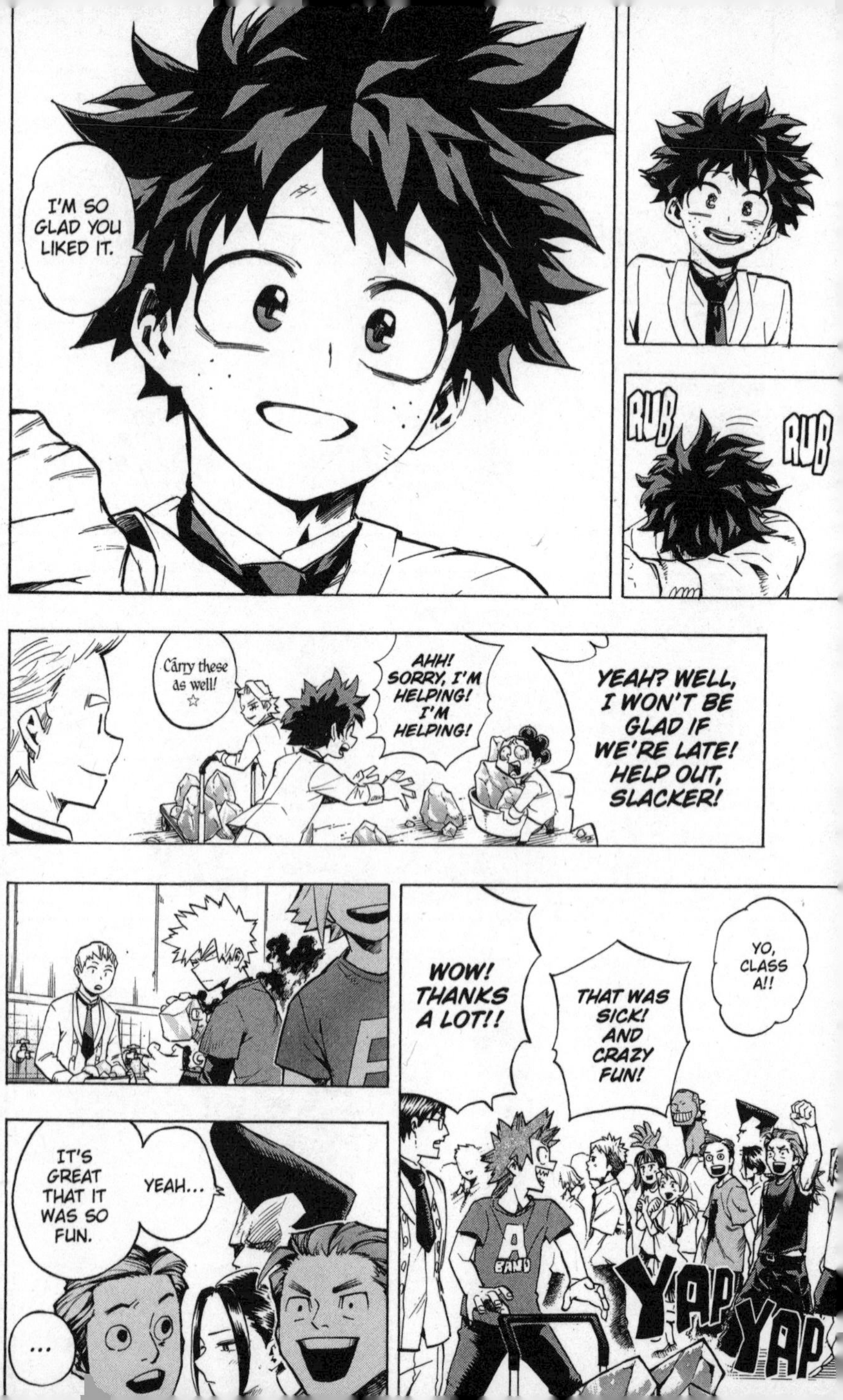
RUB RUB
I'M SO GLAD YOU LIKED IT.
YEAH? WELL, I WON'T BE GLAD IF WE'RE LATE! HELP OUT, SLACKER!
AHH! SORRY, I'M HELPING! I'M HELPING!
Carry these as well! ☆
YO, CLASS A!!
THAT WAS SICK! AND CRAZY FUN!
WOW! THANKS A LOT!!
YAP YAP
YEAH...
IT'S GREAT THAT IT WAS SO FUN.
...

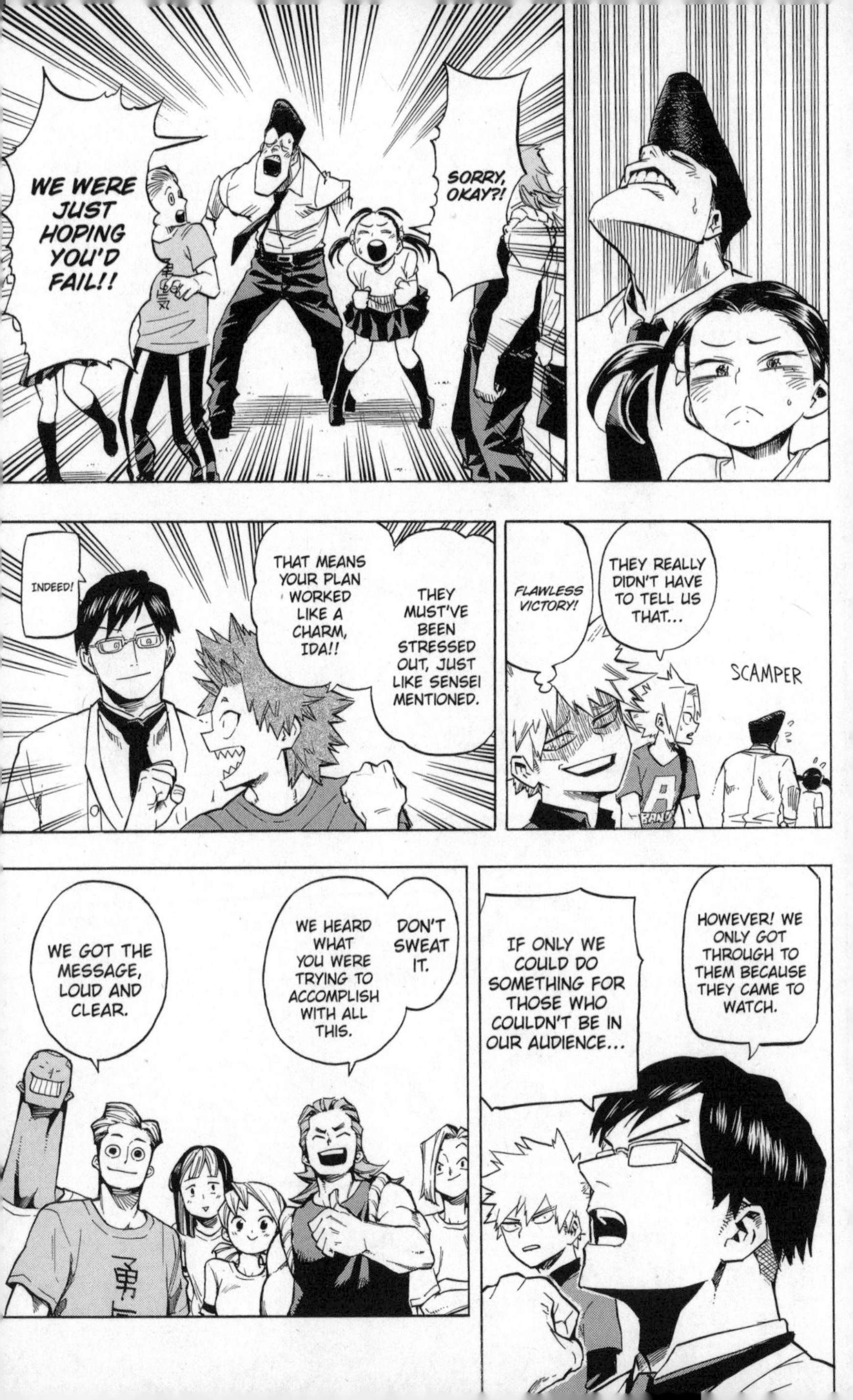
SORRY, OKAY?!
WE WERE JUST HOPING YOU'D FAIL!!
THEY REALLY DIDN'T HAVE TO TELL US THAT...
FLAWLESS VICTORY!
SCAMPER
THEY MUST'VE BEEN STRESSED OUT, JUST LIKE SENSEI MENTIONED.
THAT MEANS YOUR PLAN WORKED LIKE A CHARM, IDA!!
INDEED!
HOWEVER! WE ONLY GOT THROUGH TO THEM BECAUSE THEY CAME TO WATCH.
IF ONLY WE COULD DO SOMETHING FOR THOSE WHO COULDN'T BE IN OUR AUDIENCE...
DON'T SWEAT IT.
WE HEARD WHAT YOU WERE TRYING TO ACCOMPLISH WITH ALL THIS.
WE GOT THE MESSAGE, LOUD AND CLEAR.

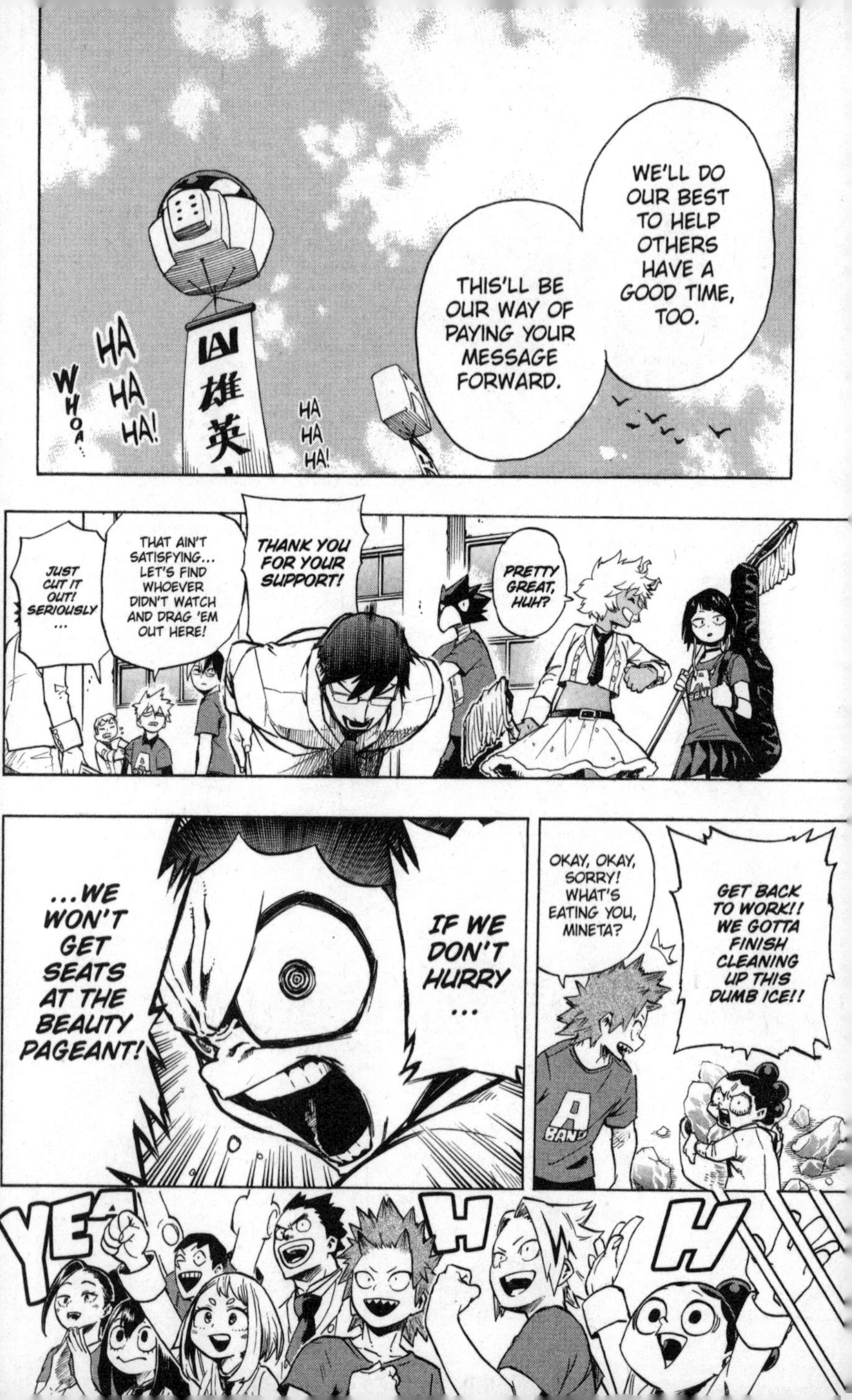
WE'LL DO OUR BEST TO HELP OTHERS HAVE A GOOD TIME, TOO.
THIS'LL BE OUR WAY OF PAYING YOUR MESSAGE FORWARD.
HA HA HA!
雄英
HA HA HA!
WHOA...
PRETTY GREAT, HUH?
THANK YOU FOR YOUR SUPPORT!
THAT AIN'T SATISFYING... LET'S FIND WHOEVER DIDN'T WATCH AND DRAG 'EM OUT HERE!
JUST CUT IT OUT! SERIOUSLY...
GET BACK TO WORK!! WE GOTTA FINISH CLEANING UP THIS DUMB ICE!!
OKAY, OKAY, SORRY! WHAT'S EATING YOU, MINETA?
IF WE DON'T HURRY...
...WE WON'T GET SEATS AT THE BEAUTY PAGEANT!
YEAHHH

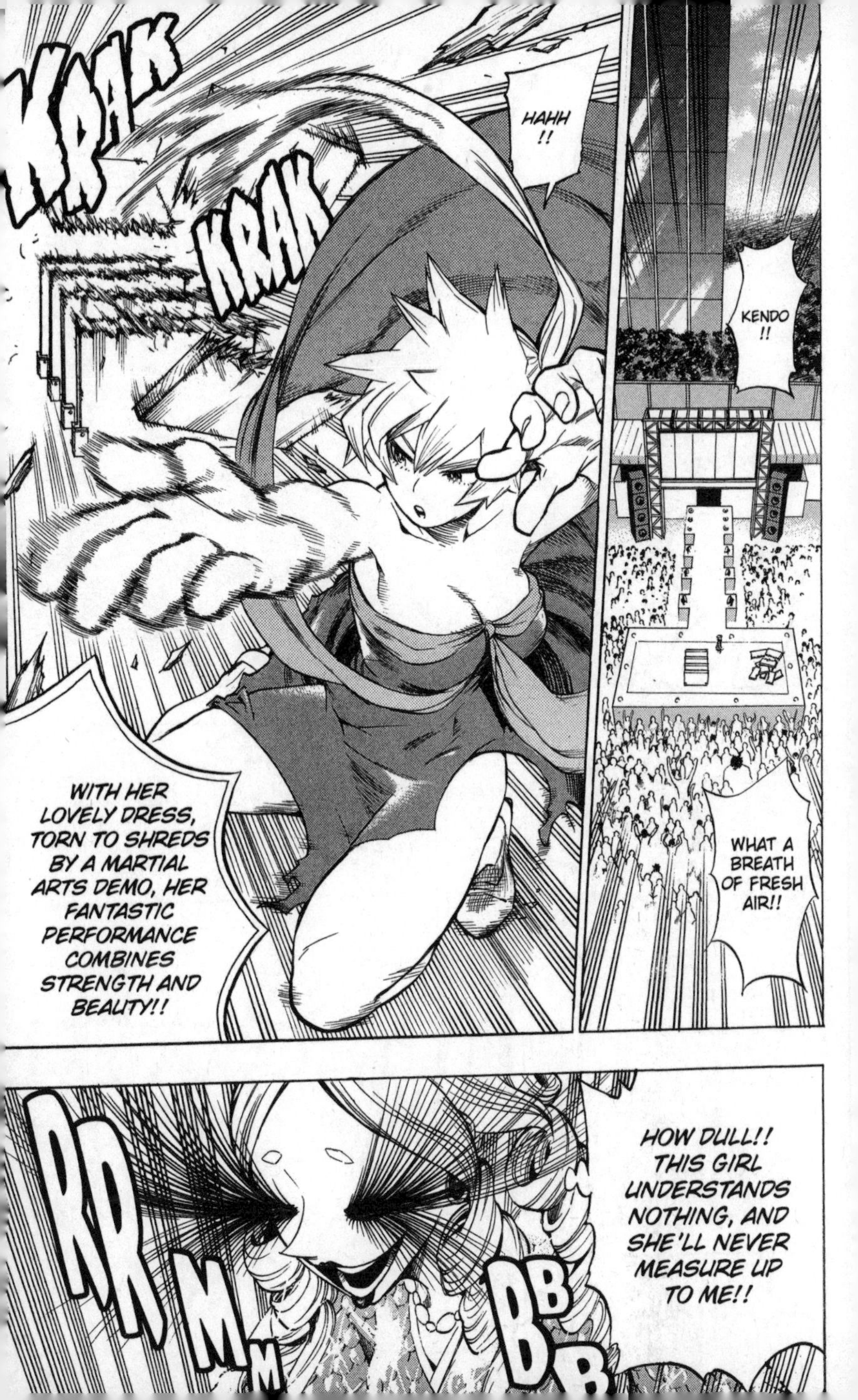
KENDO !!
WHAT A BREATH OF FRESH AIR!!
KRAK
KRAK
HAHH !!
WITH HER LOVELY DRESS, TORN TO SHREDS BY A MARTIAL ARTS DEMO, HER FANTASTIC PERFORMANCE COMBINES STRENGTH AND BEAUTY!!
HOW DULL!! THIS GIRL UNDERSTANDS NOTHING, AND SHE'LL NEVER MEASURE UP TO ME!!
RRMMM
DBBB

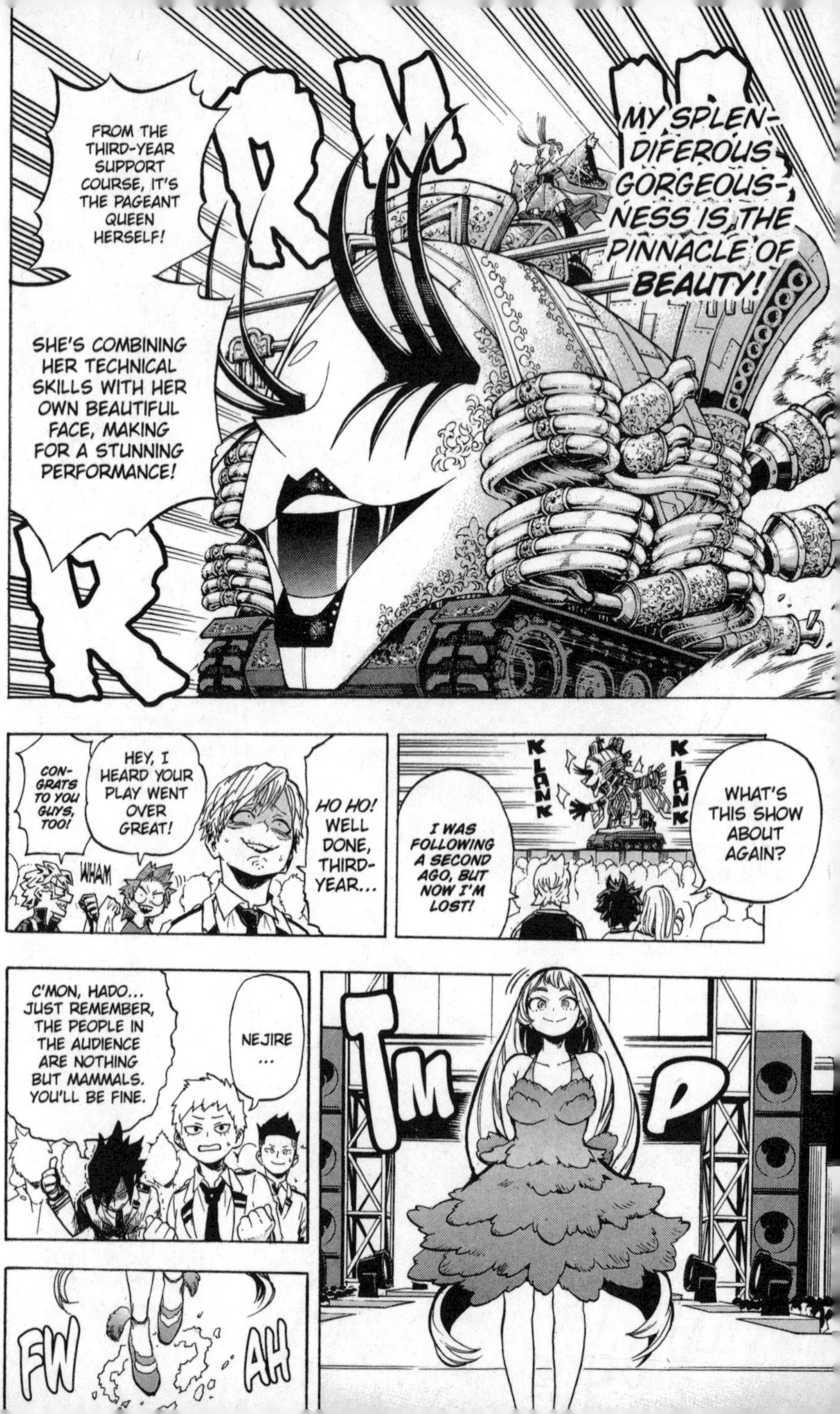
MY SPLENDIFEROUS GORGEOUSNESS IS THE PINNACLE OF BEAUTY!
FROM THE THIRD-YEAR SUPPORT COURSE, IT'S THE PAGEANT QUEEN HERSELF!
SHE'S COMBINING HER TECHNICAL SKILLS WITH HER OWN BEAUTIFUL FACE, MAKING FOR A STUNNING PERFORMANCE!
WHAT'S THIS SHOW ABOUT AGAIN?
KLANK KLANK
I WAS FOLLOWING A SECOND AGO, BUT NOW I'M LOST!
HO HO! WELL DONE, THIRD-YEAR...
HEY, I HEARD YOUR PLAY WENT OVER GREAT!
CON-GRATS TO YOU GUYS, TOO!
WHAM
TMP
NEJIRE...
C'MON, HADO... JUST REMEMBER, THE PEOPLE IN THE AUDIENCE ARE NOTHING BUT MAMMALS. YOU'LL BE FINE.
FWAH

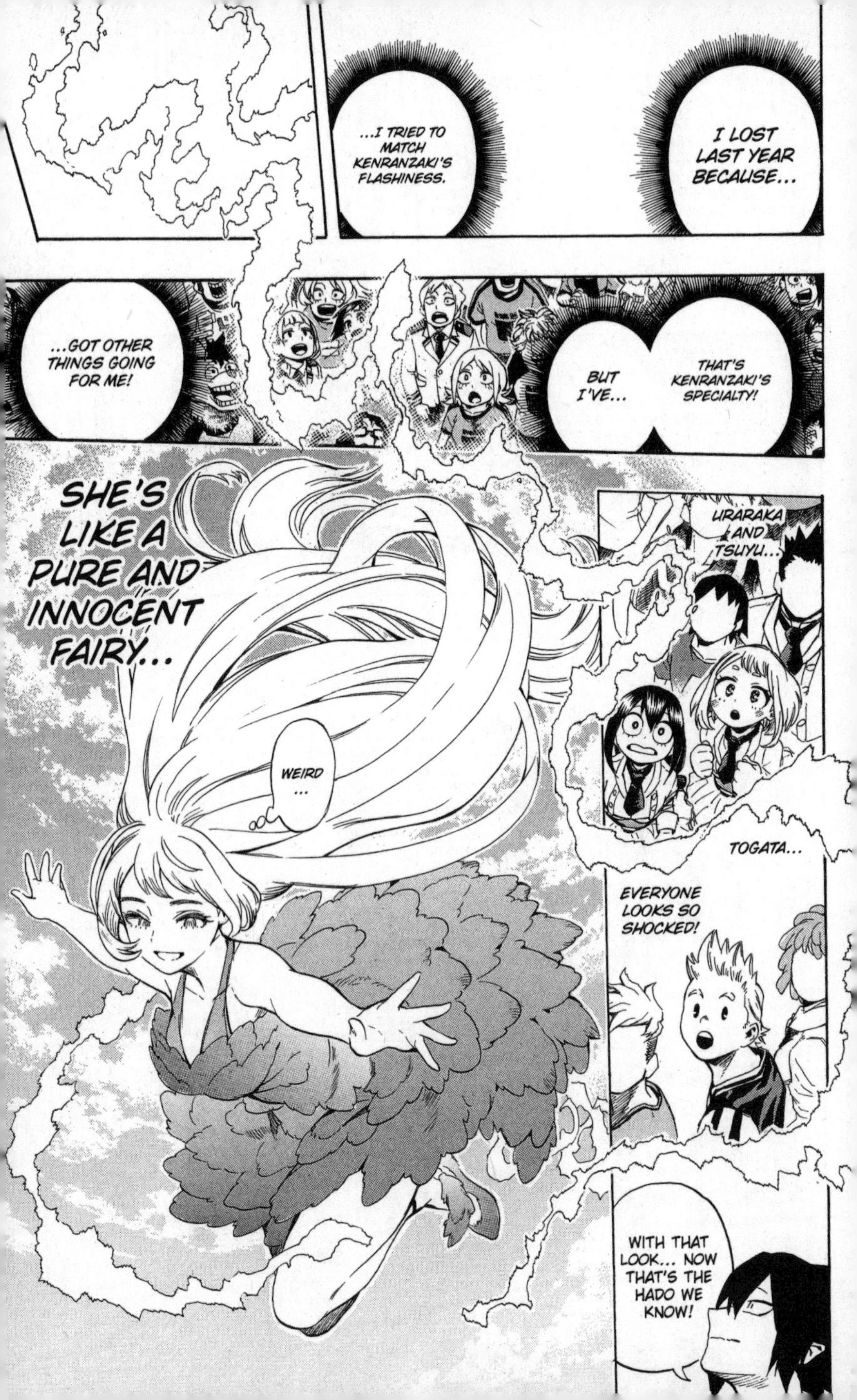
I LOST LAST YEAR BECAUSE...
...I TRIED TO MATCH KENRANZAKI'S FLASHINESS.
THAT'S KENRANZAKI'S SPECIALTY!
BUT I'VE...
...GOT OTHER THINGS GOING FOR ME!
URARAKA AND TSUYU...
TOGATA...
EVERYONE LOOKS SO SHOCKED!
WITH THAT LOOK... NOW THAT'S THE HADO WE KNOW!
SHE'S LIKE A PURE AND INNOCENT FAIRY...
WEIRD ...

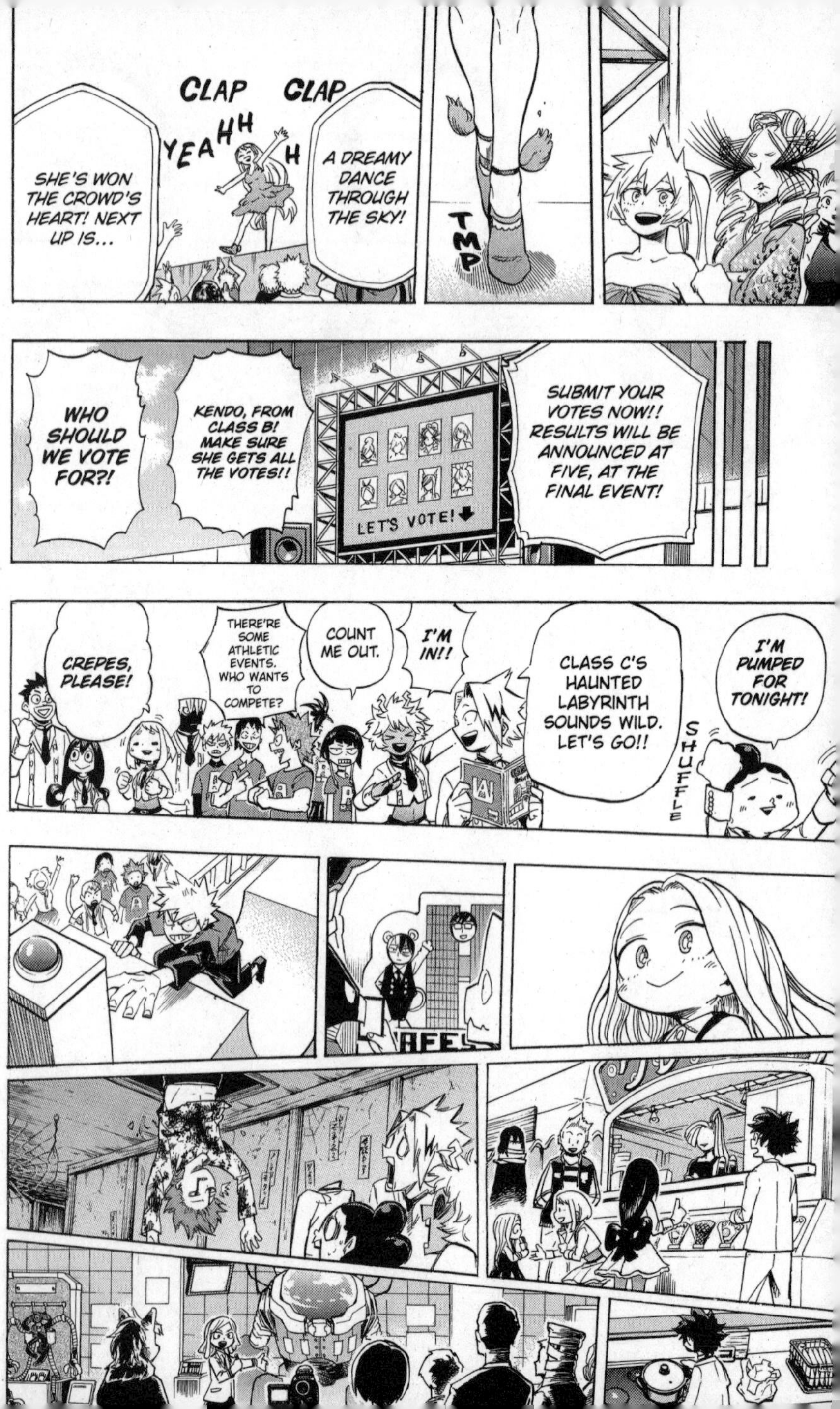
TMP
A DREAMY DANCE THROUGH THE SKY!
CLAP CLAP
YEAHHH
SHE'S WON THE CROWD'S HEART! NEXT UP IS...
SUBMIT YOUR VOTES NOW!! RESULTS WILL BE ANNOUNCED AT FIVE, AT THE FINAL EVENT!
LET'S VOTE!
KENDO, FROM CLASS B! MAKE SURE SHE GETS ALL THE VOTES!!
WHO SHOULD WE VOTE FOR?!
I'M PUMPED FOR TONIGHT!
SHUFFLE
CLASS C'S HAUNTED LABYRINTH SOUNDS WILD. LET'S GO!!
I'M IN!!
COUNT ME OUT.
THERE'RE SOME ATHLETIC EVENTS. WHO WANTS TO COMPETE?
CREPES, PLEASE!

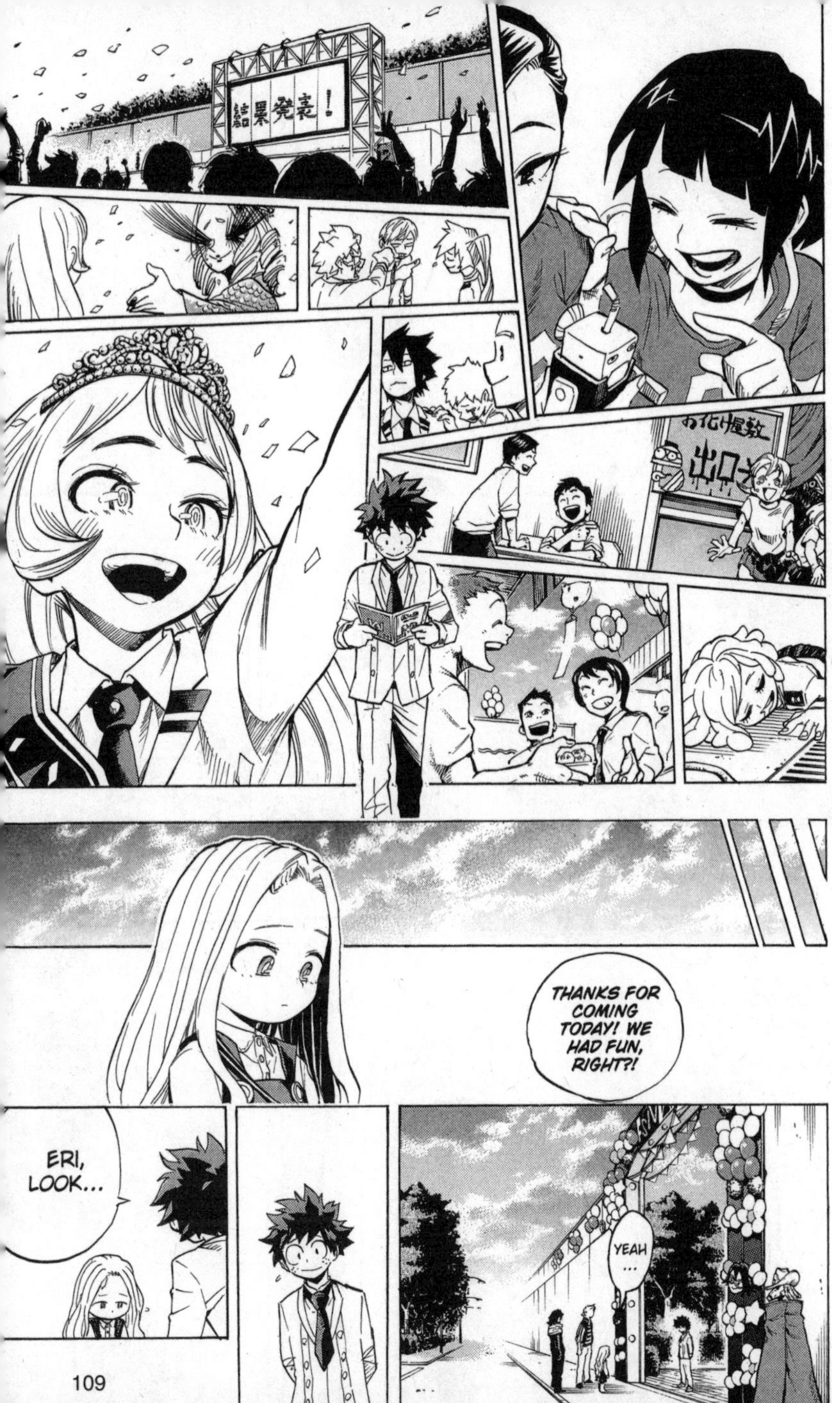
結果発表！
お化け屋敷
出口
THANKS FOR COMING TODAY! WE HAD FUN, RIGHT?!
YEAH ...
ERI, LOOK...

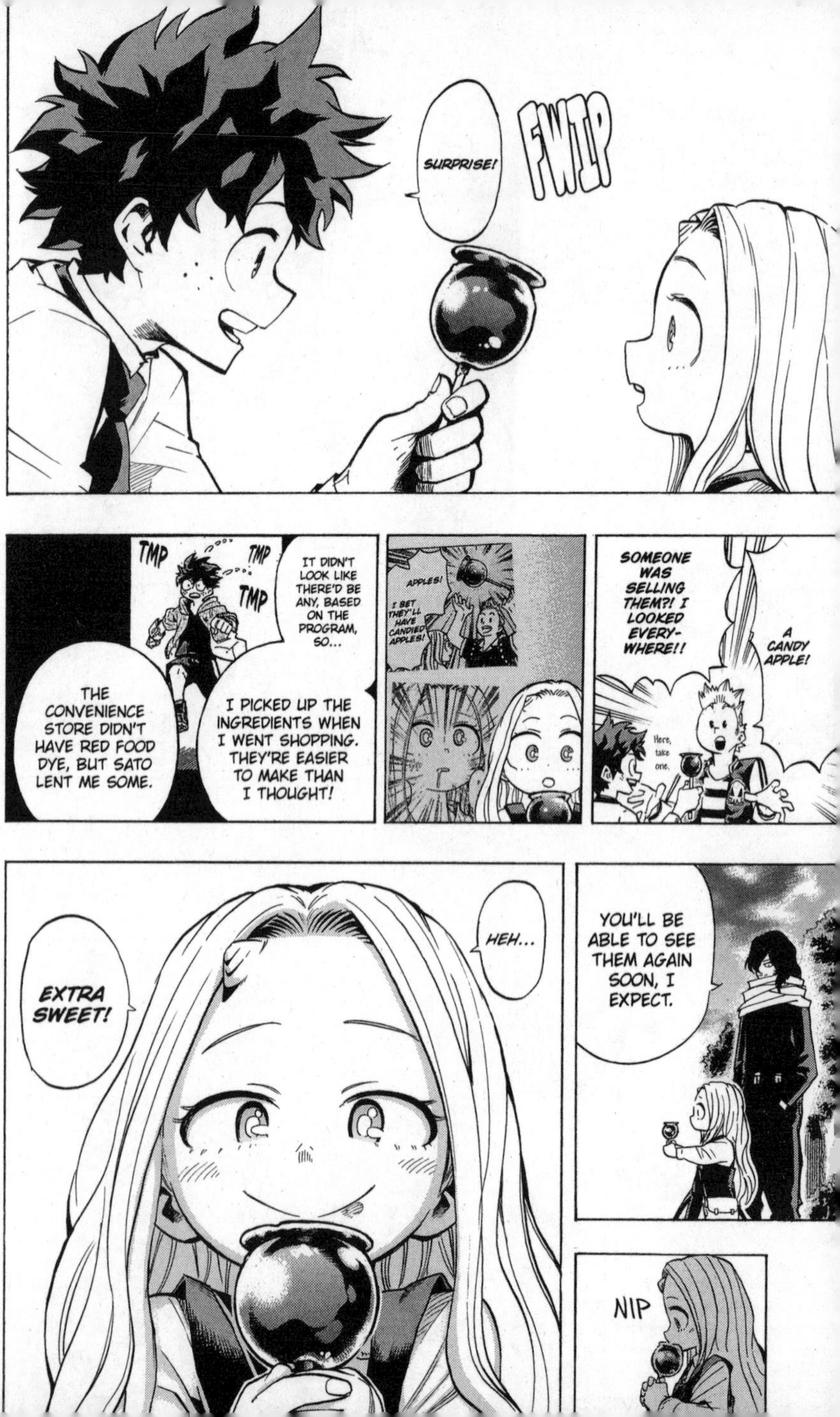
SURPRISE!
FWIP
A CANDY APPLE!
SOMEONE WAS SELLING THEM?! I LOOKED EVERY-WHERE!!
Here, take one.
APPLES!
I BET THEY'LL HAVE CANDIED APPLES!
IT DIDN'T LOOK LIKE THERE'D BE ANY, BASED ON THE PROGRAM, SO...
TMP
TMP
TMP
I PICKED UP THE INGREDIENTS WHEN I WENT SHOPPING. THEY'RE EASIER TO MAKE THAN I THOUGHT!
THE CONVENIENCE STORE DIDN'T HAVE RED FOOD DYE, BUT SATO LENT ME SOME.
YOU'LL BE ABLE TO SEE THEM AGAIN SOON, I EXPECT.
NIP
HEH...
EXTRA SWEET!

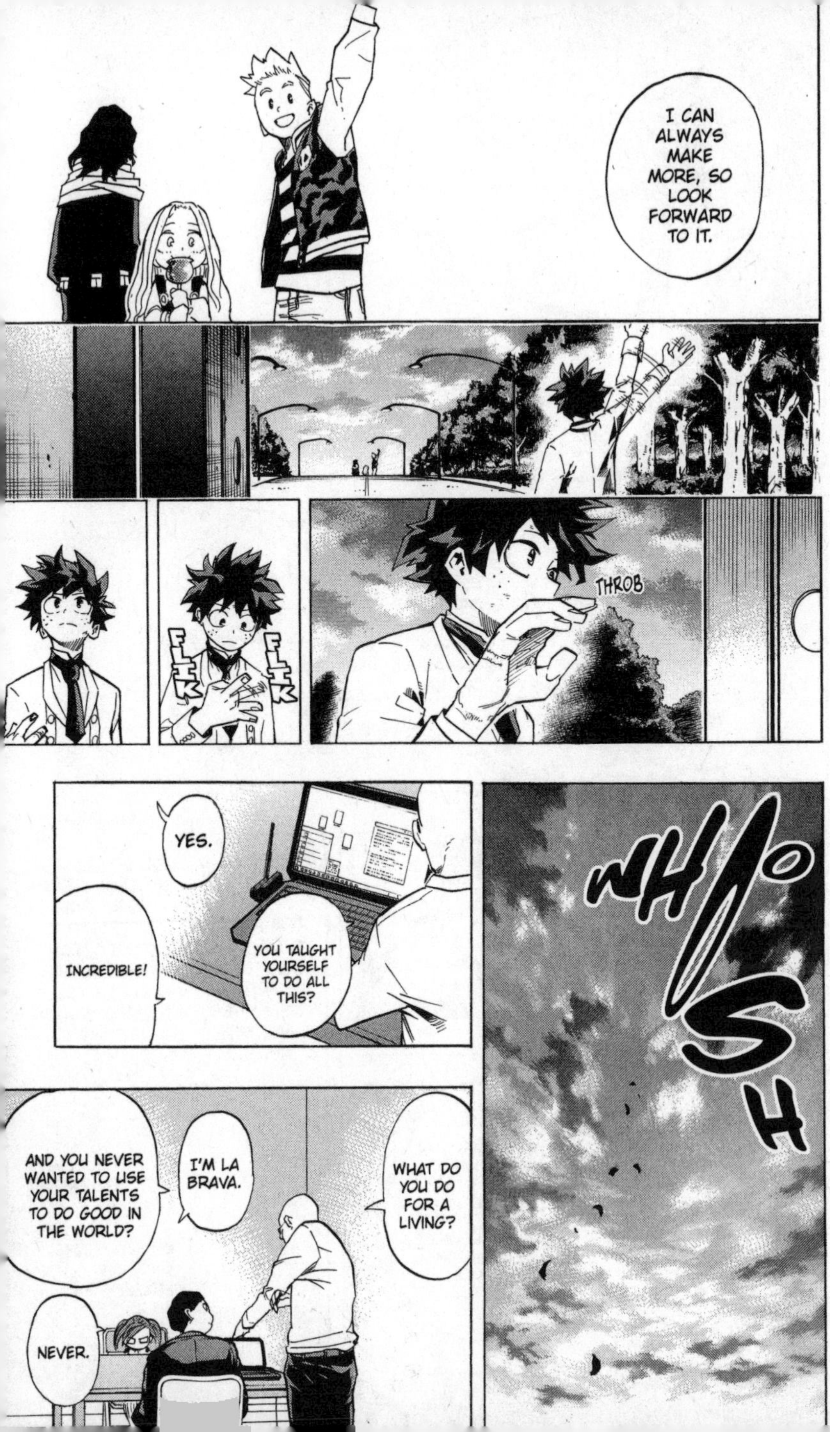
I CAN ALWAYS MAKE MORE, SO LOOK FORWARD TO IT.
THROB
FLIK FLIK
WHOOSH
INCREDIBLE!
YOU TAUGHT YOURSELF TO DO ALL THIS?
YES.
WHAT DO YOU DO FOR A LIVING?
I'M LA BRAVA.
AND YOU NEVER WANTED TO USE YOUR TALENTS TO DO GOOD IN THE WORLD?
NEVER.

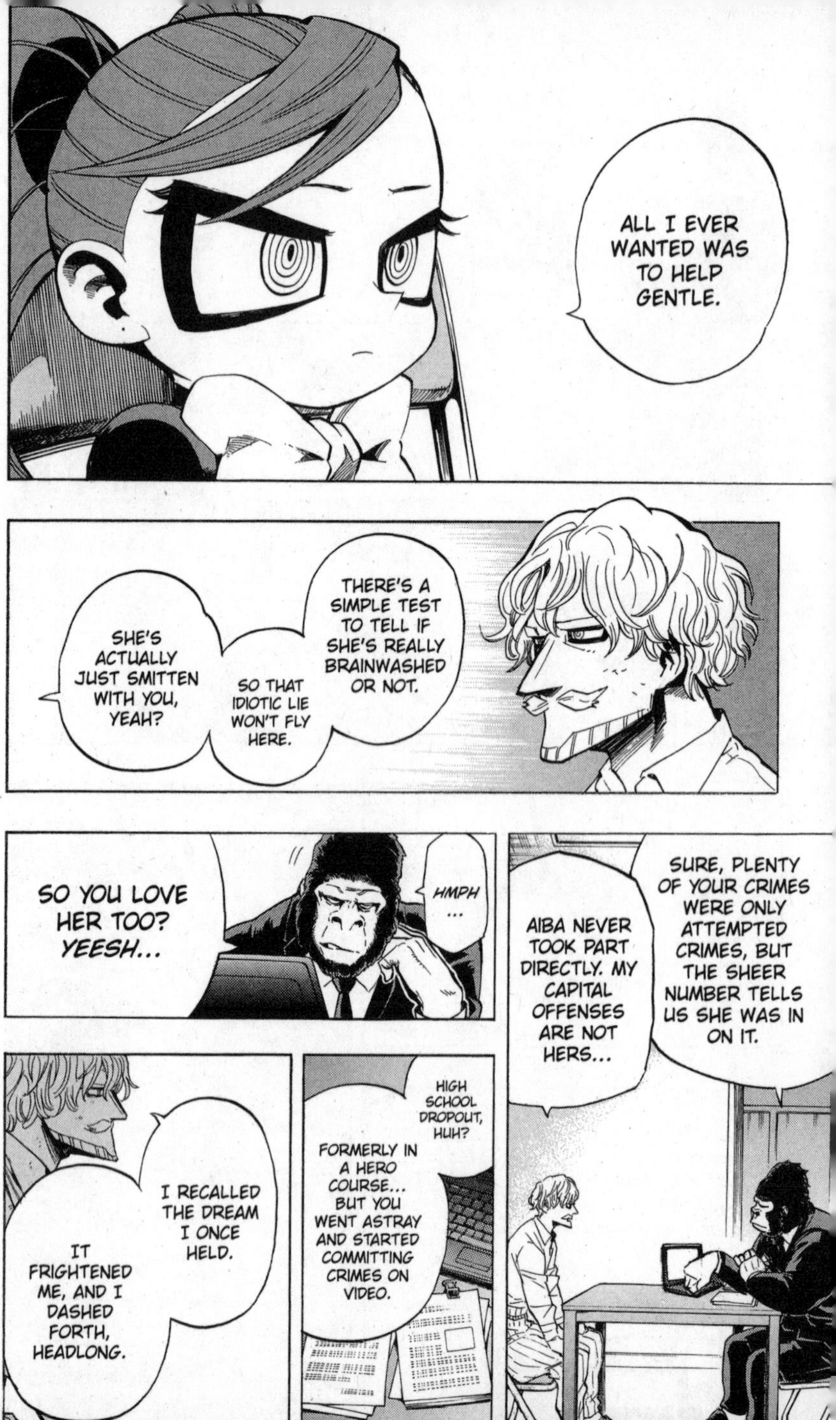
ALL I EVER WANTED WAS TO HELP GENTLE.
THERE'S A SIMPLE TEST TO TELL IF SHE'S REALLY BRAINWASHED OR NOT.
SO THAT IDIOTIC LIE WON'T FLY HERE.
SHE'S ACTUALLY JUST SMITTEN WITH YOU, YEAH?
SURE, PLENTY OF YOUR CRIMES WERE ONLY ATTEMPTED CRIMES, BUT THE SHEER NUMBER TELLS US SHE WAS IN ON IT.
AIBA NEVER TOOK PART DIRECTLY. MY CAPITAL OFFENSES ARE NOT HERS...
HMPH ...
SO YOU LOVE HER TOO? *YEESH...*
HIGH SCHOOL DROPOUT, HUH?
FORMERLY IN A HERO COURSE... BUT YOU WENT ASTRAY AND STARTED COMMITTING CRIMES ON VIDEO.
I RECALLED THE DREAM I ONCE HELD.
IT FRIGHTENED ME, AND I DASHED FORTH, HEADLONG.

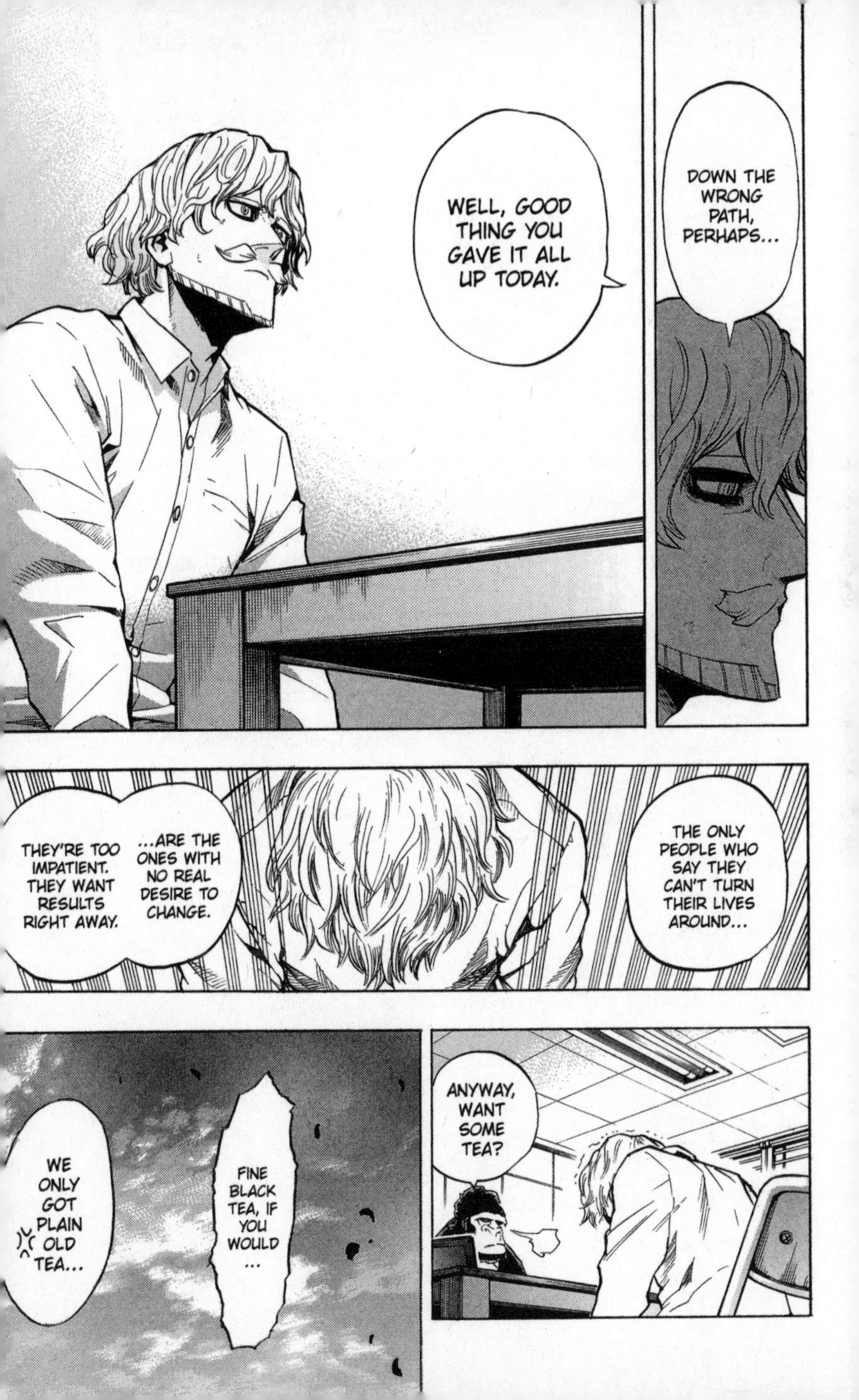
DOWN THE WRONG PATH, PERHAPS...
WELL, GOOD THING YOU GAVE IT ALL UP TODAY.
THE ONLY PEOPLE WHO SAY THEY CAN'T TURN THEIR LIVES AROUND...
...ARE THE ONES WITH NO REAL DESIRE TO CHANGE.
THEY'RE TOO IMPATIENT. THEY WANT RESULTS RIGHT AWAY.
ANYWAY, WANT SOME TEA?
FINE BLACK TEA, IF YOU WOULD...
WE ONLY GOT PLAIN OLD TEA...

YUYU HAYA [18]

THE UNIFORM

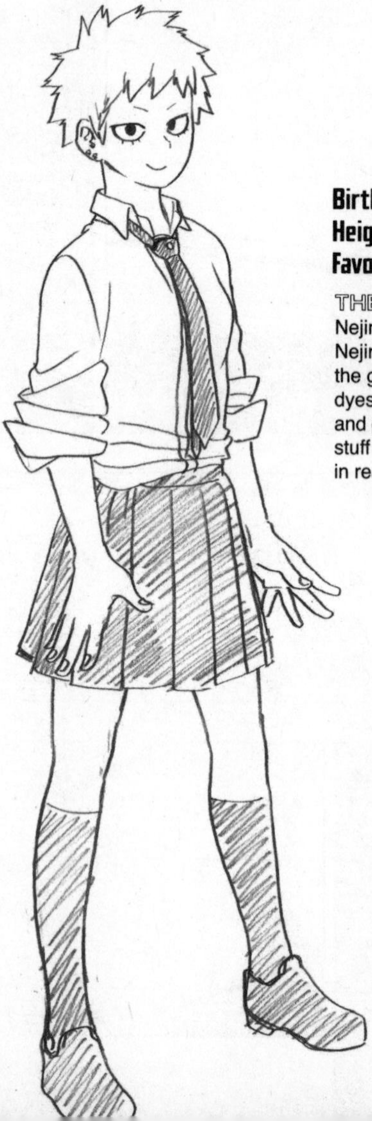

Birthday: 9/10
Height: 160 cm
Favorite Things: Everything cute

THE SUPPLEMENT

Nejire's good pal, who thinks Nejire is the cutest thing in the galaxy. Useless info: she dyes her hair, has piercings and generally does stylish stuff that wouldn't be allowed in real life.

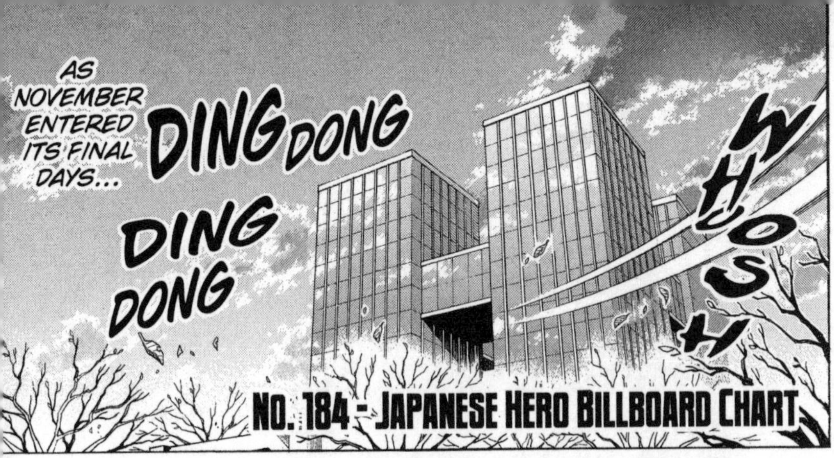
AS NOVEMBER ENTERED ITS FINAL DAYS...
DING DONG
DING DONG
WHOOSH
No. 184 - JAPANESE HERO BILLBOARD CHART
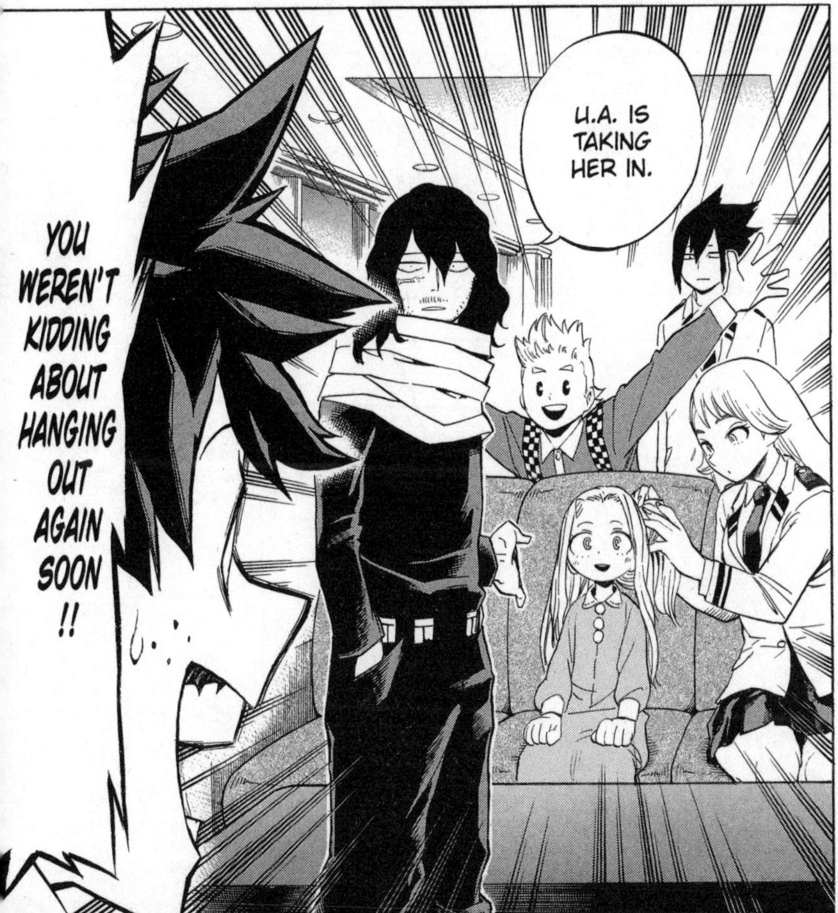
U.A. IS TAKING HER IN.
YOU WEREN'T KIDDING ABOUT HANGING OUT AGAIN SOON!!

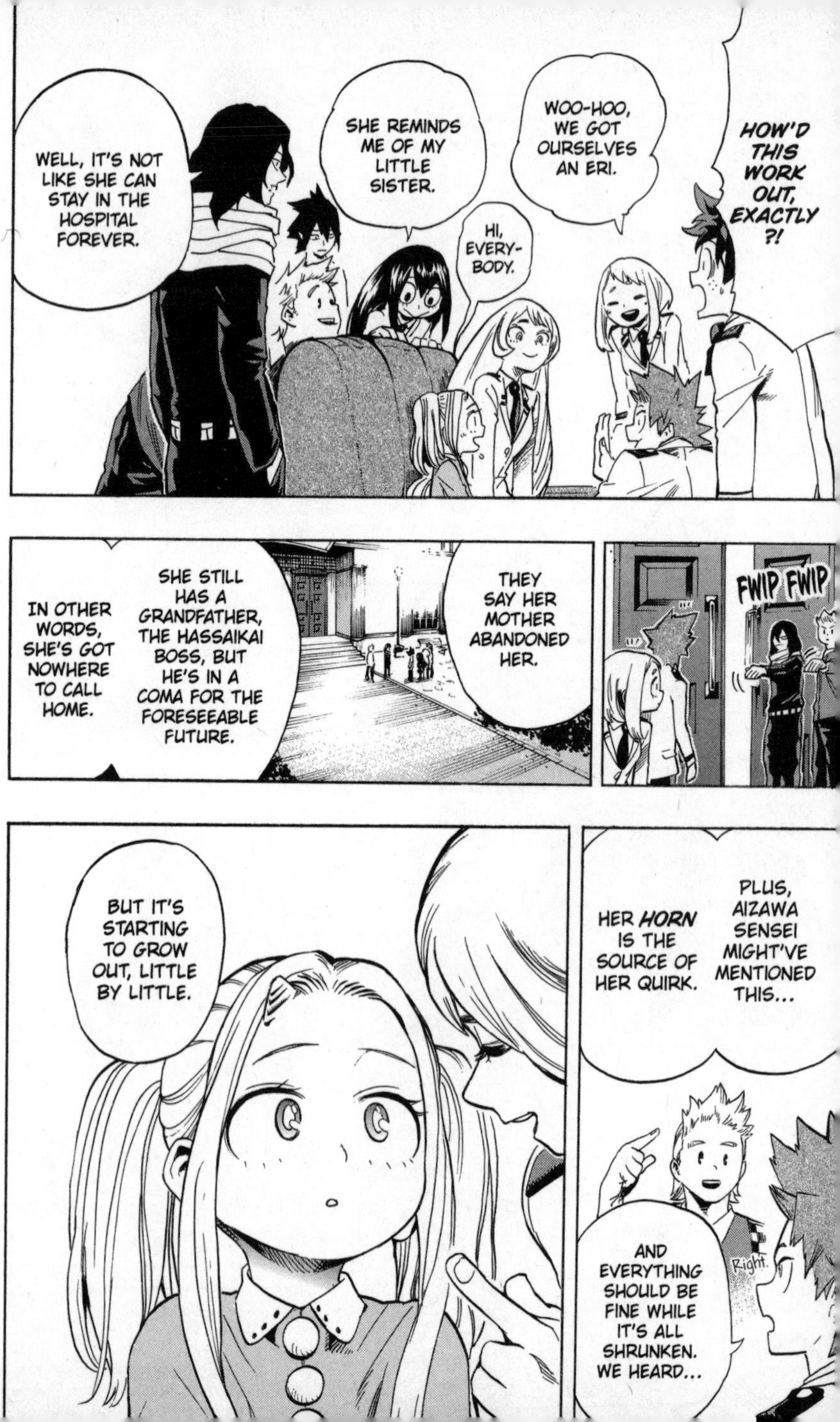
HOW'D THIS WORK OUT, EXACTLY?!
WOO-HOO, WE GOT OURSELVES AN ERI.
HI, EVERYBODY.
SHE REMINDS ME OF MY LITTLE SISTER.
WELL, IT'S NOT LIKE SHE CAN STAY IN THE HOSPITAL FOREVER.
FWIP FWIP
THEY SAY HER MOTHER ABANDONED HER.
SHE STILL HAS A GRANDFATHER, THE HASSAIKAI BOSS, BUT HE'S IN A COMA FOR THE FORESEEABLE FUTURE.
IN OTHER WORDS, SHE'S GOT NOWHERE TO CALL HOME.
PLUS, AIZAWA SENSEI MIGHT'VE MENTIONED THIS...
HER HORN IS THE SOURCE OF HER QUIRK.
Right.
AND EVERYTHING SHOULD BE FINE WHILE IT'S ALL SHRUNKEN. WE HEARD...
BUT IT'S STARTING TO GROW OUT, LITTLE BY LITTLE.

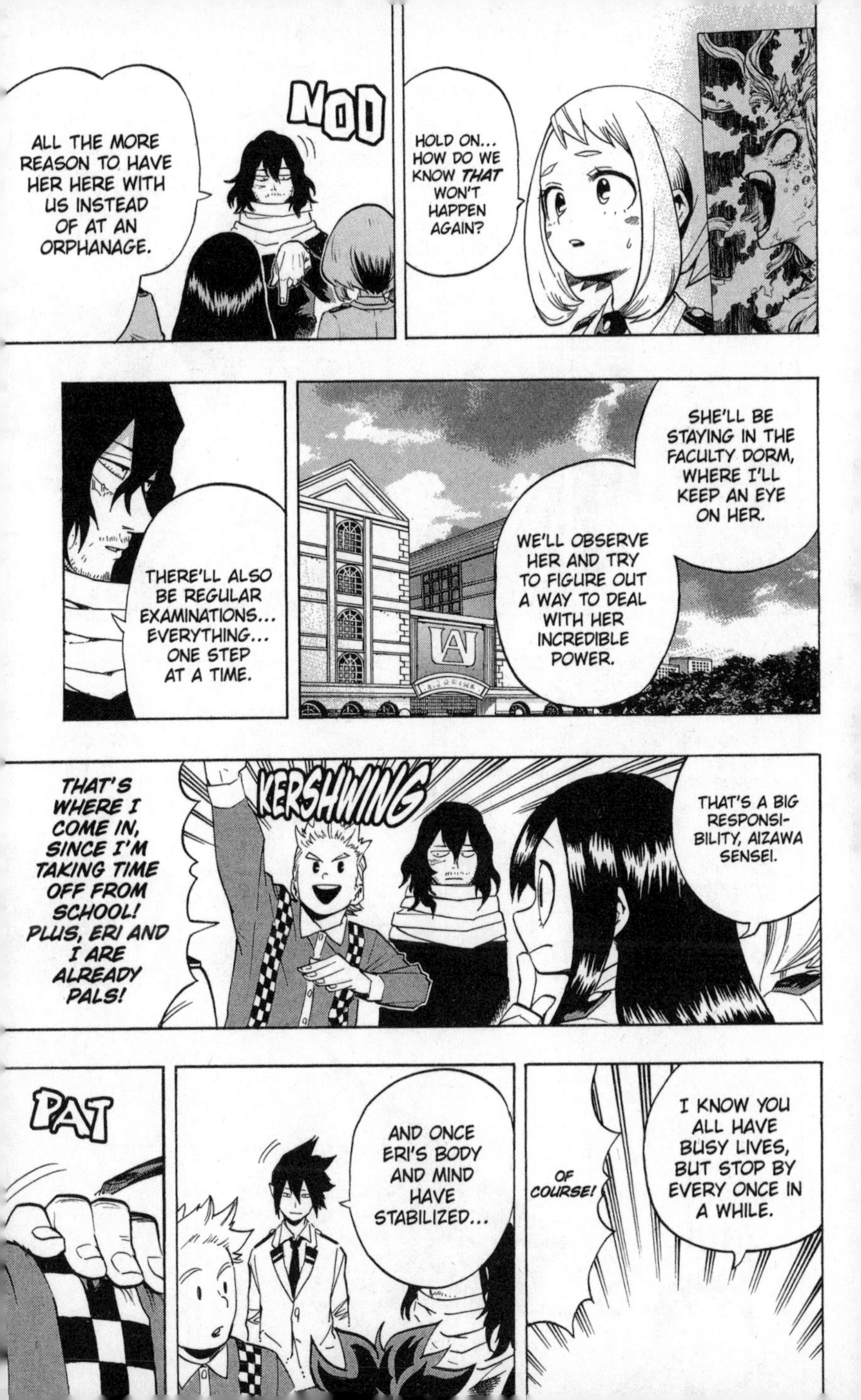
HOLD ON... HOW DO WE KNOW THAT WON'T HAPPEN AGAIN?
NOD
ALL THE MORE REASON TO HAVE HER HERE WITH US INSTEAD OF AT AN ORPHANAGE.
SHE'LL BE STAYING IN THE FACULTY DORM, WHERE I'LL KEEP AN EYE ON HER.
WE'LL OBSERVE HER AND TRY TO FIGURE OUT A WAY TO DEAL WITH HER INCREDIBLE POWER.
THERE'LL ALSO BE REGULAR EXAMINATIONS... EVERYTHING... ONE STEP AT A TIME.
THAT'S A BIG RESPONSI-BILITY, AIZAWA SENSEI.
KERSHWING
THAT'S WHERE I COME IN, SINCE I'M TAKING TIME OFF FROM SCHOOL! PLUS, ERI AND I ARE ALREADY PALS!
I KNOW YOU ALL HAVE BUSY LIVES, BUT STOP BY EVERY ONCE IN A WHILE.
OF COURSE!
AND ONCE ERI'S BODY AND MIND HAVE STABILIZED...
PAT

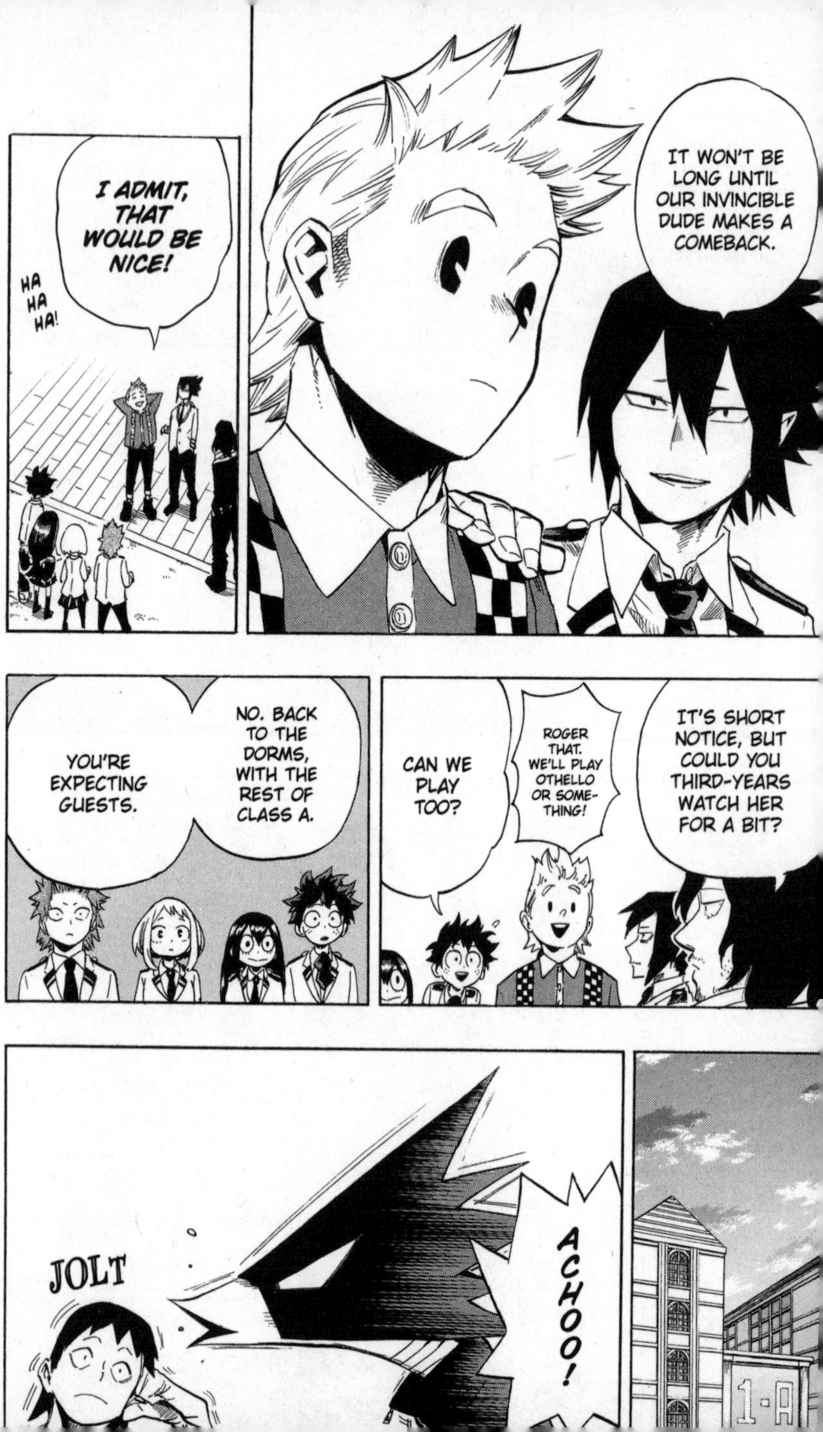
IT WON'T BE LONG UNTIL OUR INVINCIBLE DUDE MAKES A COMEBACK.
I ADMIT, THAT WOULD BE NICE!
HA HA HA!
IT'S SHORT NOTICE, BUT COULD YOU THIRD-YEARS WATCH HER FOR A BIT?
ROGER THAT. WE'LL PLAY OTHELLO OR SOME-THING!
CAN WE PLAY TOO?
NO. BACK TO THE DORMS, WITH THE REST OF CLASS A.
YOU'RE EXPECTING GUESTS.
1-A
ACHOO!
JOLT

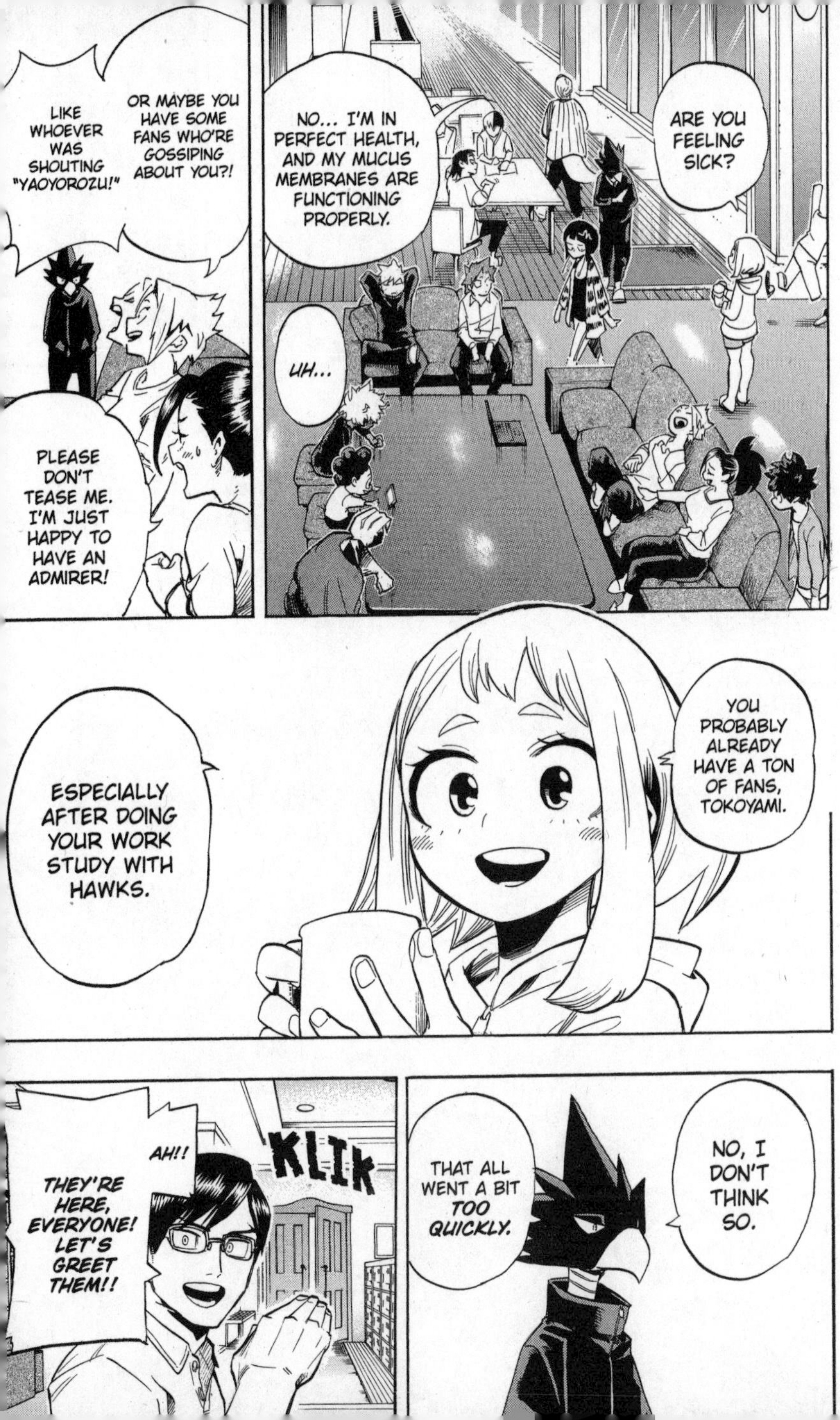
ARE YOU FEELING SICK?
NO... I'M IN PERFECT HEALTH, AND MY MUCUS MEMBRANES ARE FUNCTIONING PROPERLY.
UH...
OR MAYBE YOU HAVE SOME FANS WHO'RE GOSSIPING ABOUT YOU?!
LIKE WHOEVER WAS SHOUTING "YAOYOROZU!"
PLEASE DON'T TEASE ME. I'M JUST HAPPY TO HAVE AN ADMIRER!
YOU PROBABLY ALREADY HAVE A TON OF FANS, TOKOYAMI.
ESPECIALLY AFTER DOING YOUR WORK STUDY WITH HAWKS.
NO, I DON'T THINK SO.
THAT ALL WENT A BIT *TOO QUICKLY.*
KLIK
AH!!
THEY'RE HERE, EVERYONE! LET'S GREET THEM!!

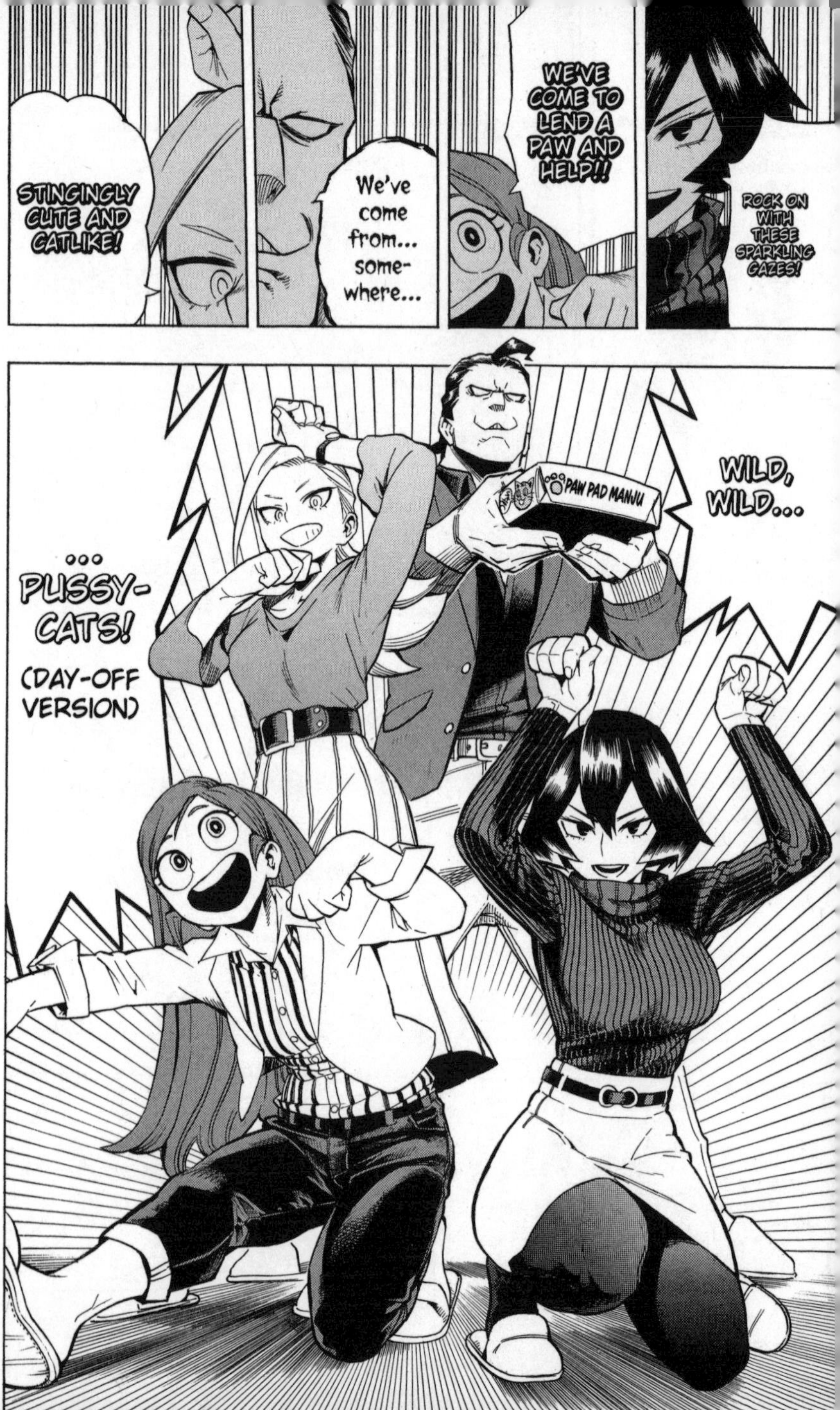
ROCK ON WITH THESE SPARKLING GAZES!
WE'VE COME TO LEND A PAW AND HELP!!
We've come from... some-where...
STINGINGLY CUTE AND CATLIKE!
WILD, WILD...
PAW PAD MANJU
...PUSSY-CATS!
(DAY-OFF VERSION)

I HOPE MY LITTLE KITTIES HAVE ALL BEEN WELL!

YAYYYY

PUSSYCATS! IT'S GREAT TO SEE YOU AFTER ALL THIS TIME!

PAW PAD MANJU!

PAW PAD MANJU!

WE'RE DOING GOOD, THANKS.

DON'T REMIND ME...

LOOM

SORRY WE COULDN'T PROTECT YOU, BACK THEN.

SURE...

UH-HUH.

THANKS FOR THAT LETTER! IT MEANT A LOT, REALLY!

HUH?

C-CUT IT OUT.

LOOK HERE, MIDORIYA.

KOTA!! LONG TIME NO SEE!!

BAM

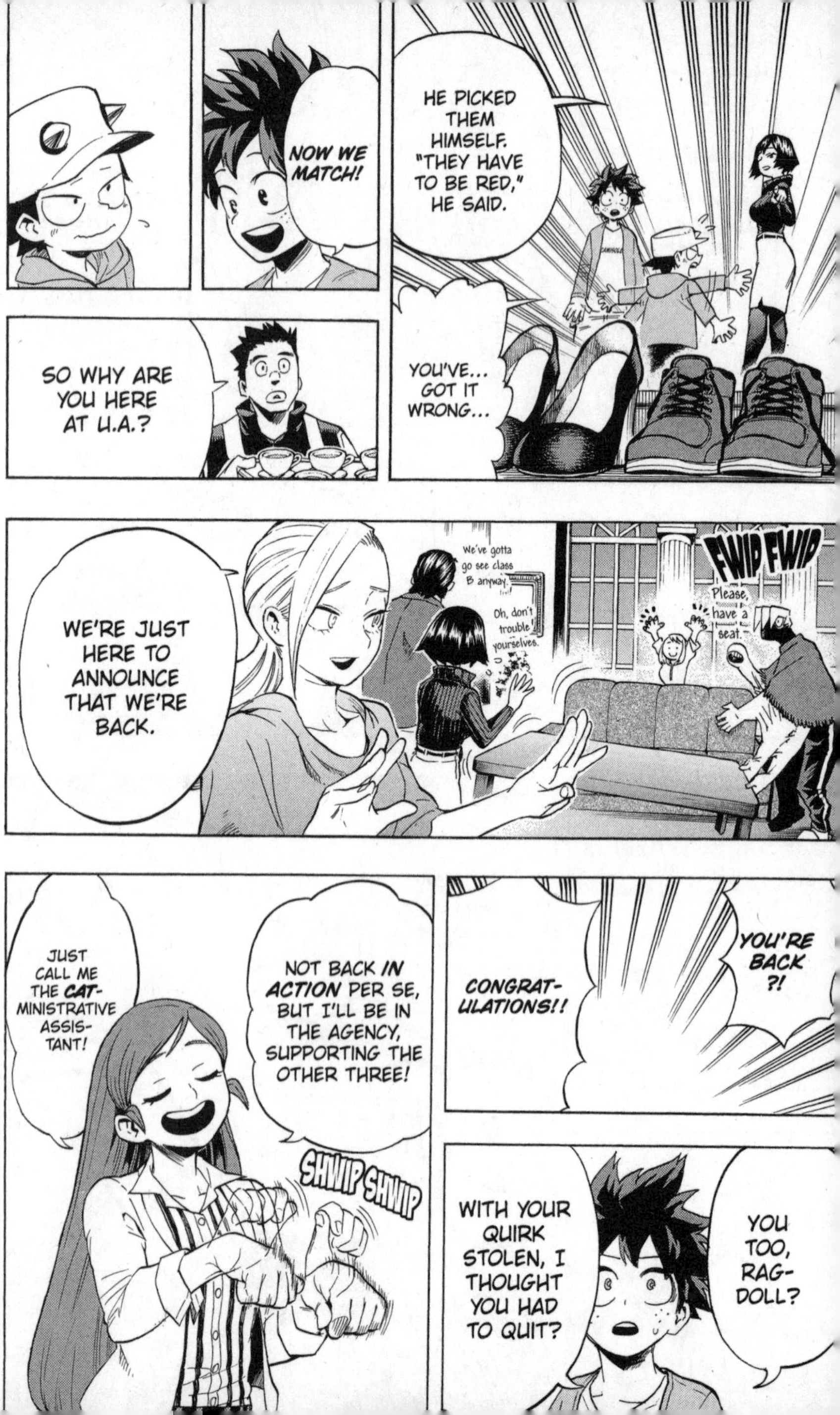
HE PICKED THEM HIMSELF. "THEY HAVE TO BE RED," HE SAID.
YOU'VE... GOT IT WRONG...
NOW WE MATCH!
SO WHY ARE YOU HERE AT U.A.?
FWIP FWIP
Please, have a seat.
We've gotta go see class B anyway.
Oh, don't trouble yourselves.
WE'RE JUST HERE TO ANNOUNCE THAT WE'RE BACK.
YOU'RE BACK?!
CONGRAT-ULATIONS!!
YOU TOO, RAG-DOLL?
WITH YOUR QUIRK STOLEN, I THOUGHT YOU HAD TO QUIT?
NOT BACK IN ACTION PER SE, BUT I'LL BE IN THE AGENCY, SUPPORTING THE OTHER THREE!
JUST CALL ME THE CAT-MINISTRATIVE ASSIS-TANT!
SHWIP SHWIP

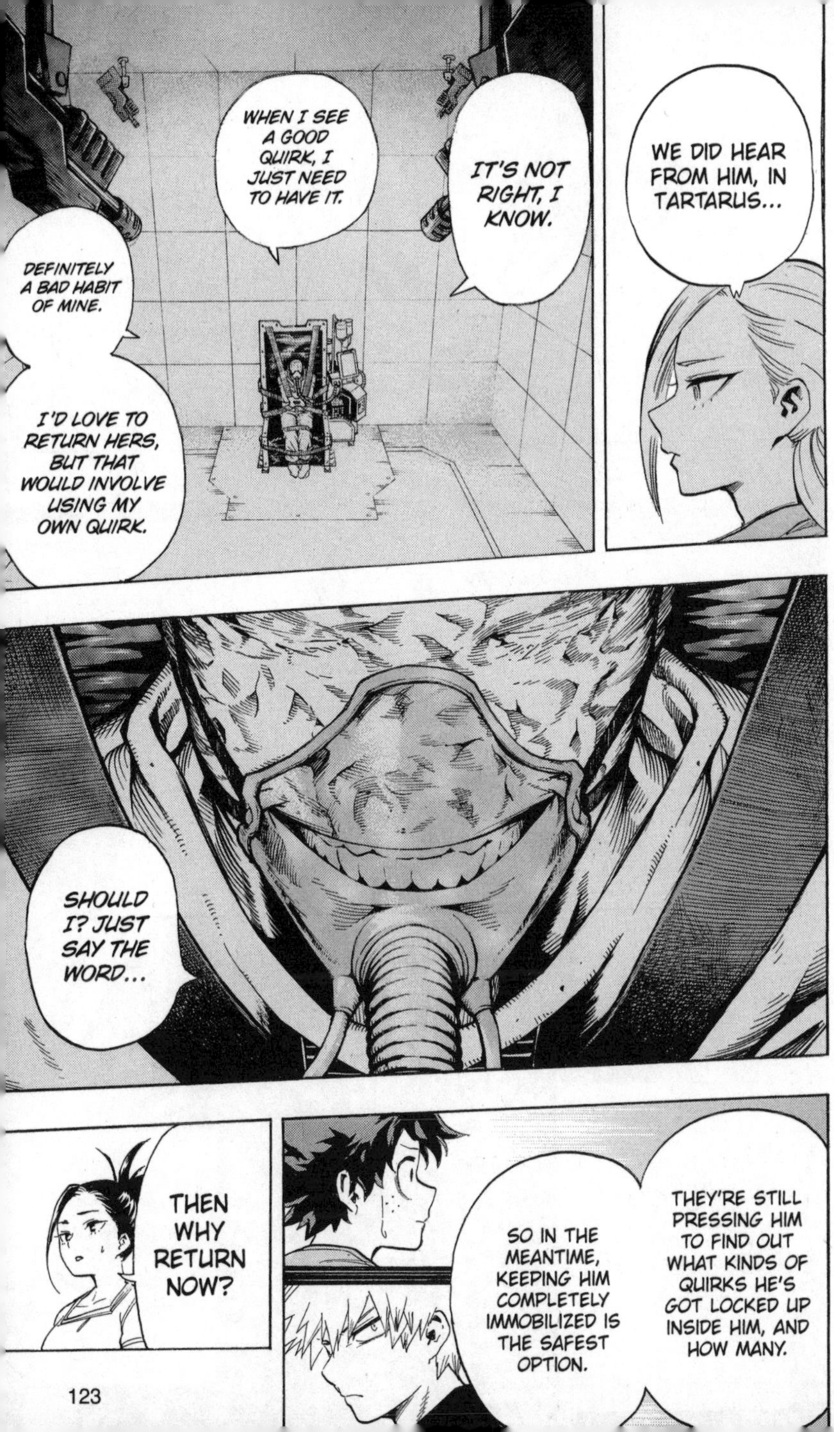
WE DID HEAR FROM HIM, IN TARTARUS...
IT'S NOT RIGHT, I KNOW.
WHEN I SEE A GOOD QUIRK, I JUST NEED TO HAVE IT.
DEFINITELY A BAD HABIT OF MINE.
I'D LOVE TO RETURN HERS, BUT THAT WOULD INVOLVE USING MY OWN QUIRK.
SHOULD I? JUST SAY THE WORD...
THEY'RE STILL PRESSING HIM TO FIND OUT WHAT KINDS OF QUIRKS HE'S GOT LOCKED UP INSIDE HIM, AND HOW MANY.
SO IN THE MEANTIME, KEEPING HIM COMPLETELY IMMOBILIZED IS THE SAFEST OPTION.
THEN WHY RETURN NOW?

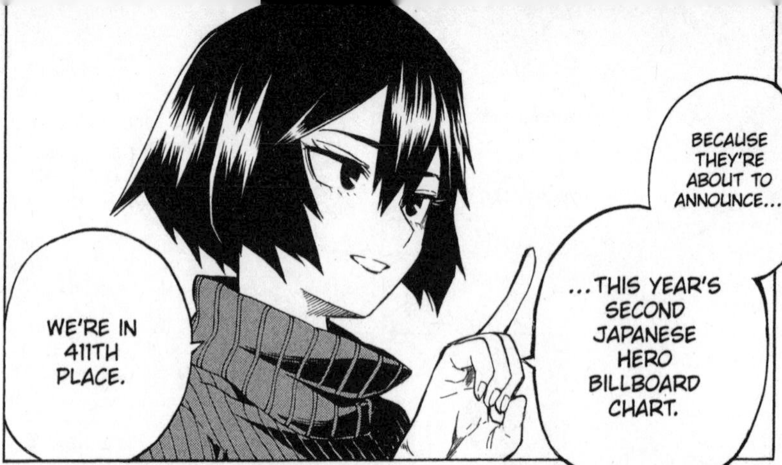
BECAUSE THEY'RE ABOUT TO ANNOUNCE...
...THIS YEAR'S SECOND JAPANESE HERO BILLBOARD CHART.
WE'RE IN 411TH PLACE.

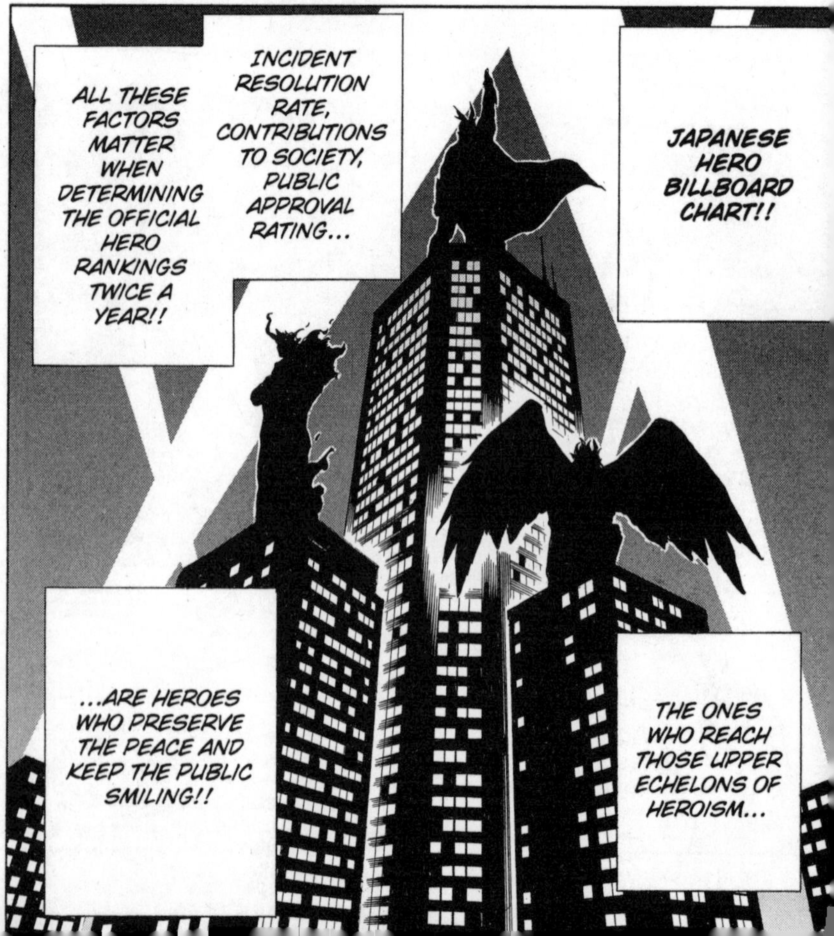
JAPANESE HERO BILLBOARD CHART!!
INCIDENT RESOLUTION RATE, CONTRIBUTIONS TO SOCIETY, PUBLIC APPROVAL RATING...
ALL THESE FACTORS MATTER WHEN DETERMINING THE OFFICIAL HERO RANKINGS TWICE A YEAR!!
THE ONES WHO REACH THOSE UPPER ECHELONS OF HEROISM...
...ARE HEROES WHO PRESERVE THE PEACE AND KEEP THE PUBLIC SMILING!!

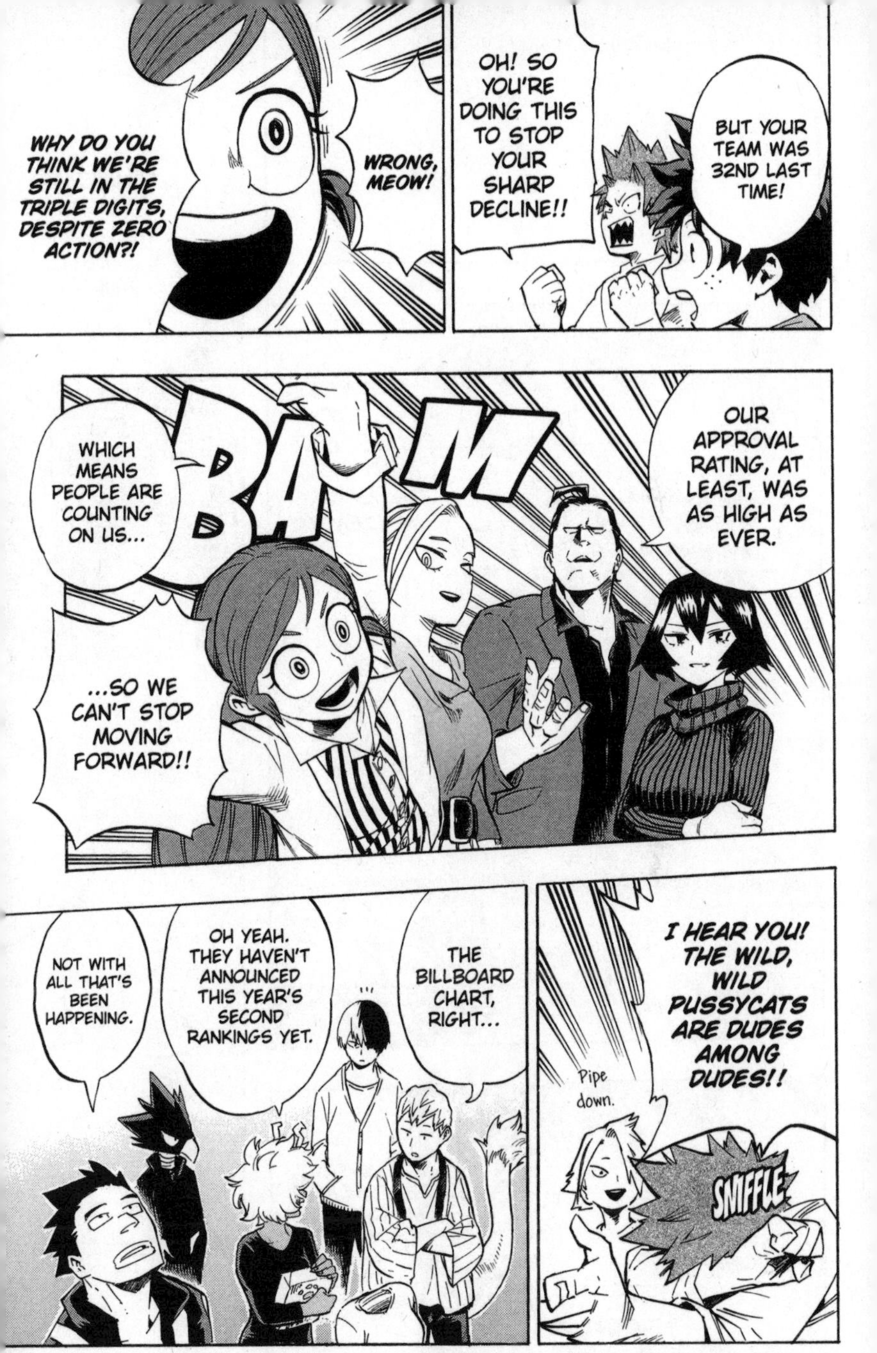
BUT YOUR TEAM WAS 32ND LAST TIME!
OH! SO YOU'RE DOING THIS TO STOP YOUR SHARP DECLINE!!
WRONG, MEOW!
WHY DO YOU THINK WE'RE STILL IN THE TRIPLE DIGITS, DESPITE ZERO ACTION?!
OUR APPROVAL RATING, AT LEAST, WAS AS HIGH AS EVER.
BAM
WHICH MEANS PEOPLE ARE COUNTING ON US...
...SO WE CAN'T STOP MOVING FORWARD!!
I HEAR YOU! THE WILD, WILD PUSSYCATS ARE DUDES AMONG DUDES!!
Pipe down.
SNIFFLE
THE BILLBOARD CHART, RIGHT...
OH YEAH. THEY HAVEN'T ANNOUNCED THIS YEAR'S SECOND RANKINGS YET.
NOT WITH ALL THAT'S BEEN HAPPENING.

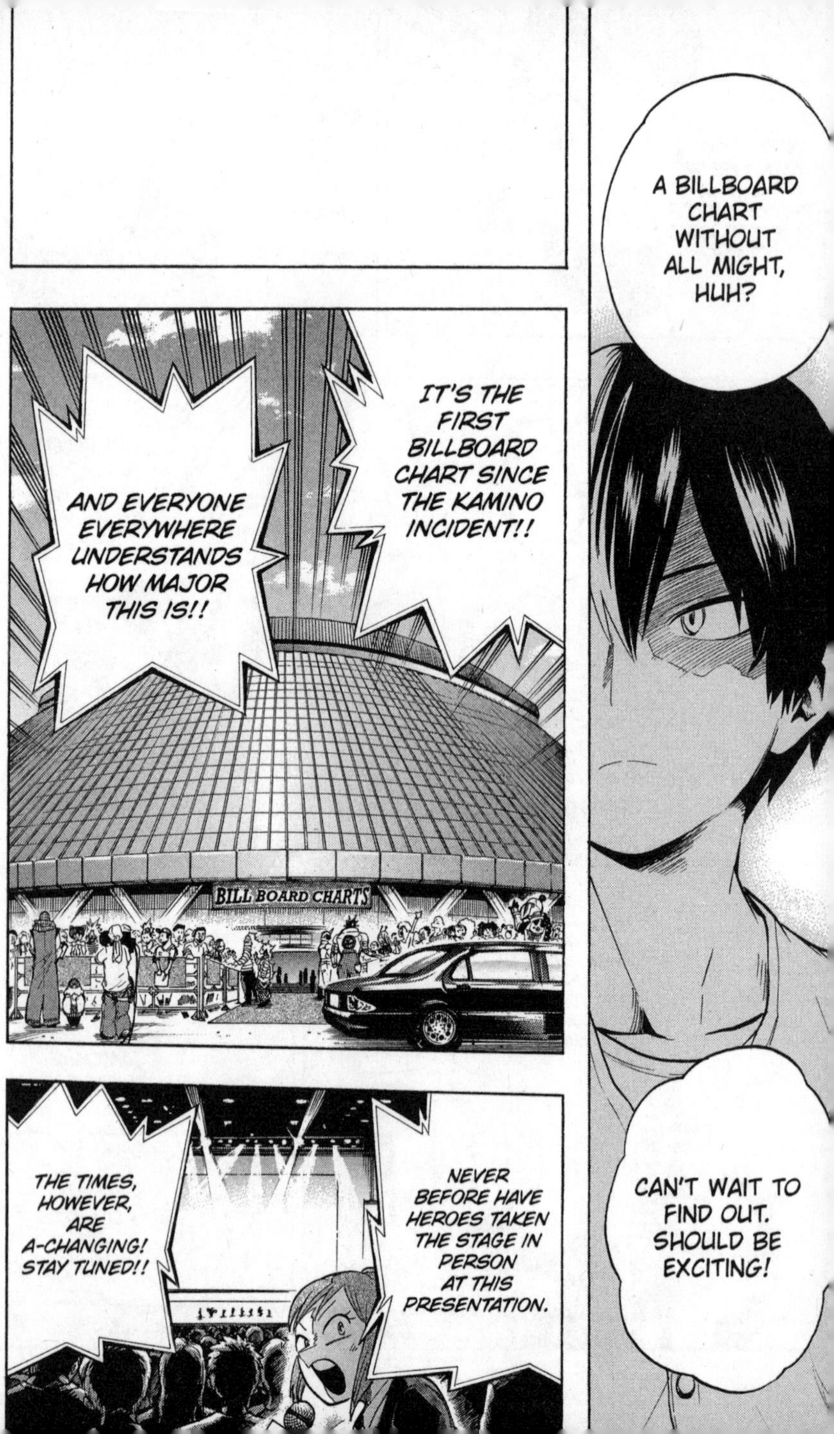
A BILLBOARD CHART WITHOUT ALL MIGHT, HUH?
CAN'T WAIT TO FIND OUT. SHOULD BE EXCITING!
IT'S THE FIRST BILLBOARD CHART SINCE THE KAMINO INCIDENT!!
AND EVERYONE EVERYWHERE UNDERSTANDS HOW MAJOR THIS IS!!
BILL BOARD CHARTS
NEVER BEFORE HAVE HEROES TAKEN THE STAGE IN PERSON AT THIS PRESENTATION.
THE TIMES, HOWEVER, ARE A-CHANGING! STAY TUNED!!

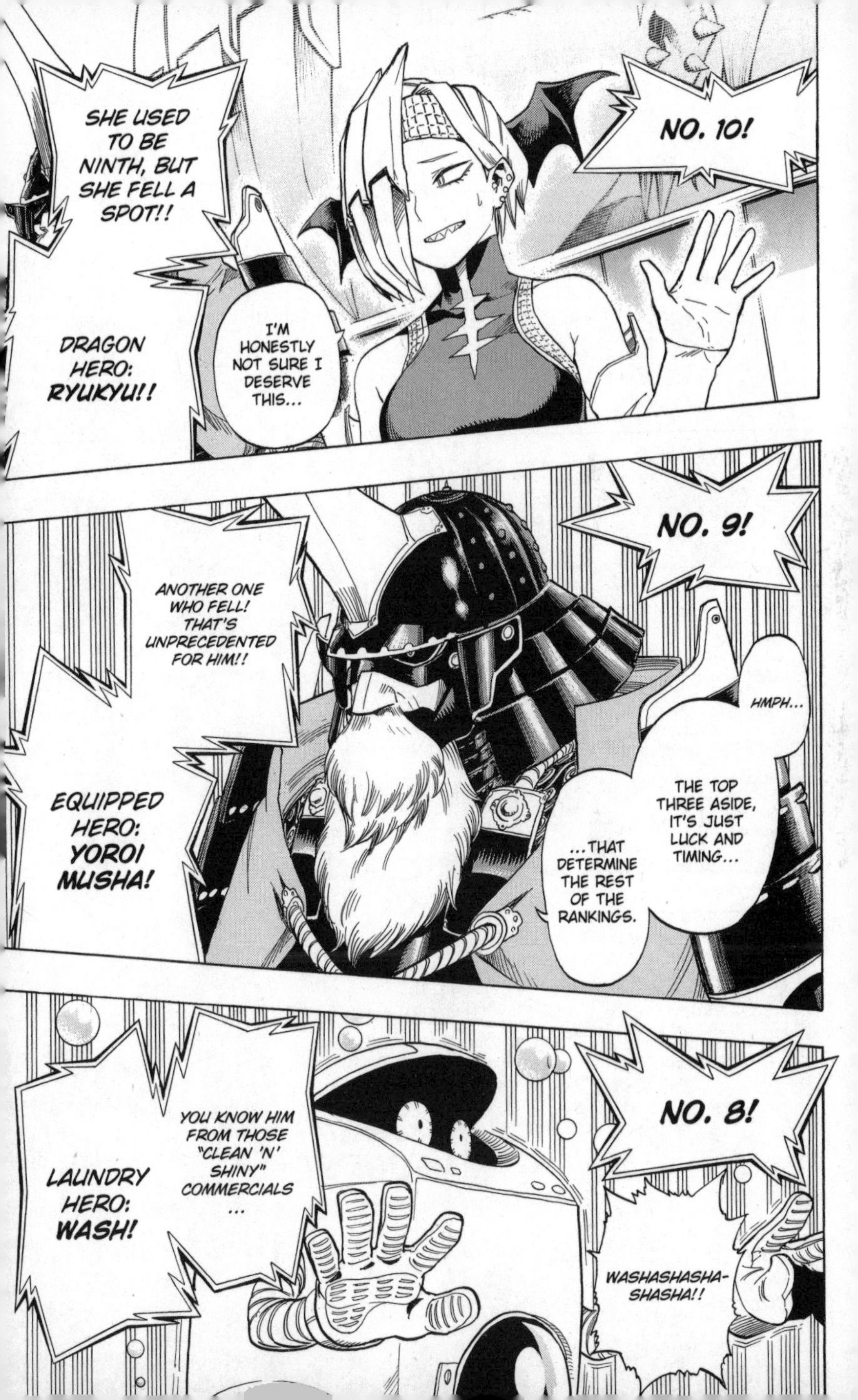
NO. 10!
SHE USED TO BE NINTH, BUT SHE FELL A SPOT!!
I'M HONESTLY NOT SURE I DESERVE THIS...
DRAGON HERO: RYUKYU!!
NO. 9!
ANOTHER ONE WHO FELL! THAT'S UNPRECEDENTED FOR HIM!!
HMPH...
THE TOP THREE ASIDE, IT'S JUST LUCK AND TIMING...
...THAT DETERMINE THE REST OF THE RANKINGS.
EQUIPPED HERO: YOROI MUSHA!
NO. 8!
YOU KNOW HIM FROM THOSE "CLEAN 'N' SHINY" COMMERCIALS...
LAUNDRY HERO: WASH!
WASHASHASHA-SHASHA!!

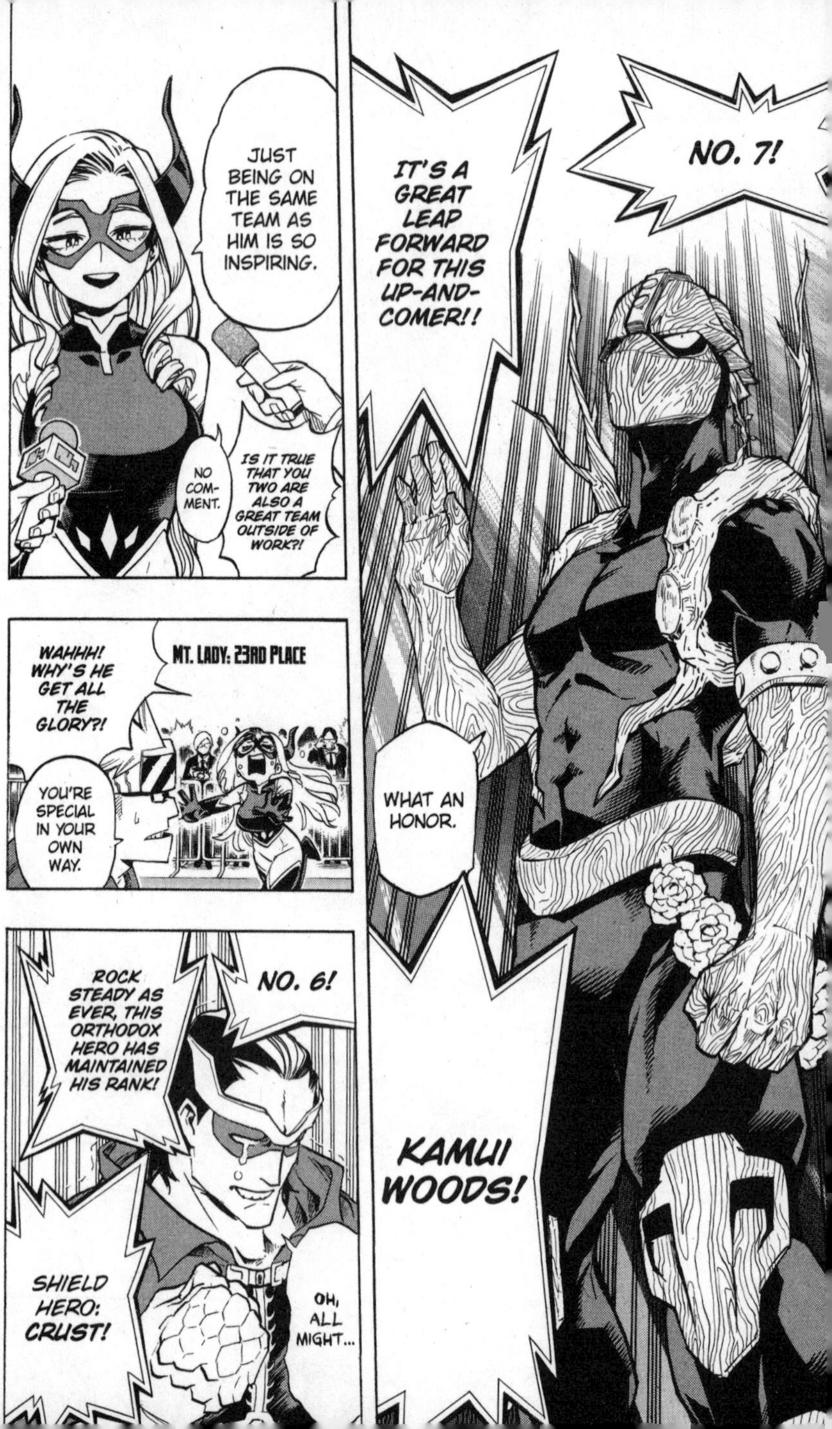
NO. 7!
IT'S A GREAT LEAP FORWARD FOR THIS UP-AND-COMER!!
WHAT AN HONOR.
KAMUI WOODS!
JUST BEING ON THE SAME TEAM AS HIM IS SO INSPIRING.
IS IT TRUE THAT YOU TWO ARE ALSO A GREAT TEAM OUTSIDE OF WORK?!
NO COMMENT.
MT. LADY: 23RD PLACE
WAHHH! WHY'S HE GET ALL THE GLORY?!
YOU'RE SPECIAL IN YOUR OWN WAY.
NO. 6!
ROCK STEADY AS EVER, THIS ORTHODOX HERO HAS MAINTAINED HIS RANK!
OH, ALL MIGHT...
SHIELD HERO: CRUST!

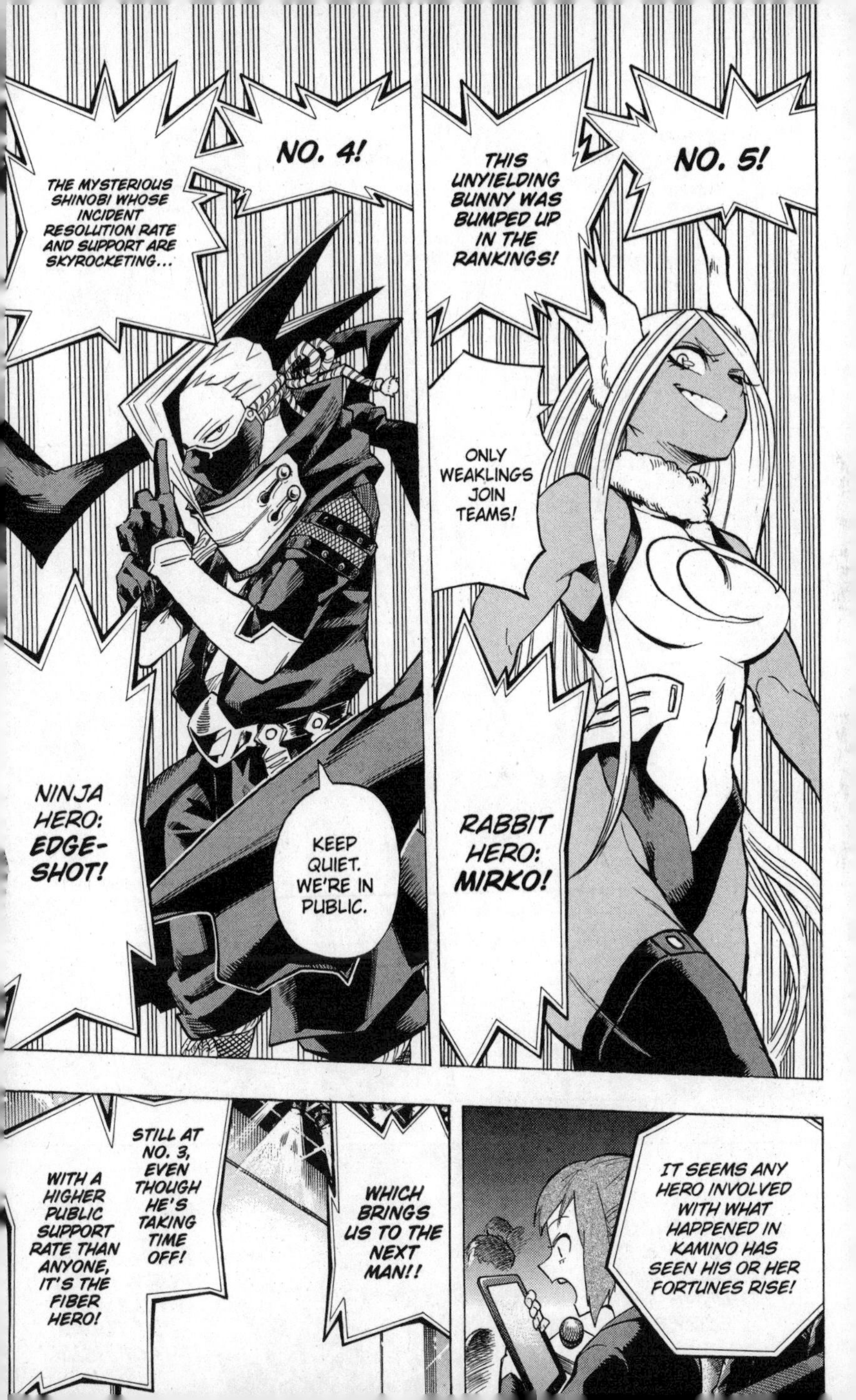
NO. 5!
THIS UNYIELDING BUNNY WAS BUMPED UP IN THE RANKINGS!
ONLY WEAKLINGS JOIN TEAMS!
RABBIT HERO: MIRKO!
NO. 4!
THE MYSTERIOUS SHINOBI WHOSE INCIDENT RESOLUTION RATE AND SUPPORT ARE SKYROCKETING...
KEEP QUIET. WE'RE IN PUBLIC.
NINJA HERO: EDGE-SHOT!
IT SEEMS ANY HERO INVOLVED WITH WHAT HAPPENED IN KAMINO HAS SEEN HIS OR HER FORTUNES RISE!
WHICH BRINGS US TO THE NEXT MAN!!
STILL AT NO. 3, EVEN THOUGH HE'S TAKING TIME OFF!
WITH A HIGHER PUBLIC SUPPORT RATE THAN ANYONE, IT'S THE FIBER HERO!

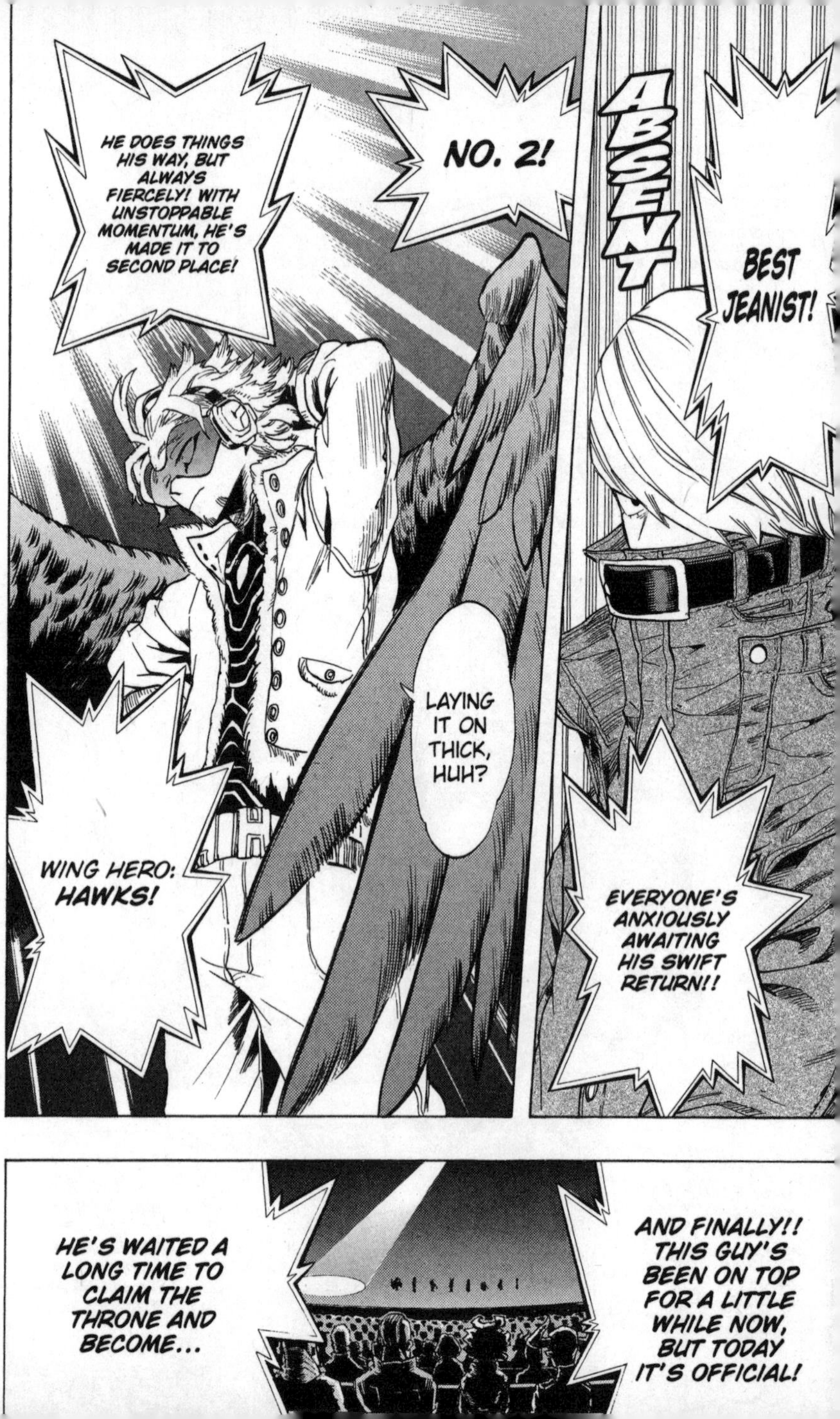
ABSENT
BEST JEANIST!
EVERYONE'S ANXIOUSLY AWAITING HIS SWIFT RETURN!!
NO. 2!
HE DOES THINGS HIS WAY, BUT ALWAYS FIERCELY! WITH UNSTOPPABLE MOMENTUM, HE'S MADE IT TO SECOND PLACE!
LAYING IT ON THICK, HUH?
WING HERO: HAWKS!
AND FINALLY!! THIS GUY'S BEEN ON TOP FOR A LITTLE WHILE NOW, BUT TODAY IT'S OFFICIAL!
HE'S WAITED A LONG TIME TO CLAIM THE THRONE AND BECOME...

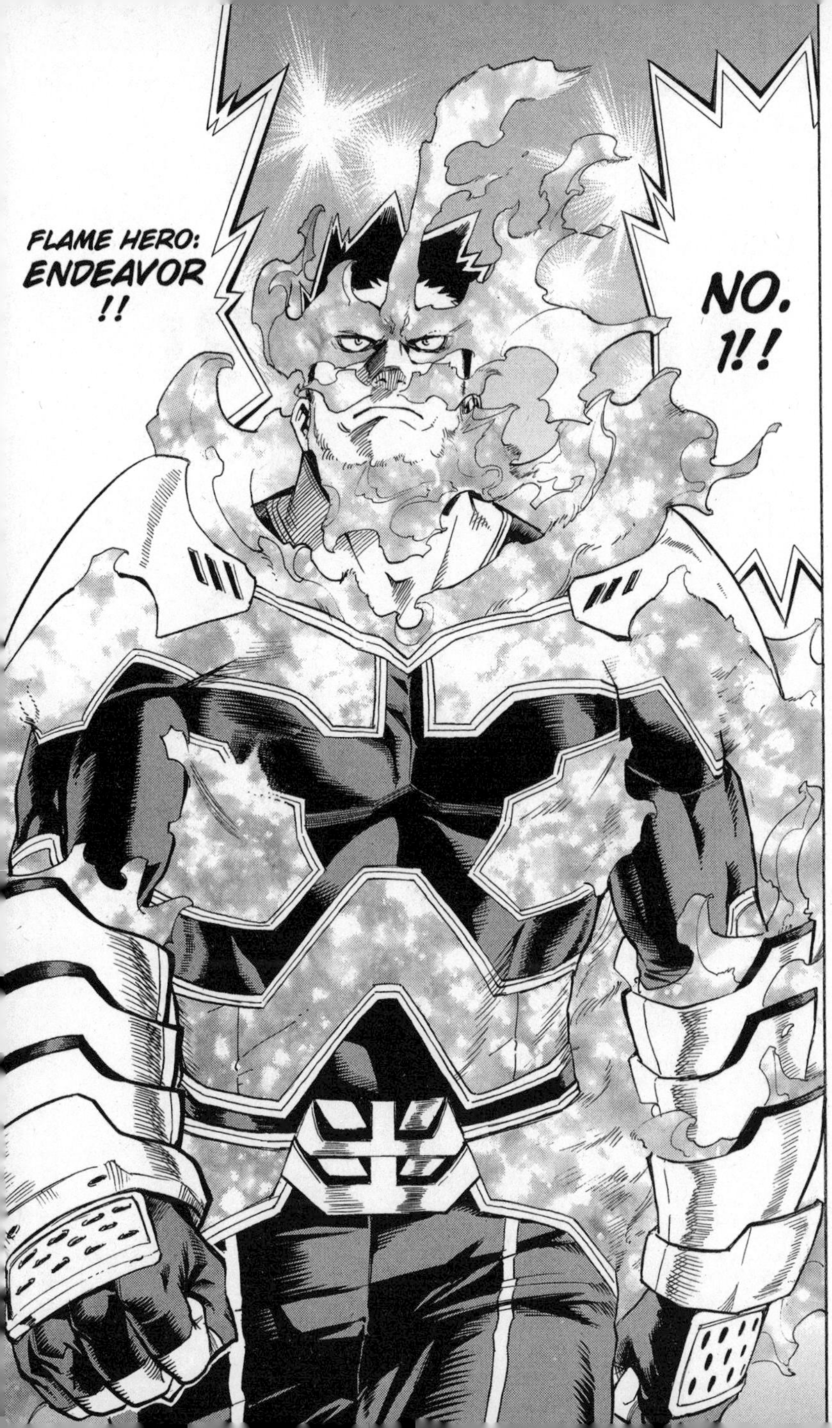
NO. 1!!
FLAME HERO: ENDEAVOR !!

WHAT ARE YOU?!

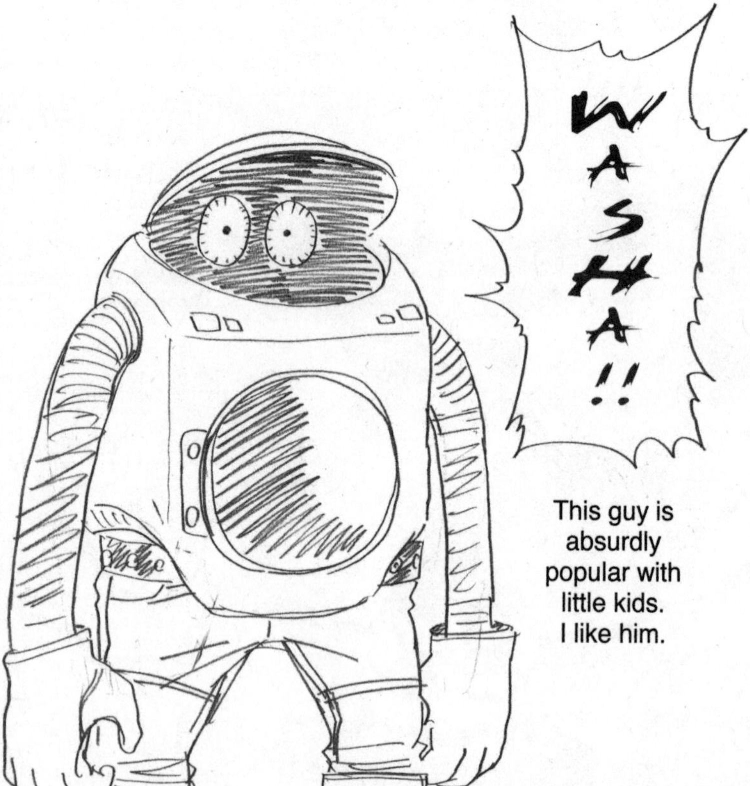
WASHA!!

This guy is absurdly popular with little kids. I like him.

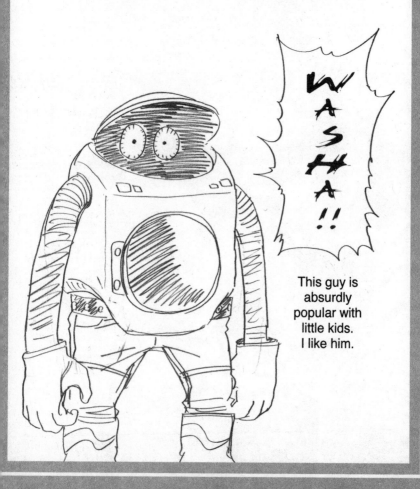

1	ENDEAVOR
2	HAWKS
3	BEST JEANIST
4	EDGESHOT
5	MIRKO
6	CRUST
7	KAMUI WOODS
8	WASH
9	YOROI MUSHA
10	RYUKYU

The Heroes Public Safety Commission looks over the past year of heroism and—after using a proprietary formula to quantify incident resolution rate, societal contributions and public approval rating—presents the results in the form of rankings.

Because incident resolution rate is the most important factor and heroes who tackle bigger incidents end up with even more public support, those involved in major crises quickly find themselves climbing the ranks.

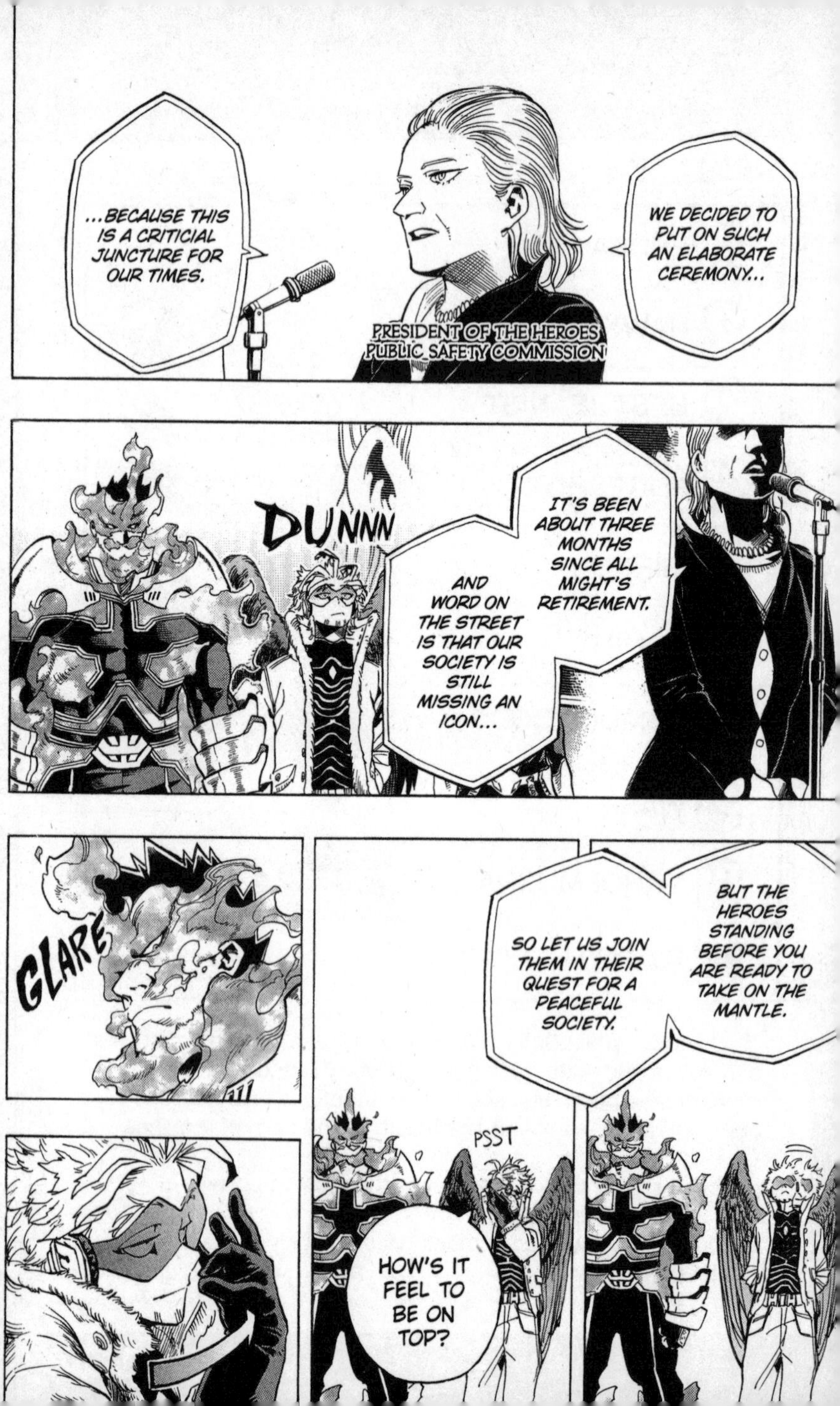
WE DECIDED TO PUT ON SUCH AN ELABORATE CEREMONY...
PRESIDENT OF THE HEROES PUBLIC SAFETY COMMISSION
...BECAUSE THIS IS A CRITICAL JUNCTURE FOR OUR TIMES.
IT'S BEEN ABOUT THREE MONTHS SINCE ALL MIGHT'S RETIREMENT.
AND WORD ON THE STREET IS THAT OUR SOCIETY IS STILL MISSING AN ICON...
DUNNN
BUT THE HEROES STANDING BEFORE YOU ARE READY TO TAKE ON THE MANTLE.
SO LET US JOIN THEM IN THEIR QUEST FOR A PEACEFUL SOCIETY.
GLARE
PSST
HOW'S IT FEEL TO BE ON TOP?

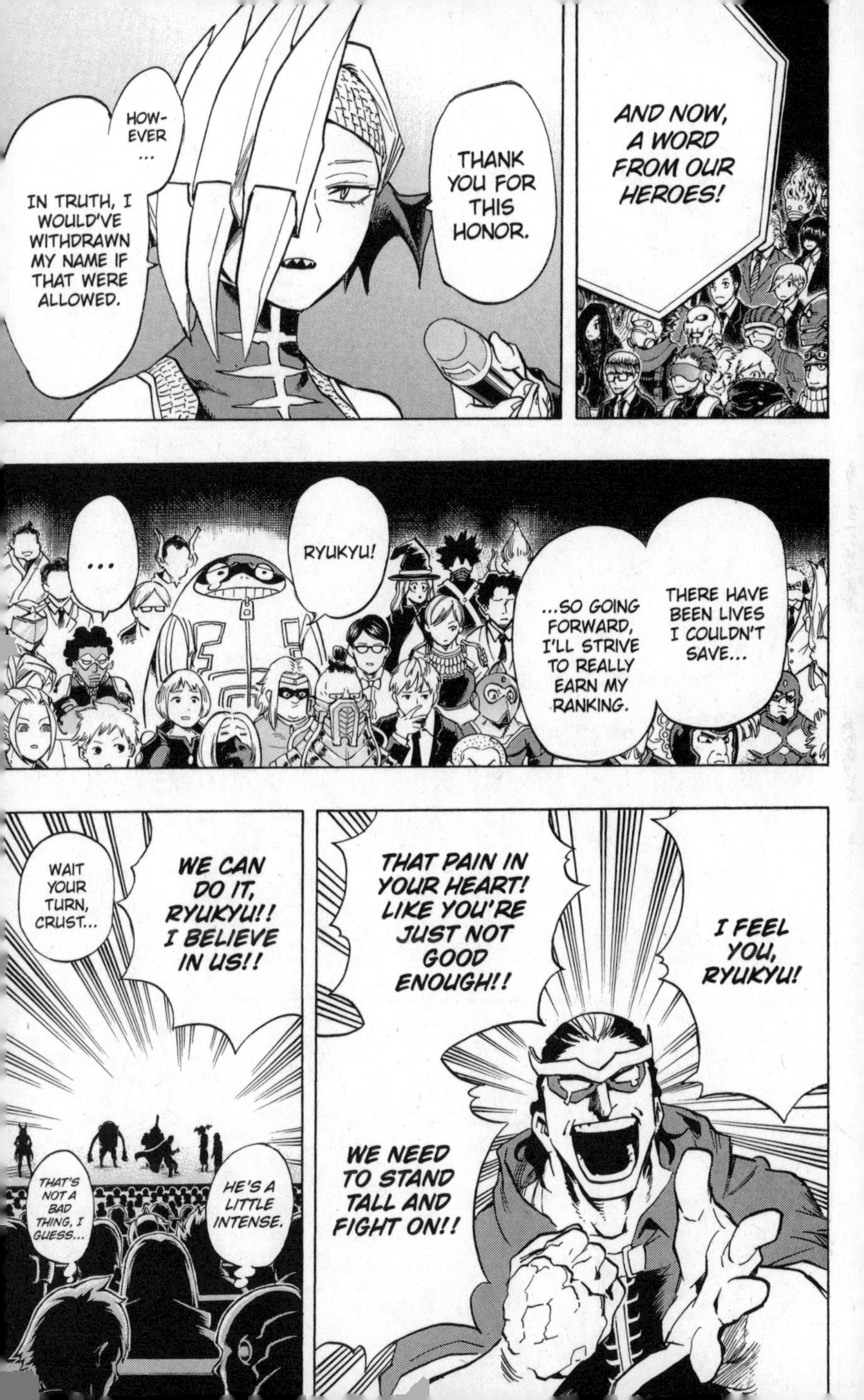
AND NOW, A WORD FROM OUR HEROES!
THANK YOU FOR THIS HONOR.
IN TRUTH, I WOULD'VE WITHDRAWN MY NAME IF THAT WERE ALLOWED.
HOW-EVER ...
THERE HAVE BEEN LIVES I COULDN'T SAVE...
...SO GOING FORWARD, I'LL STRIVE TO REALLY EARN MY RANKING.
RYUKYU!
...
I FEEL YOU, RYUKYU!
THAT PAIN IN YOUR HEART! LIKE YOU'RE JUST NOT GOOD ENOUGH!!
WE NEED TO STAND TALL AND FIGHT ON!!
WE CAN DO IT, RYUKYU!! I BELIEVE IN US!!
WAIT YOUR TURN, CRUST...
HE'S A LITTLE INTENSE.
THAT'S NOT A BAD THING, I GUESS...

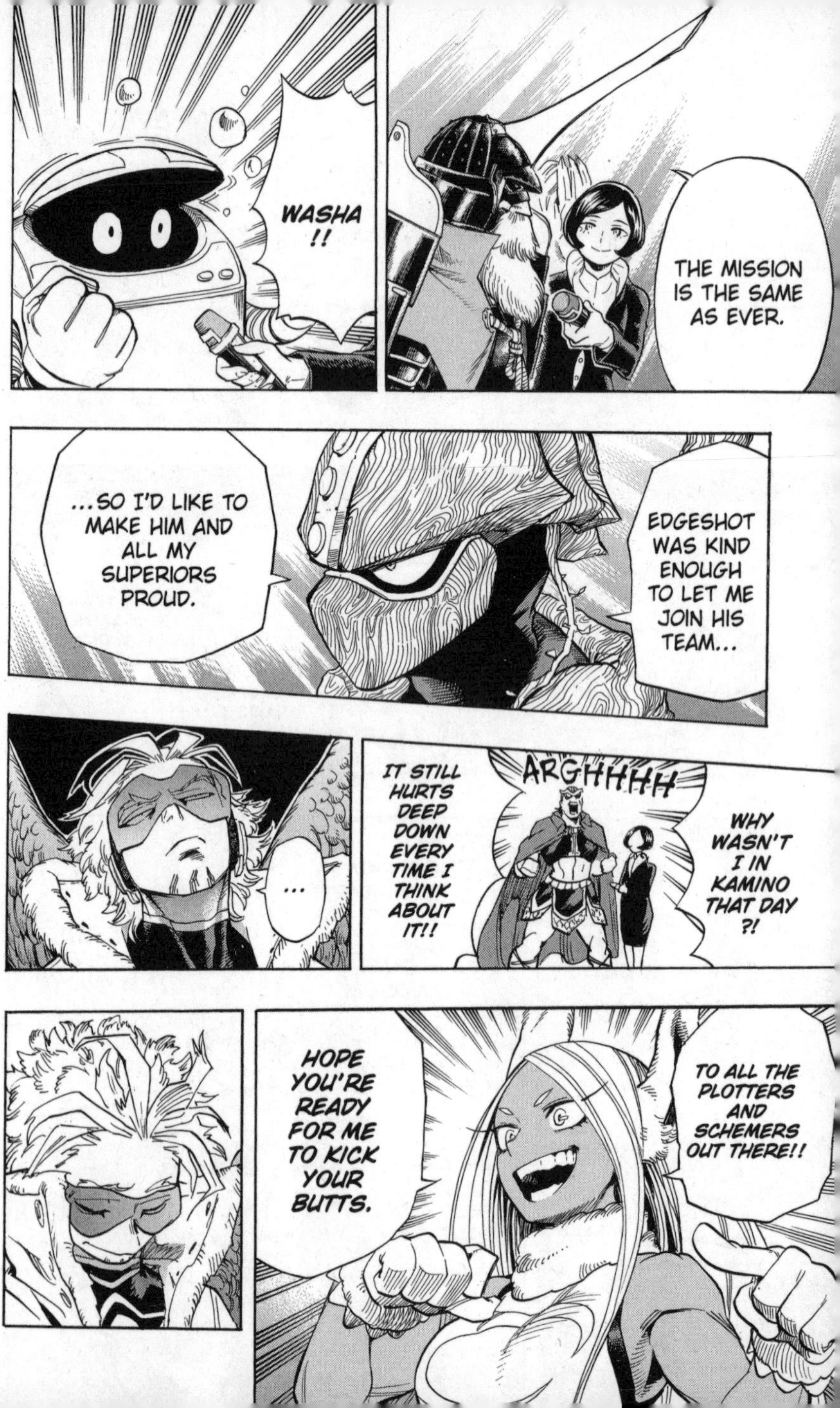
THE MISSION IS THE SAME AS EVER.
WASHA !!
EDGESHOT WAS KIND ENOUGH TO LET ME JOIN HIS TEAM...
...SO I'D LIKE TO MAKE HIM AND ALL MY SUPERIORS PROUD.
WHY WASN'T I IN KAMINO THAT DAY ?!
ARGHHHHH
IT STILL HURTS DEEP DOWN EVERY TIME I THINK ABOUT IT!!
...
TO ALL THE PLOTTERS AND SCHEMERS OUT THERE!!
HOPE YOU'RE READY FOR ME TO KICK YOUR BUTTS.

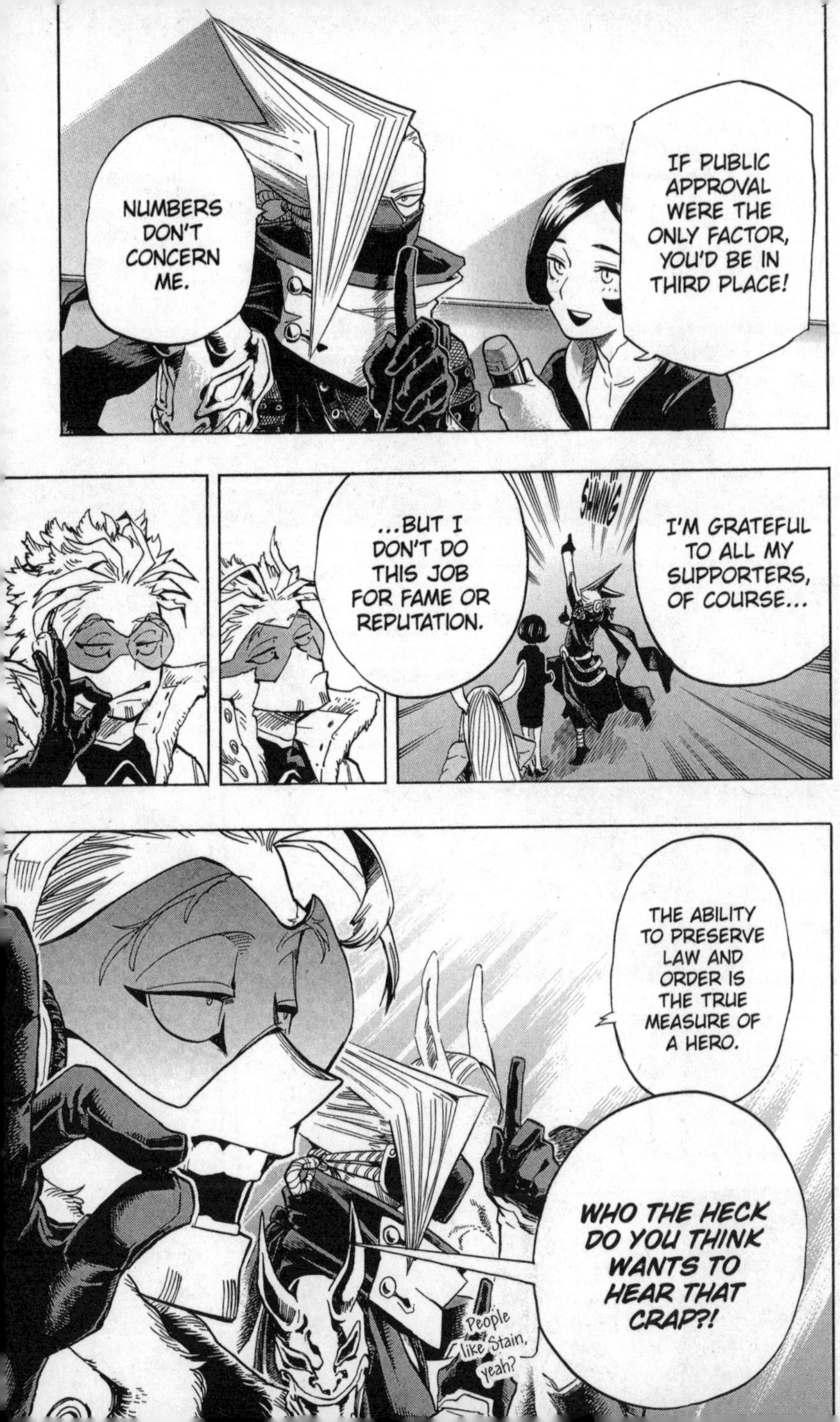
IF PUBLIC APPROVAL WERE THE ONLY FACTOR, YOU'D BE IN THIRD PLACE!
NUMBERS DON'T CONCERN ME.
SHING
I'M GRATEFUL TO ALL MY SUPPORTERS, OF COURSE...
...BUT I DON'T DO THIS JOB FOR FAME OR REPUTATION.
THE ABILITY TO PRESERVE LAW AND ORDER IS THE TRUE MEASURE OF A HERO.
WHO THE HECK DO YOU THINK WANTS TO HEAR THAT CRAP?!
People like Stain, yeah?

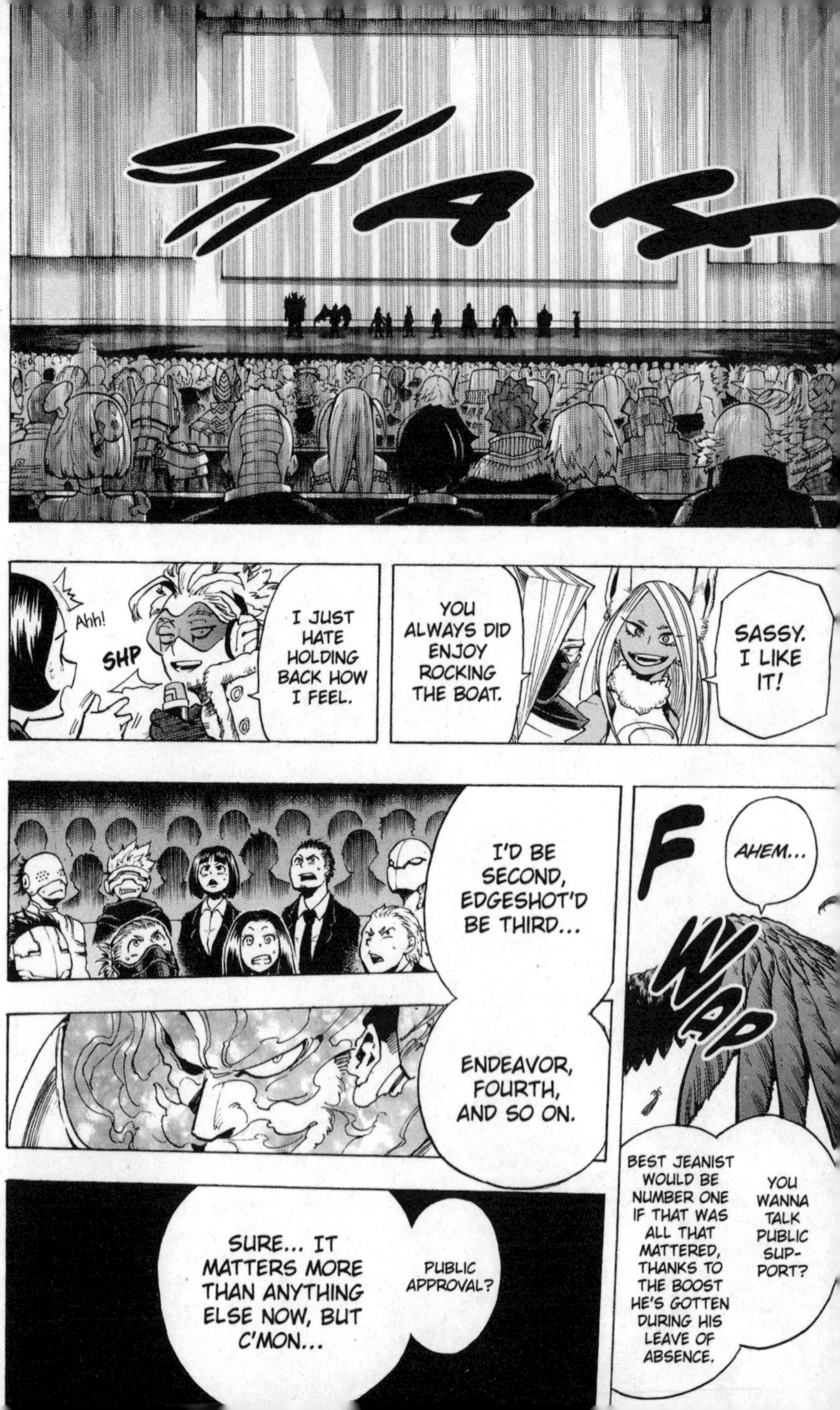

SASSY. I LIKE IT!
YOU ALWAYS DID ENJOY ROCKING THE BOAT.
I JUST HATE HOLDING BACK HOW I FEEL.
SHP
Ahh!
AHEM...
FWAP
YOU WANNA TALK PUBLIC SUP-PORT?
BEST JEANIST WOULD BE NUMBER ONE IF THAT WAS ALL THAT MATTERED, THANKS TO THE BOOST HE'S GOTTEN DURING HIS LEAVE OF ABSENCE.
I'D BE SECOND, EDGESHOT'D BE THIRD...
ENDEAVOR, FOURTH, AND SO ON.
PUBLIC APPROVAL?
SURE... IT MATTERS MORE THAN ANYTHING ELSE NOW, BUT C'MON...

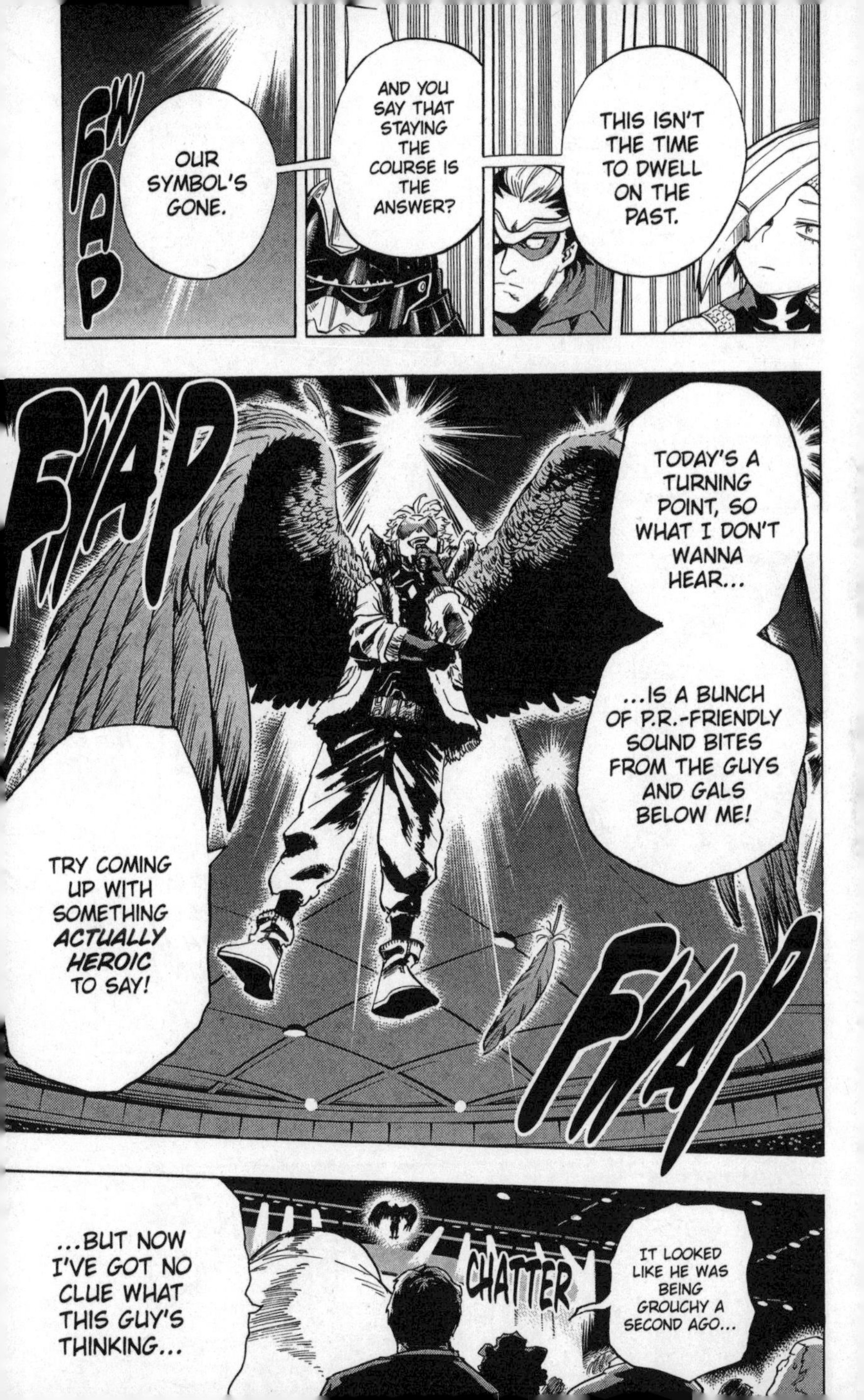
THIS ISN'T THE TIME TO DWELL ON THE PAST.
AND YOU SAY THAT STAYING THE COURSE IS THE ANSWER?
OUR SYMBOL'S GONE.
FWAP
TODAY'S A TURNING POINT, SO WHAT I DON'T WANNA HEAR...
...IS A BUNCH OF P.R.-FRIENDLY SOUND BITES FROM THE GUYS AND GALS BELOW ME!
FWAP
TRY COMING UP WITH SOMETHING *ACTUALLY HEROIC* TO SAY!
FWAP
IT LOOKED LIKE HE WAS BEING GROUCHY A SECOND AGO...
CHATTER
...BUT NOW I'VE GOT NO CLUE WHAT THIS GUY'S THINKING...

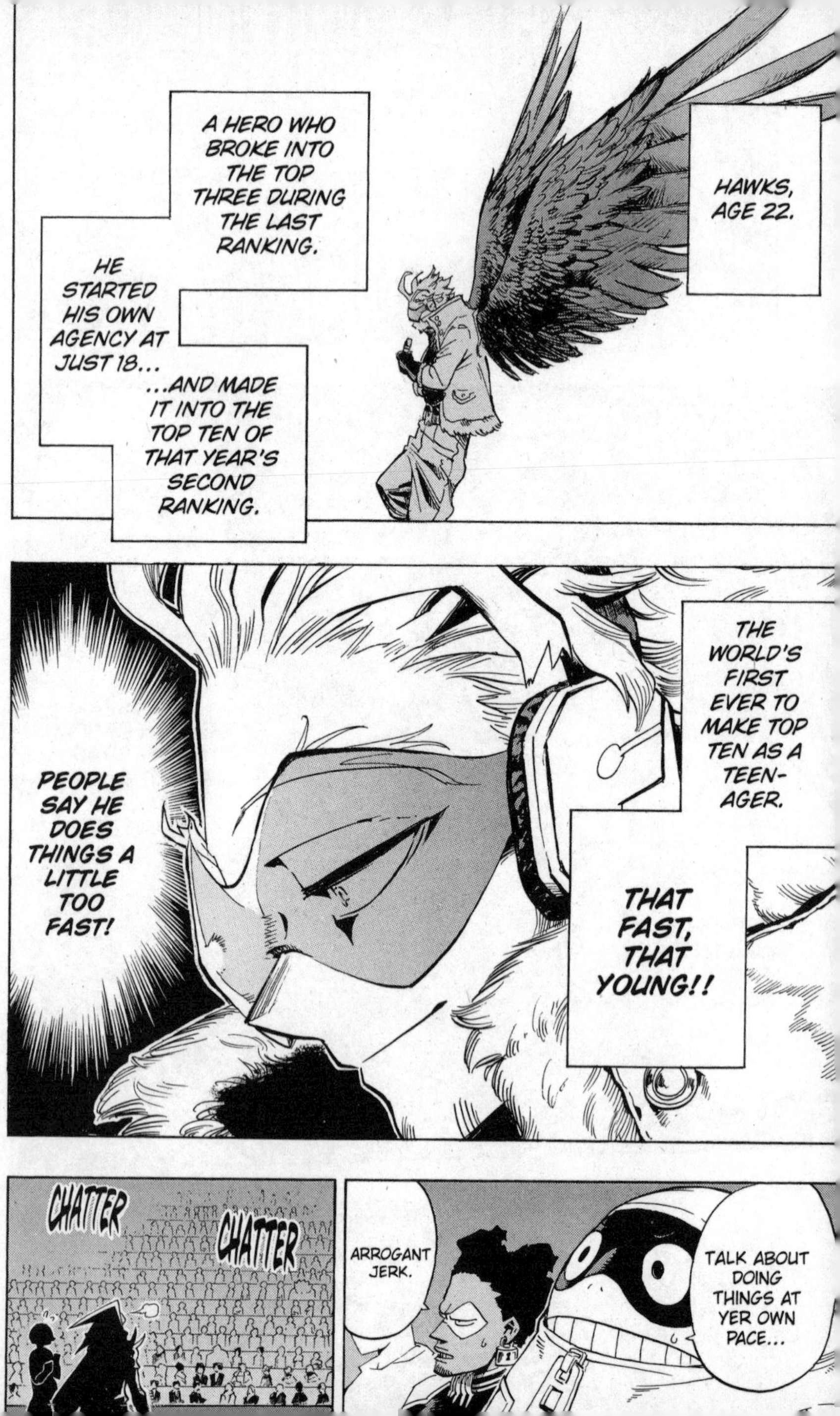
HAWKS, AGE 22.
A HERO WHO BROKE INTO THE TOP THREE DURING THE LAST RANKING.
HE STARTED HIS OWN AGENCY AT JUST 18...
...AND MADE IT INTO THE TOP TEN OF THAT YEAR'S SECOND RANKING.
THE WORLD'S FIRST EVER TO MAKE TOP TEN AS A TEEN-AGER.
THAT FAST, THAT YOUNG!!
PEOPLE SAY HE DOES THINGS A LITTLE TOO FAST!
TALK ABOUT DOING THINGS AT YER OWN PACE...
ARROGANT JERK.
CHATTER
CHATTER

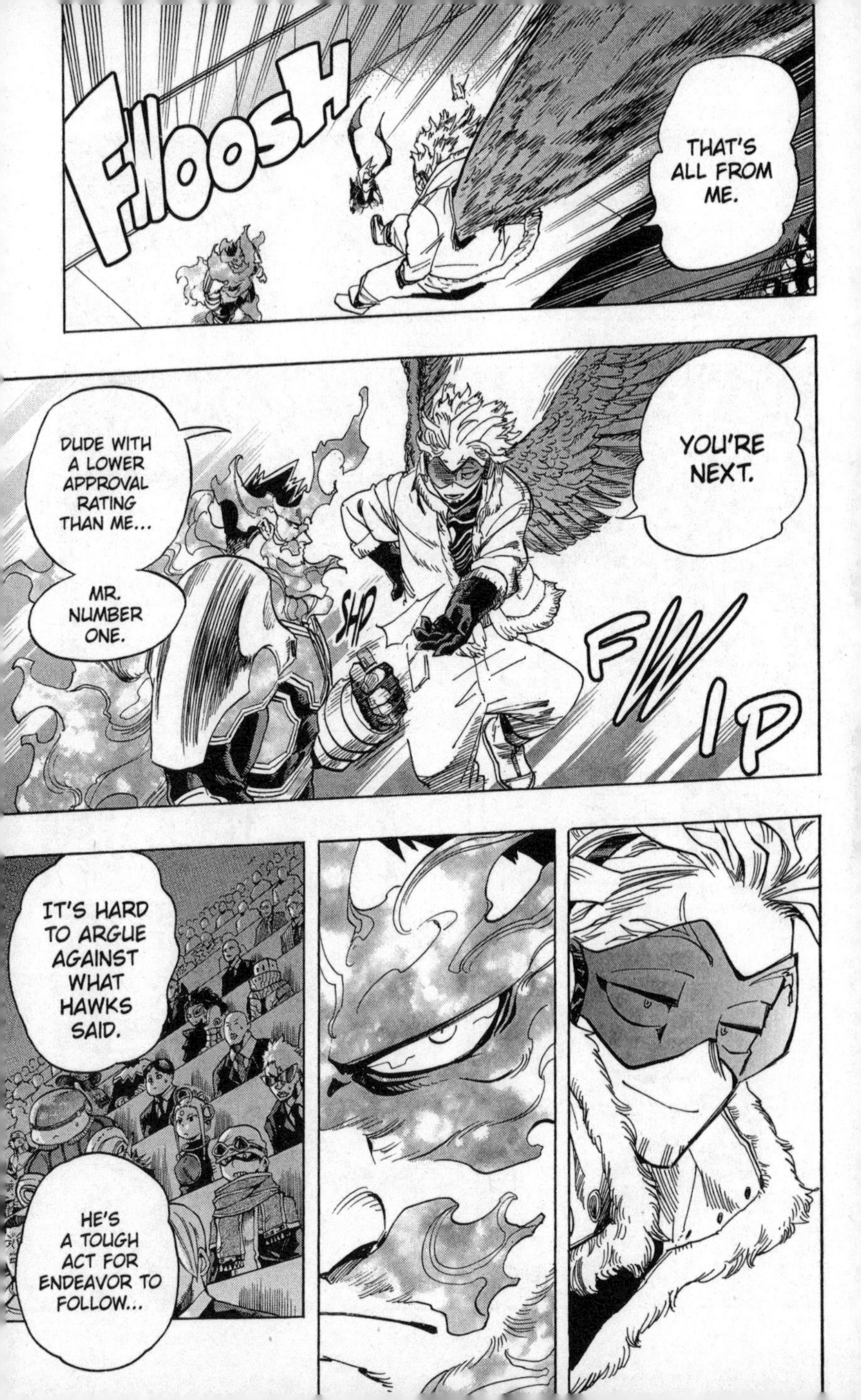
THAT'S ALL FROM ME.
FWOOSH
YOU'RE NEXT.
DUDE WITH A LOWER APPROVAL RATING THAN ME...
MR. NUMBER ONE.
FWIP
SHP
IT'S HARD TO ARGUE AGAINST WHAT HAWKS SAID.
HE'S A TOUGH ACT FOR ENDEAVOR TO FOLLOW...

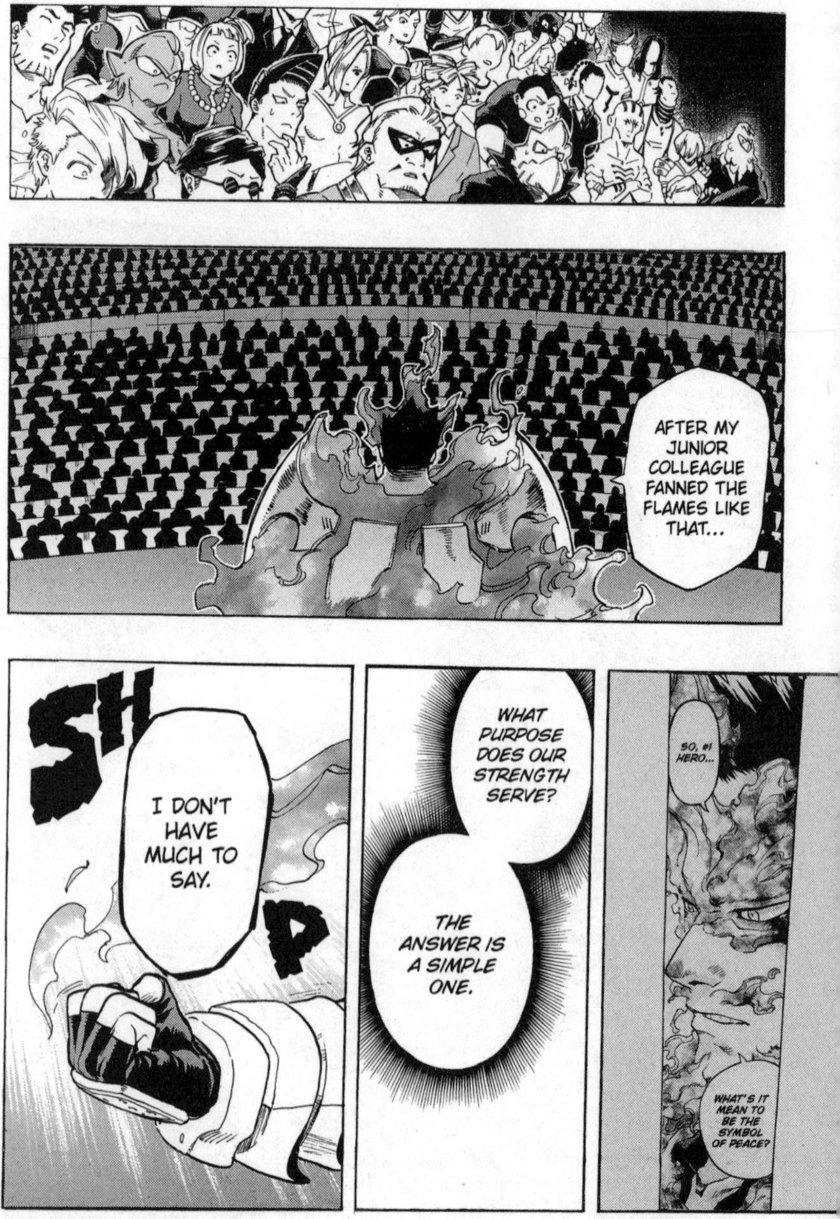
AFTER MY JUNIOR COLLEAGUE FANNED THE FLAMES LIKE THAT...
SO, #1 HERO...
WHAT'S IT MEAN TO BE THE SYMBOL OF PEACE?
WHAT PURPOSE DOES OUR STRENGTH SERVE?
THE ANSWER IS A SIMPLE ONE.
SH
P
I DON'T HAVE MUCH TO SAY.

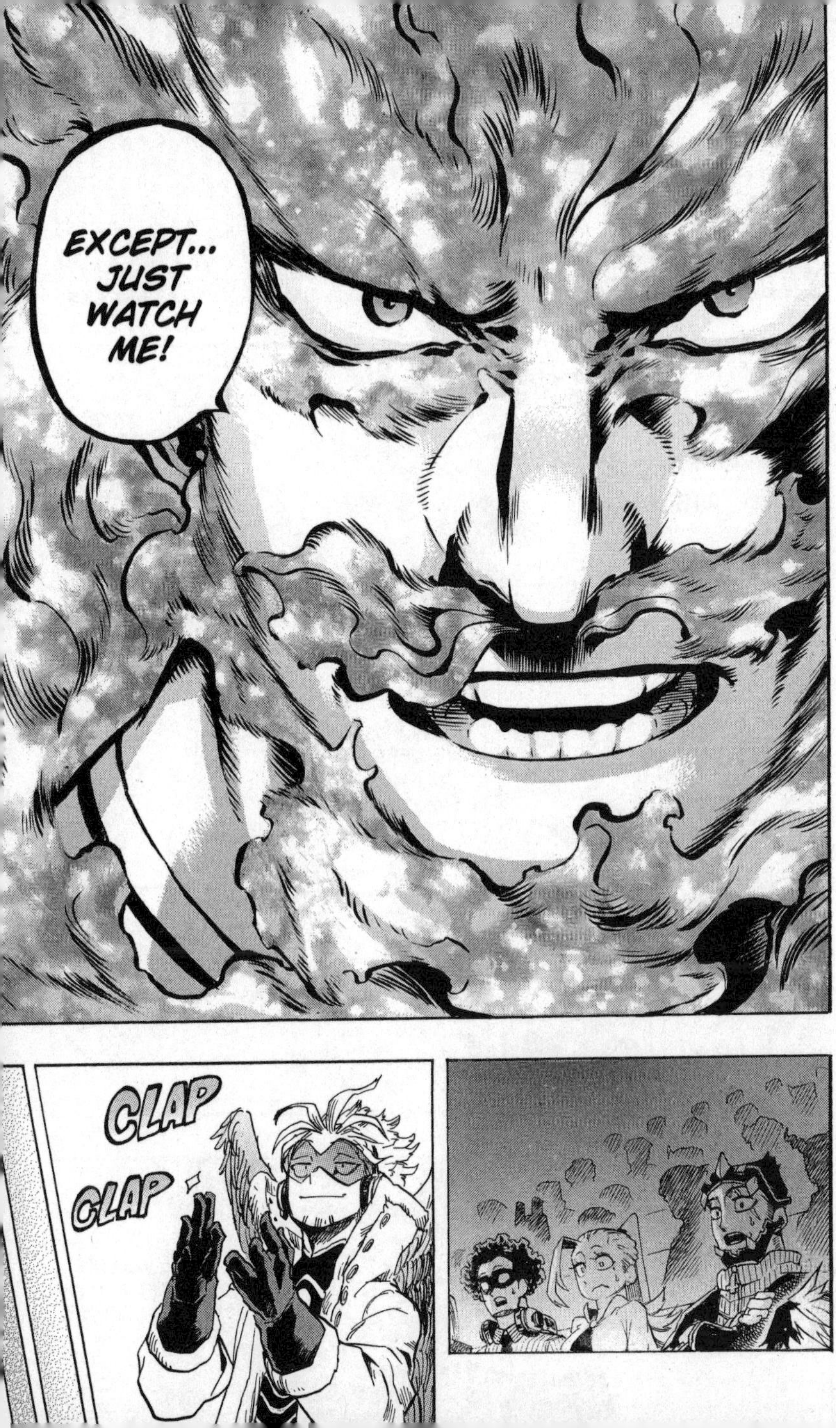
EXCEPT... JUST WATCH ME!
CLAP
CLAP

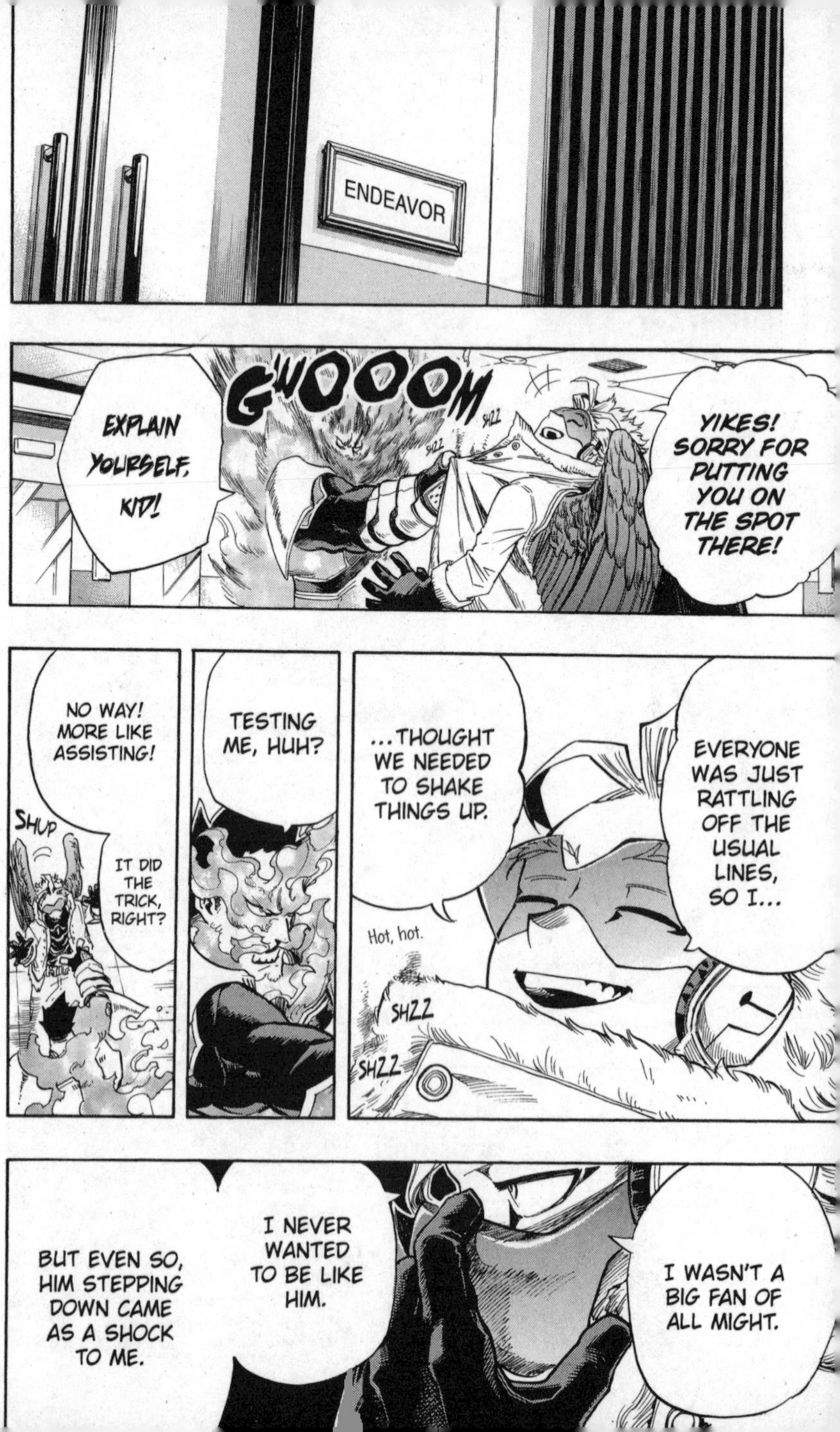
ENDEAVOR
YIKES! SORRY FOR PUTTING YOU ON THE SPOT THERE!
SHZZ
SHZZ
GWOOOM
EXPLAIN YOURSELF, KID!
EVERYONE WAS JUST RATTLING OFF THE USUAL LINES, SO I...
...THOUGHT WE NEEDED TO SHAKE THINGS UP.
Hot, hot.
SHZZ
SHZZ
TESTING ME, HUH?
NO WAY! MORE LIKE ASSISTING!
SHUP
IT DID THE TRICK, RIGHT?
I WASN'T A BIG FAN OF ALL MIGHT.
I NEVER WANTED TO BE LIKE HIM.
BUT EVEN SO, HIM STEPPING DOWN CAME AS A SHOCK TO ME.

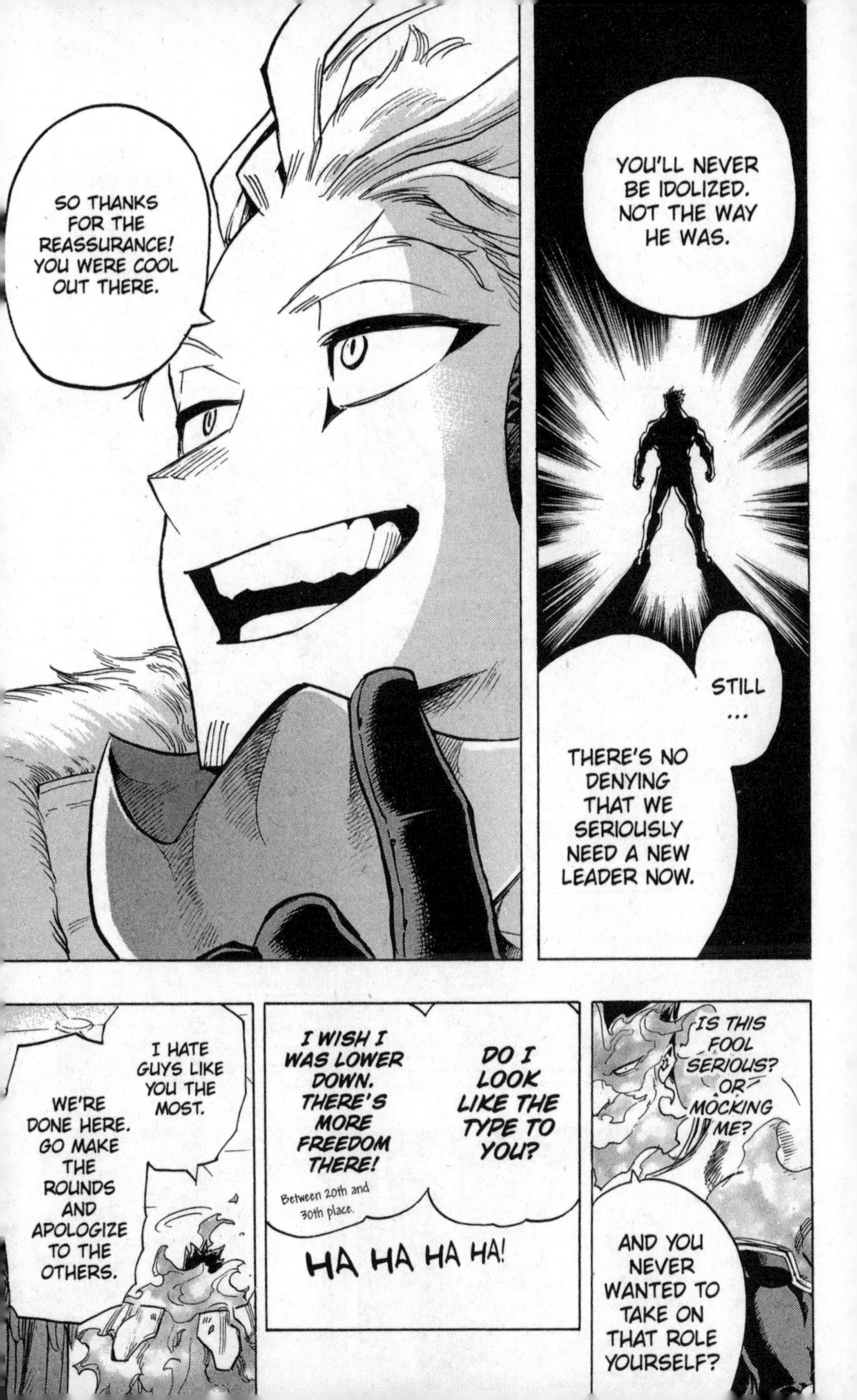
YOU'LL NEVER BE IDOLIZED. NOT THE WAY HE WAS.
STILL...
THERE'S NO DENYING THAT WE SERIOUSLY NEED A NEW LEADER NOW.
SO THANKS FOR THE REASSURANCE! YOU WERE COOL OUT THERE.
IS THIS FOOL SERIOUS? OR MOCKING ME?
AND YOU NEVER WANTED TO TAKE ON THAT ROLE YOURSELF?
DO I LOOK LIKE THE TYPE TO YOU?
I WISH I WAS LOWER DOWN. THERE'S MORE FREEDOM THERE!
Between 20th and 30th place.
HA HA HA HA!
I HATE GUYS LIKE YOU THE MOST.
WE'RE DONE HERE. GO MAKE THE ROUNDS AND APOLOGIZE TO THE OTHERS.

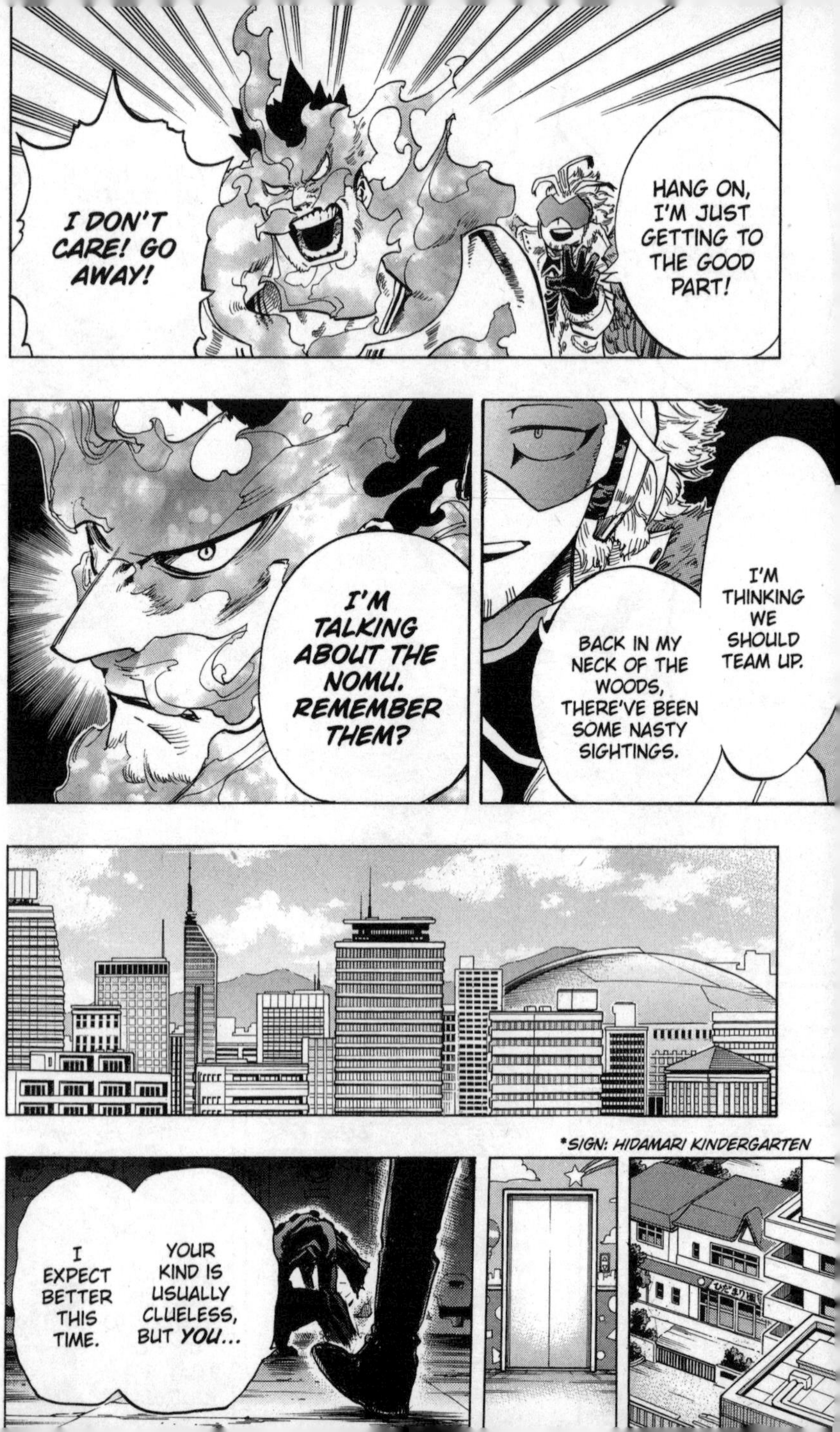
HANG ON, I'M JUST GETTING TO THE GOOD PART!
I DON'T CARE! GO AWAY!
I'M THINKING WE SHOULD TEAM UP.
BACK IN MY NECK OF THE WOODS, THERE'VE BEEN SOME NASTY SIGHTINGS.
I'M TALKING ABOUT THE NOMU. REMEMBER THEM?
*SIGN: HIDAMARI KINDERGARTEN
YOUR KIND IS USUALLY CLUELESS, BUT YOU...
I EXPECT BETTER THIS TIME.

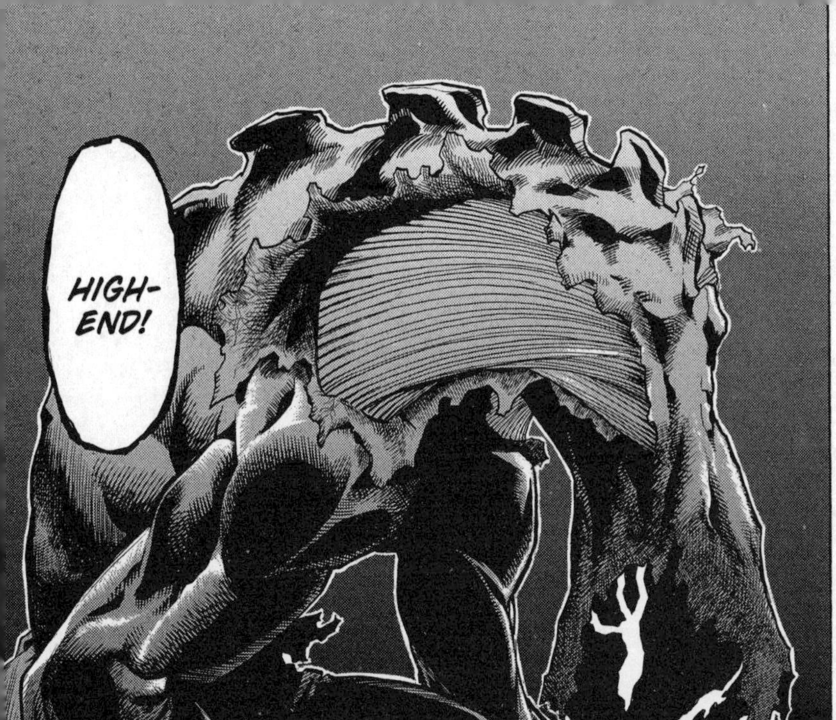
HIGH-END!

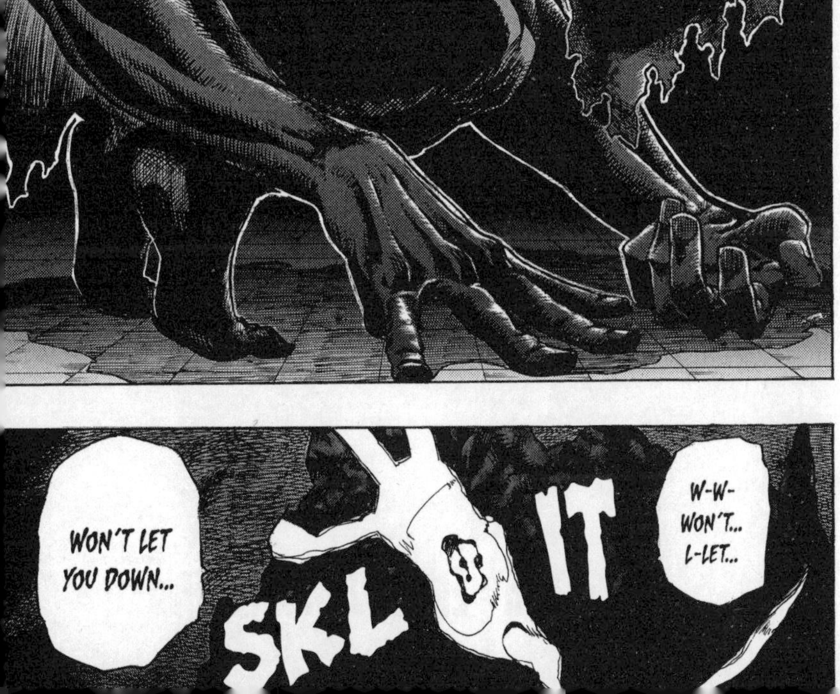
W-W-WON'T... L-LET...
WON'T LET YOU DOWN...
SKLIT

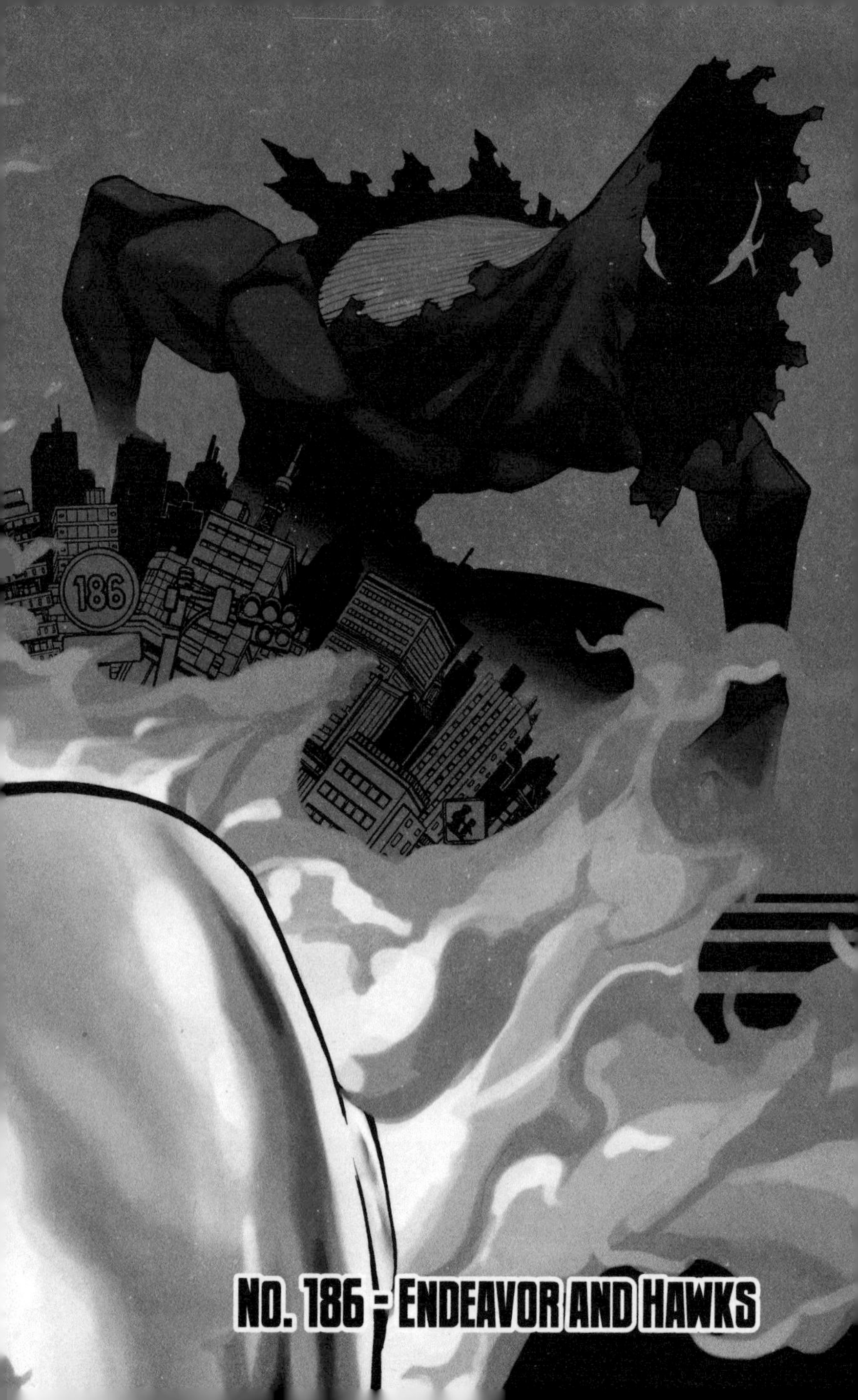
186

No. 186 - Endeavor and Hawks

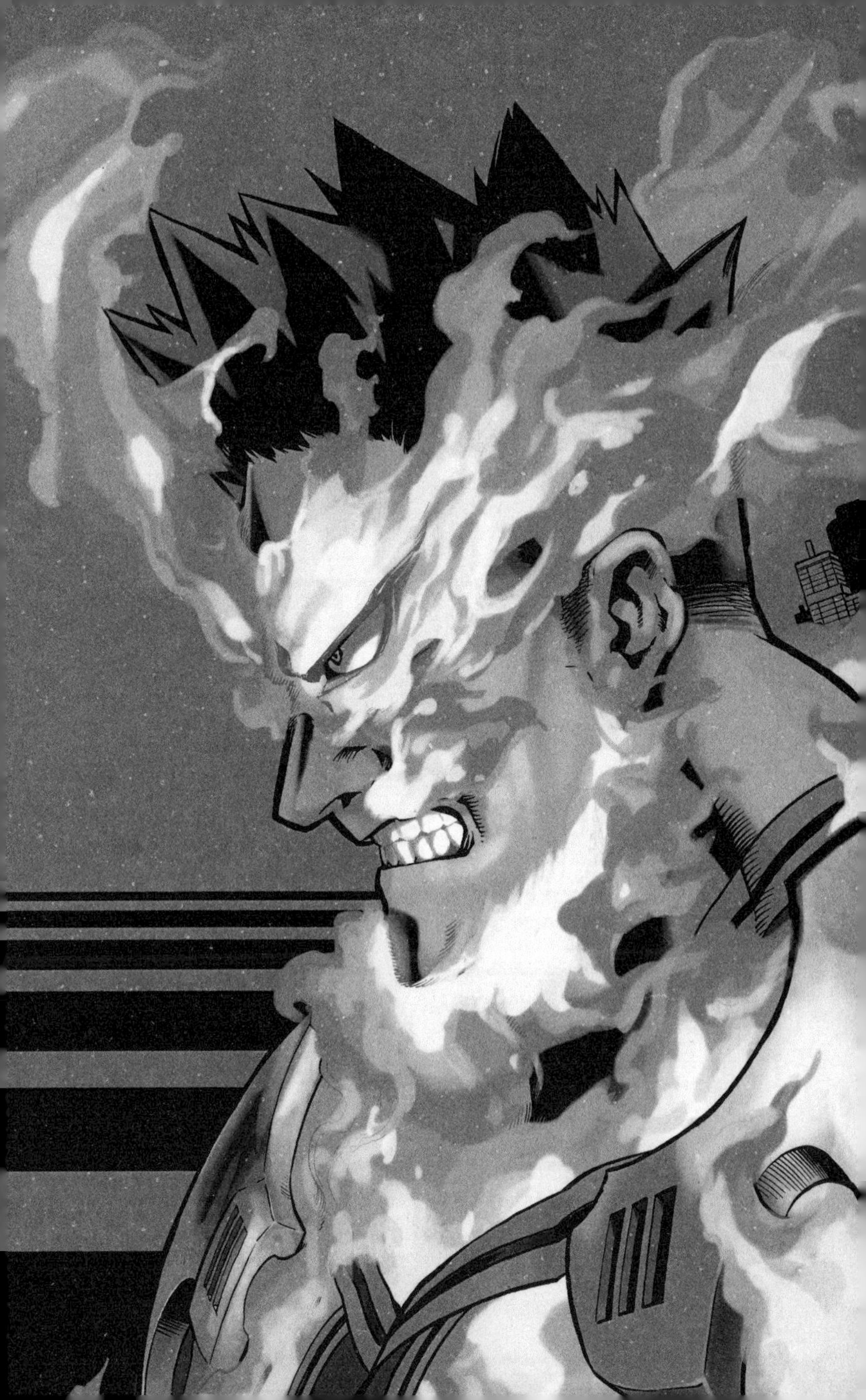

STAFF INTRODUCTION

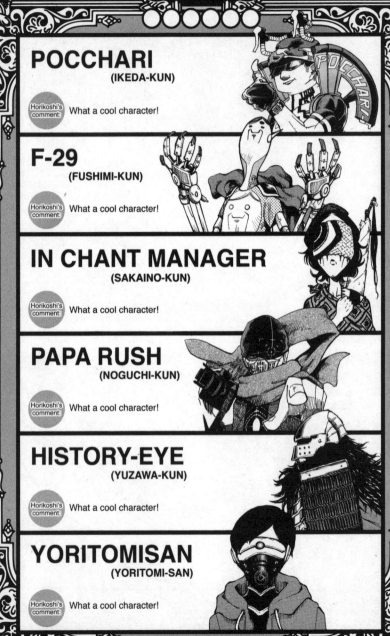

POCCHARI
(IKEDA-KUN)

Horikoshi's comment: What a cool character!

F-29
(FUSHIMI-KUN)

Horikoshi's comment: What a cool character!

IN CHANT MANAGER
(SAKAINO-KUN)

Horikoshi's comment: What a cool character!

PAPA RUSH
(NOGUCHI-KUN)

Horikoshi's comment: What a cool character!

HISTORY-EYE
(YUZAWA-KUN)

Horikoshi's comment: What a cool character!

YORITOMISAN
(YORITOMI-SAN)

Horikoshi's comment: What a cool character!

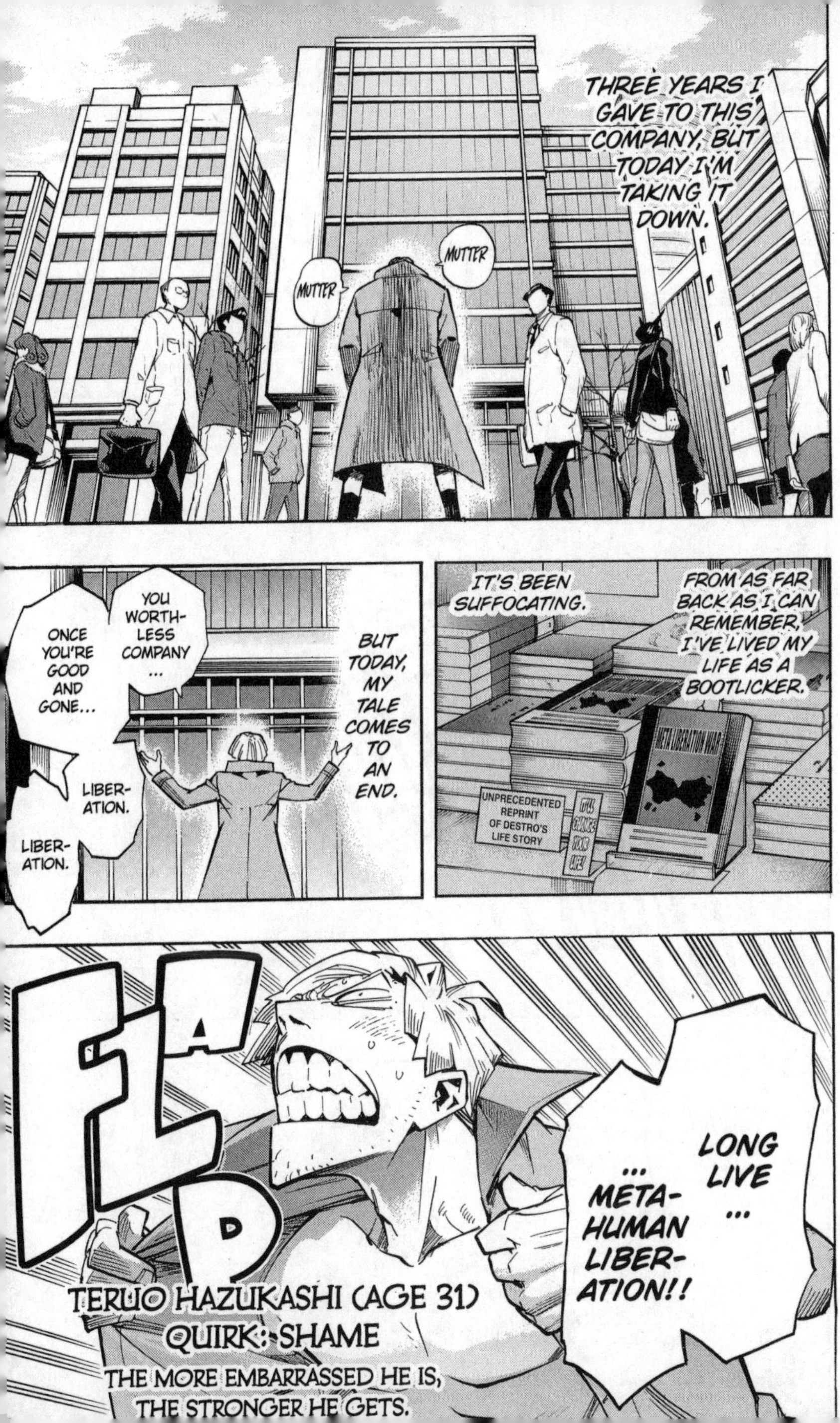
THREE YEARS I GAVE TO THIS COMPANY, BUT TODAY I'M TAKING IT DOWN.
MUTTER
MUTTER
FROM AS FAR BACK AS I CAN REMEMBER, I'VE LIVED MY LIFE AS A BOOTLICKER.
IT'S BEEN SUFFOCATING.
META LIBERATION WAR
UNPRECEDENTED REPRINT OF DESTRO'S LIFE STORY
IT'LL CHANGE YOUR LIFE!
BUT TODAY, MY TALE COMES TO AN END.
YOU WORTHLESS COMPANY...
ONCE YOU'RE GOOD AND GONE...
LIBERATION.
LIBERATION.
...LONG LIVE... META-HUMAN LIBERATION!!
FLAP
TERUO HAZUKASHI (AGE 31)
QUIRK: SHAME
THE MORE EMBARRASSED HE IS, THE STRONGER HE GETS.

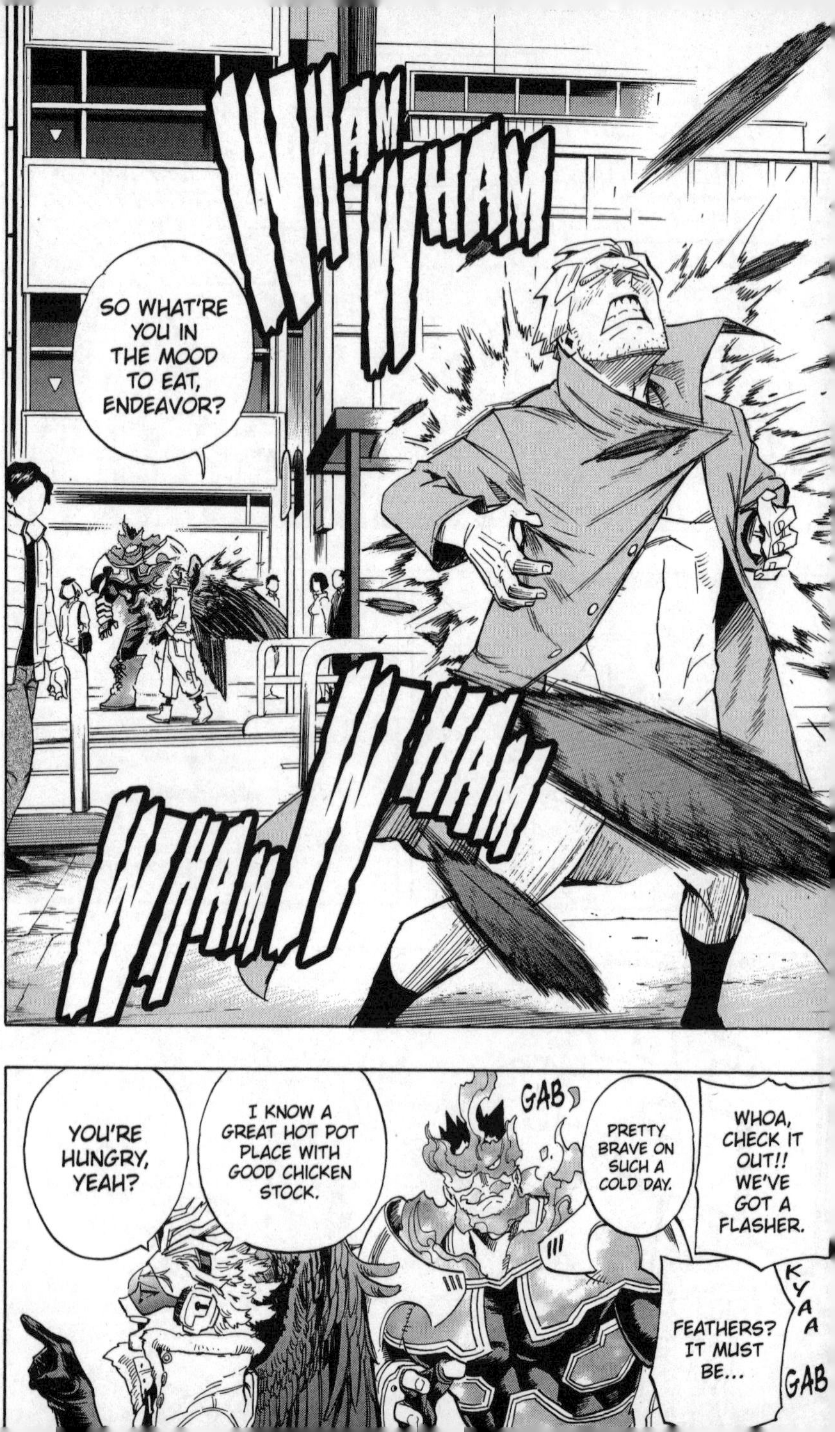
WHAM WHAM
SO WHAT'RE YOU IN THE MOOD TO EAT, ENDEAVOR?
WHAM WHAM
WHOA, CHECK IT OUT!! WE'VE GOT A FLASHER.
KYAA
FEATHERS? IT MUST BE...
GAB
GAB
PRETTY BRAVE ON SUCH A COLD DAY.
I KNOW A GREAT HOT POT PLACE WITH GOOD CHICKEN STOCK.
YOU'RE HUNGRY, YEAH?

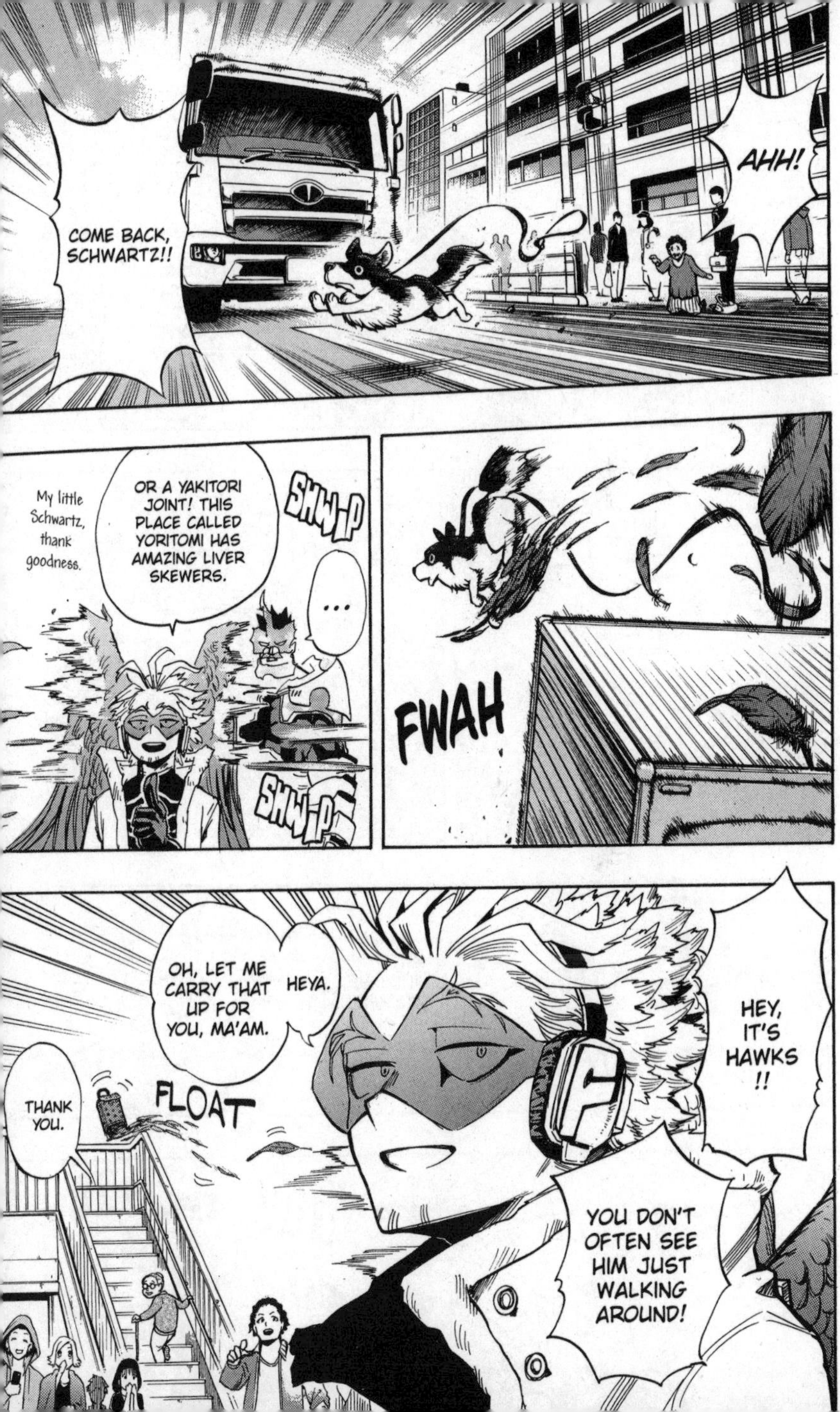
AHH!
COME BACK, SCHWARTZ!!
FWAH
SHWIP
...
OR A YAKITORI JOINT! THIS PLACE CALLED YORITOMI HAS AMAZING LIVER SKEWERS.
My little Schwartz, thank goodness.
SHWIP
HEY, IT'S HAWKS!!
YOU DON'T OFTEN SEE HIM JUST WALKING AROUND!
HEYA.
OH, LET ME CARRY THAT UP FOR YOU, MA'AM.
FLOAT
THANK YOU.

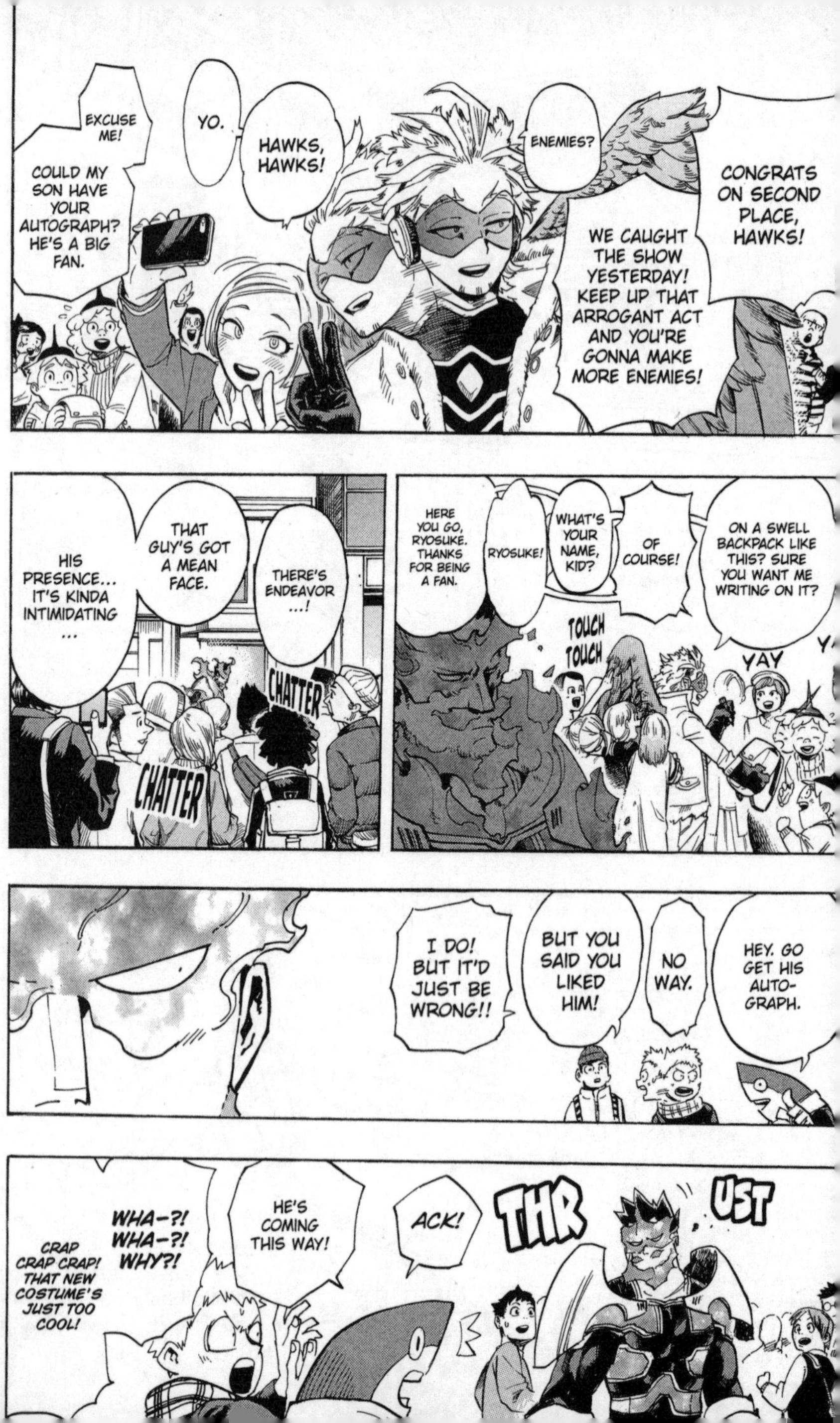
CONGRATS ON SECOND PLACE, HAWKS!
WE CAUGHT THE SHOW YESTERDAY! KEEP UP THAT ARROGANT ACT AND YOU'RE GONNA MAKE MORE ENEMIES!
ENEMIES?
HAWKS, HAWKS!
YO.
EXCUSE ME!
COULD MY SON HAVE YOUR AUTOGRAPH? HE'S A BIG FAN.
ON A SWELL BACKPACK LIKE THIS? SURE YOU WANT ME WRITING ON IT?
YAY
OF COURSE!
WHAT'S YOUR NAME, KID?
RYOSUKE!
HERE YOU GO, RYOSUKE. THANKS FOR BEING A FAN.
TOUCH TOUCH
THERE'S ENDEAVOR ...!
CHATTER
THAT GUY'S GOT A MEAN FACE.
HIS PRESENCE... IT'S KINDA INTIMIDATING ...
CHATTER
HEY. GO GET HIS AUTO-GRAPH.
NO WAY.
BUT YOU SAID YOU LIKED HIM!
I DO! BUT IT'D JUST BE WRONG!!
THR UST
ACK!
HE'S COMING THIS WAY!
WHA-?! WHA-?! WHY?!
CRAP CRAP CRAP! THAT NEW COSTUME'S JUST TOO COOL!

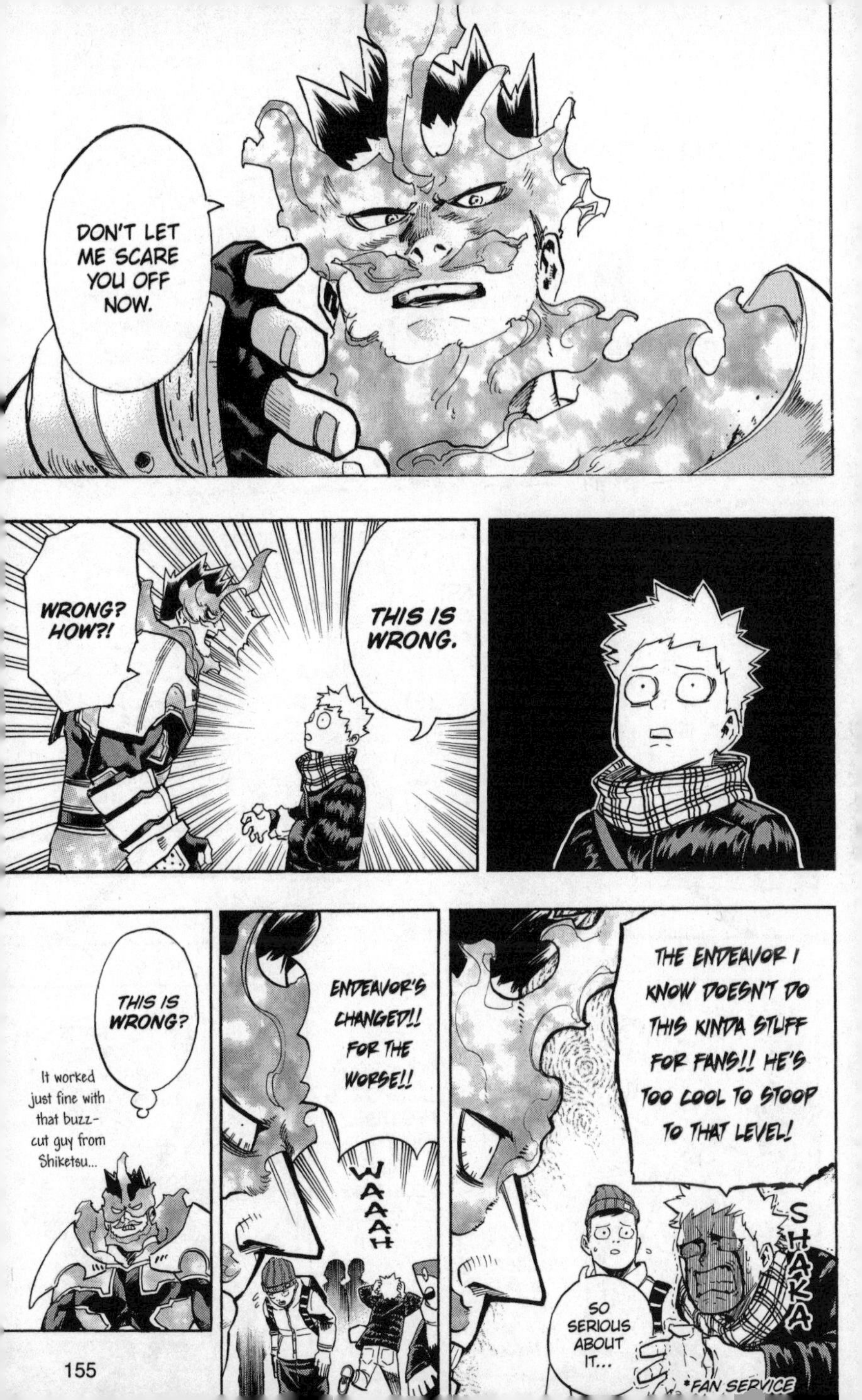
DON'T LET ME SCARE YOU OFF NOW.
THIS IS WRONG.
WRONG? HOW?!
THE ENDEAVOR I KNOW DOESN'T DO THIS KINDA STUFF FOR FANS!! HE'S TOO COOL TO STOOP TO THAT LEVEL!
SHAKA
SO SERIOUS ABOUT IT...
*FAN SERVICE
ENDEAVOR'S CHANGED!! FOR THE WORSE!!
WAAAAH
THIS IS WRONG?
It worked just fine with that buzz-cut guy from Shiketsu...

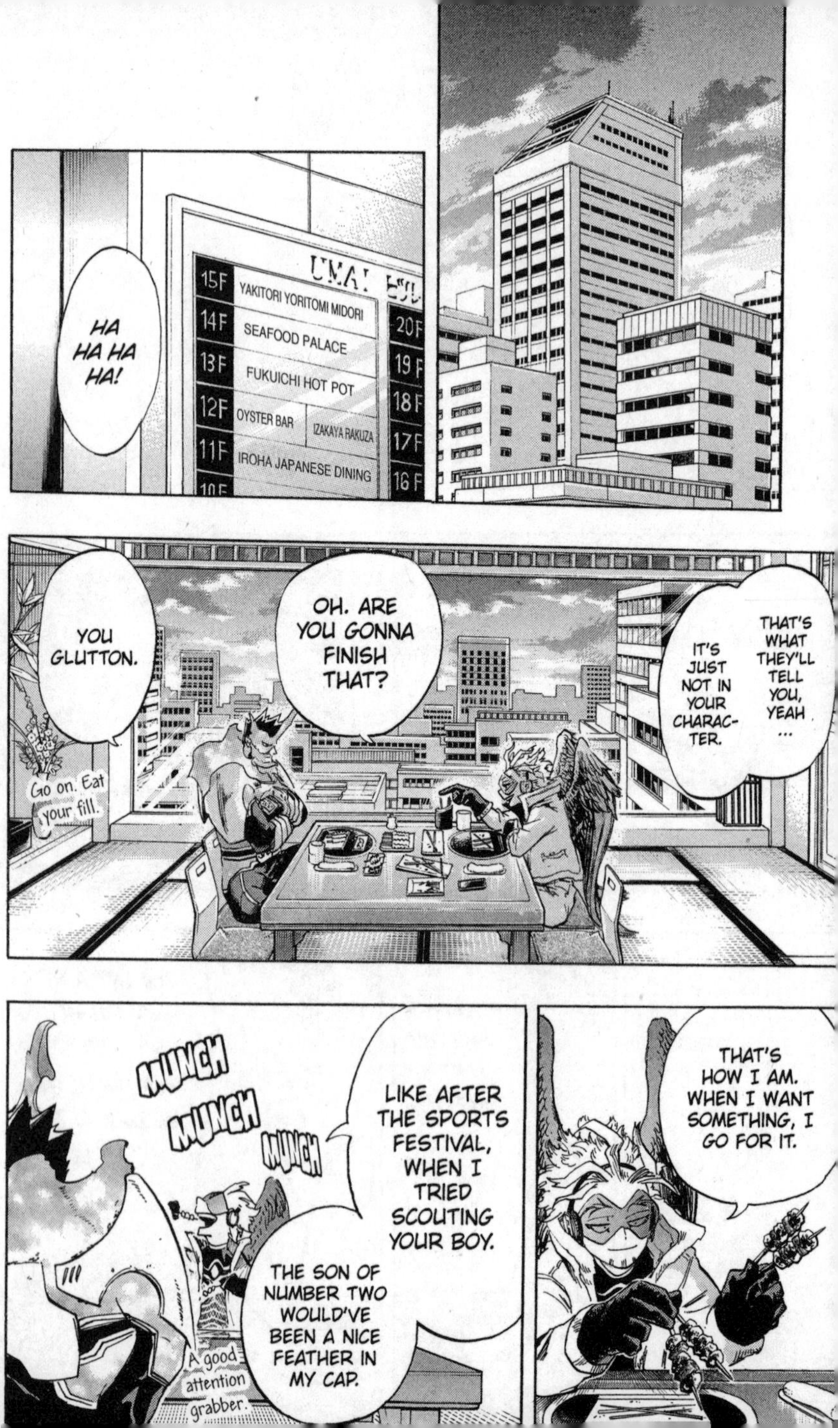

HA HA HA HA!
UMAI
15F YAKITORI YORITOMI MIDORI
14F SEAFOOD PALACE
13F FUKUICHI HOT POT
12F OYSTER BAR
IZAKAYA RAKUZA
11F IROHA JAPANESE DINING
20F
19F
18F
17F
16F
THAT'S WHAT THEY'LL TELL YOU, YEAH...
IT'S JUST NOT IN YOUR CHARAC-TER.
OH. ARE YOU GONNA FINISH THAT?
YOU GLUTTON.
Go on. Eat your fill.
THAT'S HOW I AM. WHEN I WANT SOMETHING, I GO FOR IT.
LIKE AFTER THE SPORTS FESTIVAL, WHEN I TRIED SCOUTING YOUR BOY.
MUNCH
MUNCH
MUNCH
THE SON OF NUMBER TWO WOULD'VE BEEN A NICE FEATHER IN MY CAP.
A good attention grabber.

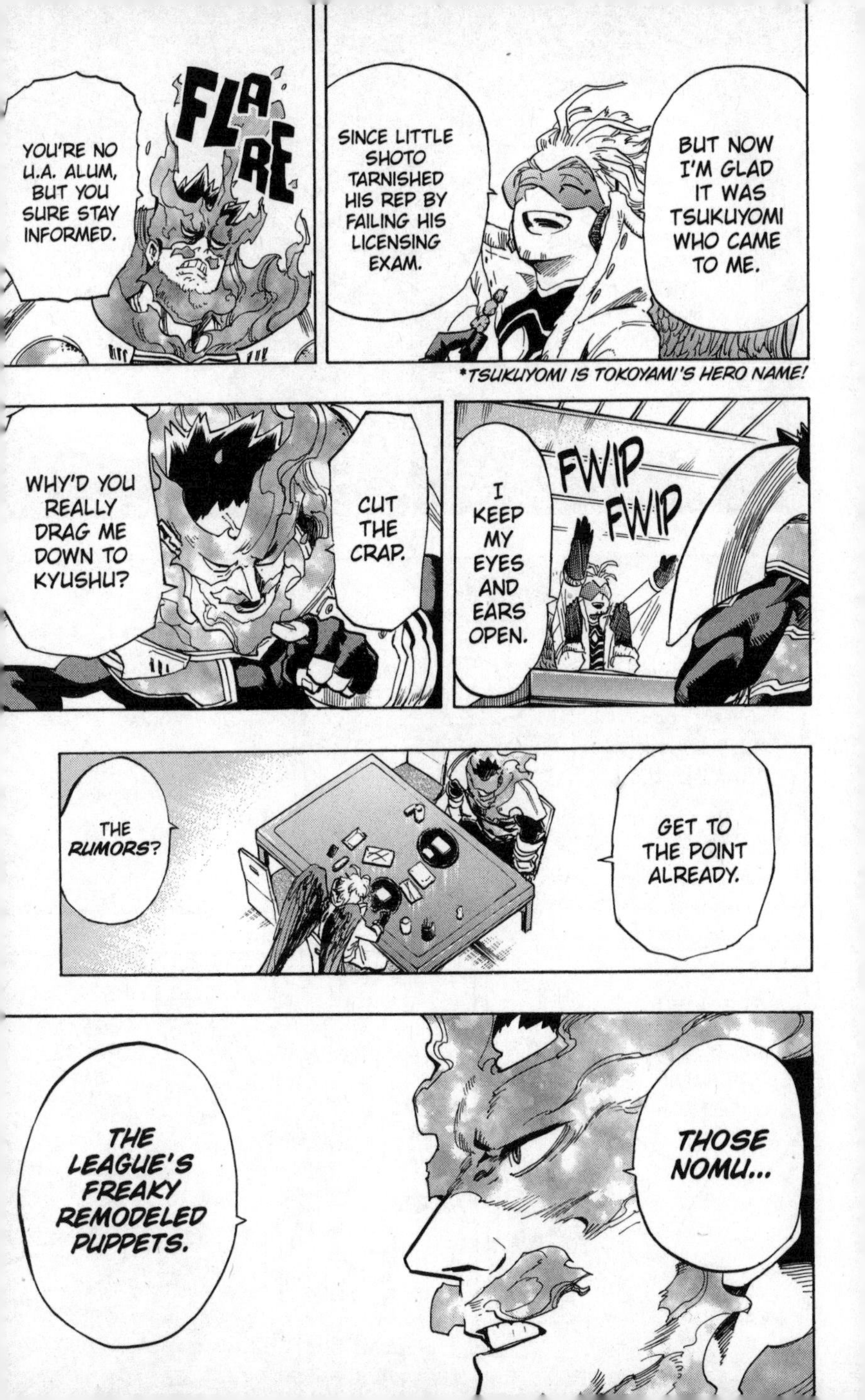
BUT NOW I'M GLAD IT WAS TSUKUYOMI WHO CAME TO ME.
SINCE LITTLE SHOTO TARNISHED HIS REP BY FAILING HIS LICENSING EXAM.
*TSUKUYOMI IS TOKOYAMI'S HERO NAME!
FLARE
YOU'RE NO U.A. ALUM, BUT YOU SURE STAY INFORMED.
FWIP FWIP
I KEEP MY EYES AND EARS OPEN.
CUT THE CRAP.
WHY'D YOU REALLY DRAG ME DOWN TO KYUSHU?
GET TO THE POINT ALREADY.
THE *RUMORS*?
THOSE NOMU...
THE LEAGUE'S FREAKY REMODELED PUPPETS.

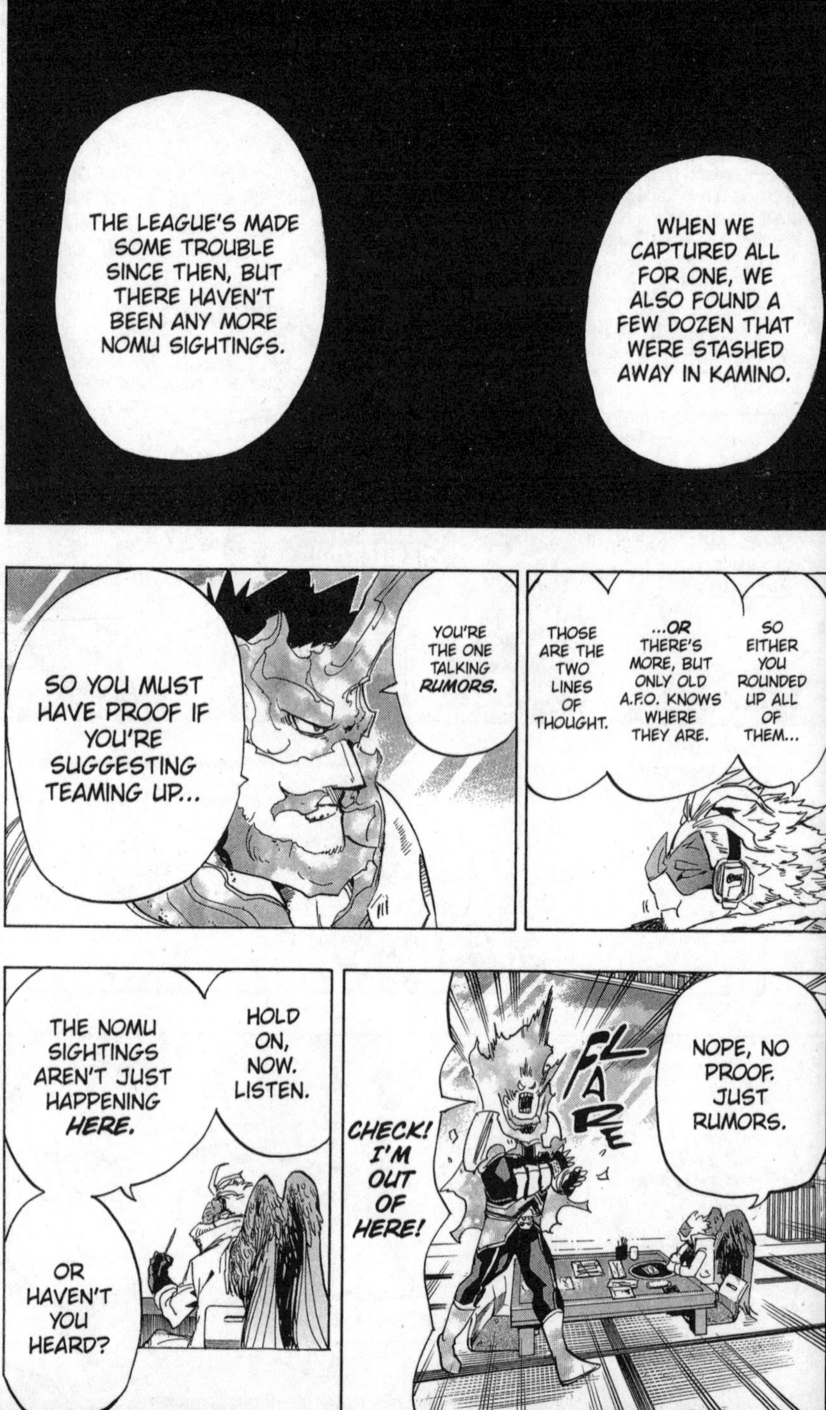
WHEN WE CAPTURED ALL FOR ONE, WE ALSO FOUND A FEW DOZEN THAT WERE STASHED AWAY IN KAMINO.
THE LEAGUE'S MADE SOME TROUBLE SINCE THEN, BUT THERE HAVEN'T BEEN ANY MORE NOMU SIGHTINGS.
SO EITHER YOU ROUNDED UP ALL OF THEM...
...*OR* THERE'S MORE, BUT ONLY OLD A.F.O. KNOWS WHERE THEY ARE.
THOSE ARE THE TWO LINES OF THOUGHT.
YOU'RE THE ONE TALKING *RUMORS.*
SO YOU MUST HAVE PROOF IF YOU'RE SUGGESTING TEAMING UP...
NOPE, NO PROOF. JUST RUMORS.
FLARE
CHECK! I'M OUT OF HERE!
HOLD ON, NOW. LISTEN.
THE NOMU SIGHTINGS AREN'T JUST HAPPENING *HERE.*
OR HAVEN'T YOU HEARD?

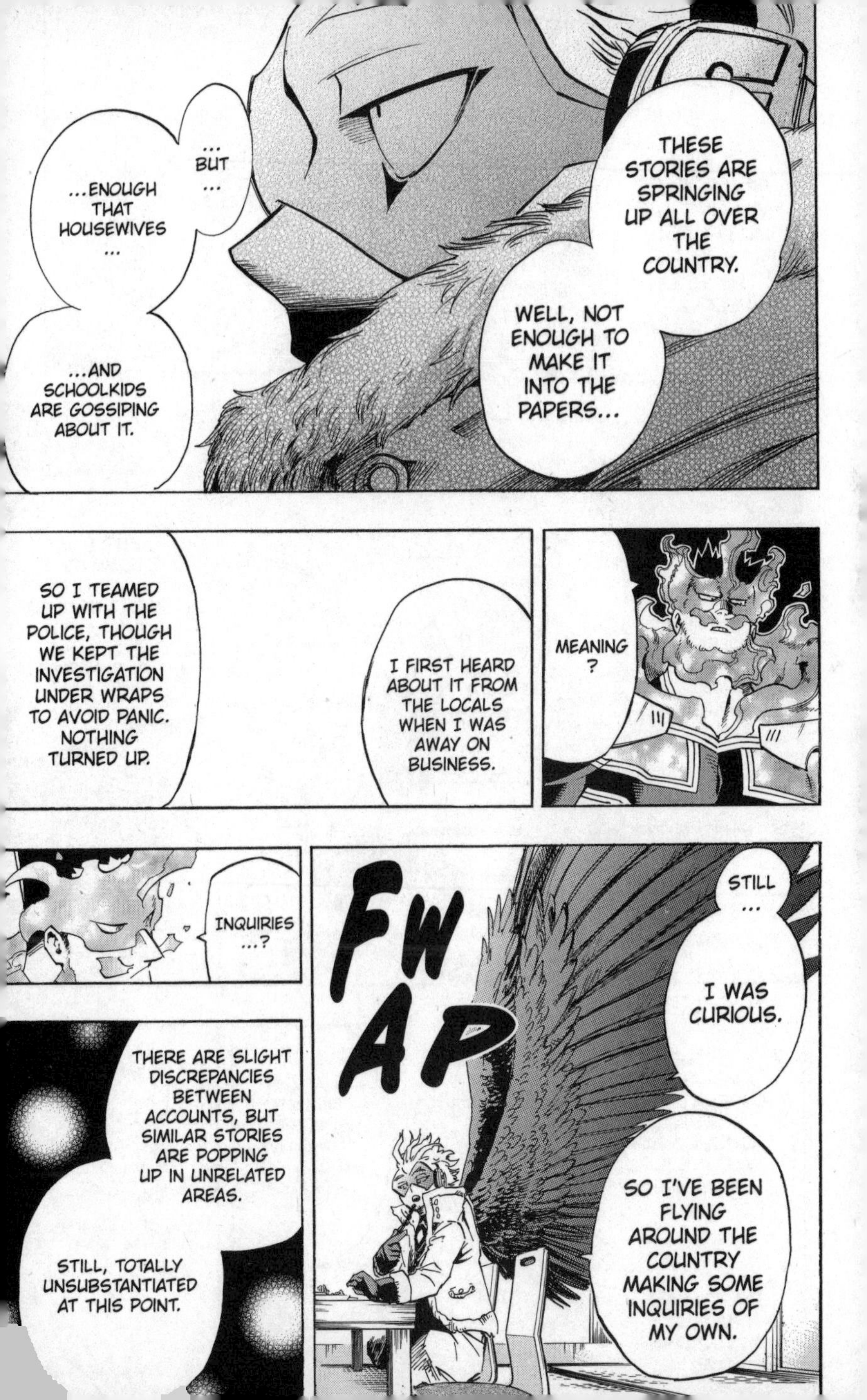
THESE STORIES ARE SPRINGING UP ALL OVER THE COUNTRY.
WELL, NOT ENOUGH TO MAKE IT INTO THE PAPERS...
...BUT...
...ENOUGH THAT HOUSEWIVES...
...AND SCHOOLKIDS ARE GOSSIPING ABOUT IT.
MEANING?
I FIRST HEARD ABOUT IT FROM THE LOCALS WHEN I WAS AWAY ON BUSINESS.
SO I TEAMED UP WITH THE POLICE, THOUGH WE KEPT THE INVESTIGATION UNDER WRAPS TO AVOID PANIC. NOTHING TURNED UP.
STILL...
FWAP
I WAS CURIOUS.
SO I'VE BEEN FLYING AROUND THE COUNTRY MAKING SOME INQUIRIES OF MY OWN.
INQUIRIES...?
THERE ARE SLIGHT DISCREPANCIES BETWEEN ACCOUNTS, BUT SIMILAR STORIES ARE POPPING UP IN UNRELATED AREAS.
STILL, TOTALLY UNSUBSTANTIATED AT THIS POINT.

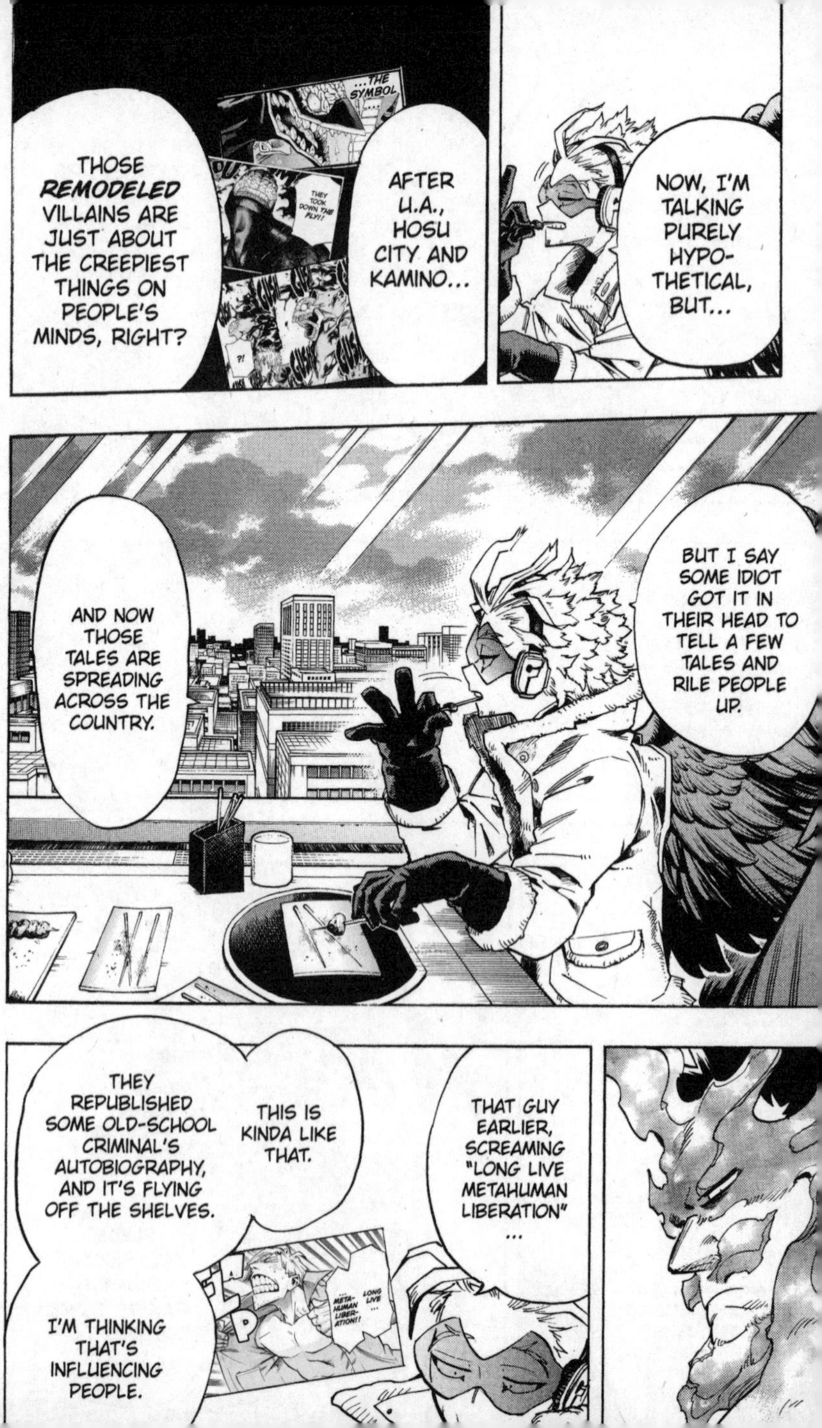

NOW, I'M TALKING PURELY HYPOTHETICAL, BUT...
AFTER U.A., HOSU CITY AND KAMINO...
...THE SYMBOL
THEY TOOK DOWN THE FLY!?
?!
THOSE ***REMODELED*** VILLAINS ARE JUST ABOUT THE CREEPIEST THINGS ON PEOPLE'S MINDS, RIGHT?
BUT I SAY SOME IDIOT GOT IT IN THEIR HEAD TO TELL A FEW TALES AND RILE PEOPLE UP.
AND NOW THOSE TALES ARE SPREADING ACROSS THE COUNTRY.
THAT GUY EARLIER, SCREAMING "LONG LIVE METAHUMAN LIBERATION" ...
LONG LIVE ...
... METAHUMAN LIBERATION!!
THIS IS KINDA LIKE THAT.
THEY REPUBLISHED SOME OLD-SCHOOL CRIMINAL'S AUTOBIOGRAPHY, AND IT'S FLYING OFF THE SHELVES.
I'M THINKING THAT'S INFLUENCING PEOPLE.

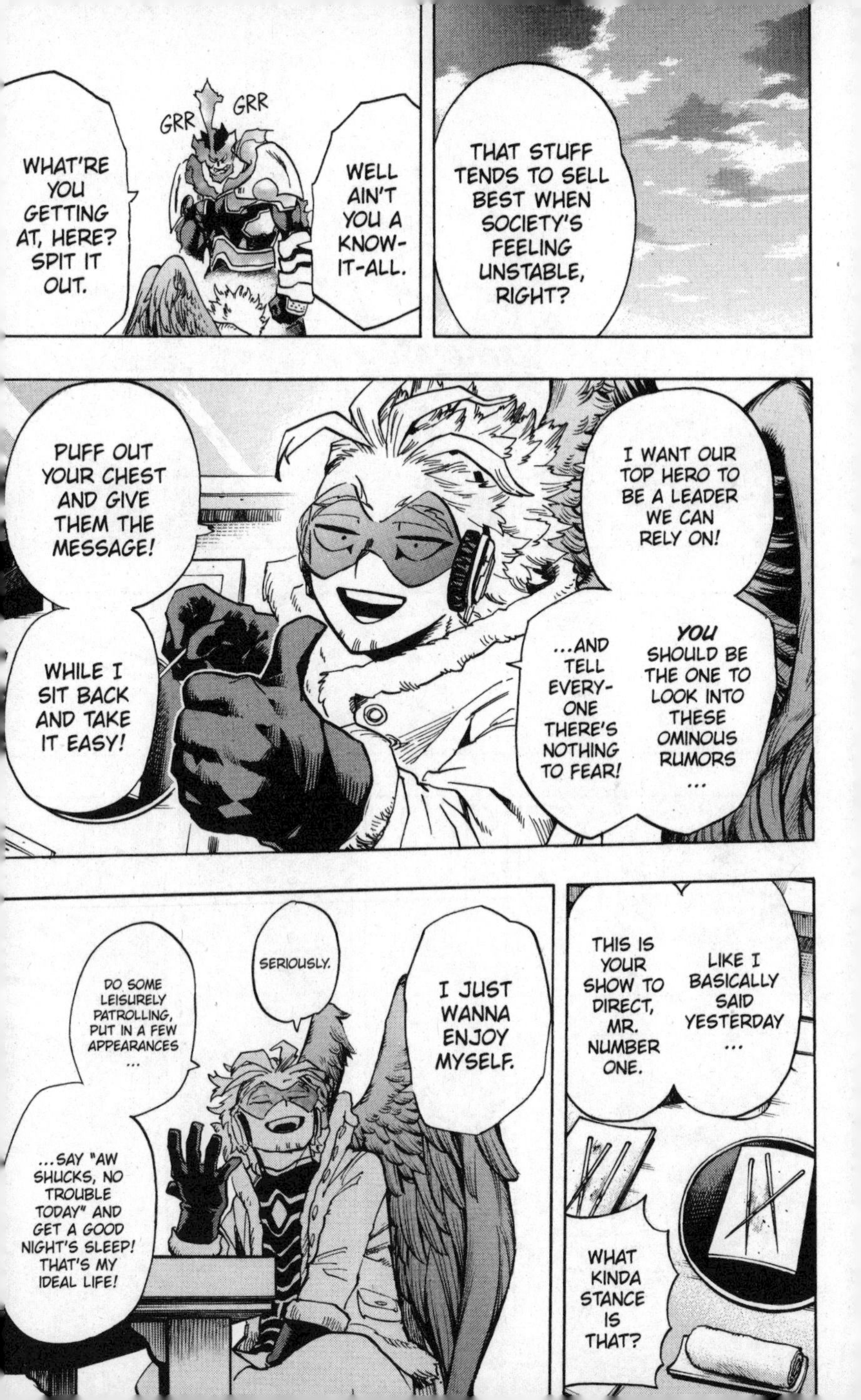
THAT STUFF TENDS TO SELL BEST WHEN SOCIETY'S FEELING UNSTABLE, RIGHT?
WELL AIN'T YOU A KNOW-IT-ALL.
GRR GRR
WHAT'RE YOU GETTING AT, HERE? SPIT IT OUT.
I WANT OUR TOP HERO TO BE A LEADER WE CAN RELY ON!
YOU SHOULD BE THE ONE TO LOOK INTO THESE OMINOUS RUMORS ...
...AND TELL EVERY-ONE THERE'S NOTHING TO FEAR!
PUFF OUT YOUR CHEST AND GIVE THEM THE MESSAGE!
WHILE I SIT BACK AND TAKE IT EASY!
LIKE I BASICALLY SAID YESTERDAY ...
THIS IS YOUR SHOW TO DIRECT, MR. NUMBER ONE.
WHAT KINDA STANCE IS THAT?
I JUST WANNA ENJOY MYSELF.
SERIOUSLY.
DO SOME LEISURELY PATROLLING, PUT IN A FEW APPEARANCES ...
...SAY "AW SHUCKS, NO TROUBLE TODAY" AND GET A GOOD NIGHT'S SLEEP! THAT'S MY IDEAL LIFE!

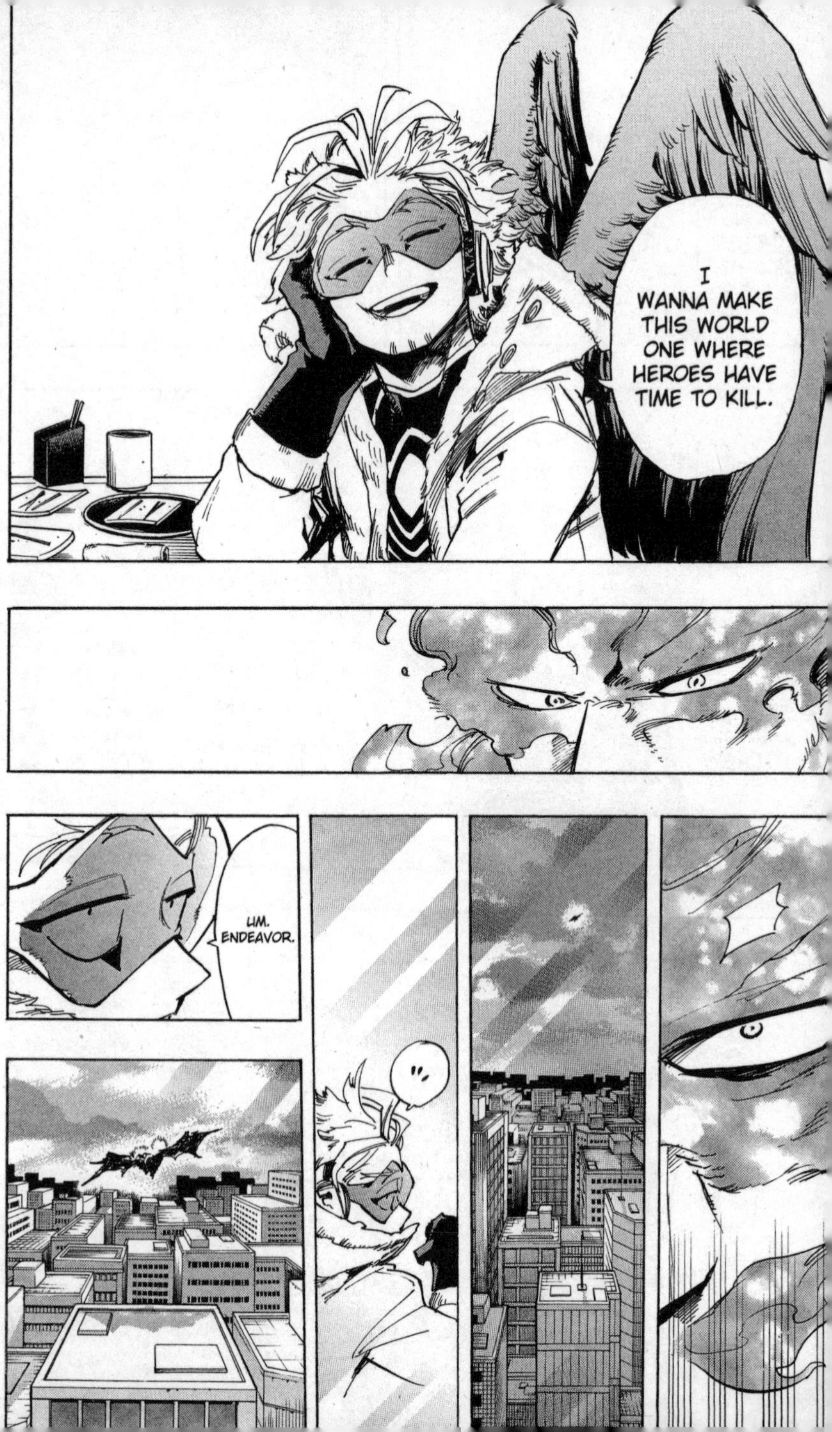
I WANNA MAKE THIS WORLD ONE WHERE HEROES HAVE TIME TO KILL.
UM. ENDEAVOR.

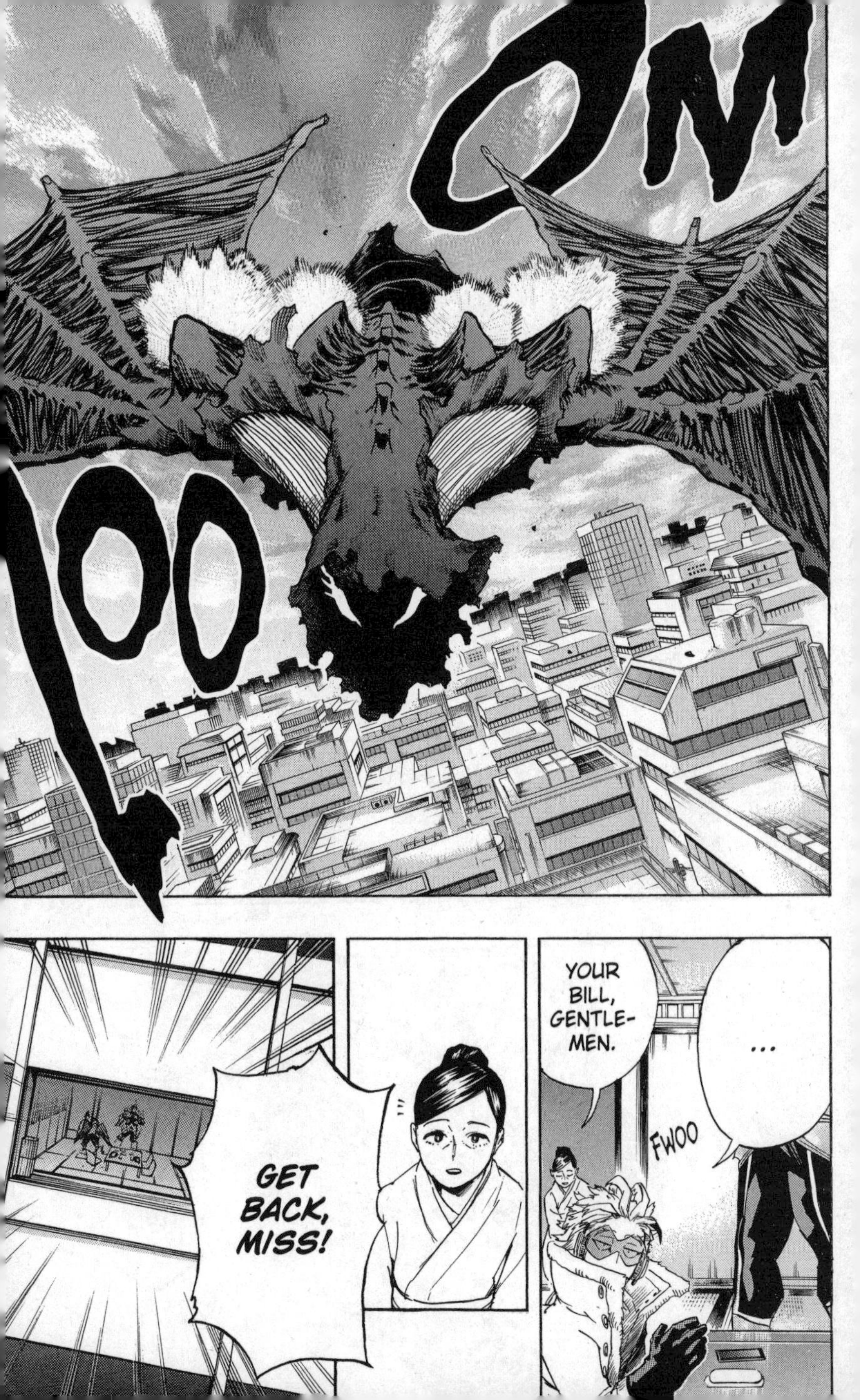
DOOOM
YOUR BILL, GENTLE-MEN.
...
FWOO
GET BACK, MISS!

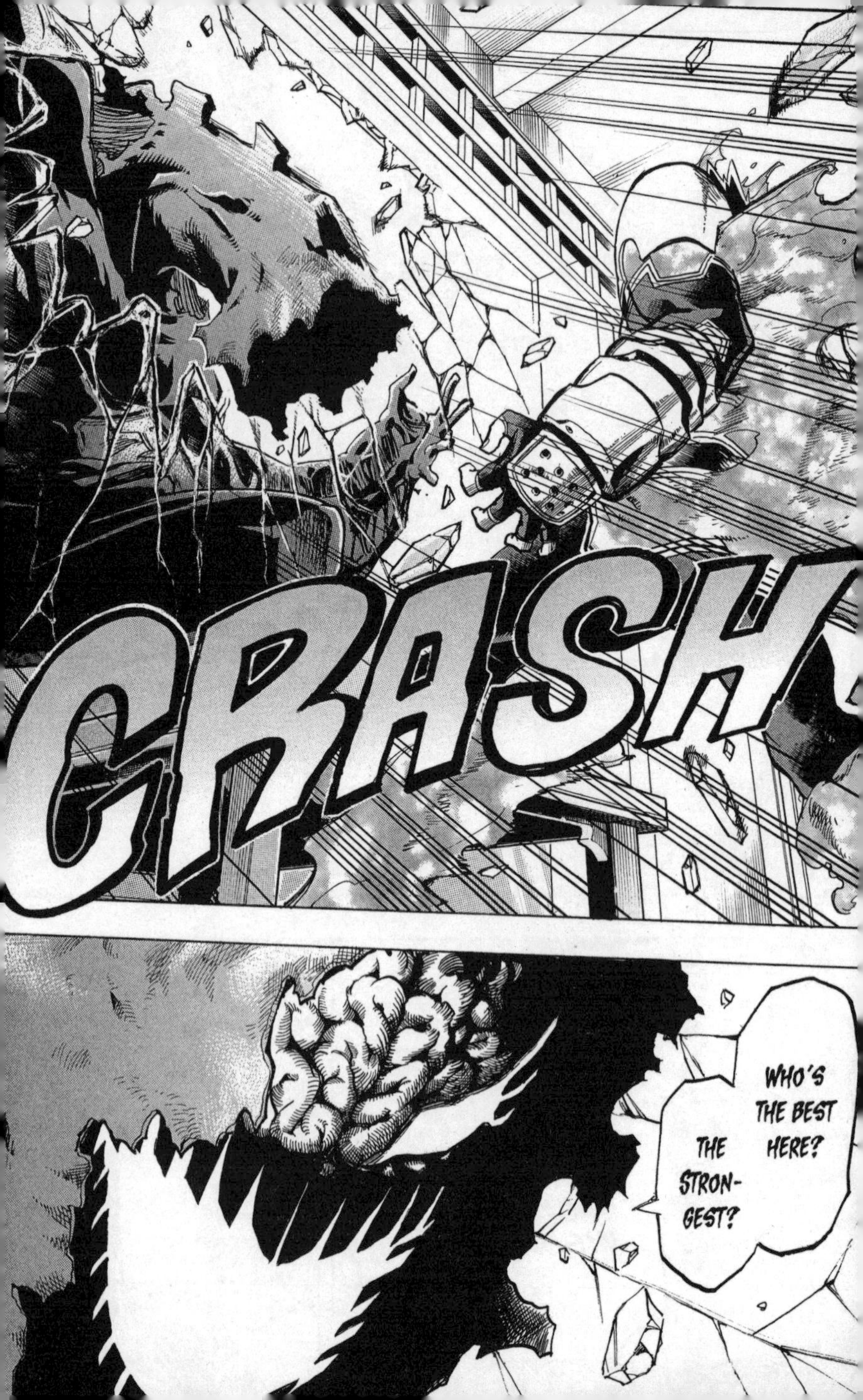
CRASH
WHO'S THE BEST HERE?
THE STRONGEST?

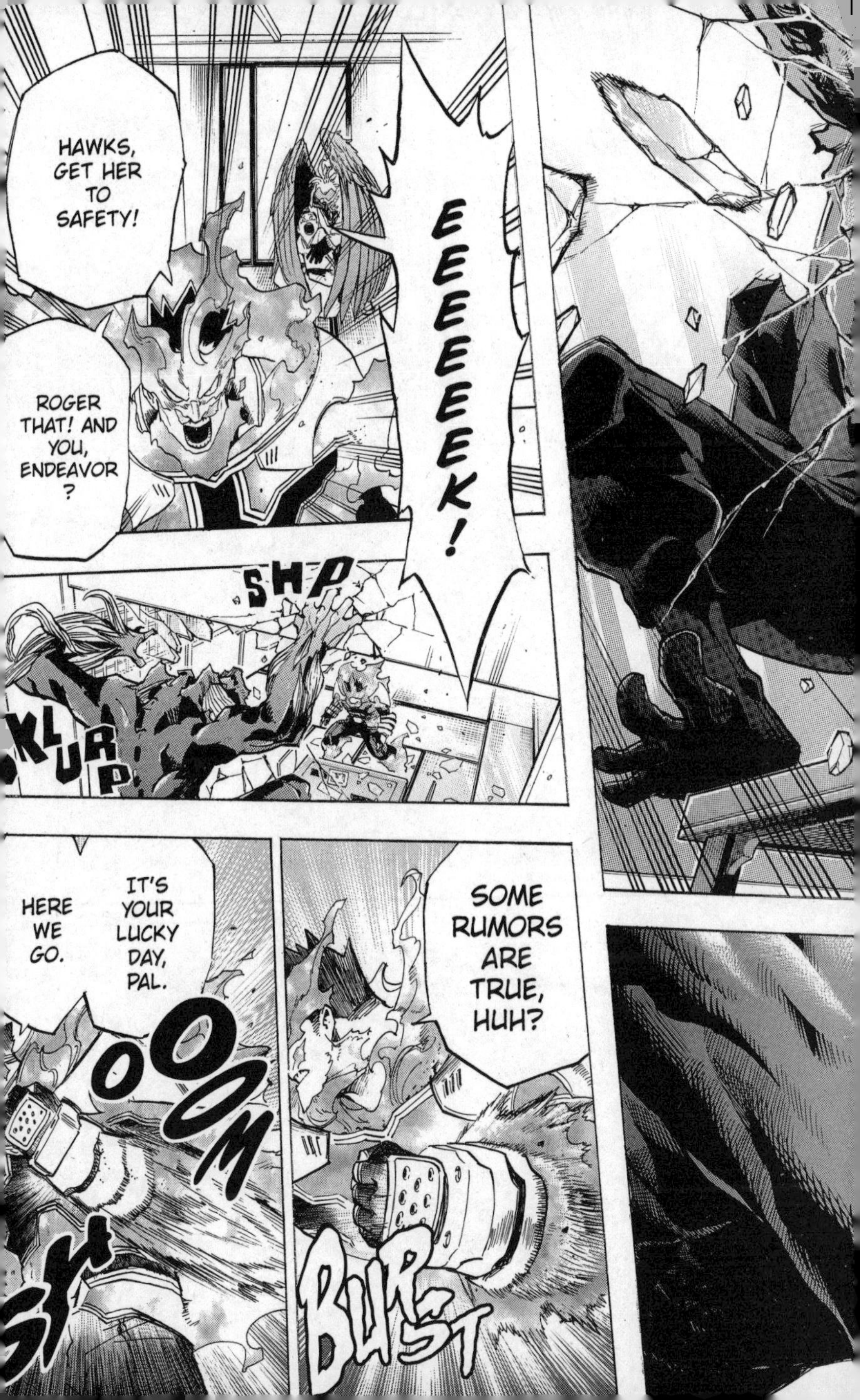
HAWKS, GET HER TO SAFETY!
ROGER THAT! AND YOU, ENDEAVOR?
EEEEEEEK!
SHP
KLURUP
SOME RUMORS ARE TRUE, HUH?
BURST
IT'S YOUR LUCKY DAY, PAL.
HERE WE GO.
OOOM

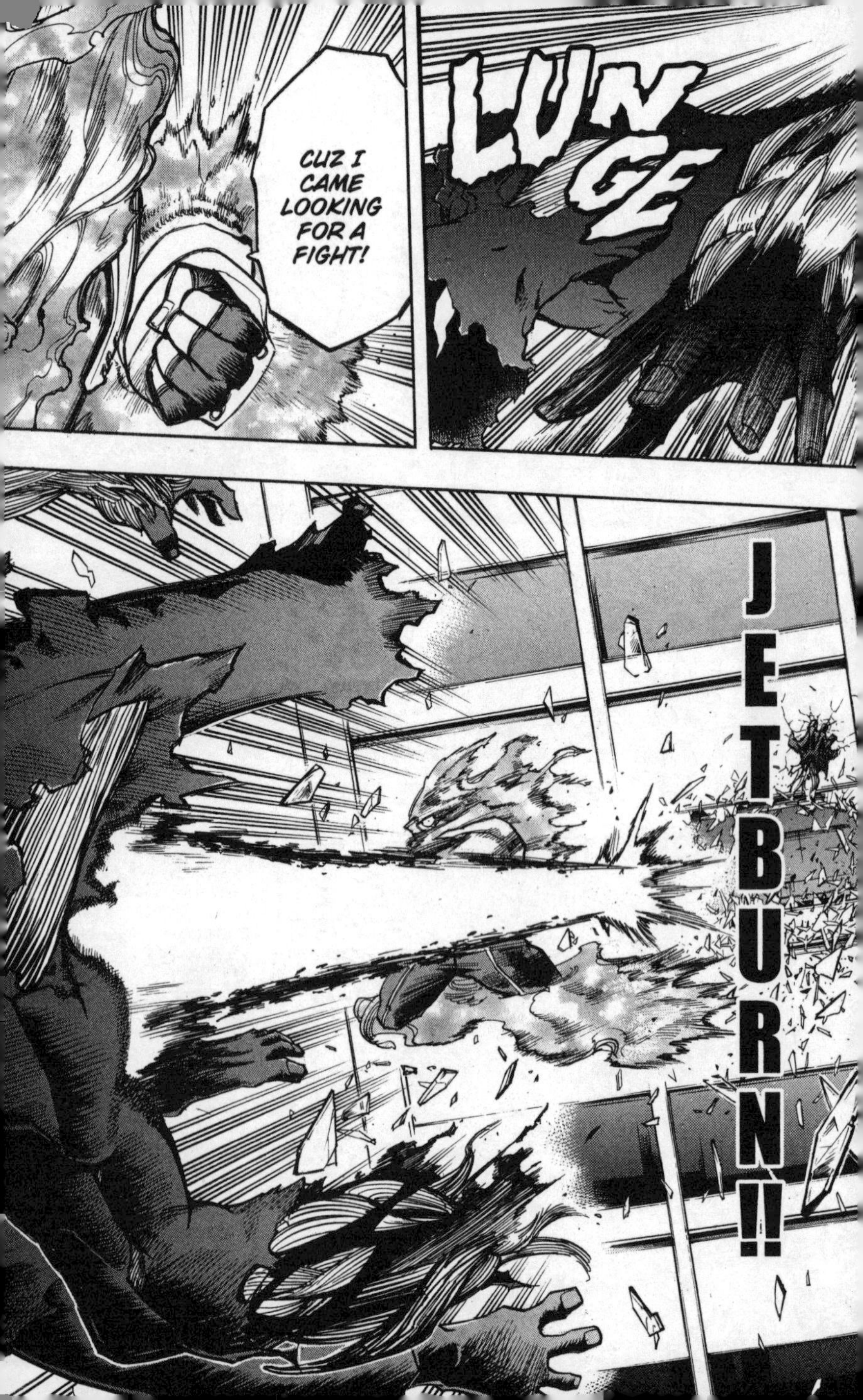
LUNGE
CUZ I CAME LOOKING FOR A FIGHT!
JET BURN!!

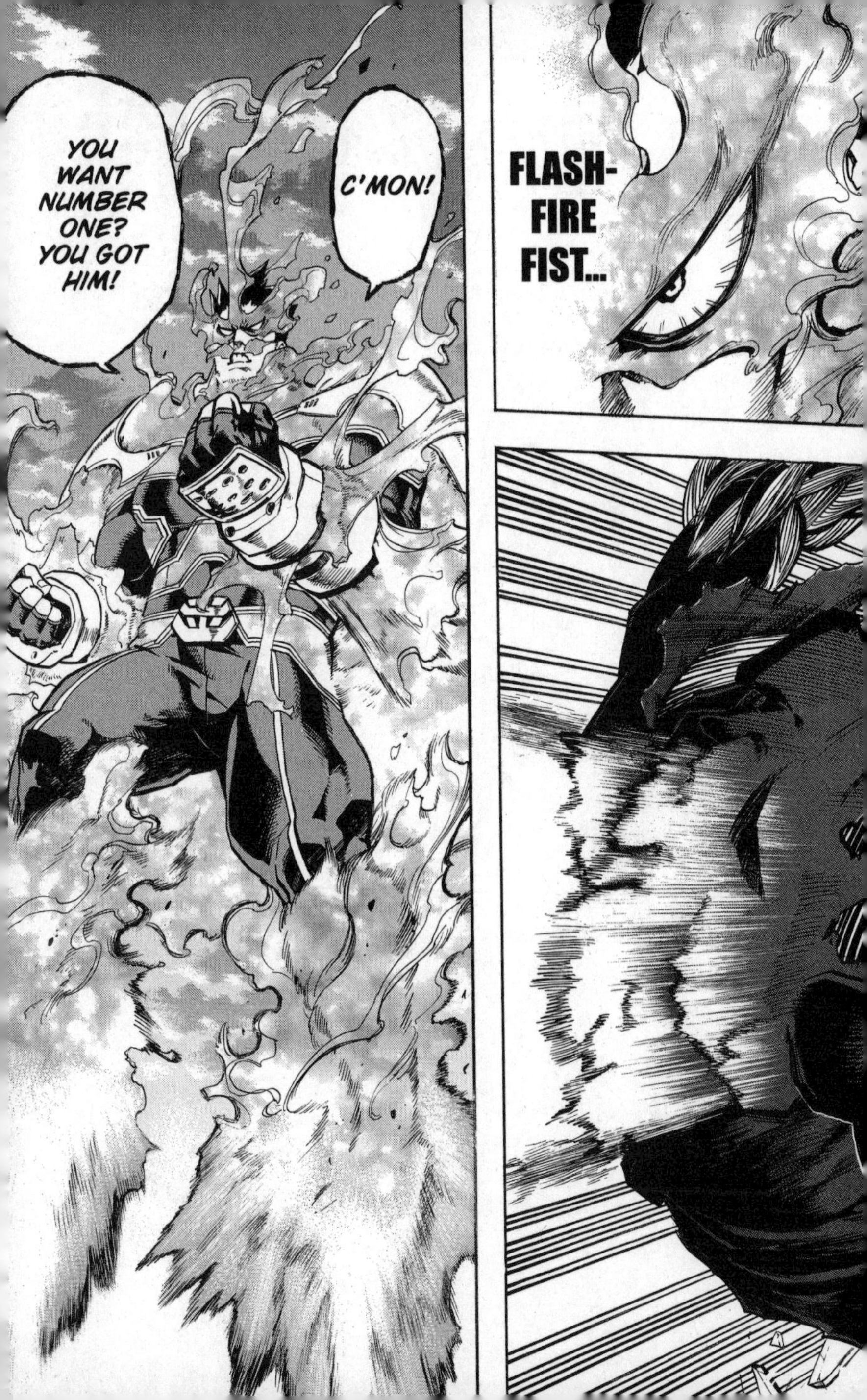
FLASH-FIRE FIST...
C'MON!
YOU WANT NUMBER ONE? YOU GOT HIM!

HERO

MIRKO (26) (RUMI USAGIYAMA)

STREET CLOTHES

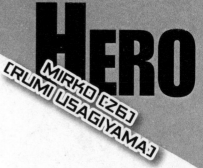

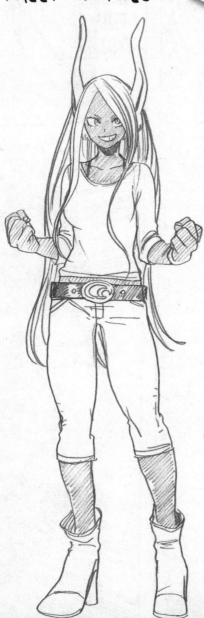

Birthday: 3/1
Height: 159 cm
Favorite Thing: Carrots

THE SUPPLEMENT

Designwise, she's an amalgamation of my likes and preferences.

Her hero name is a reference to a certain MMA fighter.

No. 187 - Flaming Roar! vs. Nomu: High-End

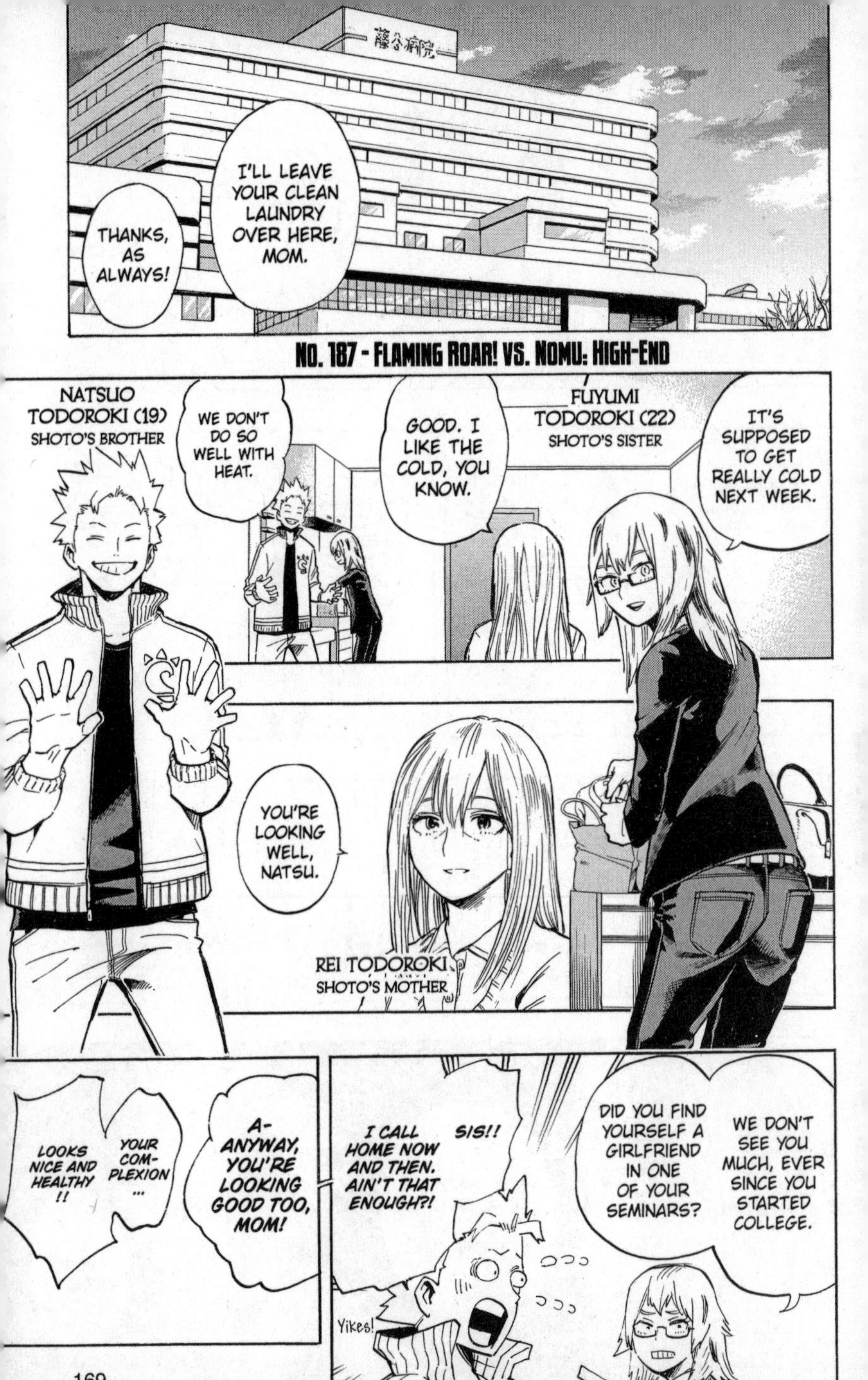

I'LL LEAVE YOUR CLEAN LAUNDRY OVER HERE, MOM.
THANKS, AS ALWAYS!
藤谷病院
IT'S SUPPOSED TO GET REALLY COLD NEXT WEEK.
FUYUMI TODOROKI (22) SHOTO'S SISTER
GOOD. I LIKE THE COLD, YOU KNOW.
WE DON'T DO SO WELL WITH HEAT.
NATSUO TODOROKI (19) SHOTO'S BROTHER
YOU'RE LOOKING WELL, NATSU.
REI TODOROKI SHOTO'S MOTHER
WE DON'T SEE YOU MUCH, EVER SINCE YOU STARTED COLLEGE.
DID YOU FIND YOURSELF A GIRLFRIEND IN ONE OF YOUR SEMINARS?
SIS!!
I CALL HOME NOW AND THEN. AIN'T THAT ENOUGH?!
Yikes!
A- ANYWAY, YOU'RE LOOKING GOOD TOO, MOM!
YOUR COMPLEXION...
LOOKS NICE AND HEALTHY!!

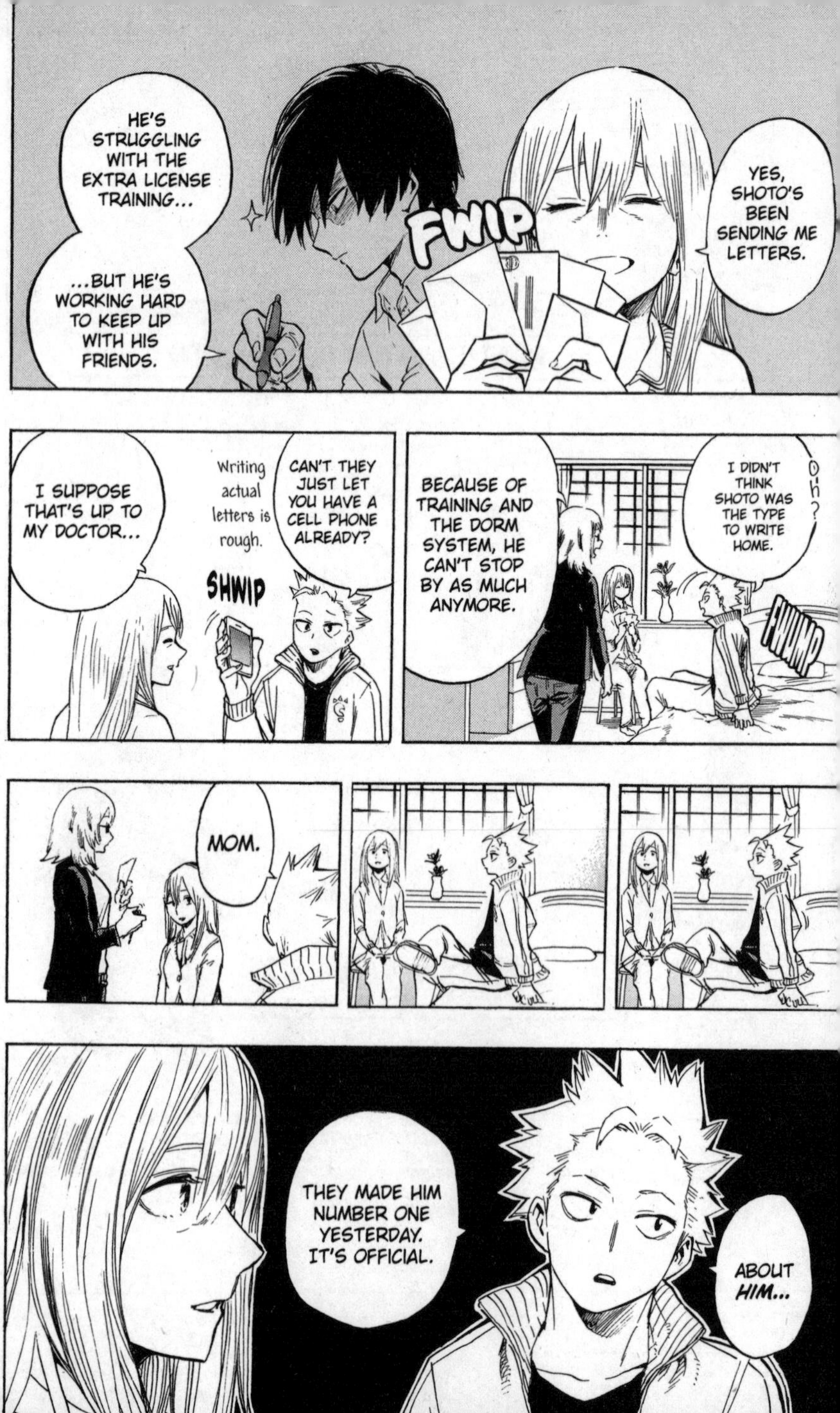
YES, SHOTO'S BEEN SENDING ME LETTERS.
FWIP
HE'S STRUGGLING WITH THE EXTRA LICENSE TRAINING...
...BUT HE'S WORKING HARD TO KEEP UP WITH HIS FRIENDS.
Oh?
I DIDN'T THINK SHOTO WAS THE TYPE TO WRITE HOME.
FWUMP
BECAUSE OF TRAINING AND THE DORM SYSTEM, HE CAN'T STOP BY AS MUCH ANYMORE.
CAN'T THEY JUST LET YOU HAVE A CELL PHONE ALREADY?
Writing actual letters is rough.
SHWIP
I SUPPOSE THAT'S UP TO MY DOCTOR...
MOM.
ABOUT HIM...
THEY MADE HIM NUMBER ONE YESTERDAY. IT'S OFFICIAL.

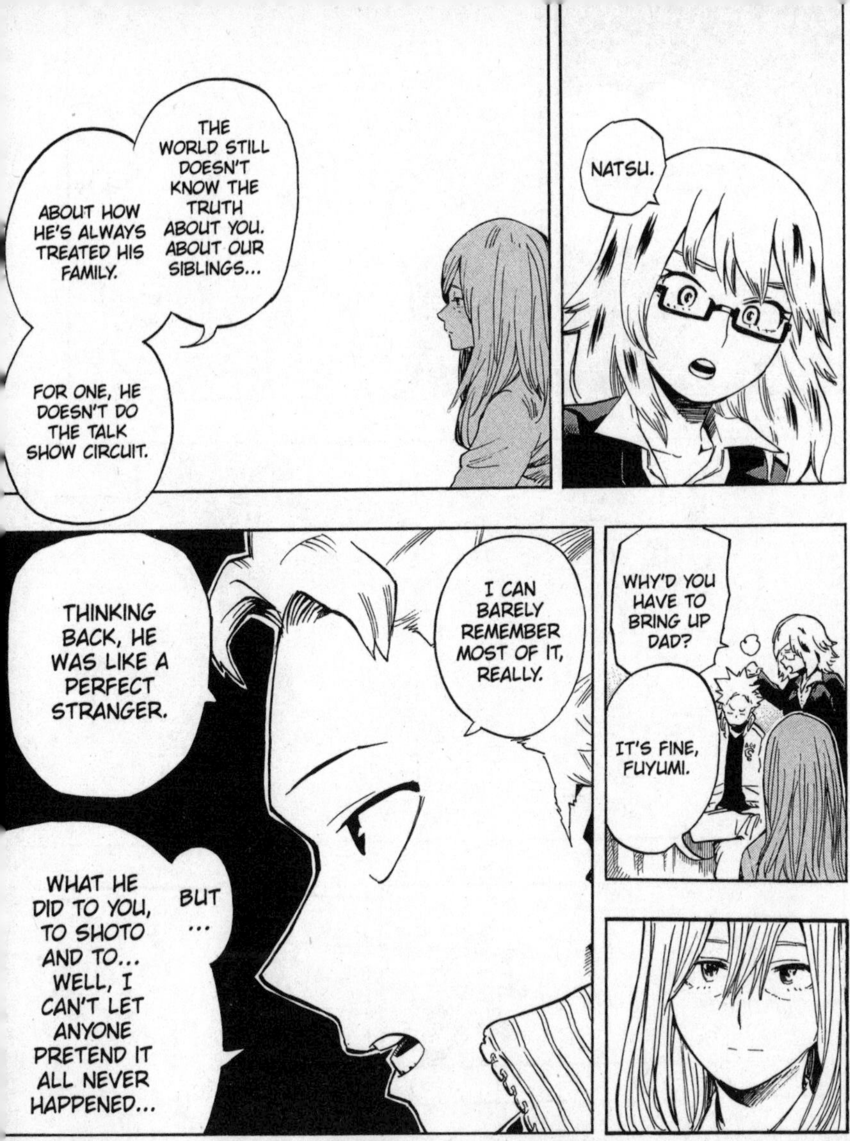
NATSU.
THE WORLD STILL DOESN'T KNOW THE TRUTH ABOUT YOU. ABOUT OUR SIBLINGS...
ABOUT HOW HE'S ALWAYS TREATED HIS FAMILY.
FOR ONE, HE DOESN'T DO THE TALK SHOW CIRCUIT.
WHY'D YOU HAVE TO BRING UP DAD?
IT'S FINE, FUYUMI.
I CAN BARELY REMEMBER MOST OF IT, REALLY.
THINKING BACK, HE WAS LIKE A PERFECT STRANGER.
BUT...
WHAT HE DID TO YOU, TO SHOTO AND TO... WELL, I CAN'T LET ANYONE PRETEND IT ALL NEVER HAPPENED...

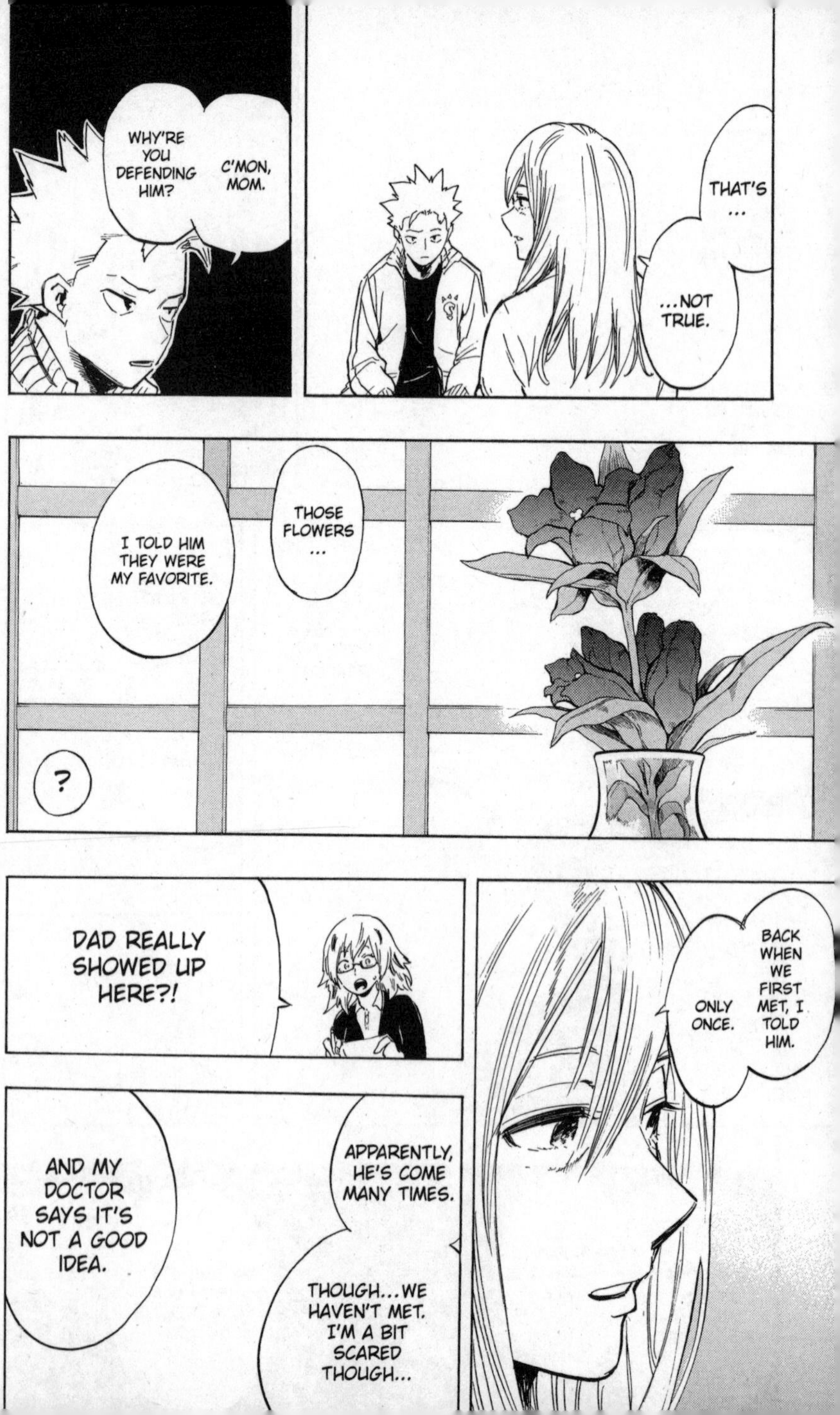
THAT'S ...
...NOT TRUE.
C'MON, MOM.
WHY'RE YOU DEFENDING HIM?
THOSE FLOWERS ...
I TOLD HIM THEY WERE MY FAVORITE.
?
BACK WHEN WE FIRST MET, I TOLD HIM.
ONLY ONCE.
DAD REALLY SHOWED UP HERE?!
APPARENTLY, HE'S COME MANY TIMES.
AND MY DOCTOR SAYS IT'S NOT A GOOD IDEA.
THOUGH...WE HAVEN'T MET. I'M A BIT SCARED THOUGH...

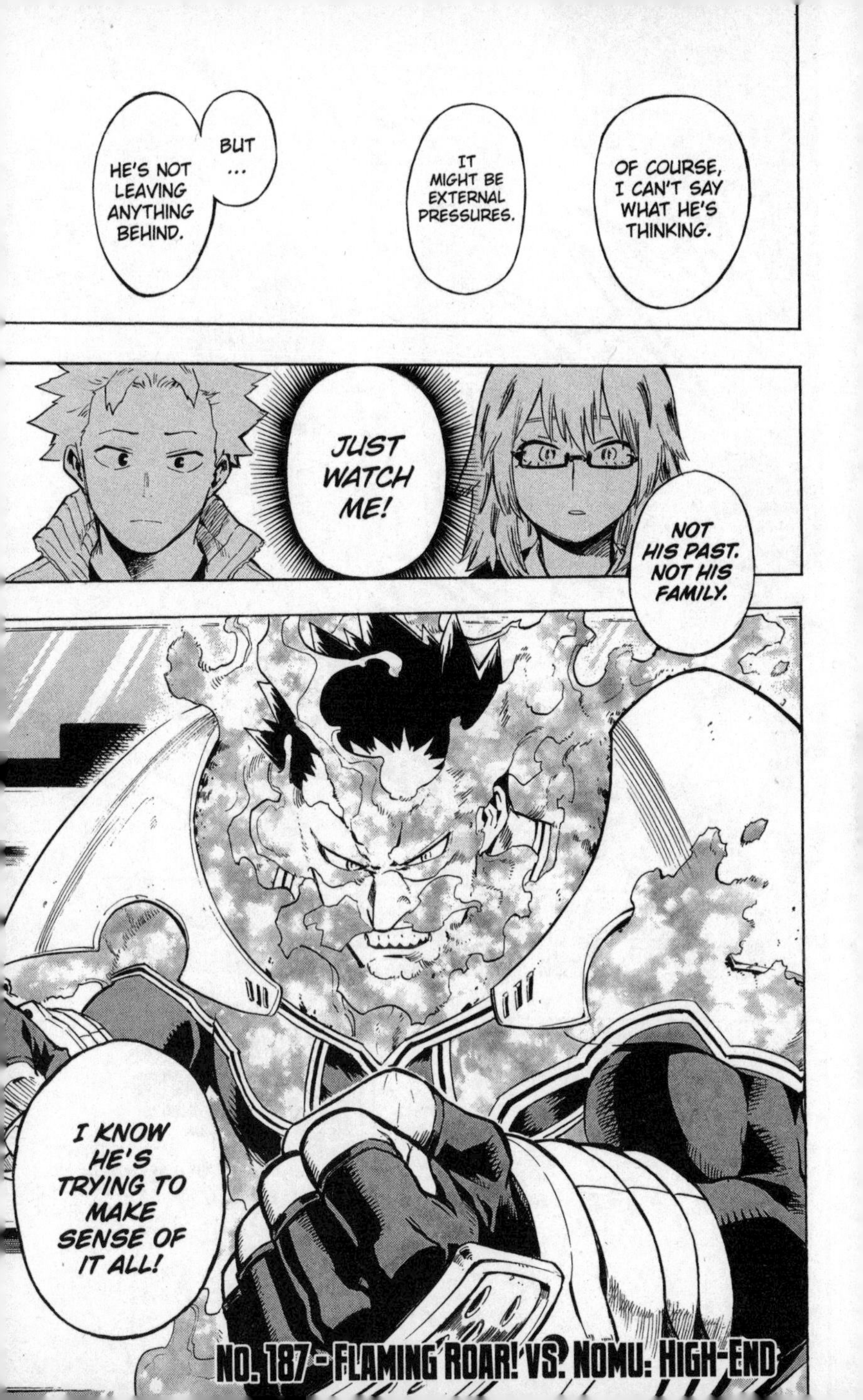
OF COURSE, I CAN'T SAY WHAT HE'S THINKING.
IT MIGHT BE EXTERNAL PRESSURES.
BUT ...
HE'S NOT LEAVING ANYTHING BEHIND.
NOT HIS PAST. NOT HIS FAMILY.
JUST WATCH ME!
I KNOW HE'S TRYING TO MAKE SENSE OF IT ALL!
NO. 187 - FLAMING ROAR! VS. NOMU: HIGH-END

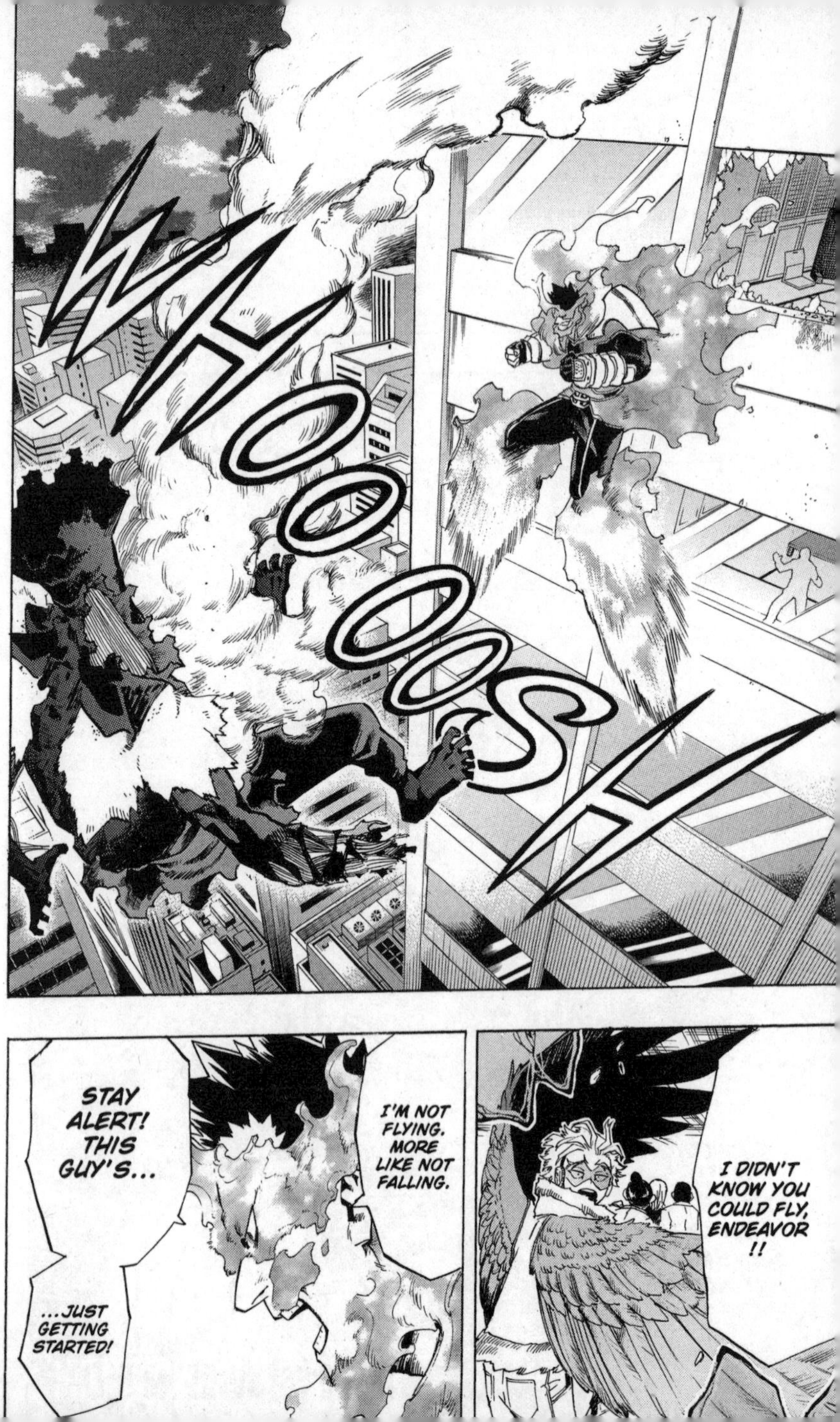
WHOOOOOSH
I DIDN'T KNOW YOU COULD FLY, ENDEAVOR!!
I'M NOT FLYING. MORE LIKE NOT FALLING.
STAY ALERT! THIS GUY'S...
...JUST GETTING STARTED!

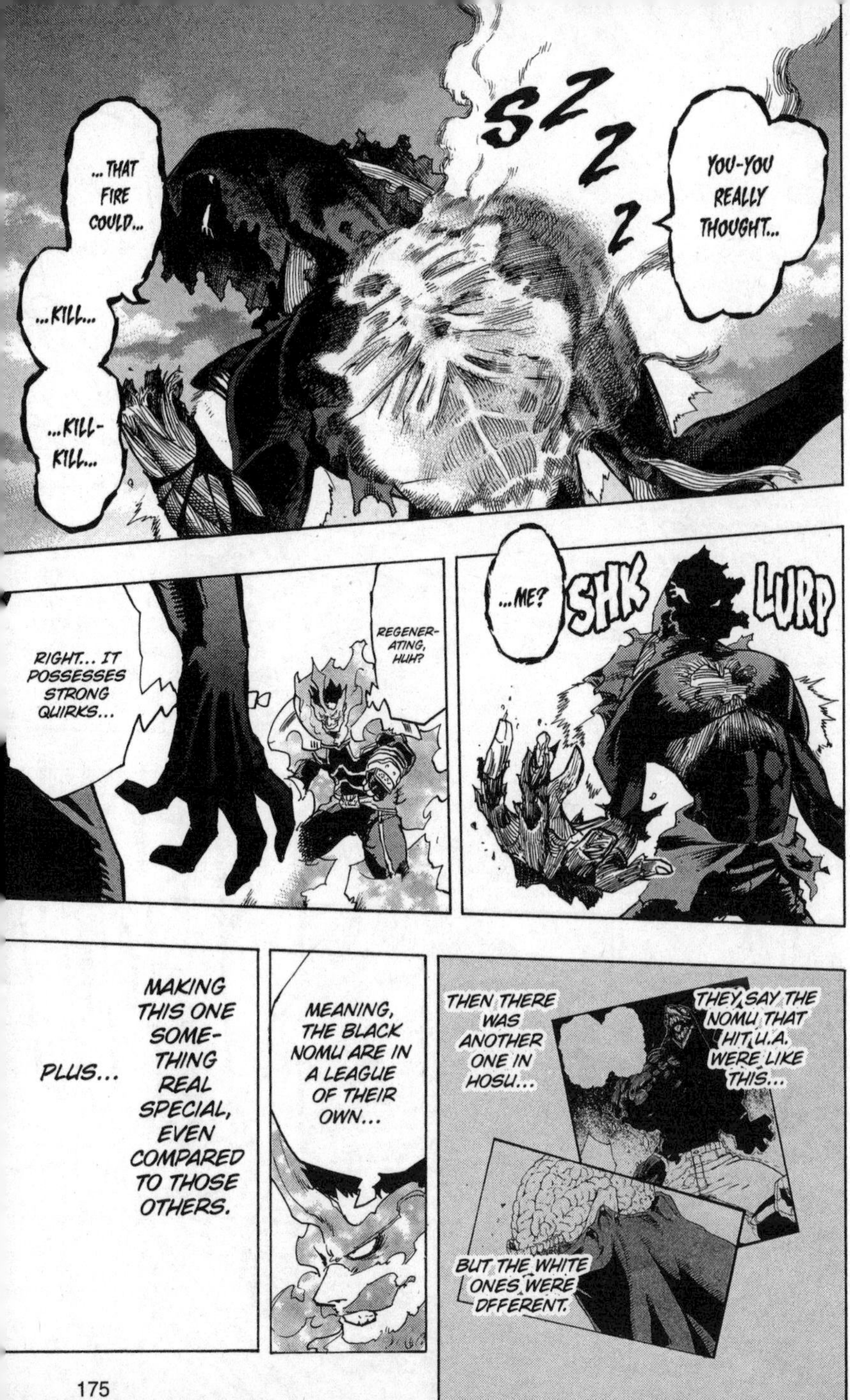
YOU-YOU REALLY THOUGHT...
SZZZZ
...THAT FIRE COULD...
...KILL...
...KILL-KILL...
...ME?
SHK
LURP
REGENER-ATING, HUH?
RIGHT... IT POSSESSES STRONG QUIRKS...
THEY SAY THE NOMU THAT HIT U.A. WERE LIKE THIS...
THEN THERE WAS ANOTHER ONE IN HOSU...
BUT THE WHITE ONES WERE DFFERENT.
MEANING, THE BLACK NOMU ARE IN A LEAGUE OF THEIR OWN...
MAKING THIS ONE SOME-THING REAL SPECIAL, EVEN COMPARED TO THOSE OTHERS.
PLUS...

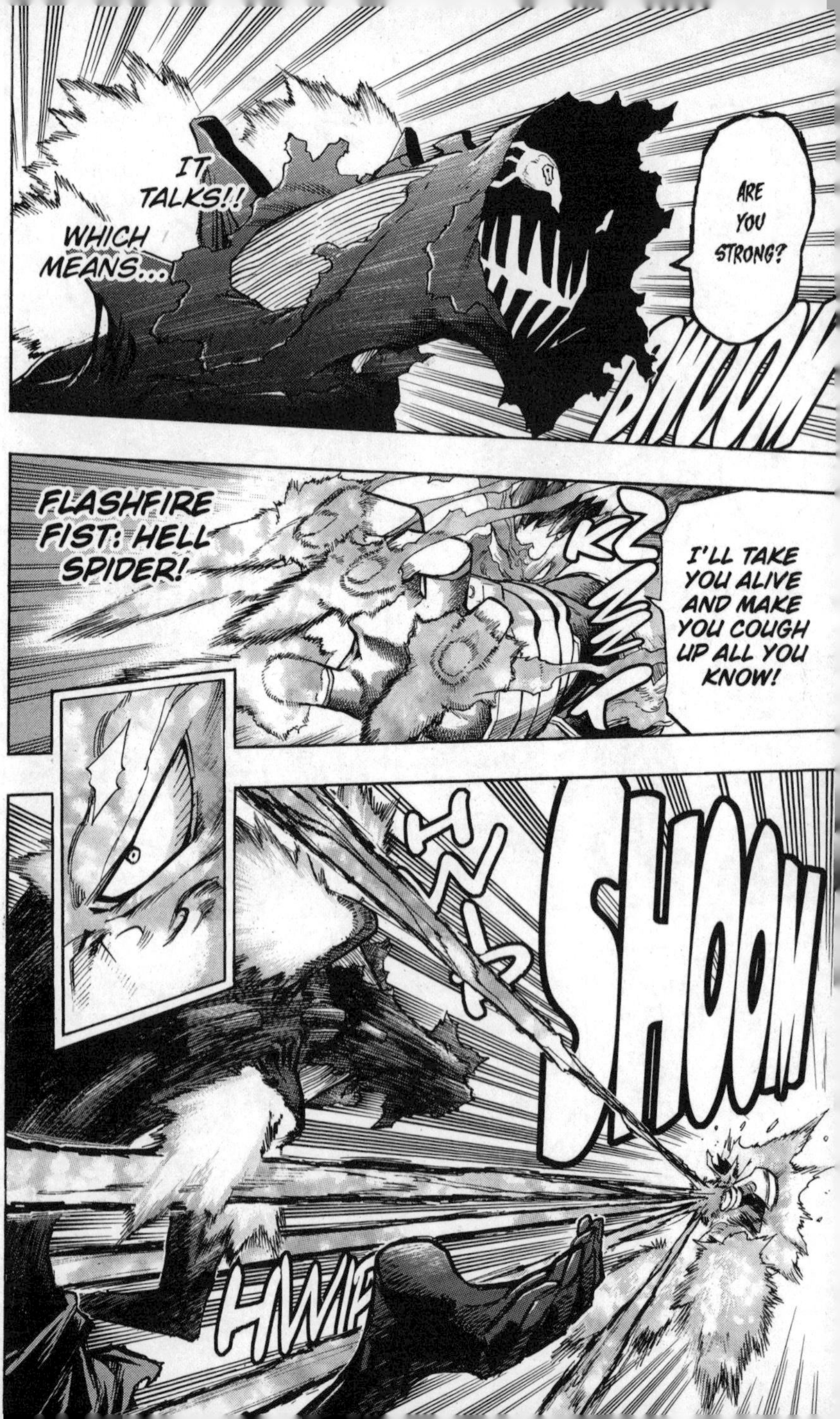
ARE YOU STRONG?
IT TALKS!!
WHICH MEANS...
DWOOM
I'LL TAKE YOU ALIVE AND MAKE YOU COUGH UP ALL YOU KNOW!
FLASHFIRE FIST: HELL SPIDER!
SHOOM

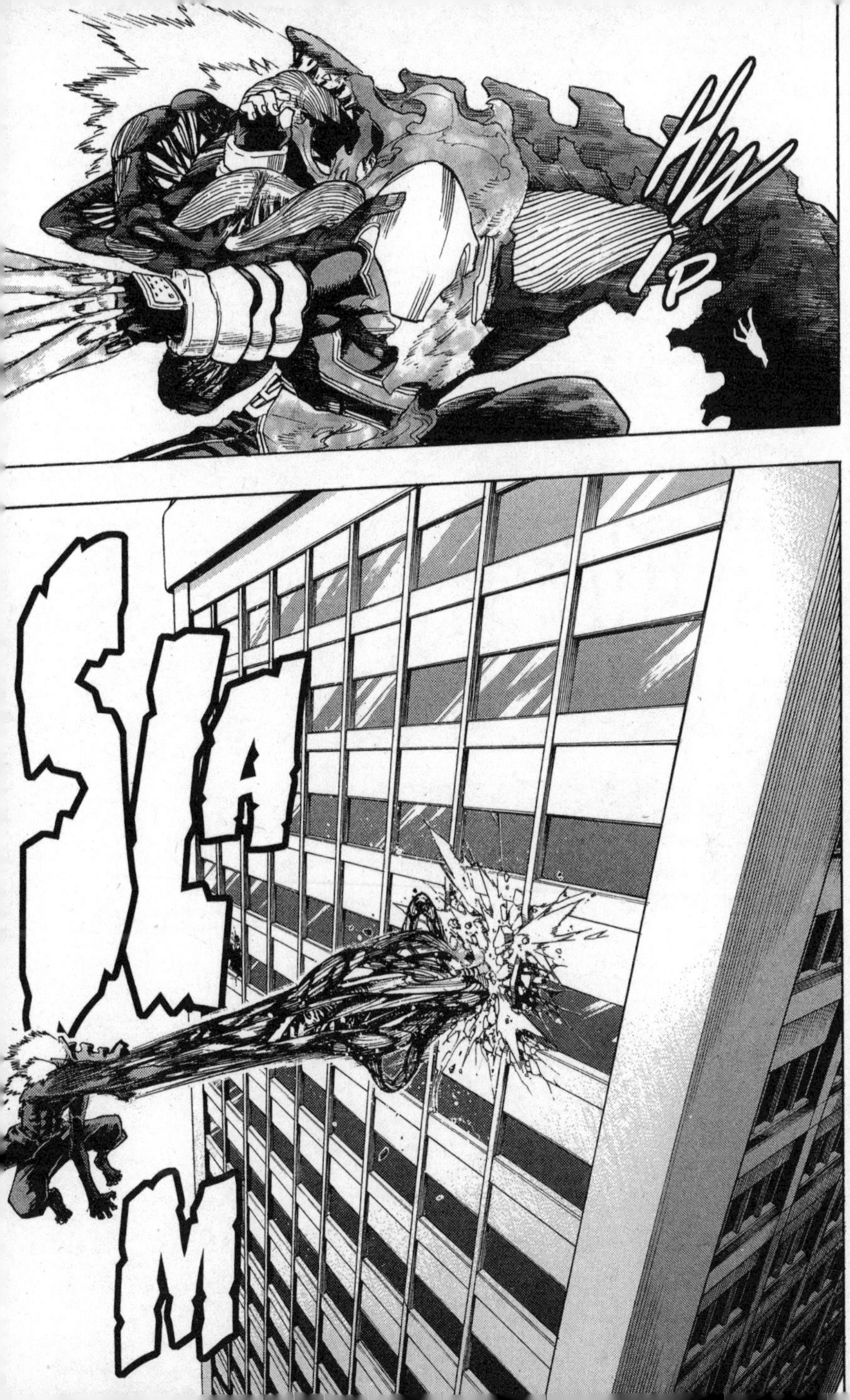
WHIP
SLAM

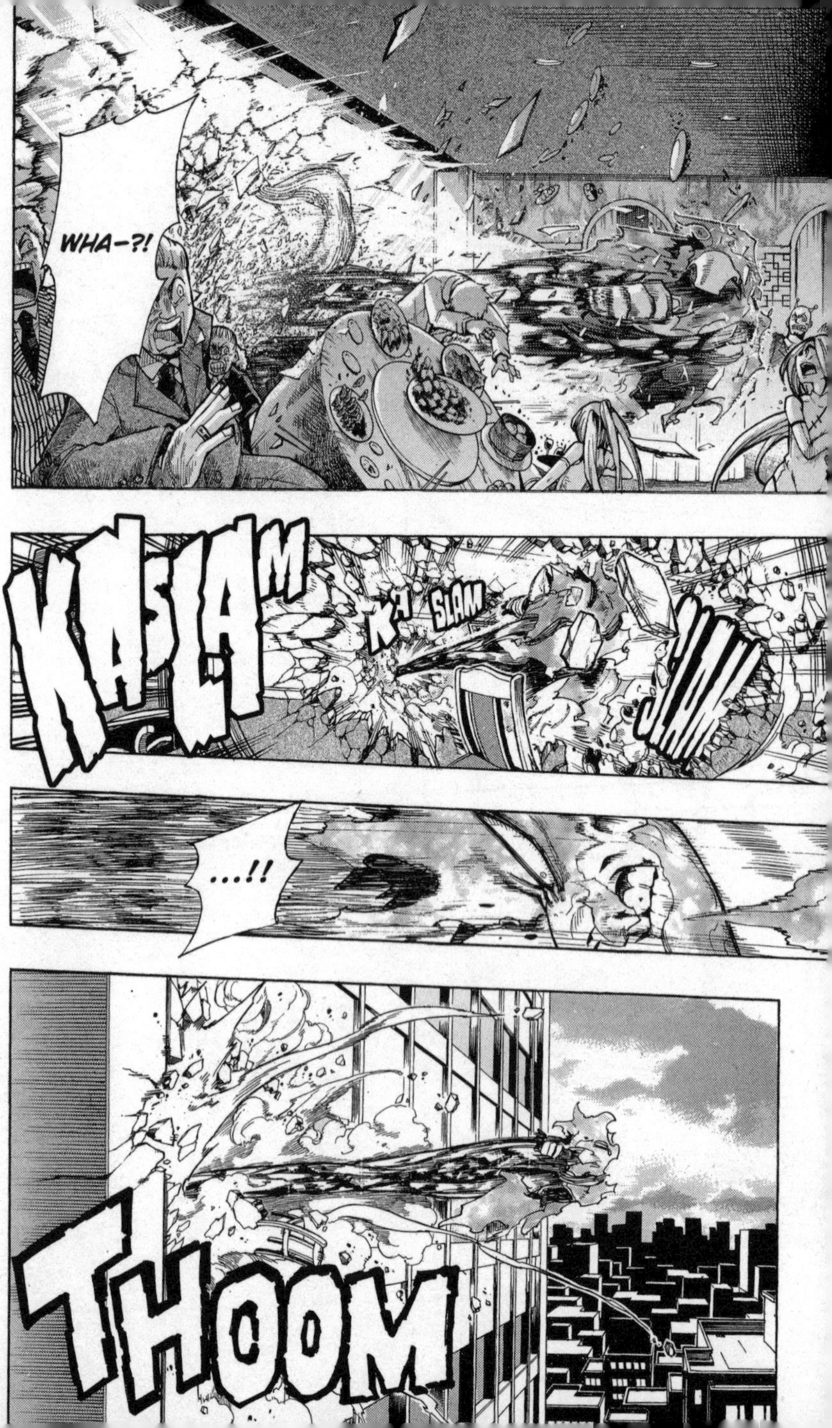
WHA-?!
WHAM
KA SLAM
KASLAM
...!!
THOOM

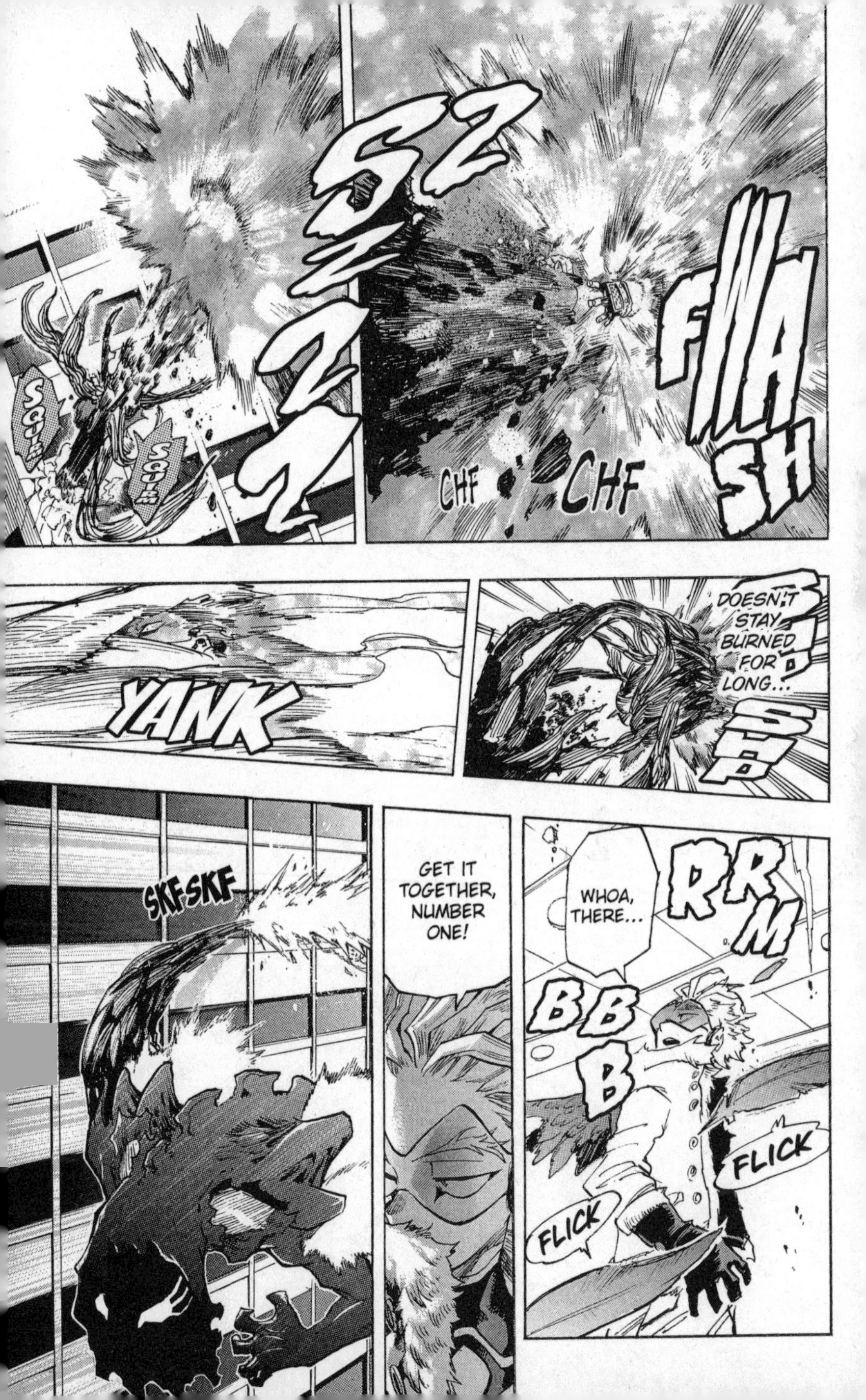
FLASH
CHF
CHF
SQUIRM
SQUIRM
DOESN'T STAY BURNED FOR LONG...
YANK
RRM
WHOA, THERE...
BBB
FLICK
FLICK
GET IT TOGETHER, NUMBER ONE!
SKFSKF

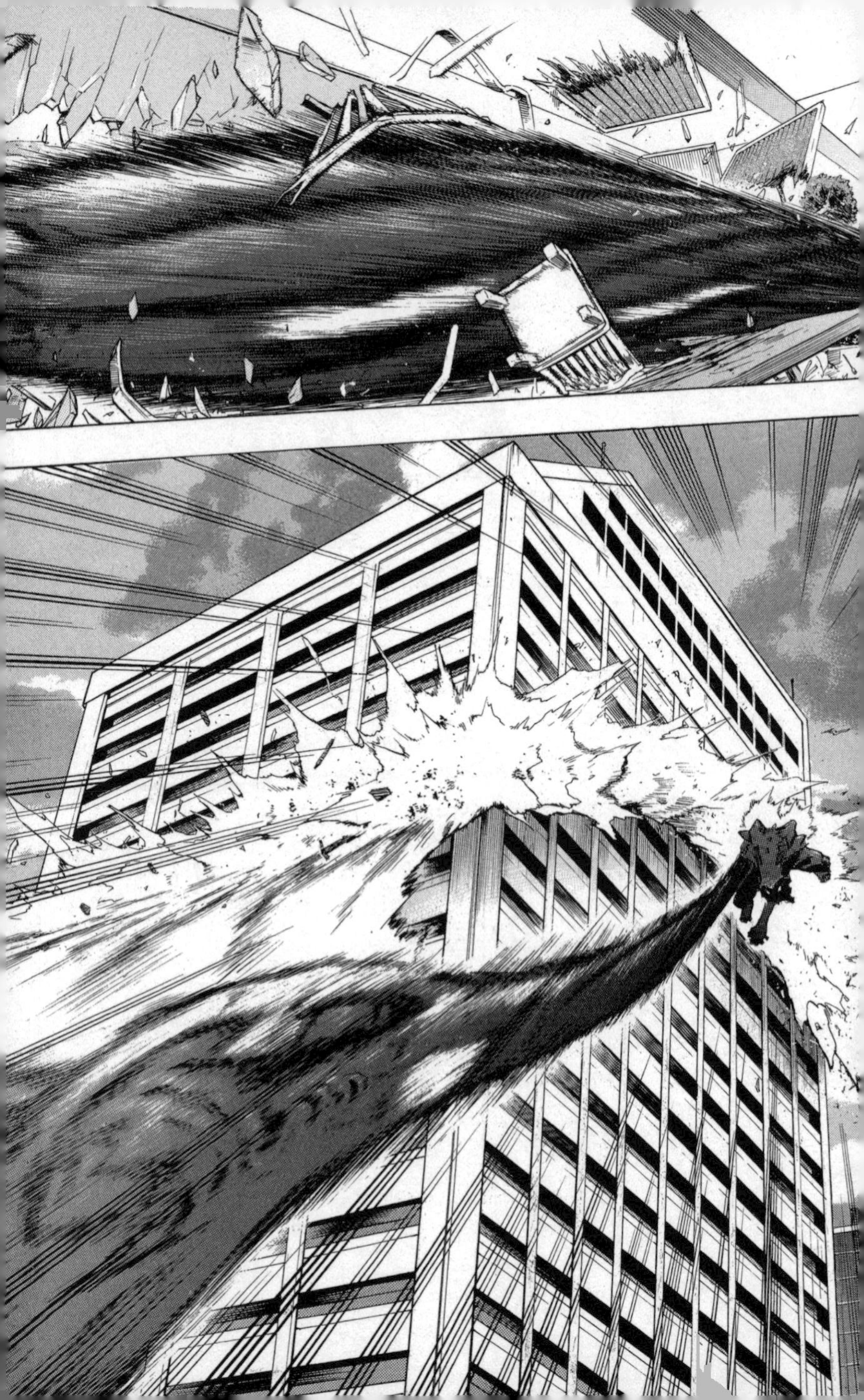

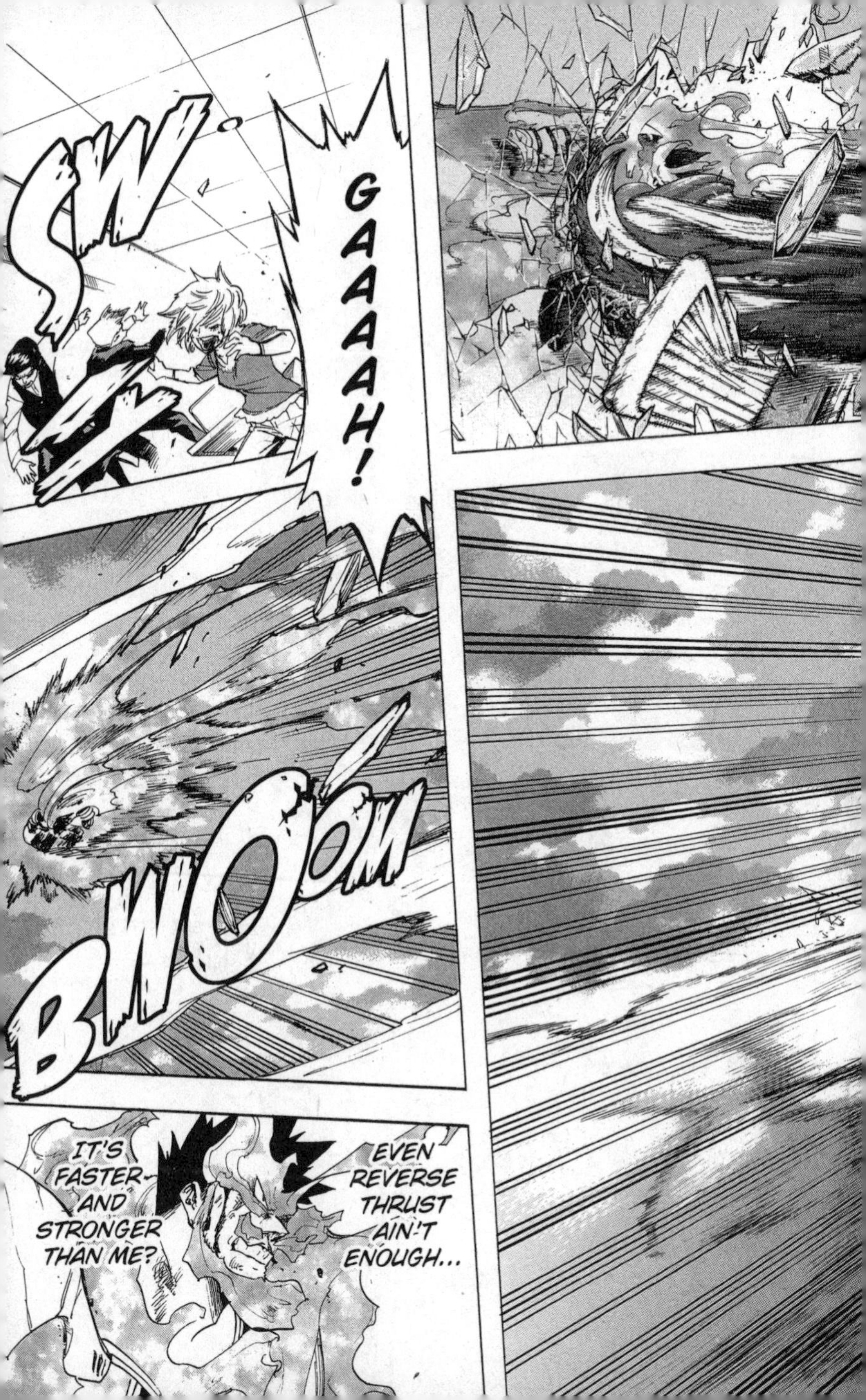
GAAAAAH!
SW
BWOOM
EVEN REVERSE THRUST AIN'T ENOUGH...
IT'S FASTER AND STRONGER THAN ME?

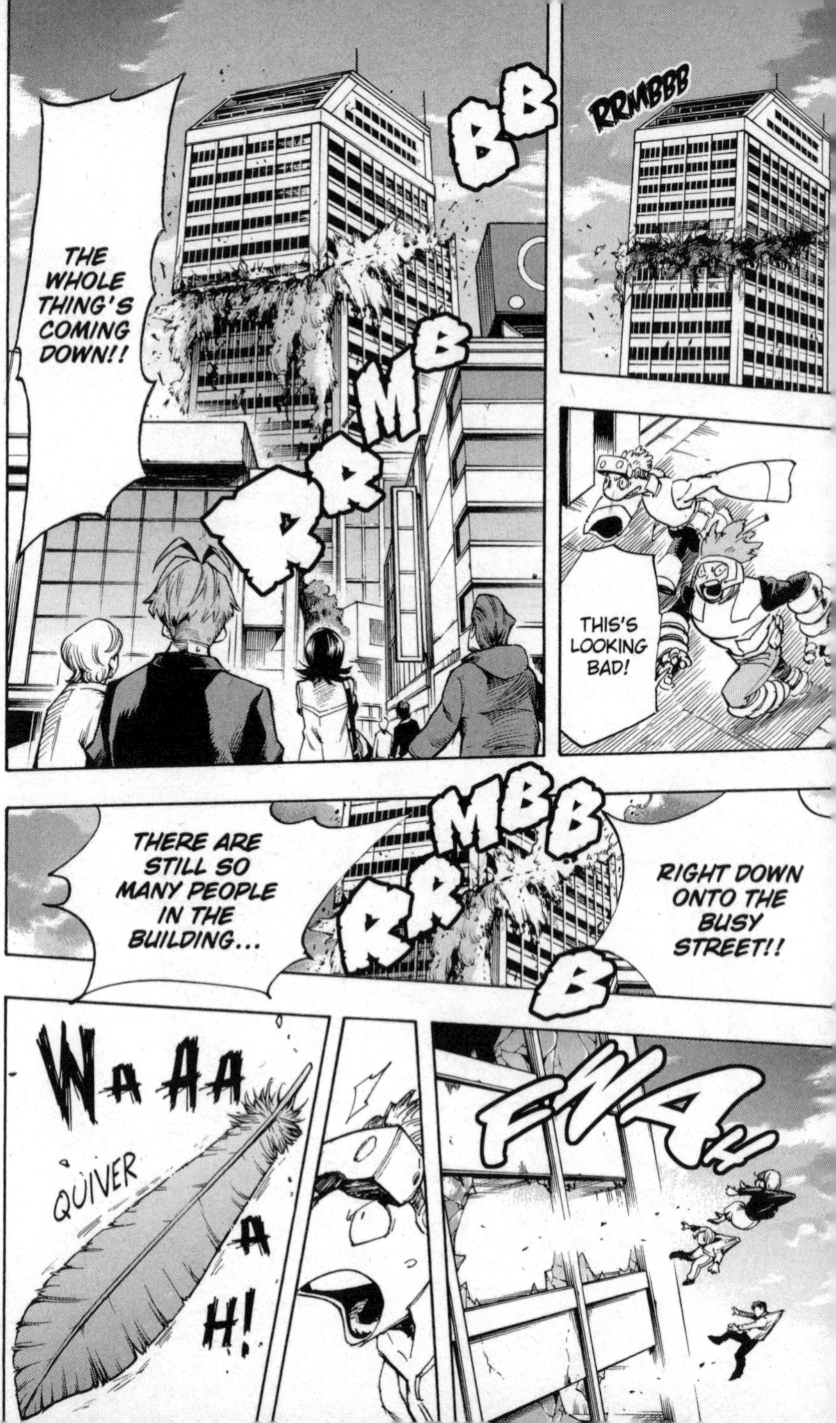
RRMBBB
THIS'S LOOKING BAD!
RRMBBB
THE WHOLE THING'S COMING DOWN!!
RIGHT DOWN ONTO THE BUSY STREET!!
RRMBBB
THERE ARE STILL SO MANY PEOPLE IN THE BUILDING...
FWAH
WAAAAH!
QUIVER

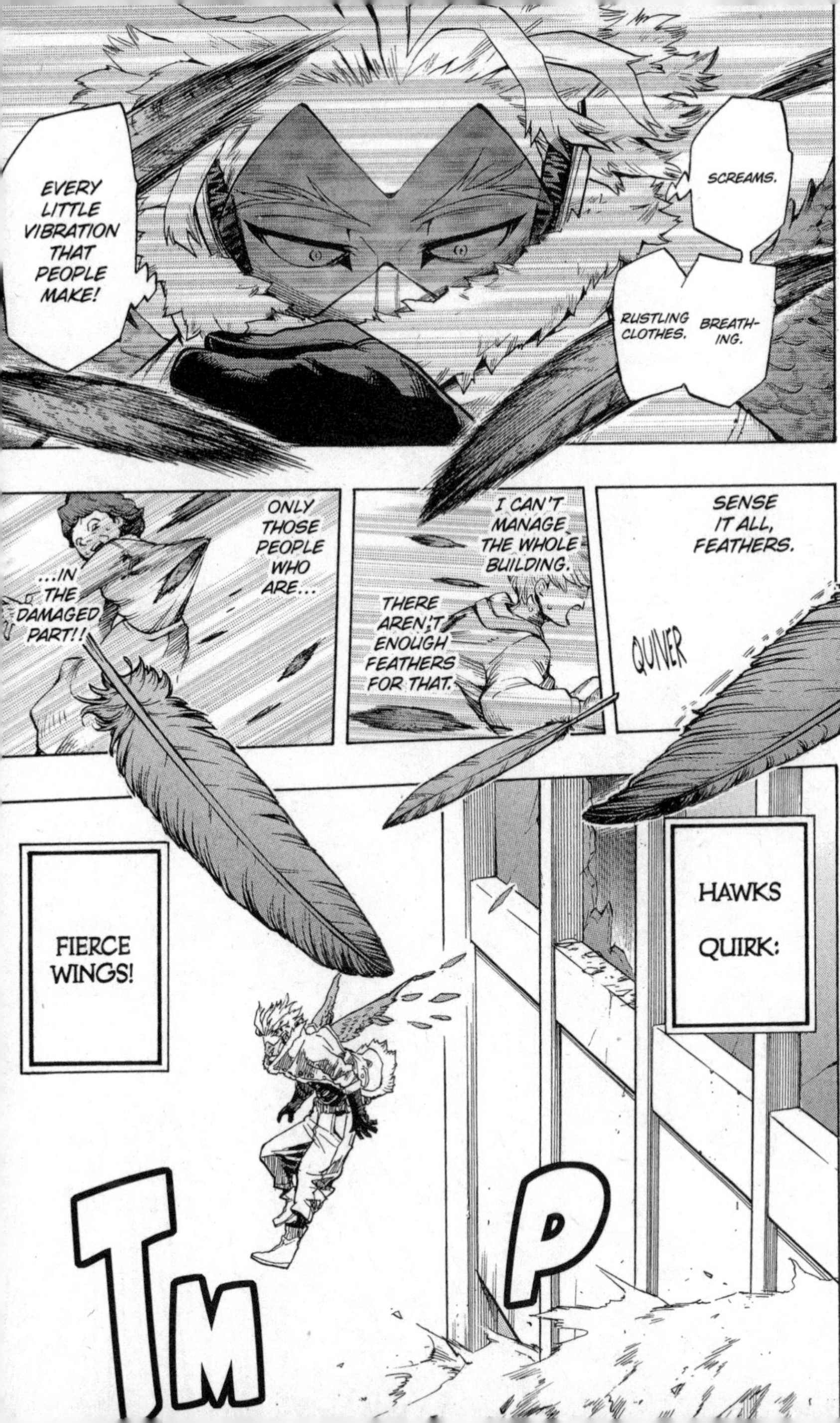

SCREAMS.
BREATHING.
RUSTLING CLOTHES.
EVERY LITTLE VIBRATION THAT PEOPLE MAKE!
SENSE IT ALL, FEATHERS.
QUIVER
I CAN'T MANAGE THE WHOLE BUILDING.
THERE AREN'T ENOUGH FEATHERS FOR THAT.
ONLY THOSE PEOPLE WHO ARE...
...IN THE DAMAGED PART!!
HAWKS QUIRK:
FIERCE WINGS!
TMP

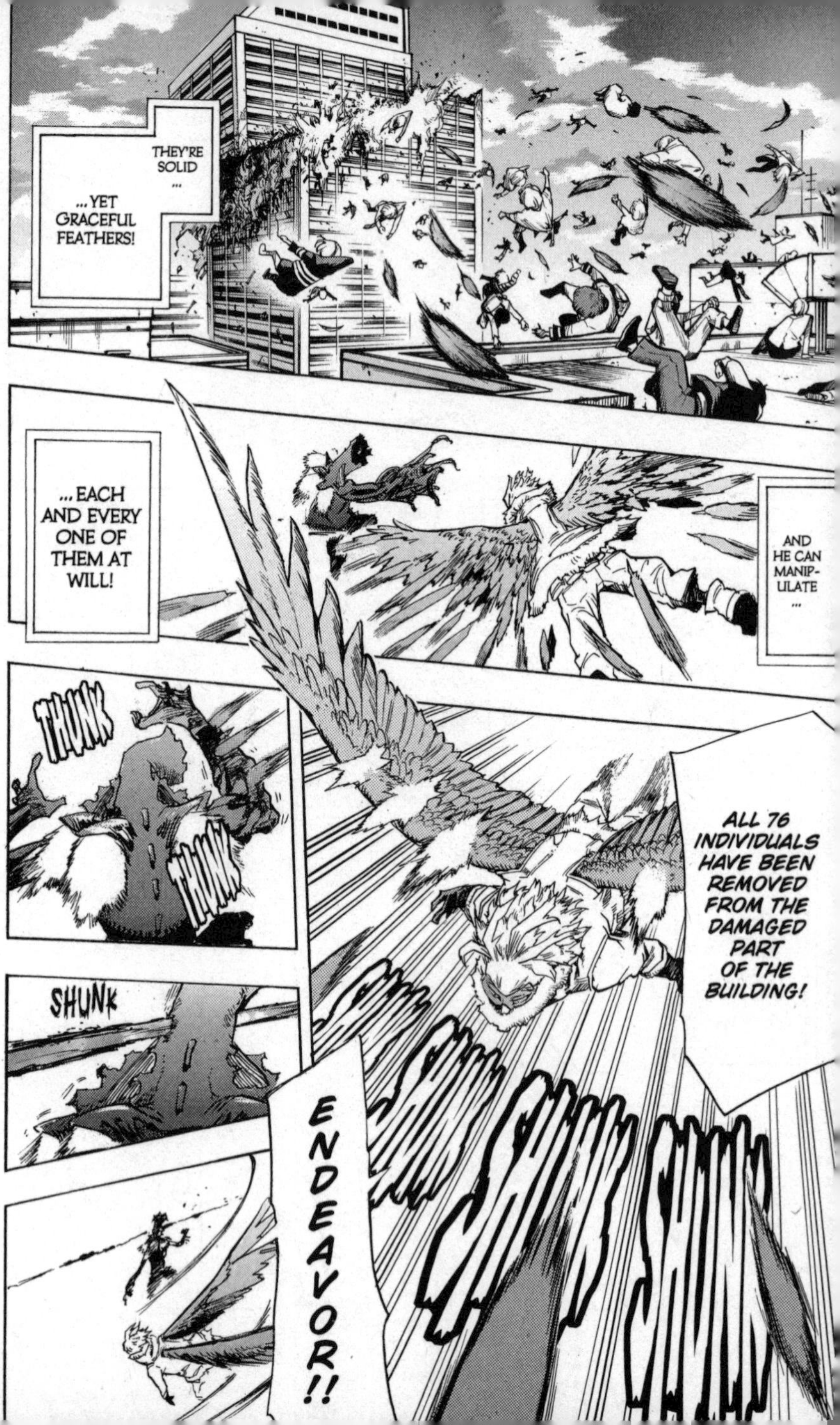
THEY'RE SOLID ...
...YET GRACEFUL FEATHERS!
AND HE CAN MANIP-ULATE ...
...EACH AND EVERY ONE OF THEM AT WILL!
ALL 76 INDIVIDUALS HAVE BEEN REMOVED FROM THE DAMAGED PART OF THE BUILDING!
ENDEAVOR!!
THUNK
THUNK
SHUNK

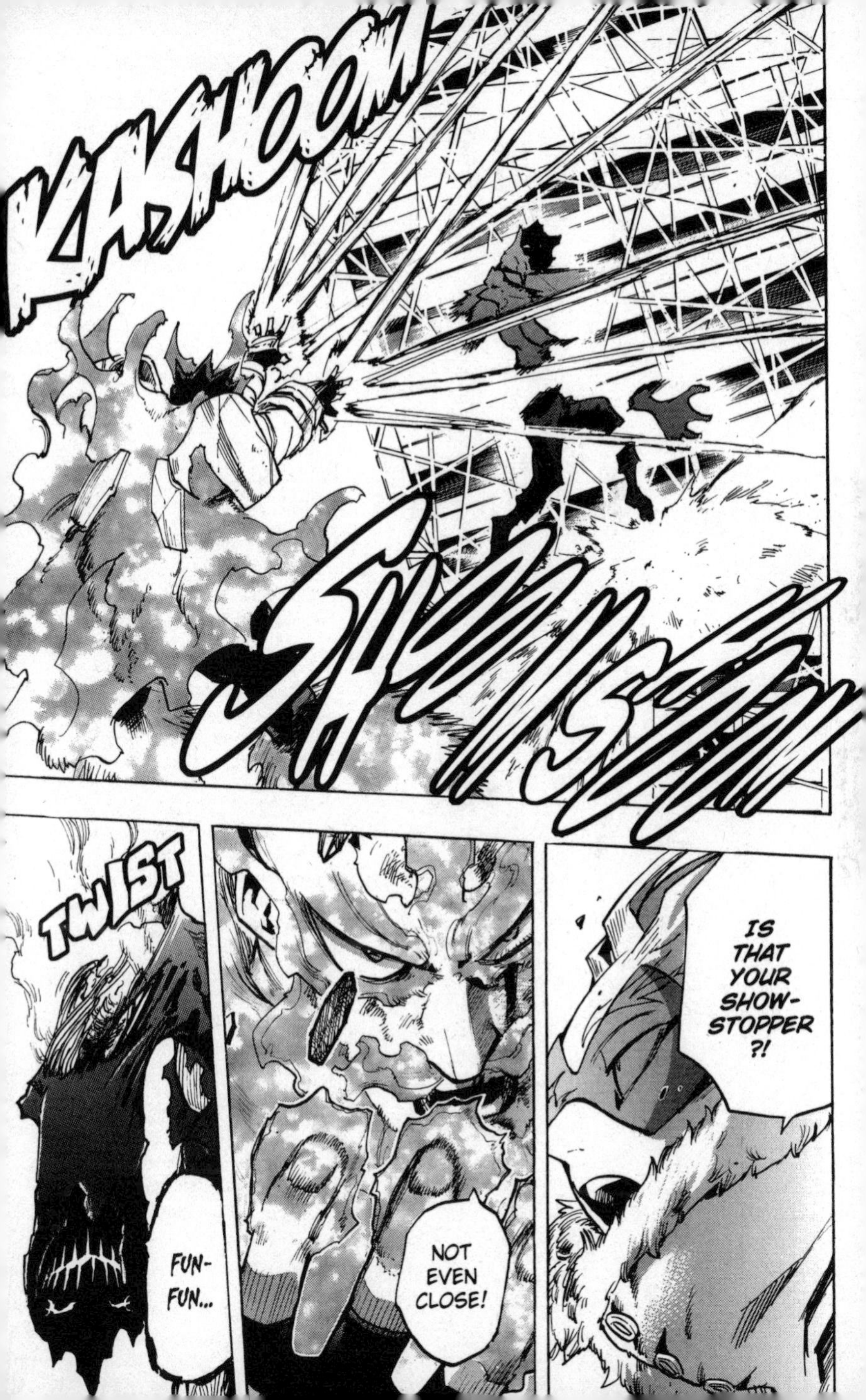
IS THAT YOUR SHOW-STOPPER?!
NOT EVEN CLOSE!
TWIST
FUN-FUN...

STREET CLOTHES

Birthday: 12/28
Height: 172 cm
Favorite Thing: Chicken (as food)

DEEP BEHIND THE SCENES

He was originally going to be a man with a bird head. Basically, the reappropriated design of Takahiro, from one of my older series. I'll be honest—I love bird people. You can blame *Mashin Hero Wataru* for that.

So how'd he get this human head? Well, during production of the movie, the anime staff came to me and asked, "Can we use Takahiro?" It was deeply moving to think that they had read my earlier series and wanted to show it some love. My life is basically peaking with this movie, so of course I agreed with enthusiasm. Not a big deal to change Hawks' design, after all.

After that, my staff had a lukewarm reaction to the idea of a birdman being number two, but I settled on this safe and sound (?) design for the guy.

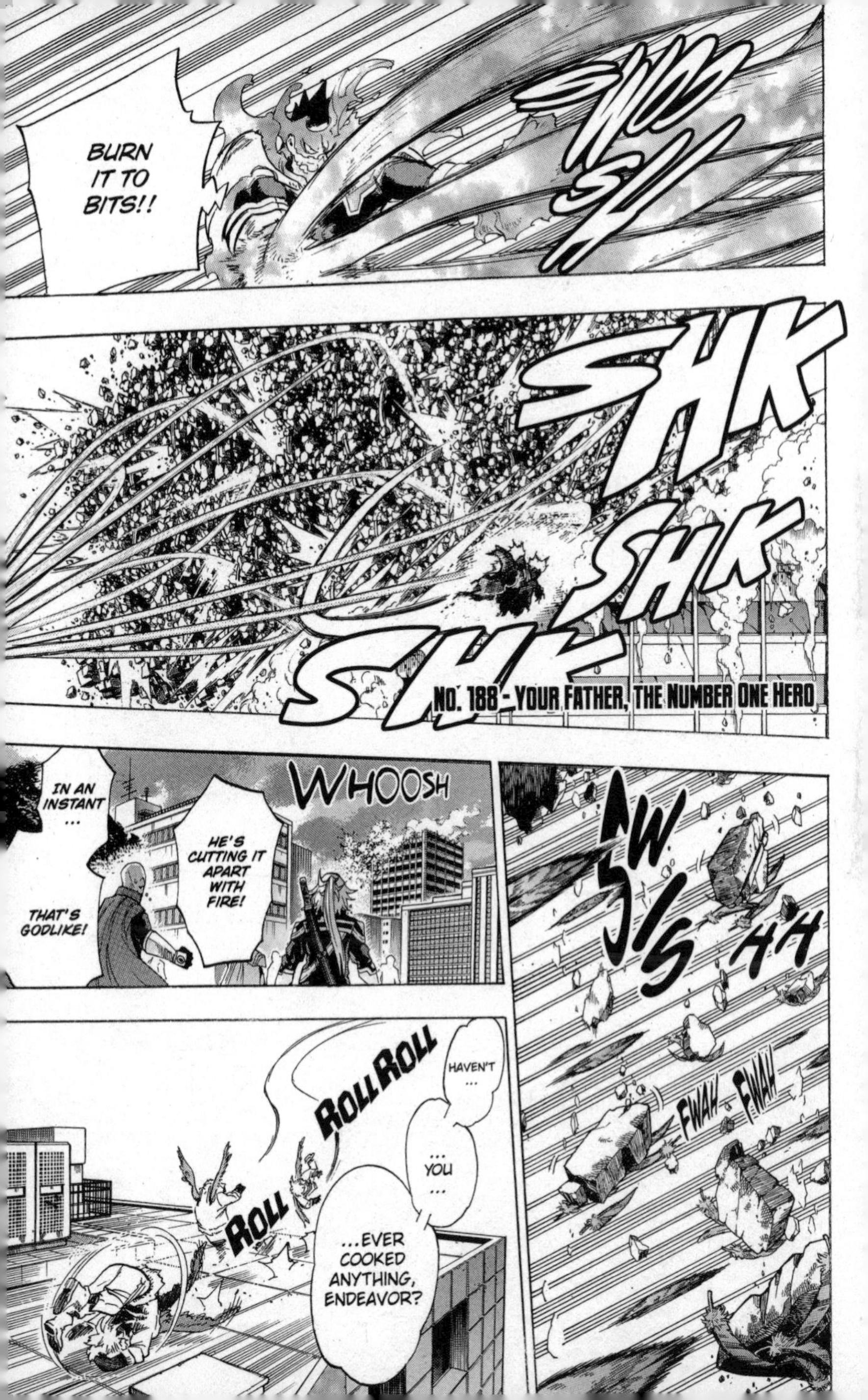
SWOOSH
BURN IT TO BITS!!
SHK
SHK
SHK
No. 188 - Your Father, the Number One Hero
SWISH
FWAH FWAH
WHOOSH
HE'S CUTTING IT APART WITH FIRE!
IN AN INSTANT ...
THAT'S GODLIKE!
HAVEN'T ...
... YOU ...
...EVER COOKED ANYTHING, ENDEAVOR?
ROLL ROLL
ROLL

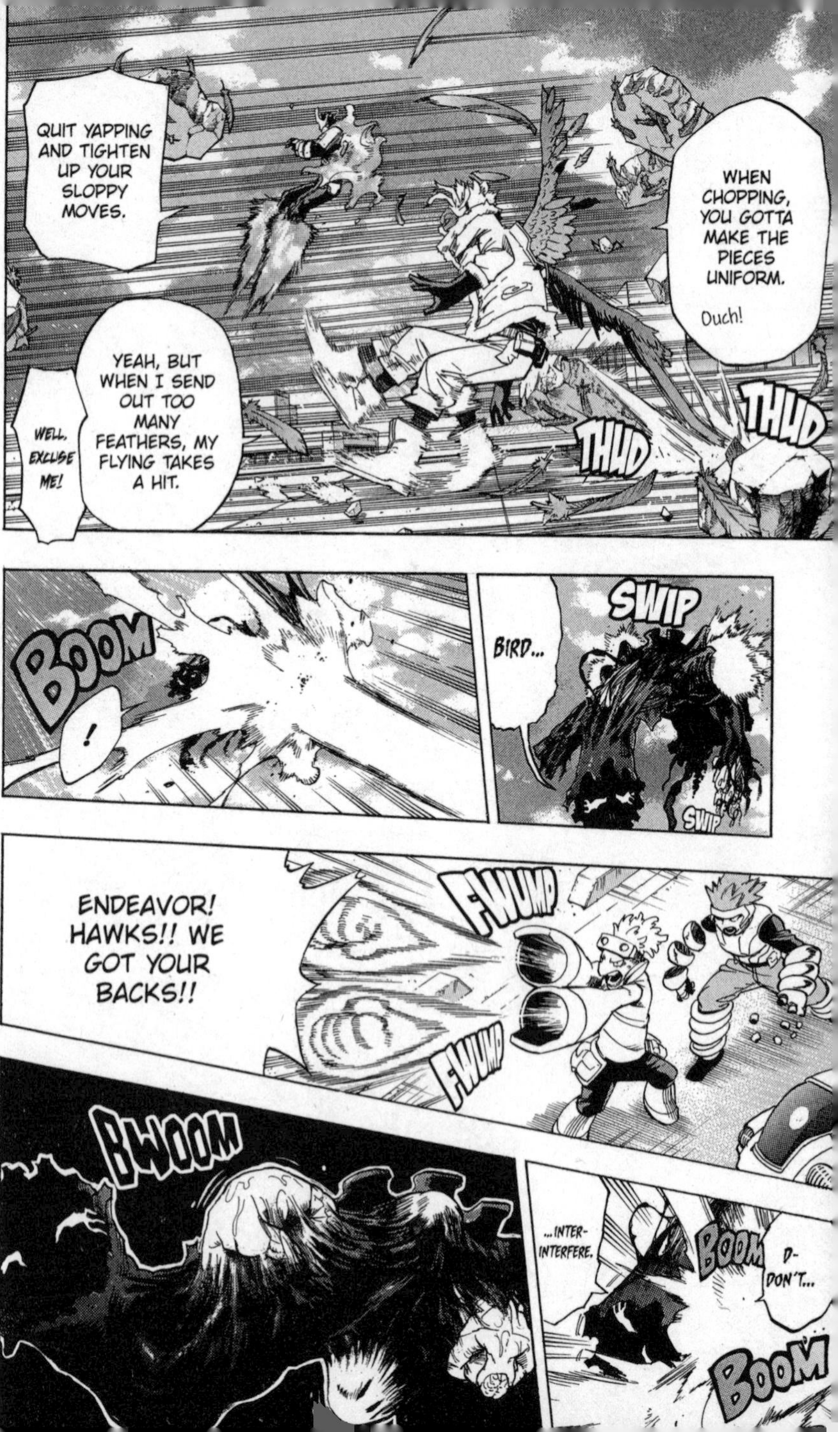
WHEN CHOPPING, YOU GOTTA MAKE THE PIECES UNIFORM.
Ouch!
THUD
THUD
QUIT YAPPING AND TIGHTEN UP YOUR SLOPPY MOVES.
YEAH, BUT WHEN I SEND OUT TOO MANY FEATHERS, MY FLYING TAKES A HIT.
WELL, EXCUSE ME!
SWIP
BIRD...
SWIP
BOOM
!
FWUMP
FWUMP
ENDEAVOR! HAWKS!! WE GOT YOUR BACKS!!
D-DON'T...
BOOM
...INTER-INTERFERE.
BOOM
BWOOM

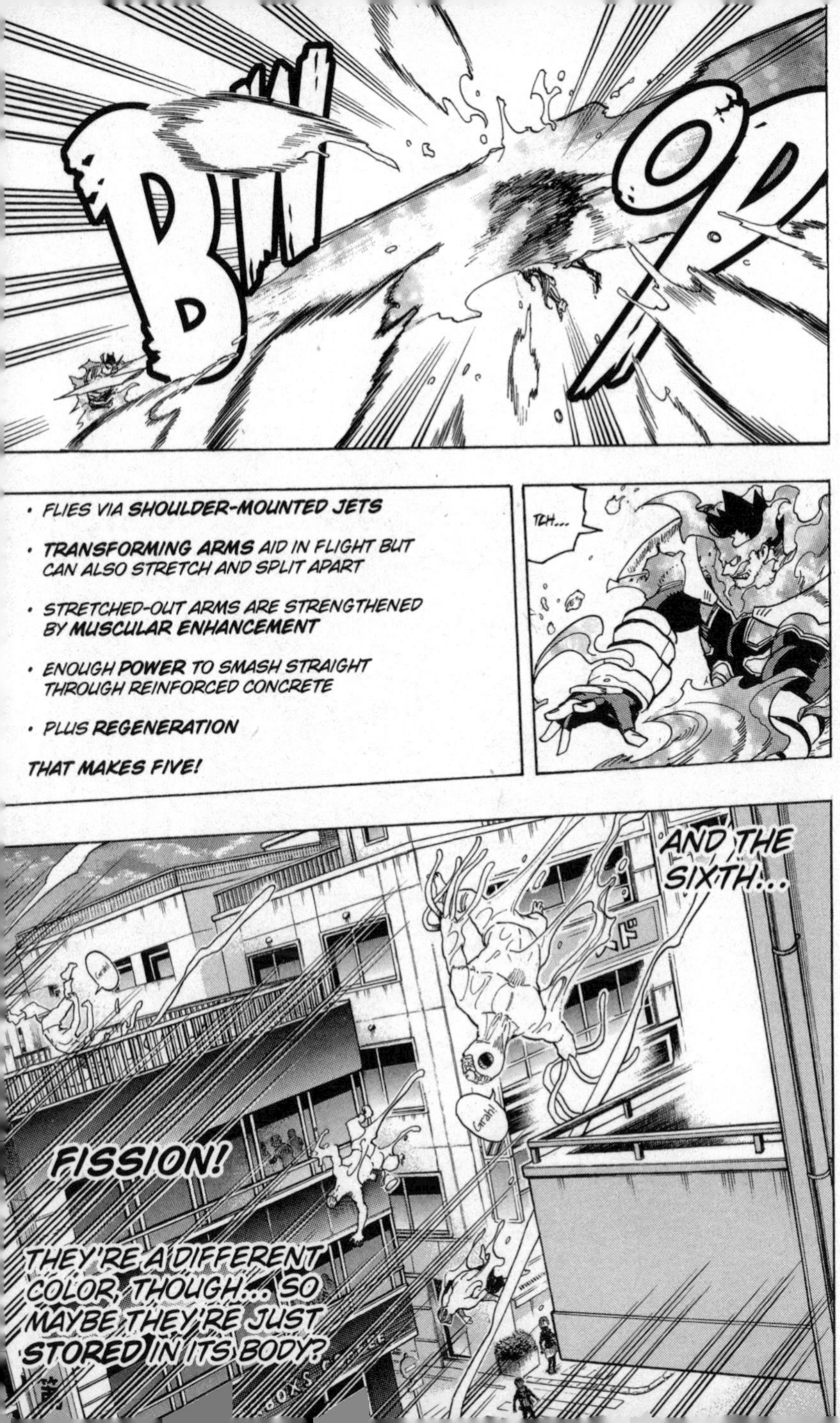

TCH...
• FLIES VIA SHOULDER-MOUNTED JETS
• TRANSFORMING ARMS AID IN FLIGHT BUT CAN ALSO STRETCH AND SPLIT APART
• STRETCHED-OUT ARMS ARE STRENGTHENED BY MUSCULAR ENHANCEMENT
• ENOUGH POWER TO SMASH STRAIGHT THROUGH REINFORCED CONCRETE
• PLUS REGENERATION
THAT MAKES FIVE!
AND THE SIXTH...
Grah!
Grah!
FISSION!
THEY'RE A DIFFERENT COLOR, THOUGH... SO MAYBE THEY'RE JUST STORED IN ITS BODY?

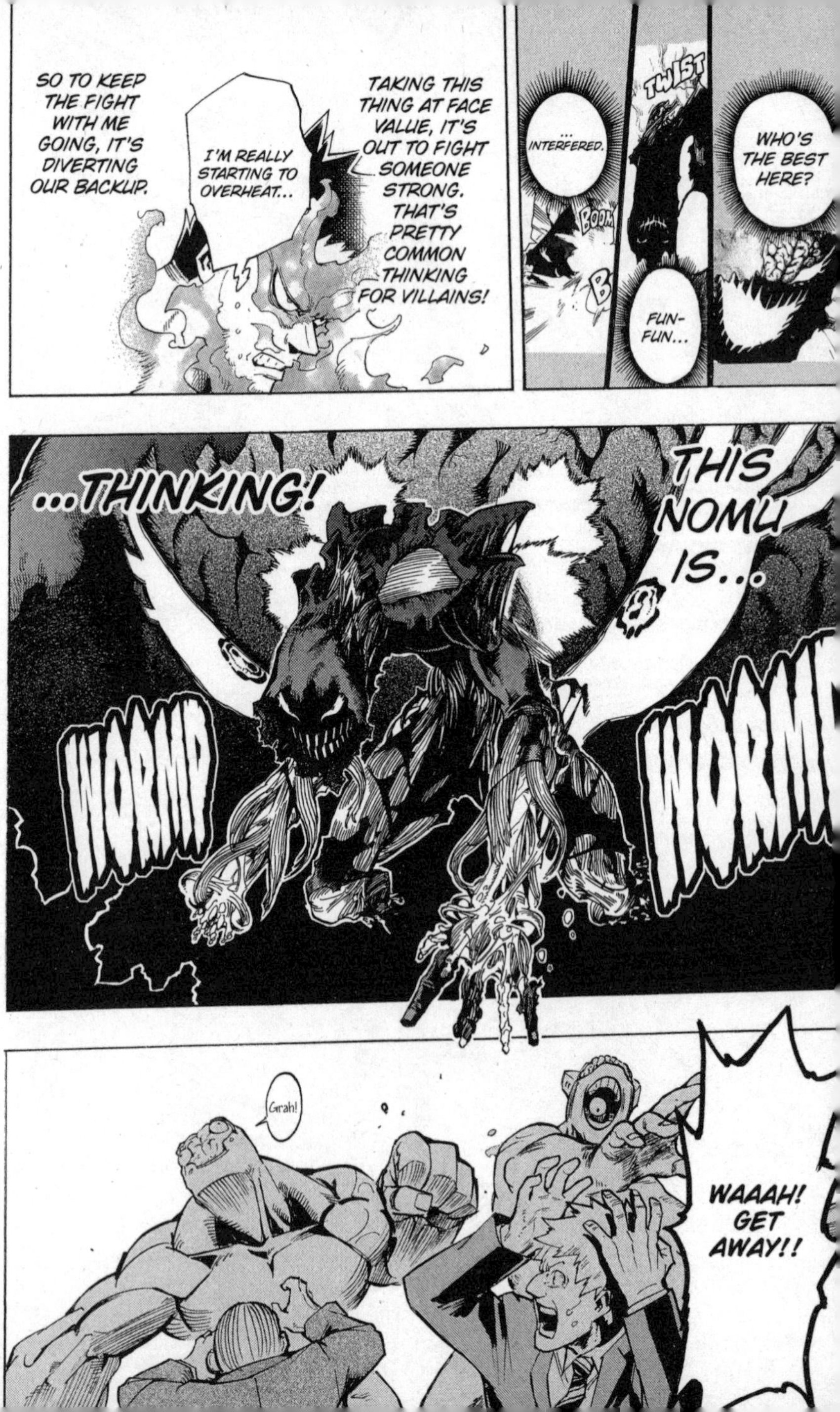
WHO'S THE BEST HERE?
FUN-FUN...
TWIST
...INTERFERED.
BOOM
B
TAKING THIS THING AT FACE VALUE, IT'S OUT TO FIGHT SOMEONE STRONG. THAT'S PRETTY COMMON THINKING FOR VILLAINS!
I'M REALLY STARTING TO OVERHEAT...
SO TO KEEP THE FIGHT WITH ME GOING, IT'S DIVERTING OUR BACKUP.
THIS NOMU IS...
...THINKING!
WORMP
WORMP
WAAAH! GET AWAY!!
Grah!

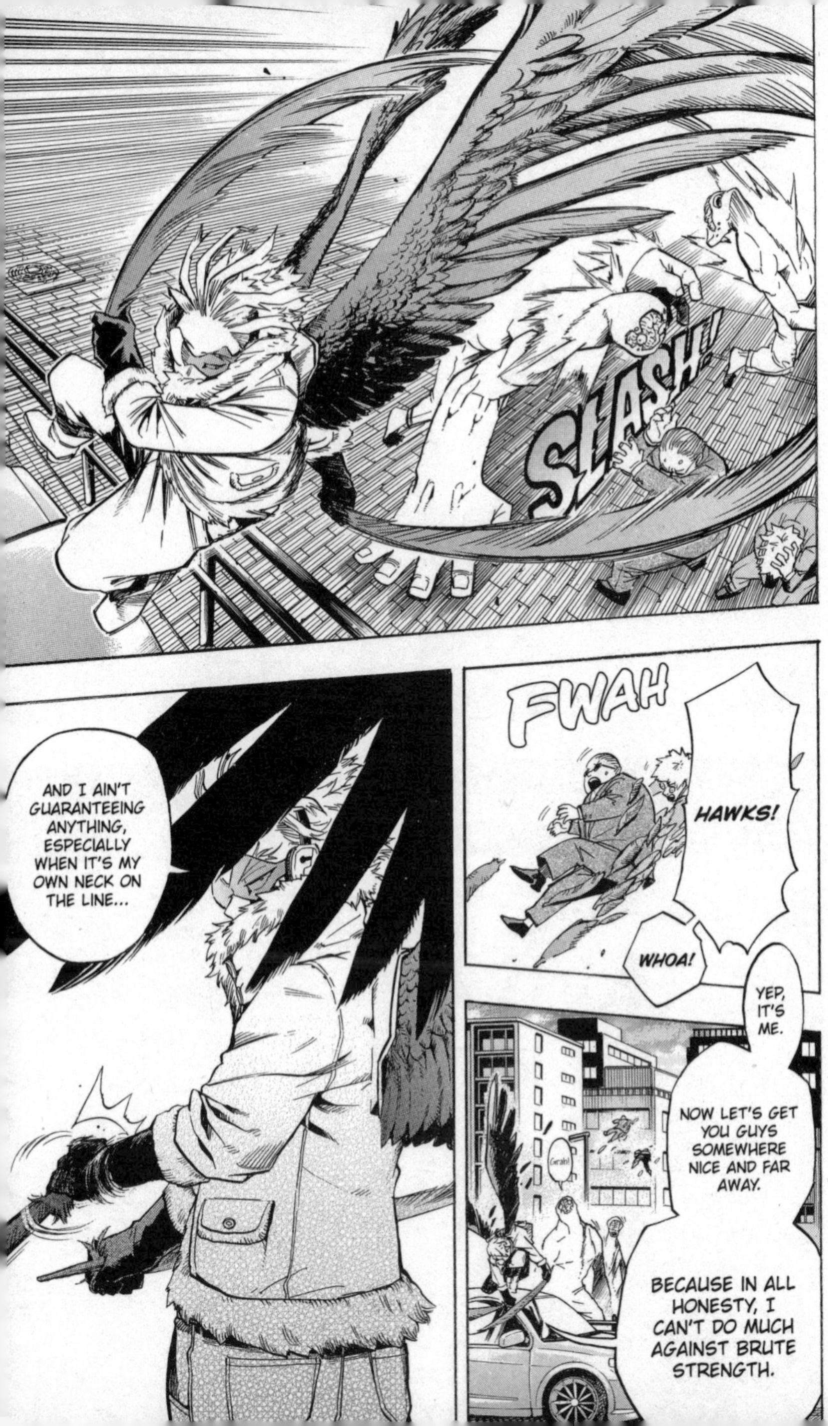
SLASH!!
FWAH
HAWKS!
WHOA!
YEP, IT'S ME.
NOW LET'S GET YOU GUYS SOMEWHERE NICE AND FAR AWAY.
BECAUSE IN ALL HONESTY, I CAN'T DO MUCH AGAINST BRUTE STRENGTH.
AND I AIN'T GUARANTEEING ANYTHING, ESPECIALLY WHEN IT'S MY OWN NECK ON THE LINE...

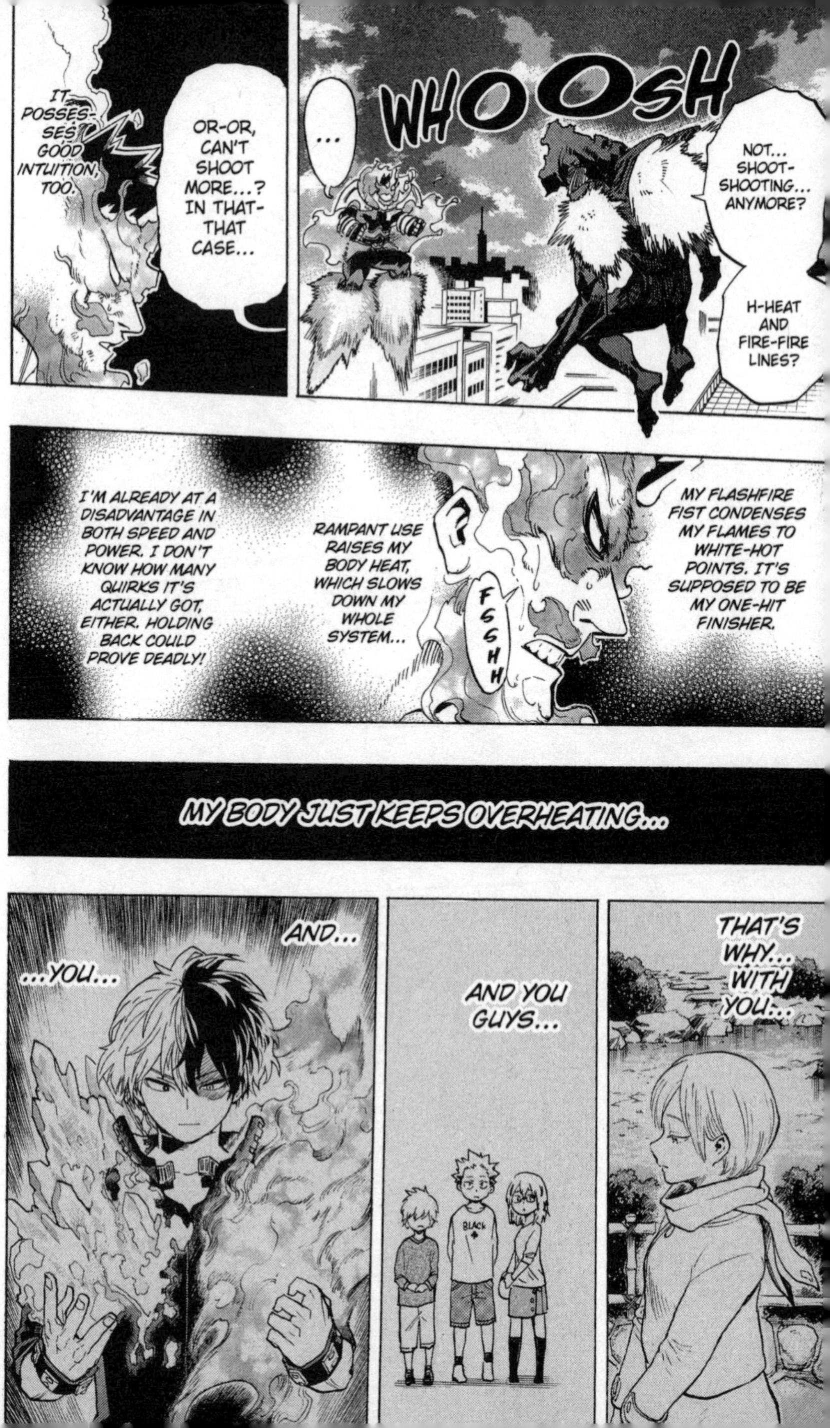
NOT... SHOOT-SHOOTING... ANYMORE?
H-HEAT AND FIRE-FIRE LINES?
WHOOOSH
...
OR-OR, CAN'T SHOOT MORE...? IN THAT-THAT CASE...
IT POSSES-SES GOOD INTUITION, TOO.
MY FLASHFIRE FIST CONDENSES MY FLAMES TO WHITE-HOT POINTS. IT'S SUPPOSED TO BE MY ONE-HIT FINISHER.
FSSHH
RAMPANT USE RAISES MY BODY HEAT, WHICH SLOWS DOWN MY WHOLE SYSTEM...
I'M ALREADY AT A DISADVANTAGE IN BOTH SPEED AND POWER. I DON'T KNOW HOW MANY QUIRKS IT'S ACTUALLY GOT, EITHER. HOLDING BACK COULD PROVE DEADLY!
MY BODY JUST KEEPS OVERHEATING...
THAT'S WHY... WITH YOU...
AND YOU GUYS...
AND...
...YOU...

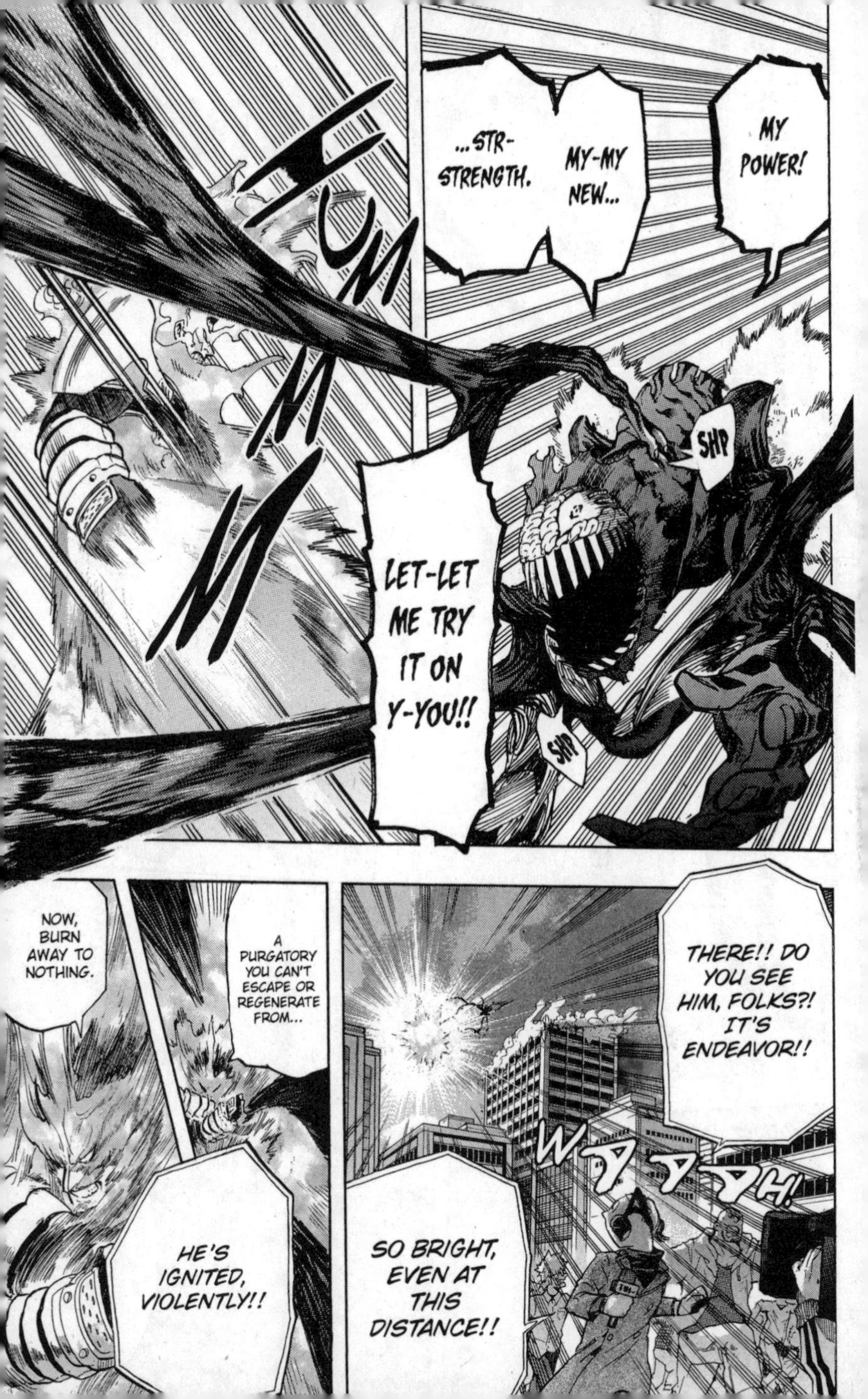
MY POWER!
MY-MY NEW...
...STR- STRENGTH.
SHP
LET-LET ME TRY IT ON Y-YOU!!
SHP
HUMMM
THERE!! DO YOU SEE HIM, FOLKS?! IT'S ENDEAVOR!!
WAAAH!
SO BRIGHT, EVEN AT THIS DISTANCE!!
A PURGATORY YOU CAN'T ESCAPE OR REGENERATE FROM...
NOW, BURN AWAY TO NOTHING.
HE'S IGNITED, VIOLENTLY!!

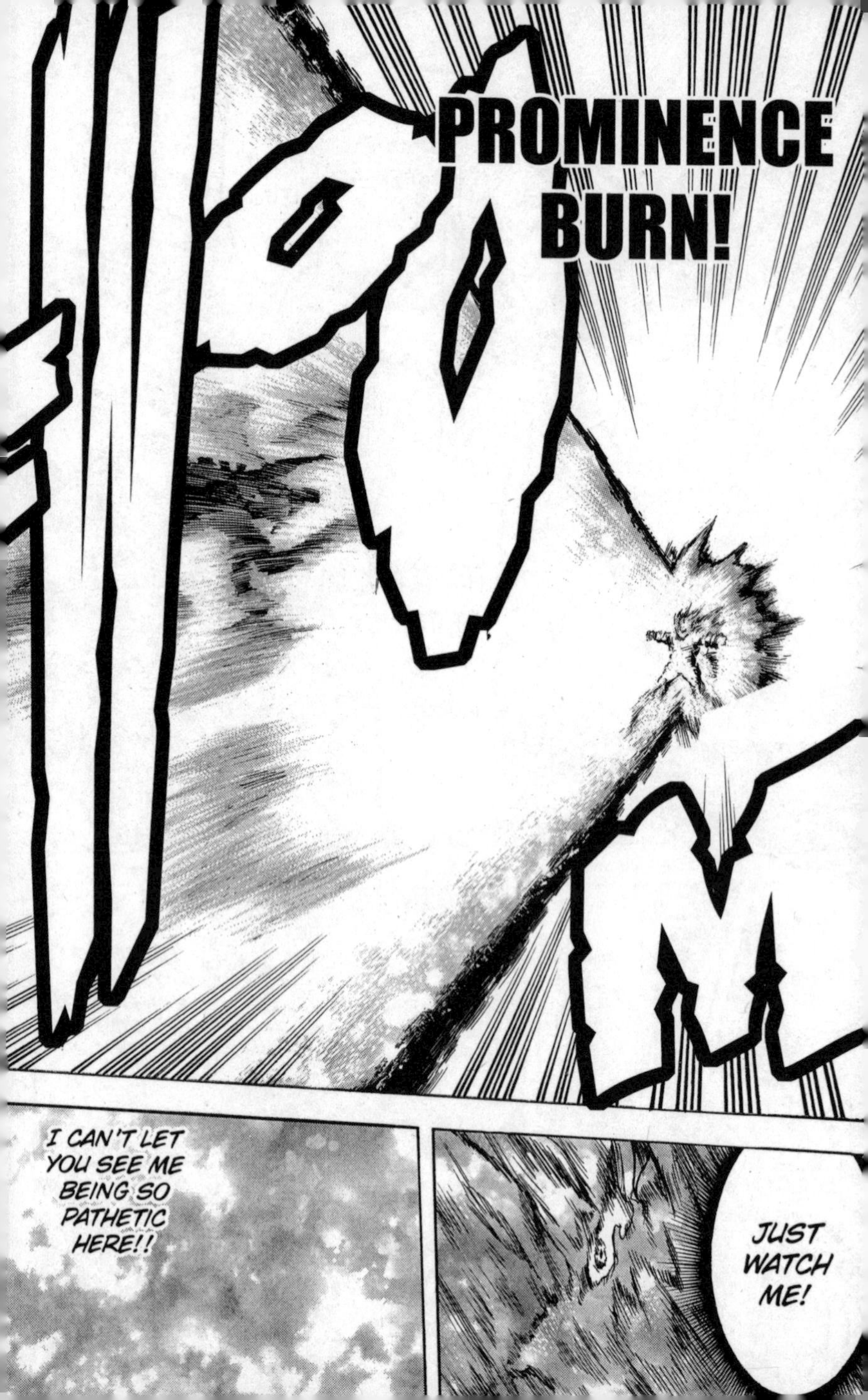
PROMINENCE BURN!
JUST WATCH ME!
I CAN'T LET YOU SEE ME BEING SO PATHETIC HERE!!

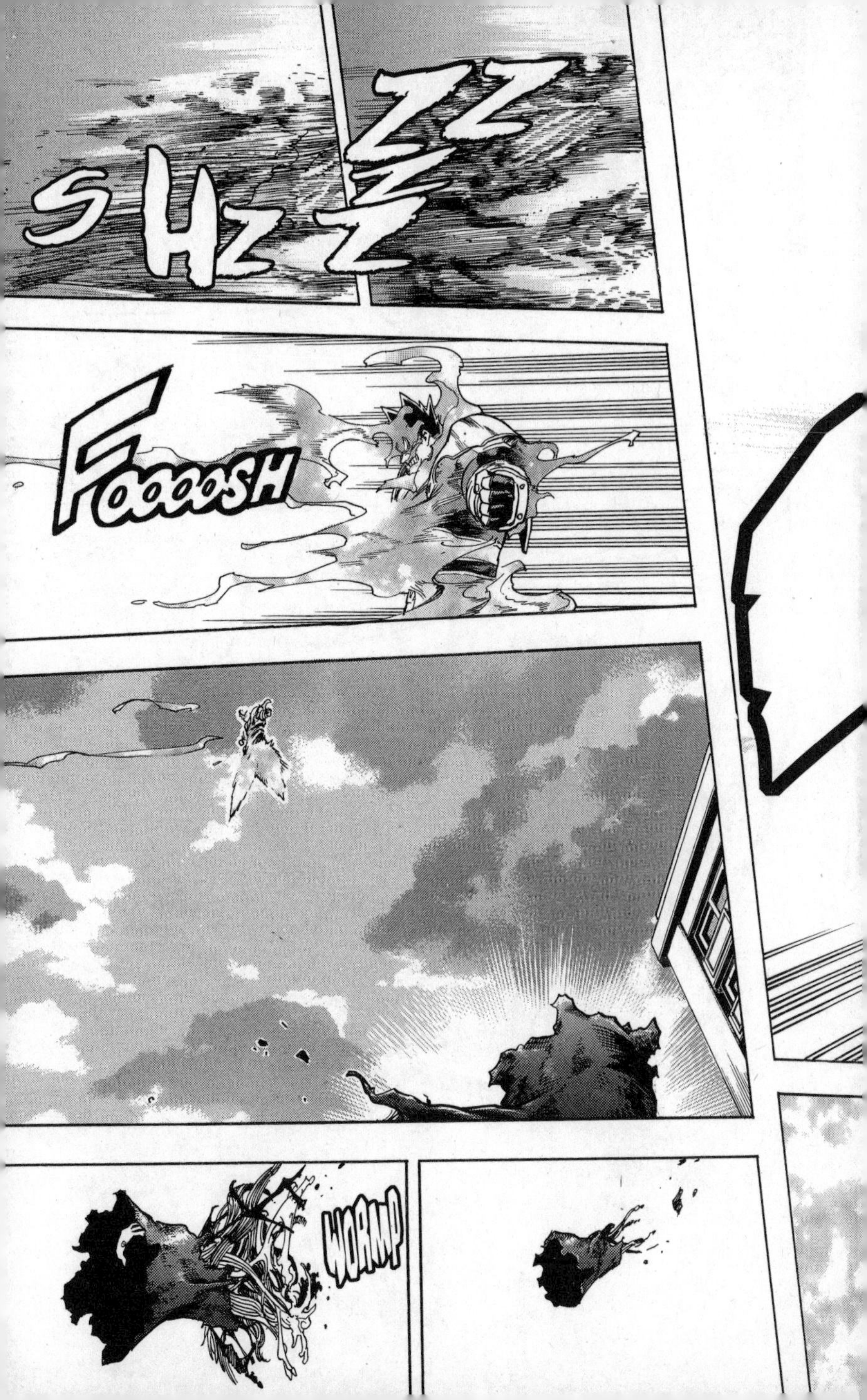
SHZZZZZ
FOOOOSH
WOMP

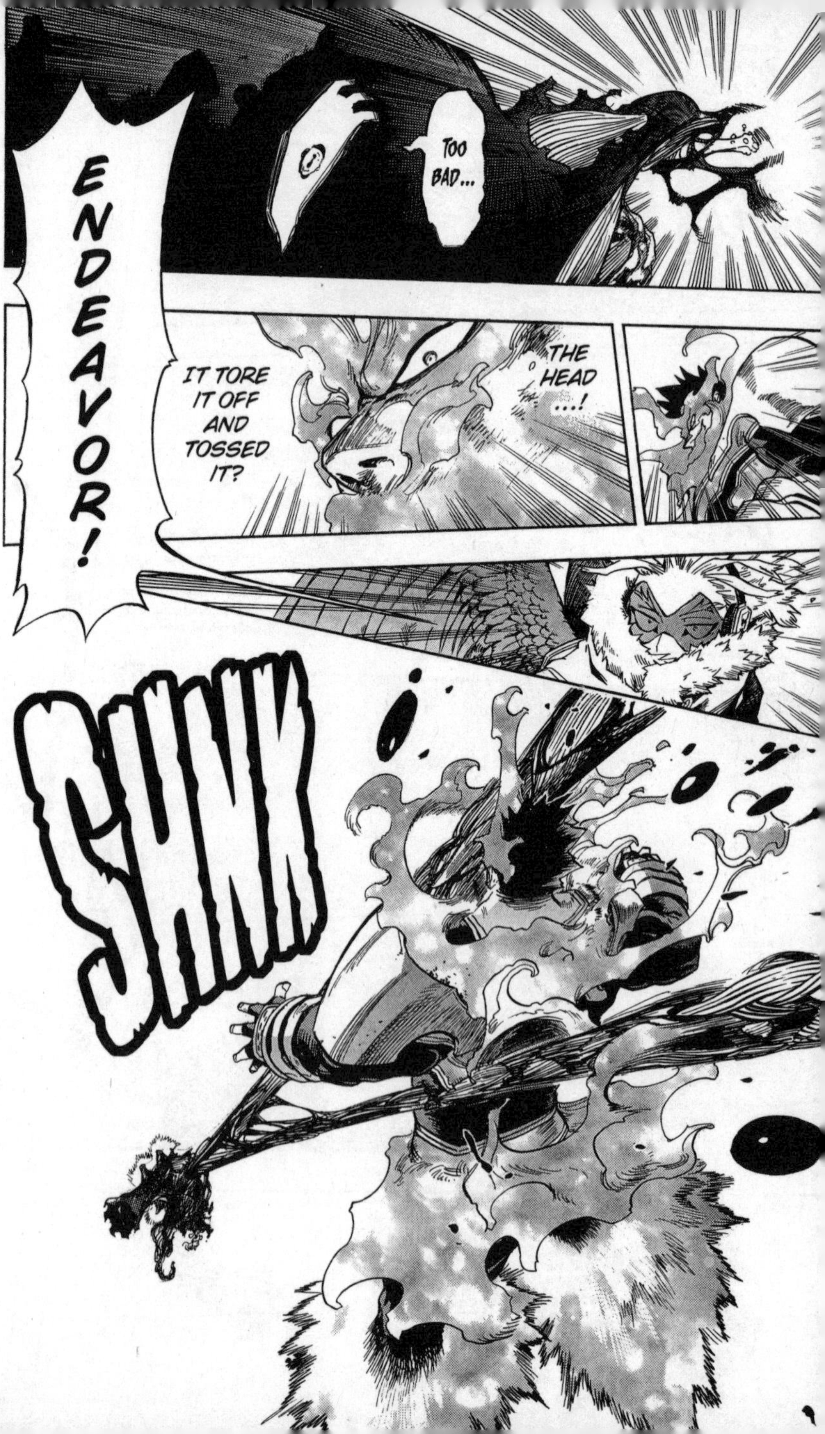
TOO BAD...
THE HEAD ...!
IT TORE IT OFF AND TOSSED IT?
ENDEAVOR!
SHNK

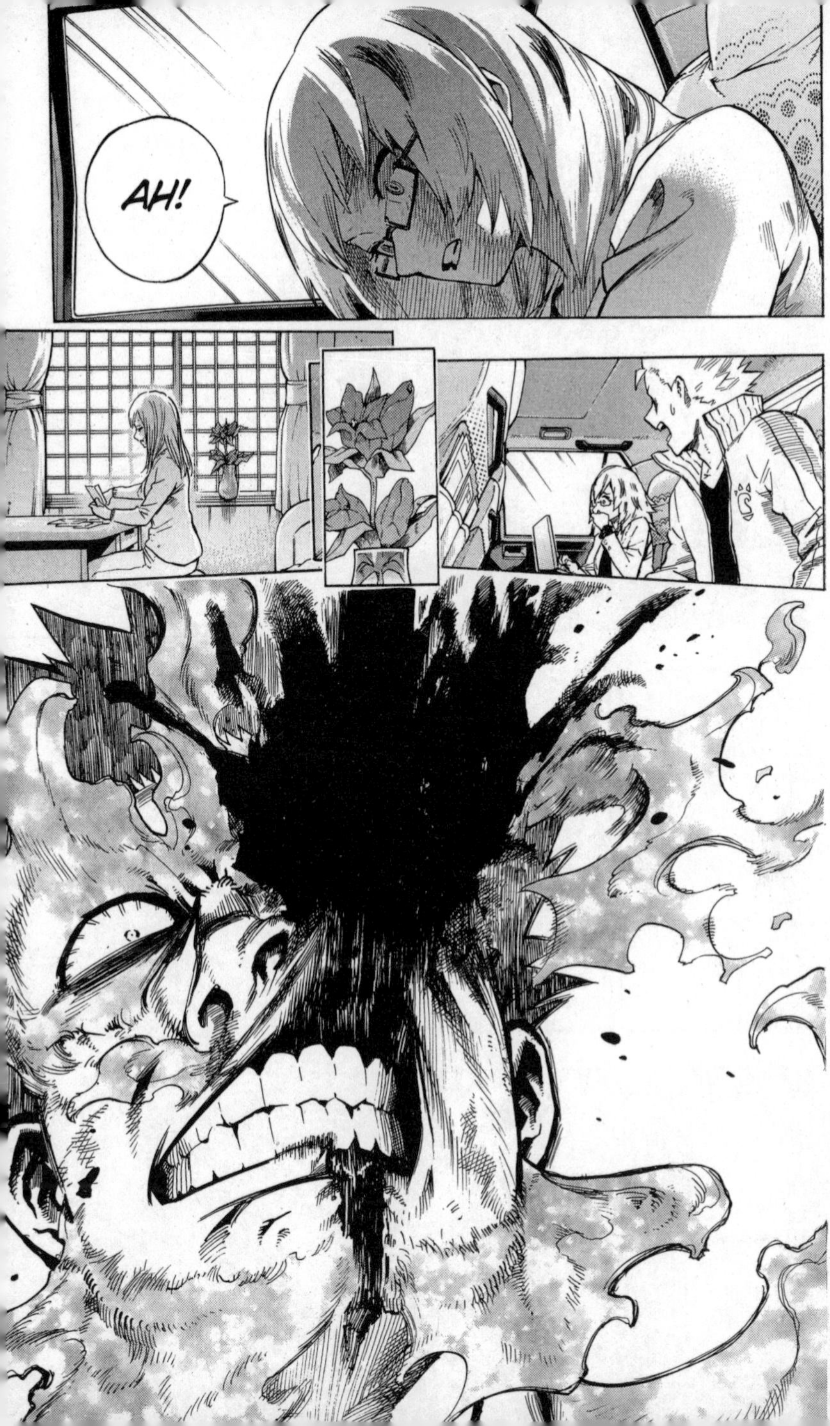
AH!

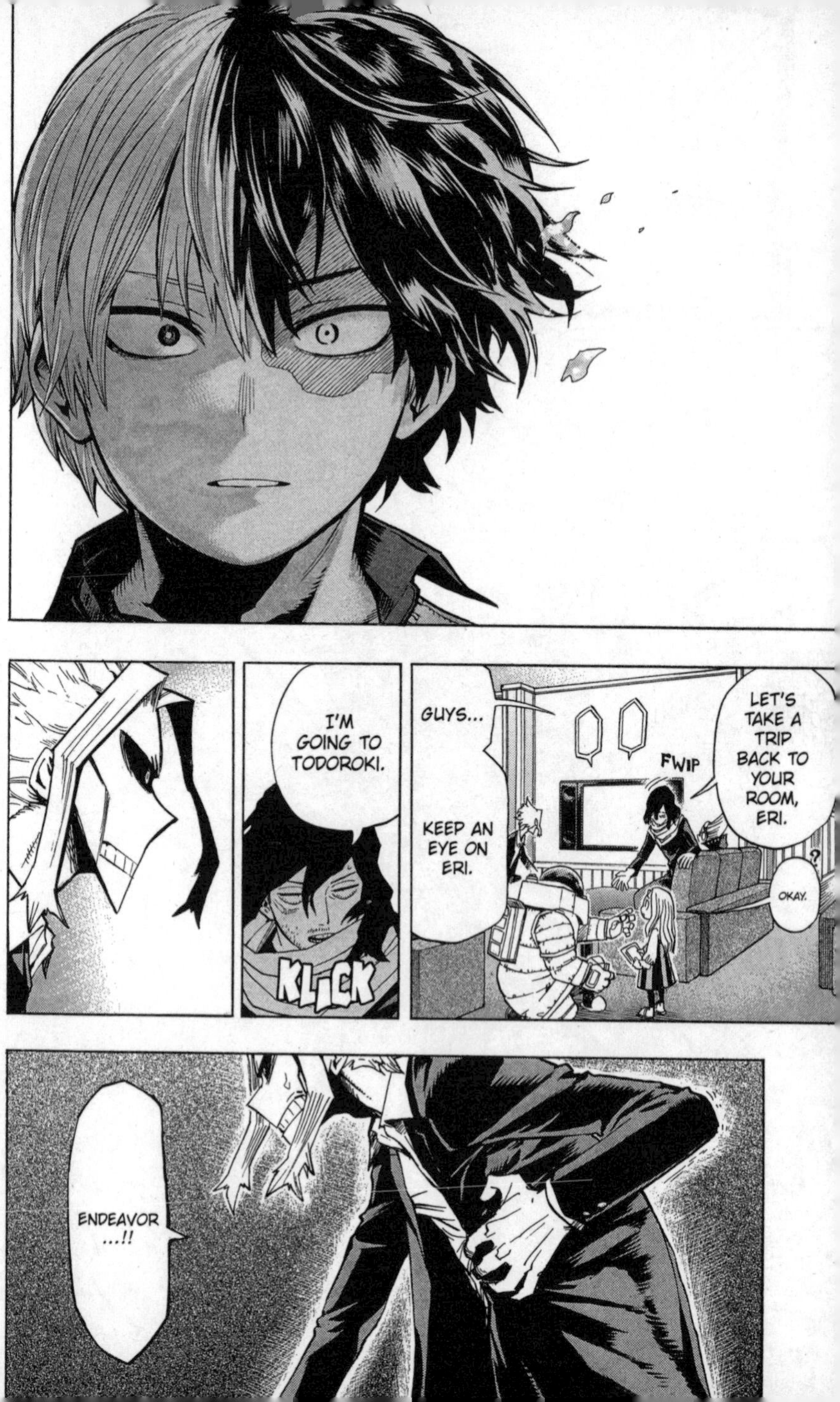
LET'S TAKE A TRIP BACK TO YOUR ROOM, ERI.
FWIP
GUYS...
?
OKAY.
KEEP AN EYE ON ERI.
I'M GOING TO TODOROKI.
KLICK
ENDEAVOR ...!!

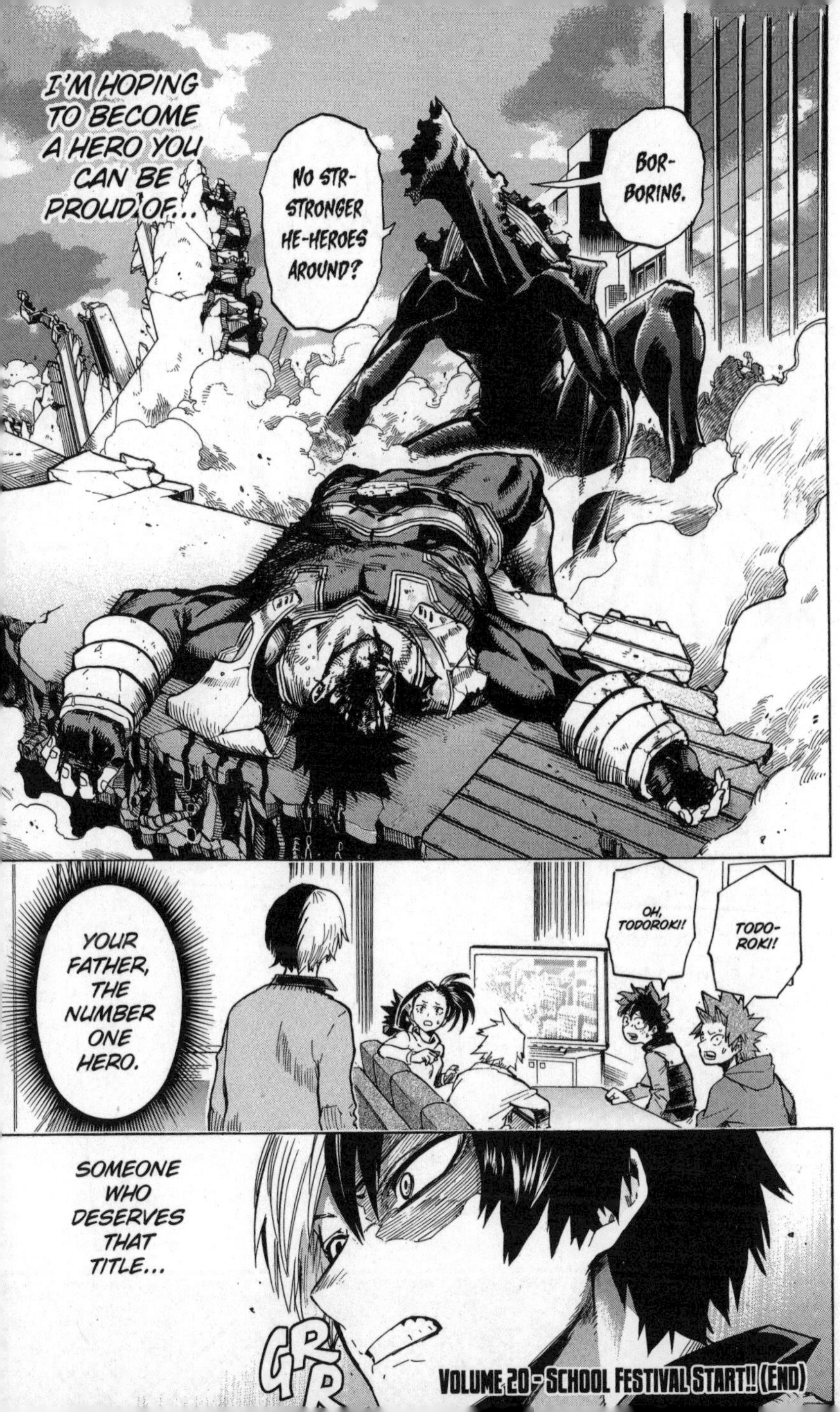
BOR- BORING.
NO STR- STRONGER HE-HEROES AROUND?
I'M HOPING TO BECOME A HERO YOU CAN BE PROUD OF...
TODO- ROKI!
OH, TODOROKI!
YOUR FATHER, THE NUMBER ONE HERO.
SOMEONE WHO DESERVES THAT TITLE...
GRR
VOLUME 20 - SCHOOL FESTIVAL START!! (END)

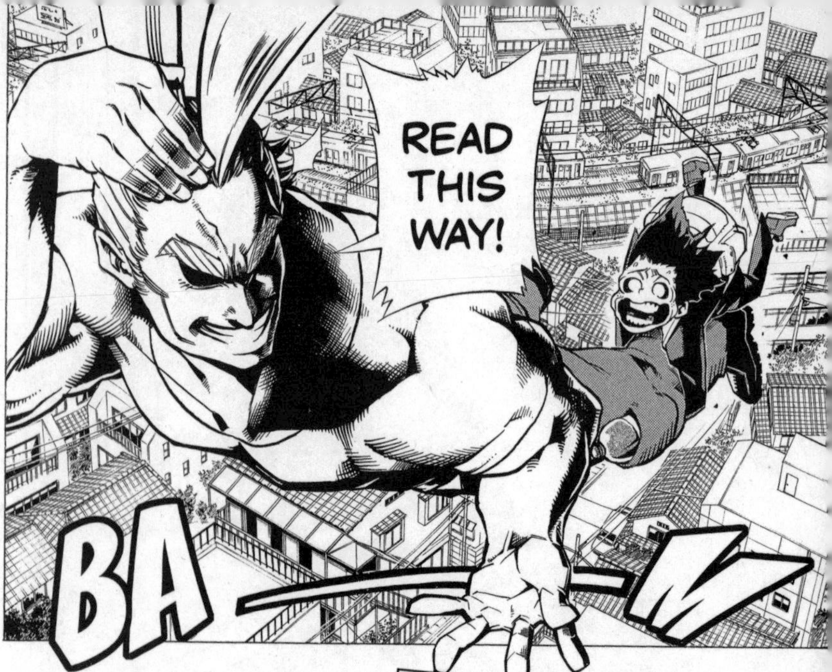
READ THIS WAY!
BA—M

MY HERO ACADEMIA reads from right to left, starting in the upper-right corner. Japanese is read from right to left, meaning that action, sound effects and word-balloon order are completely reversed from English order.

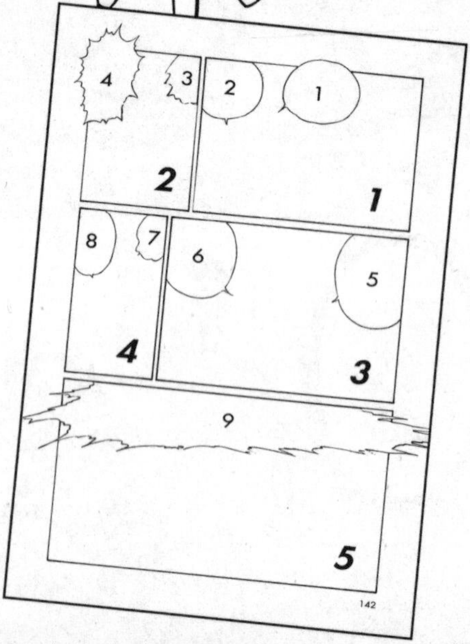
1
2
3
4
1
2
5
6
7
8
3
4
9
5
142